DEFENDING
PORNOGRAPHY

Second Child Coming, copyright © 1998 by Saelon Renkes. This hand-painted photograph is posted on the website of Art on the Net, a plaintiff in three ACLU lawsuits challenging state cybercensorship laws (in Michigan, New Mexico, and New York) that endangered all online nudity, even in fine art.

DEFENDING PORNOGRAPHY

*Free Speech, Sex, and the Fight
for Women's Rights*

Nadine Strossen

New York University Press

NEW YORK

NEW YORK UNIVERSITY PRESS
New York
www.nyupress.org

Defending Pornography was originally published in hardcover by Scribner
in 1995, and in paperback by Anchor Books in 1996.

Library of Congress Cataloging-in-Publication Data
Strossen, Nadine
Defending Pornography: free speech, sex, and the fight for
women's rights / Nadine Strossen.
p.   cm.
Includes bibliographical references and index.
ISBN 9781479830763 (hardback) | ISBN 9781479829903 (paperback) |
ISBN 9781479830794 (ebook) | ISBN 9781479830800 (ebook other)
1. Pornography—Social aspects—United States.   2. Feminism—United States.
3. Feminist criticism—United States.   I. Title.
HQ472.U6.S87 2000
363.4'7—dc21   00-036067

This book is printed on acid-free paper, and its binding materials are
chosen for strength and durability. We strive to use environmentally responsible
suppliers and materials

Manufactured in the United States of America
10 9 8 7 6 5 4

Also available as an ebook

Contents

Preface to the 2024 Edition   vii

Foreword to the Second Edition by Wendy Kaminer   xxix

Introduction to the Second Edition   xxxiii

Acknowledgments   1

Introduction   5

1. The Sex Panic and the Feminist Split   11

2. Sexual Speech and the Law   29

3. The Fatally Flawed Feminist Antipornography Laws   49

4. The Growing Suppression of "Sexpression"   71

5. Revealing Views of Women, Men, and Sex   93

6. Defining Sexual Harassment: Sexuality Does Not Equal Sexism   105

7. "Different Strokes for Different Folks": The Panoply
   of Pornographic Imagination   125

8. Positive Aspects of Pornographic Imagery   145

9. Posing for Pornography: Coercion or Consent?   163

10. Would-Be Censors Subordinate Valuable Works
    to Their Agenda   181

11. Lessons from Enforcement: When the Powerful
    Get More Power   197

12. Why Censoring Pornography Would Not Reduce
    Discrimination or Violence against Women   225

13. Toward Constructive Approaches to Reducing
    Discrimination and Violence against Women   241

Notes   255

Index   281

Preface to the 2024 Edition

I'm afraid this book will always be timely.... [T]he urge to censor ... seems to come as naturally to people as the diverse sexual desires censors condemn.

> —WENDY KAMINER,
> Foreword to the Second Edition
> of *Defending Pornography* (2000)

During the first half of the 2022–23 school year ... books [in public school libraries or classrooms] are more frequently labeled "pornographic" or "indecent" [by] ... activists and politicians to justify removing books that do not remotely fit the well-established legal and colloquial definitions of "pornography." Rhetoric about "porn in schools" has also been advanced as justification for ... new state laws, some of which would bar any books with sexual content [including] ... health-related content.... Overwhelmingly, book banners continue to target stories by and about people of color and LGBTQ+ individuals.

> —PEN America,
> *2023 Banned Books Update* (2023)

The limitations on free speech caused by FOSTA [a 2018 federal statute, the "Fight Online Sex Trafficking Act"] have essentially censored harm reduction and safety information sharing, removed tools that sex workers used to keep themselves and others safe, and interrupted organizing and legislative endeavors to ... enhance the wellbeing of sex workers and trafficking survivors alike. [FOSTA] has had a devastating impact on already marginalized and vulnerable communities.

—Brief filed by Decriminalize Sex Work et al.,
in constitutional challenge to FOSTA (2022)

FOSTA's . . . censorial effect has resulted in the removal [from online platforms] of speech created by LGBTQ+ people and discussions of sexuality and gender identity. This is the continuation of a long history of the silencing and oppression of LGBTQ+ people through vague and overbroad laws.

—Brief filed by Transgender Law Center,
in constitutional challenge to FOSTA (2022)

PEN America's recent statement on banned books and the two constitutional challenges to FOSTA by Decriminalize Sex Work[1] and the Transgender Law Center[2] illustrate the enduring nature of the problems that *Defending Pornography* chronicled. Today, measures censoring sexual expression continue to abound from across the ideological spectrum, not only violating free speech rights but also undermining the health and safety of women, LGBTQ+ people, young people, and others who are the avowed beneficiaries of such censorship. Alas, Wendy Kaminer's prediction that *Defending Pornography* "will always be timely" has proven prescient. In this new preface, I will flag its major themes and trace their resonance throughout the three decades since I wrote it, noting some of the multifarious, ideologically diverse attacks on sexual expression that have prevailed when each reissue went to press (1994, 1999, and 2023).

Defending Pornography, 1995

I wrote *Defending Pornography* to present the feminist case against the then-widespread view, originated by writer Andrea Dworkin and law professor Catharine MacKinnon, that "pornography"—which they defined as sexual expression that is "subordinating" to women—should be suppressed because it causes discrimination and violence against women. In contrast with this strain of so-called "radical" feminism, anti-censorship feminists espoused classical liberal values of free speech and equality; we maintained that censoring sexual expression, no matter how well-intended, would do more harm than good for women's rights and safety. As *Defending Pornography* explained, the term "radical" is inaccurate, since the pro-censorship feminists' views were conservative in key respects, even reactionary; accordingly, I will continue to put the term in quotation marks.

To be sure, liberal free speech principles would permit the government to restrict sexual expression—along with other forms of expression—if it could show that the expression directly, imminently caused or threatened great harm, such as discrimination or violence against women, and that the restriction was necessary to avert the harm. Despite substantial analysis of any potential causal connection between sexual expression and harm by relevant experts, however, the evidence fails to show any such causal link.

The lack of evidence substantiating any harmful impact of sexual expression, which *Defending Pornography* discussed in detail, was reaffirmed by a federal judge just before this preface went to print. On August 31, 2023, US District Judge David Alan Ezra issued a preliminary injunction against a Texas law requiring age verification to access sexual expression content online. The law's stated aim was to protect children from the alleged adverse impacts of such expression; the judge ruled that the law violates the First Amendment. Considering the evidence in the most favorable light from the government's perspective, Judge Ezra explained that "the relevant science shows, at best, substantial disagreement amongst physicians and psychologists regarding the effects of pornography."[3] He cited a 2022 study of anti-pornography advocacy from 1984 to 2018, which concluded that "the anti-pornography movement is growing 'more connected to religious conservatism than views about scientific authority.'"[4] Moreover, just as *Defending Pornography* quoted some feminist scholars who explicated pornography's positive impacts specifically for women, Judge Ezra quoted recent feminist scholarship in the same vein.[5]

Definitions and Legal Concepts

"Pornography" has no specific legal meaning, because the Supreme Court has never defined a category of sexual speech in order to restrict its use under the First Amendment. In contrast, the Supreme Court has held that "child pornography"—sexually explicit photographs or films of actual minors—is constitutionally unprotected because of its inherent exploitation of the minors who are (ab)used in the production process. A typical dictionary definition of "pornography" (from Dictionary.com) is "sexually explicit [expression] whose purpose is to elicit sexual arousal."

The only subset of sexual expression that is constitutionally unprotected because of what it depicts or describes—in contrast with child pornography, which is constitutionally unprotected because of the minors who were (ab)used to produce it—is labeled "obscenity." To restrict a book or other expressive work as "obscene," the government must show that it satisfies all elements of a multi-pronged Supreme Court definition. Among other things, the government must show that, when considered as a whole, the work lacks "serious literary, artistic, political, or scientific value."[6] Importantly, the work's value is assessed under national standards, not those of any local community, thus shielding sexual expression from adverse judgments by particular communities with relatively intolerant perspectives about such expression.

In sum, almost all sexual expression—including almost all such expression that satisfies any definition of pornography—is constitutionally protected. Explaining that "[t]he portrayal of sex . . . is not itself sufficient reason to deny material . . . constitutional protection," the Supreme Court has observed that "[s]ex, a great and mysterious motive force in human life, . . . is one of the vital problems of human interest and public concern."[7]

Dictionary and legal definitions aside, the term "pornography" in everyday speech generally has negative connotations, so that people of varying viewpoints apply it to whatever sexual expression they personally dislike. Correspondingly, politicians regularly invoke the term to designate whatever sexual expression they seek to suppress. As one wit put it: "What turns *me* on is 'erotica,' but what turns *you* on is 'pornography.'"

The inherent ambiguity of the term "pornography," and the resulting reality that any restriction on it relies on the enforcing authority's subjective viewpoint, is exemplified by what is probably the most famous description of that term: former Supreme Court Justice Potter Stewart's much-quoted statement that "I [can] not . . . define [it] . . . .[b]ut I know it when I see it."[8] The problem is that every one of us sees a different "it," thus endangering essentially all sexual expression.

The Distinctive Feminist Anti-Censorship Perspective

Traditionally, anti-censorship arguments against pornography restrictions—including the "radical" feminist laws—have been based on First Amendment principles, which do indeed invalidate such laws, as reviewing courts have consistently ruled. Among other First Amendment flaws, these laws violate the "bedrock"[9] legal principle of "viewpoint neutrality": that the government may neither favor nor disfavor speech based on its views or ideas. Directly flouting this principle, the Dworkin-MacKinnon concept of "illegal pornography" explicitly singles out sexual expression because of its "subordinating" view toward women.

The fact that the "radical" feminist anti-pornography laws blatantly violated the First Amendment fed a misconception that these feminists purveyed: that there is an inevitable clash between free speech and gender equality, and hence, supporters of women's rights must endorse the censorial measures. Feminists who supported censorship attacked those of us in the anti-censorship camp, calling us "scabs," "Uncle Toms,"[10] and even accusing us of not being authentic women. For example, one leader of a feminist pro-censorship group called me an "honorary man."[11]

At the same time that these debates about sexual expression were raging among feminists, we saw similar, burgeoning debates in the broader context of "hate speech"—speech conveying hateful or discriminatory ideas about members of historically marginalized groups. Between 1982 and 1990, three law professors wrote influential law review articles supporting hate speech restrictions on campus and beyond, premised on the same broad claim that the pro-censorship feminists made: that free speech and equality principles necessarily conflict with each other.[12] Indeed, the "radical" feminist concept of pornography constituted a specific type of hate speech: sexual expression that conveyed hateful or discriminatory views about women.

In response to these increasingly prevalent perspectives about the negative interrelationship between free speech and gender equality (as well as equality more generally), anti-censorship feminists raised counterarguments that were expressly grounded on concerns of gender equality: that the censorial schemes, far from promoting women's equality and safety, would actually undermine them. For example, in 1992, the National Organization for Women (NOW) of New York State declared: "Censorship has been, throughout history, the single most widely used patriarchal tool for 'protecting' women—from birth control, abortion, sexual satisfaction and non-heterosexual relationships. Without free speech we can have no feminist movement."[13]

In a 1992 essay in *The Nation*, renowned Harvard professor Henry Louis Gates, Jr. praised the "distinctive feminist contribution" that anti-censorship feminists made to debates about sexual expression. He wrote: "The strain of anti-pornologism is hardly what's distinctive about feminism; whereas anti-anti-pornology—the critique of the anti-porn movement on grounds other than constitutional formalism or First Amendment pietism—is a distinctive feminist contribution."[14] Given the importance of the specifically feminist anti-censorship perspective, I was delighted to have the opportunity to write *Defending Pornography*, to present to a broader audience the arguments that I, along with many other anti-censorship feminists, had been raising in other forums, including scholarly articles and legal briefs.

Defending Pornography, 2000

The book was reissued only five years later, highlighting the widespread arrival of the internet as urgent, and hotly contested, new terrain for government censorship. Both new elements of the second edition— Wendy Kaminer's foreword and my new introduction—focused on this theme. As the internet became more widely accessible after the World Wide Web was launched into the public domain in 1993, sexual expression faced increasingly severe attacks from across the ideological spectrum. Public awareness of the internet added fuel to these raging censorial fires.

As *Defending Pornography* described, starting in the late 1970s and continuing throughout the 1980s and beyond, an unprecedented, yet influential, coalition formed between anti-pornography "radical" feminists and Christian and Republican conservatives. While the first group attacked sexual expression that they considered inconsistent with their feminist values, the latter attacked sexual expression that, in their view, undermined traditional family values. Their dramatically different views about which sexual expression posed particular dangers notwithstanding, the two factions repeatedly teamed up to support various censorial initiatives, including those recommended by the 1986 report of the Meese Pornography Commission, spearheaded by President Ronald Reagan's attorney general Ed Meese. From 1991 to 1993, responsive to pressures from these vocal anti-pornography advocates on both ends of the ideological spectrum, Congress considered enacting a Dworkin-MacKinnon-style law, which had significant bipartisan support.

Given this broad cross-partisan support for censoring sexual expression at the time that the internet burst upon public, press, and political radars, both factions unsurprisingly greeted fears about "cyberporn" in particular. The result was the 1996 Communications Decency Act (CDA), a sweeping federal legislation restricting online sexual expression, as well as multiple similar state laws and local regulations. These measures were passed by overwhelming bipartisan majorities. In light of these developments, I welcomed the opportunity to write a new introduction to *Defending Pornography*, explaining why the censorship of online sexual expression was as dangerous for women's rights—and LGBTQ+ rights—as the censorship of sexual expression had always been in any other media.

The CDA's threat to historically disempowered sexual and gender identities was highlighted by the roster of clients in the successful American Civil Liberties Union (ACLU) First Amendment challenge to the CDA provisions outlawing "indecent" or "patently offensive" online expression, which the Supreme Court unanimously struck down in a landmark 1997 decision.[15] These clients, whose expression would have been suppressed under the CDA, included important organizations advancing women's rights, as well as reproductive freedom and LGBTQ+ rights. They joined the many mainstream free speech-oriented organizations that also challenged the law, such as the American Booksellers Association and the American Library Association.

To illustrate the CDA's adverse impact on expression of particular importance for women, thus continuing the historic pattern of all laws censoring sexual expression, I will cite one passage from the second edition introduction. It refers to the 1873 Comstock Act, initiated by the controversial "anti-vice" crusader Anthony Comstock. In the same phrase, the Act outlaws both "obscene, lewd, or lascivious" materials, and "any article . . . intended for the prevention of conception or procuring of abortion," as well as "any . . . information" about any of the prohibited materials. The law thus expressly conflates expression about contraception and abortion with other expression outlawed as "obscene," and moreover equates expression about contraception and abortion with contraceptives and abortifacients. The introduction explained the links between the Comstock Act and the CDA:

> As *Defending Pornography* recounts, during the ACLU's first decade of our existence, one of our clients was Margaret Sanger. She was repeatedly harassed and prosecuted under the Victorian-era Comstock Act, the first federal anti-obscenity law, which criminalized the information she conveyed about women's reproductive health and options. Sadly, more than three-quarters of a century later, we had to defend the organization that Sanger founded [Planned Parenthood] against the Internet era's first federal cybercensorship law, which criminalized the very same information.[16]

Even more sadly, this passage from *Defending Pornography*'s second edition is still pertinent. In 2023, the 1873 Comstock Act—which is still on the books—has been continuously wielded in multiple courts to further curb women's reproductive options, already severely diminished by the Supreme Court's 2022 *Dobbs* decision overturning *Roe v. Wade*.[17] This nineteenth-century law has been invoked to curb women's access to mifepristone, which the Food and Drug Administration (FDA) approved in 2000 for use in terminating a pregnancy during its early stages. In February 2023, twenty Republican lawmakers cited the Act in letters to CVS and Walgreens pharmacies, threatening them with legal action if they distributed mifepristone.[18] And in April 2023, a federal judge in Texas ordered a hold on the FDA's approval of mifepristone, citing the Comstock Act in his opinion.[19]

Just as the Comstock Act equated the distribution of contraceptives and abortifacients with the distribution of information about them, we are now witnessing the same false, dangerous equation between conduct and expression. Shortly after the *Dobbs* decision, the National Right to Life Committee circulated a model state statute, which included bans on certain expression about abortion on the rationale that it could "aid and abet" illegal abortions.[20]

Restricting speech on the rationale that it is tantamount to illegal conduct is a tactic that has also been deployed by advocates with very different perspectives about abortion and other issues relating to sex and gender. As this new preface discusses, some feminists have supported restrictions on wide-ranging expression—such as classroom discussions of rape and LGBTQ+ rights—on the grounds that it is tantamount to illegal discrimination or even violence. This issue illustrates why all people who depend on robust free speech to advocate their causes—including women, feminists, LGBTQ+ individuals, and reproductive rights activists—have a special stake in resisting speech-suppressive tactics, even when the immediate result might accord with their policy goals. Given the deep societal division around issues concerning sex and gender, and the shifting political winds, a speech-suppressive measure that in a certain community at a certain time might aid supporters of a particular cause will, in another community or at another time, aid opponents of that very same cause.

Defending Pornography, 2024

When NYU Press expressed interest in publishing a new preface for another reissue of *Defending Pornography*, I was forced to acknowledge the book's ongoing timeliness, consistent with Wendy Kaminer's 2000 prediction.

Recent Assaults on Sexual Expression

To illustrate the ongoing efforts to censor sexual expression since this book's prior reissue, I will list some additional examples, beyond those I have already noted. In most of these situations, the stigmatizing term pornography has been deployed against the targeted material to convey the view that it lacks value and, even worse, is harmful to individuals and society. Following the pattern of earlier eras, some of these censorial efforts are supported mostly by people on the left, others supported mostly by people on the right, and still others receiving broad support from across the political spectrum.

- In addition to suppressing sexual expression in public and school libraries, some state legislation has also suppressed such expression in bookstores. For example, a 2022 Arkansas law made it a crime for a bookseller or a library to make any books "available" to minors that could be deemed "harmful" to them. Given the law's severe penalties, it was clearly designed to deter booksellers and librarians from making any books with any sexual content available to minors. As a practical matter, considering the difficulties of enforcing such restrictions to minors only, these laws will also impede adults' access to the same material.
- A 2023 Arkansas statute empowers anyone who claims to be "affected by" any material in a library's collection to "challenge the appropriateness" of such material, without defining "appropriateness." The executive director of the Garland County, Arkansas Library reported that, pursuant to this sweeping provision, his library had received a "blanket request" to remove "all materials with LGBTQ+ characters."[21]
- Even mere nudity has been the basis for removing books and artworks from public schools and other public settings, even when the nudity is a minor element of the work and the work has serious value. Perhaps the most notorious case in point is Art Spiegelman's Pulitzer Prize-winning graphic novel *Maus*, which depicts the horrors of the Holocaust. *Maus* has been repeatedly removed from public schools due to one small cartoon drawing of a naked woman in a bathtub, in which her breasts and legs are visible

above the water. This drawing depicts Spiegelman's mother after she had committed suicide.

- In July 2023, the US House of Representatives passed a proposal to block military schools from purchasing or having "pornographic and radical gender ideology books" in their libraries.[22]
- Legislation in multiple states have banned "drag" performances, using broad, vague language that encompasses any cross-dressing, even without sexual connotations. These laws therefore endanger wide-ranging artistic expression, including, for example, the plays of William Shakespeare. As author Charles P. Pierce commented in a 2023 essay, "Shakespeare is just collateral damage for transphobic laws against drag shows."[23]
- Multiple state laws have imposed age verification requirements for accessing online sites with sexual content. Because these measures invade privacy, they deter adults, as well as minors, from accessing constitutionally protected expression. In his 2023 decision striking down Texas's age verification law, federal judge David Alan Ezra explained that the law's deterrent effect "is particularly acute because access to sexual material could reveal intimate desires and preferences." Noting that Texas still has not repealed its criminal "anti-sodomy" law, despite the Supreme Court's 2003 decision invalidating it, Judge Ezra concluded: "Given Texas's ongoing criminalization of homosexual intercourse, it is apparent that people who wish to view homosexual material will be profoundly chilled from doing so if they must first affirmatively identify themselves to the state."[24]
- Overly broad concepts of punishable sexual harassment have been enforced either formally, through means such as campus regulations, or informally, through campaigns such as the #MeToo movement. As *Defending Pornography* stressed, sexual harassment is indeed a type of illegal sex discrimination, but the key goal of countering such discrimination is undermined by falsely equating sex*ual* expression with sex*ist* conduct.

This double distortion wrongly conflates not only expression with conduct, but also sexuality with sexism, despite the Supreme Court's clear warning to the contrary. In a unanimous 1998 decision (which was joined by the Court's two female justices at the time, Sandra Day O'Connor and Ruth Bader Ginsburg), the Court explained that Title VII, the federal statute that outlaws gender-based discrimination in the workplace, "does not prohibit all verbal or physical harassment in the workplace," but only such harassment that constitutes "*discriminat[ion]* . . . because of . . . sex." The Court stressed that even harassing expression doesn't "automatically" constitute "discrimination because of sex merely because the words used have sexual content or connotations."[25] On campus, though, it is precisely this wrongheaded equation between sexually themed words and sex discrimination that has instigated sexual harassment investigations and even punishments—including of women and feminist faculty members—simply for their nonviolent expression about sex or gender with which complainants disagree.

Likewise, some participants in the #MeToo movement have failed to sufficiently distinguish those convicted of serial rape (such as Harvey Weinstein) from those accused of misogynistic or insensitive expression (such as Al Franken), and have accordingly subjected the latter to disproportionately harsh punishment. In 2018, one hundred prominent French women, including the film star Catherine Deneuve, published a column in the leading French newspaper *Le Monde*, complaining that the #MeToo movement and its French counterpart "put on exactly the same level as sexual aggressors" men whose "only wrong was to have . . . talked about 'intimate' things at a professional dinner or sent messages with sexual connotations to women in whom the attraction was not reciprocated." This letter also complained that #MeToo violated the free speech rights not only of men who had allegedly engaged in inappropriate sexual expression, but also women who critiqued such excesses. It stated:

> Following the Weinstein affair, there was a legitimate awareness of sexual violence against women, especially in the workplace, where some men abuse their power. It was necessary. But this freedom of speech today turns into its opposite: we are told to speak properly, to silence what is upsetting, and those who refuse to comply . . . are regarded as traitors, accomplices![26]

The Enduring, Expanding Influence of the Feminist Anti-Pornography Ideology

In light of the persistent and ever-expanding efforts to censor sexual expression in this new millennium, the remainder of this preface offers some observations about the ongoing relevance of several key themes in *Defending Pornography.* Although the courts swiftly struck it down as a violation of core First Amendment principles,[27] the Dworkin-MacKinnon model anti-pornography law has had an abiding and even increasing cultural impact as a worldview; it has continued to foster speech-suppressive attitudes and actions toward many types of controversial expression, in addition to sexual expression. This preface concludes by noting some encouraging countercurrents.

Just as the "radical" feminist movement to censor certain sexual expression fueled the general movement to censor hate speech more broadly, it also pioneered several interrelated ideas that have now become widely accepted, far beyond the pornography context, with ongoing impacts to speech suppression. At the time, these ideas were generally viewed as extreme and even as hyperbolic rhetoric, but more recently they have influenced important policy decisions, including not to permit certain people to speak on campus, and not to permit certain ideas or sexual identities to be discussed in classrooms. As is true for the feminist anti-pornography perspective in general, these ideas actually undermine women's and LGBTQ+ people's rights and safety, far from advancing them.

Dangerous Blurrings of Key Distinctions . . .

. . . Between Words and Violence, and Between Intentional and Unintentional acts

The then-novel ideas that the feminist pro-censorship movement launched have increasingly influenced policies regarding not only sexual expression, but also other controversial expression. Examples include the following: that women should be shielded from sexually themed expression that makes them "uncomfortable"; that words have the potential to not only lead to violence and other harm, but also that words themselves can *be* harmful and violent; and that a speaker's intent is irrelevant, so that even campus speech with an important educational purpose may be proscribed or punished if it makes a member of the campus community "uncomfortable."

. . . Between Rape and Expression about It

Detrimental to women's rights and safety, pro-censorship feminists have discounted—if not outright denied—distinctions between actual rape and depictions or descriptions of rape. These same groups advance interrelated arguments that women should be shielded from any expression about rape on the theory that it causes them "discomfort" and "harm."

In more recent years, this elision between expression about rape and actual rape has become increasingly accepted—including at law schools, where one would expect students and faculty members to sharply distinguish any illegal act from expression that describes or depicts it. The introduction to the second edition of *Defending Pornography* described a then-novel situation (arising in 1999), in which a prominent Columbia Law School professor faced serious sexual harassment accusations for including a question about sexual violence (based on actual cases that had been discussed in class) on the take-home final exam in his criminal law course.

Unfortunately, that Columbia incident is no longer novel. It is now all too common for law students and faculty members to deem academic discussions about sexual violence sufficiently harmful enough to outweigh the benefits of educating future lawyers and policymakers so that they can effectively defend and protect against sexual violence. As Harvard Law Professor Jeannie Suk Gersen explained in a 2014 *New Yorker* article, many female law students have objected to studying cases about rape and other sexual assault in their criminal law courses on the grounds that reading about and discussing the crime "might be traumatic." Gersen pointed out that many criminal law professors are even declining to cover this important topic, for fear of being accused of (unintentionally) harming some students. In a nod toward the sustained impact that the pro-censorship feminists have had on our culture, Gersen observed: "[M]any students and teachers appear to be absorbing a cultural signal that . . . discussion of sexual misconduct . . . [creates] the risk . . . of a traumatic injury analogous to sexual assault itself."

Gersen concludes that the removal of sexual assault cases from a student's legal education "would be a tremendous loss—above all to victims of sexual assault."[28] For many of us older feminists, this is a bitterly ironic development, since the important topic of rape and sexual violence has too often been excluded from criminal law courses, reduced instead to a "women's issue," deemed of insufficient general interest. It was thanks to advocacy by the growing numbers of women law students and faculty members, starting in the 1970's (of whom I was one), that the law of sexual violence was recognized as eminently deserving of study—not least to spur efforts to reform the law to facilitate fair prosecutions—equipping lawyers to effectively pursue such prosecutions.

. . . Between Sexual Expression and Sexist Conduct

Defending Pornography contains one of the earliest discussions of the conflation of these issues. It bears repeating that, although sexual harassment does constitute illegal sex discrimination, it has often been too broadly defined as extending to any expression with any sexual content or connotation. Since Catharine MacKinnon played a leading (and commendable) role in the legal system's recognition of sexual harassment as a form of illegal sex discrimination, it is not surprising that she and others have construed excessive sexual expression as punishable sexual harassment.

Restricting speech on the rationale that it is tantamount to illegal conduct is a tactic that has also been deployed by advocates with widely varying perspectives on issues relating to sex and gender. For example, anti-abortion activists are seeking to outlaw expression about abortion in states that severely restrict abortions. Even beyond providing general support for the dangerous blurring of the distinction between illegal conduct and speech about it in the anti-abortion context, this blurring in the context of sexual harassment itself endangers women's rights.

Appropriately, the Supreme Court has worked to narrowly hem in the conduct—including expression—that may be considered illegal sexual harassment in specific contexts. In the workplace, the Court has held that the expression must be "severe or pervasive" enough to create a "hostile or abusive work environment."[29] In the educational context, the Court has ruled that the expression must be "so severe, pervasive, and objectively offensive, and [it must] so undermine[ ] and detract[ ] from the victims' educational experience, that the victim-students are effectively denied equal access to [the] institution's resources and opportunities."[30]

A broader concept of speech that constitutes sexual harassment does not promote the key goal of countering sex discrimination, but rather undermines it. Vesting enforcement authorities with further discretion to restrict sexual expression under the rationale of harassment has the same predictable result as any measure that censor sexual expression: it too broadly suppresses speech that is especially important for women. Both prior editions of *Defending Pornography* recount multiple instances where complaints of sexual harassment have assailed expression by women feminists, ranging from artistic creations to academic lectures.

Since the book's second edition, an unduly expansive concept of proscriptive sexual harassment has become increasingly widespread, including in campus policies. A 2017 report by the American Association of University Professors concludes that universities have shown "a tendency to treat academic discussion of sex and sexuality as contributing to a hostile environment," a form of illegal sexual harassment.[31] Universities have continued to punish students and faculty members for all manner of sexual expression, even when it has an important academic purpose—and even when it has a feminist perspective.

Perhaps the most egregious example is the prolonged sexual harassment investigation that Northwestern University conducted against film professor Laura Kipnis in 2015 following an article she published in the *Chronicle of Higher Education* in which, ironically, she criticized the exaggerated, distorted concept of sexual harassment that is common on campus. For months, the university subjected her to Star Chamber-type interrogations, pursuing the charge that her essay somehow constituted unlawful harassment.

Symptomatic of the expanding impact of the "radical" feminist theories, well beyond the context of the sexual expression they directly

targeted, colleges and universities have incorporated the dangerous
equation between conduct and expression into their codes barring
"discriminatory harassment." Amplifying the problem, these policies
typically define prohibited expression in broad, vague terms. They thus
have enormous, chilling impacts on virtually any expression that refers
to sex or gender (among myriad identity factors).

Let me cite one example from the University of Central Florida that
a federal appellate court struck down in 2022. In all-too-nebulous
language, this policy barred any student's speech that "unreasonably
altered another student's educational experience" on the basis of multiple identity factors, including sex or gender. At oral argument, one of
the judges asked the University's lawyer whether a student would violate
this policy by stating that "abortion is immoral." The university counsel
responded that "he couldn't say for sure." As the court commented: "If
UCF's own attorney . . . can't tell whether a particular statement would
violate the policy, it seems eminently fair to conclude that the school's
students can't either."[32]

Regardless of whether a particular university expressly incorporates an unduly broad concept of sexual harassment into its policies,
such concepts have become widely accepted across college campuses.
Therefore, many students and faculty members avoid discussing topics
related to sex and gender altogether, for fear of being accused of making
someone "uncomfortable" or causing them "harm" (even if unintentionally). Surveys confirm rampant self-censorship around these concepts, even when they entail key public policy issues. For example, in
a 2022 comprehensive survey of college and university students, which
College Pulse conducted for the Foundation for Individual Rights and
Expression (FIRE), 49 percent of students named abortion as a topic
about which it is "difficult to have an open and honest conversation" on
their campus.[33]

Another current topic of special importance to women and feminists, as well as LGBTQ+ people, is the potential impact that various
policies concerning trans people have on gender-segregated entities.
Prime examples include policies about the participation of trans women
in women's sports and about accommodating trans women in certain
facilities for women where safety concerns are acute, such as prisons
and shelters for domestic violence victims. Feminists, cis women, and

trans women have sharply disagreed about these policies, with some in each group expressing their support for and opposition to these policies, respectively. Yet too many people—including some in each of these groups—refrain from expressing any views on such important issues. For instance, in the College Pulse survey cited above, 44 percent of respondents said that it is difficult to candidly discuss transgender issues on their campus.[34]

To be sure, the expression of views on such sensitive, important topics—across the ideological spectrum—could make any listener uncomfortable. But such discomfort is a small price to pay for the equal rights we all have, regardless of identity or ideology, to not only express our own views, but also to listen to other speakers' views, and to live in a society whose public policies are shaped by vigorous debates among "We the People." As the Supreme Court observed in a 2011 case: "As a Nation we have chosen . . . to protect even hurtful speech on public issues to ensure that we do not stifle public debate."

Eternal Anti-Censorship Vigilance—and Victories

Eternal vigilance is the price of liberty.
—THOMAS JEFFERSON

Although many recent measures have been proposed to curtail sexual expression in contravention of fundamental First Amendment rights, a silver lining appears in the high success rate of lawsuits which have been filed to reverse these attempts. As in the past, these lawsuits have been supported by a broad array of organizations advocating for the rights of the people who are the most adversely affected by the censorship of sexual expression, including women, reproductive rights advocates, LGBTQ+ people, feminists, librarians, booksellers, teachers, and students.

Notably, the judges who have held that the First Amendment bars these speech-suppressive measures have been appointed by ideologically diverse US presidents. For example, the federal judges who struck down three state laws restricting sexual expression in the summer of

2023—Tennessee's anti-drag law, Arkansas's law against materials in libraries and bookstores deemed "harmful to minors," and Texas's age verification law for online sexual material—were appointed by former presidents Trump, Obama, and Reagan, respectively. To be sure, too many people—including too many politicians—tend to support "freedom of speech for *me*, but not for *thee*." Fortunately, though, many other people—including federal judges—recognize the golden rule of free speech: that we cannot enjoy freedom for the speech we love unless we also protect freedom for the speech we loathe.

Complementing the lawsuits enforcing First Amendment rights, there have been proliferating efforts to foster a robust free speech culture to counter the speech-suppressive climate that has hampered discussions on campus and elsewhere. These include: new campus centers, programs, and even academic departments and dedicated schools focusing on free speech, intellectual freedom, and civil discourse; new civil society organizations with the same mission; and the development of resources for every educational level, readily available online, to not only bolster knowledge about free speech rights, but also to gain skills for exercising them. Key to these efforts is education about the essential benefits that flow from robust free speech for every individual, for our democracy overall, and specifically for groups that have traditionally lacked political power, including women and LGBTQ+ people. I hope that this most recent reissue of *Defending Pornography* will contribute to these vital educational efforts, and will help to deflect future developments that would warrant another edition.

—Nadine Strossen
New Milford, Connecticut
August 2023

NOTES

Deep thanks are due to the following colleagues and friends for their meaningful contributions to this preface: for their comments on prior versions of it, Ronald K.L. Collins, Bob Corn-Revere, Chrissy Cunningham, and Chris Finan; and for helpful background materials and analysis, Bob Corn-Revere, Vera Eidelman, and Michael McCarthy.

1. *Woodhull Freedom Foundation v. United States*, Case No. 22-5105, United States Court of Appeals, D.C. Cir., filed 14 September 2022, Brief of Decriminalize Sex Work, et al. in Support of Appellants, at p. 8.

2. Ibid. Brief of *Amicus Curiae*, Transgender Law Center, et al. in Support of Appellants, p. 1.

3. *Free Speech Coalition v. Colmenero*, Case No. 1:23-CV-917-DAE, United States District Court, W. D. TX, filed 31 August 2023, at p. 69.

4. Ibid. at p. 67. (Quoting Samuel L. Perry, "Banning Because of Science or In Spite of It?: Scientific Authority, Religious Conservatism, and Support for Outlawing Pornography, 1984–2018," *Social Forces* 100, no. 3 (March 2022): p. 1385.)

5. Ibid. (Quoting Athanasia Daskalopoulou and Maria Carolina Zanette, "Women's Consumption of Pornography: Pleasure, Contestation, and Empowerment," *Sociology* 54, no. 5 (May 2020): p. 969. The authors note that female consumption of pornography is both "empowering and disciplining" for women.)

6. *Miller v. California*, 413 U.S. 15, 24 (1973).

7. *Roth v. United States*, 354 U.S. 476, 487 (1957).

8. *Jacobellis v. Ohio*, 378 U.S. 184, 197 (1964) (concurring).

9. *Texas v. Johnson*, 491 U.S. 397, 414 (1989).

10. Catharine MacKinnon, quoted in Pete Hamill, "Women on the Verge of a Legal Breakdown," *Playboy*, January 1993, p. 186.

11. Patrick Cooke, "Defending the L-Word," *Vogue*, December 1992, pp. 156–160, at p. 158 (quoting Norma Ramos).

12. Charles R. Lawrence III, *If He Hollers Let Him Go: Regulating Racist Speech on Campus*, 33 Duke Law Journal 431–483 (1990); Mari J. Matsuda, *Public Response to Racist Speech: Considering the Victim's Story*, 1989 Michigan Law Review 2320–2381 (1989); Richard Delgado, *Words that Wound: A Tort Action for Racial Insults, Epithets, and Name-Calling*, 1982 Harvard Civil Rights-Civil Liberties Law Review 133–181 (1982). For a response to these arguments, see Nadine Strossen, *HATE: Why We Should Resist It with Free Speech, Not Censorship* (New York: Oxford University Press, 2020).

13. NOW-New York State, "Canada Sounds Death-Knell for Free Speech," press release, 28 February 1992.

14. Henry Louis Gates, Jr., "To Deprave and Corrupt," review of *Girls Lean Back Everywhere: The Law of Obscenity and the Assault on Genius*, by Edward de Grazia, *The Nation*, 29 June 1992, pp. 898–903, at p. 898.

15. *Reno v. ACLU*, 521 U.S. 824 (1997).

16. At pp. XX in this volume.

17. *Roe v. Wade*, 410 U.S. 113 (1973).

18. Jim Salter, "20 attorneys general warn Walgreens, CVS over abortion pills," *AP News*, 1 February 2023, https://apnews.com/article/abortion-missouri-state-government -west-virginia-united-states-us-food-and-drug-administration-a1b1a387788bb5aaa3 9c9ce4128d77ab.

19. *Alliance for Hippocratic Medicine, v. FDA*, Case No. 22-CV-223-Z, N.D. Tex. Issued 7 April 2023.

20. National Right to Life Committee, "National Right to Life Committee Proposes Legislation to Protect the Unborn Post-Roe," press release, 15 June 2022. The press release links to the text of the model law. The model law includes language such as, "Aiding or abetting an unlawful abortion should include, but not be limited to: giving instructions over the telephone, the internet, or any other medium of communication regarding self administered abortions or means to obtain an unlawful abortion; hosting or maintaining a website, or providing internet service, regarding how to obtain

an unlawful abortion; . . . and providing referrals to an unlawful abortion provider."
For full text of the model law, see www.nrlc.org/wp-content/uploads/NRLC-Post-Roe
-Model-Abortion-Law-Version-2.pdf.

21. Memorandum Opinion and Order, *Fayetteville Public Library v. Crawford County, Arkansas* (W.D. Ark.) Case 5:23-cv-05086-TLB Document 53, filed 29 July 2023, at p. 23.
22. Jonathan Oosting, "Tudor Dixon eyes banning 'pornographic' books in Michigan schools," *Bridge Michigan,* 20 September, 2022, www.bridgemi.com.
23. Charles P. Pierce, "Transphobic, Anti-Drag Laws May Affect Performances of Shakespeare, Too," *Esquire,* 26 January 2023, www.esquire.com.
24. *Free Speech Coalition v. Colmenero,* at pp. 40–41.
25. *Oncale v. Sundowner Offshore Services, Inc.,* 523 U.S. 75, 80 (1998) (emphasis in original).
26. Valeriya Safronova, "Catherine Deneuve and Others Denounce the #MeToo Movement," *The New York Times,* 9 January 2018.
27. *American Booksellers Association v. Hudnut,* 598 F. Supp. 1316, 1340–41 (D. Ind. 1984), *aff'd,* 771 F. 2d 323 (7th Cir. 1985), *aff'd mem.,* 475 U.S. 10001 (1986).
28. Jeannie Suk Gersen, "The Trouble with Teaching Rape Law," *New Yorker,* 15 December 2014.
29. *Harris v. Forklift Sys., Inc.,* 510 U.S. 17, 21–22 (1993).
30. *Davis v. Monroe County Board of Education,* 526 U.S. pp. 629, 633 (1999).
31. American Association of University Professors, "The History, Uses, and Abuses of Title IX," report, June 2016.
32. *Speech First, Inc. v. Cartwright,* USCA11 Case: 21-1258, filed 21 April 2022, pp. 21–22.
33. College Pulse and FIRE, 2022–2023 "College Free Speech Rankings: What is the State of Free Speech on America's College Campuses?," at p. 37.
34. Ibid.

Foreword to the Second Edition

Wendy Kaminer

Imagine no religion, as John Lennon suggested. Imagine no authoritarianism. Now imagine no sex. You've just imagined no censorship, and, all things considered, it's a rather dystopian vision. Forced to choose, you might prefer sexual pleasure and the hope of salvation to uncontested free expression. But the prospect of no censorship is merely hypothetical; I'm afraid this book will always be timely. Driven by fear of sex, love of God, and lust for power, the urge to censor is a constant in social relations. It seems to come as naturally to people as the diverse sexual desires censors condemn.

But if censoriousness is perennial and practically universal, it waxes and wanes in response to particular social trends. What, in particular, fuels censorship campaigns in America today? Consider the obvious effects of feminism and the digital revolution, as well as the subtler influences of popular therapies.

An ideologically fractured movement, feminism has fought both for and against rights of speech. In the Victorian 1880s and, a century later, in the postmodern 1980s, some feminists demanded the censorship of whatever sexually explicit material they considered "vicious" or "pornographic." Some nineteenth-century women's rights advocates also opposed contraception, in the belief that it would facilitate sexual abuse. But over the past hundred years, other feminists have championed free love and free speech, while efforts to censor abortion rights advocates and sex educators like Margaret Sanger and Mary Ware Dennett have made clear the connection between freedom of speech and reproductive choice. In the 1960s and 1970s, the first generation of contemporary feminists sought sexual liberation along with economic equality. Then, antipornography feminists advanced in the 1980s (with the aid of the Reagan Administration, the President's Commission on

Pornography, and various censors on the right), but they were soon upstaged by the prosex Cosmo-feminists of the 1990s.

Neither the prosex nor the procensorship wing considers the other representative of "true feminism," and each is beset with internal contradictions. Considering its exaltation of conventional feminine beauty, Cosmo-feminism doesn't further the sexual liberation of homely women or celebrate nontraditional female achievement. (At its worst, it devolves into bimbo feminism.) The antiporn movement is more repressive, embracing traditional notions of female fragility and perverting the feminist drive to expand rights into a crusade to restrict them. Still, each of these opposing camps represents a historic force within the women's movement. Torn between concern about sexual violence and desire for sexual liberation, feminism has always had a rather conflicted relationship with liberty.

Technology also works for and against free speech (particularly speech about sex), as campaigns to censor cyberspace demonstrate. The introduction of the Internet into many American homes has exacerbated public concern about the welfare of children and the dangers of exposing them to "pornography," defined differently by different interest groups. It's hardly a surprising development. New technologies that aid the flow of information inevitably inspire renewed demands for censorship. For free speech advocates, that is the irony of progress.

What is it about the Internet in particular that inspires calls for censorship? It's not just that the Net brings its ideas and images directly into the home; radio and television have been doing that for decades. It's not just that minors may enjoy increased access to sexual explicitness in cyberspace; exposure of young children, in particular, to what many consider "adults only" content is a common concern, but also a familiar one that predates the Internet. I suspect that what greatly intensifies anxiety about harm to minors today is the fact that children are often more adept at using computers than their parents.

Censorship, after all, reflects the need to exert control over what others read and think and how they behave. The more people feel controlled by culture (and the less they feel in sync with it), the more intense their drive to censor. Antiporn feminists feel under attack by a predominantly sexist, violent culture. Right-wing Christians who began agitating for censorship of sex education and Darwinism in the 1970s feel besieged by a Godless culture and want to gain control of it. Parents left and right worry about controlling and protecting their kids. Their worries are naturally exacerbated as children enter their teens. Who can control a horny teenager, especially one who can exert more control of new technologies than his parents? Kids who've grown up with computers often have a sense of mastery in cyberspace that adults struggle to approximate.

Technology can facilitate unsettling familial role reversals. Some children teach their parents how to use computers (and other electronic devices) the way parents once taught their children how to read. Like first-generation Americans who grew up translating for their immigrant parents and guiding them through bureaucracies, some computer-savvy children have guided their parents through cyberspace.

I don't want to exaggerate the digital mastery of children, or the incompetence of adults (especially those under forty). There are many kids who are not yet online; the less affluent, in particular, have been left out of the digital culture. There are also families in which every member is computer literate. And a few adults, like Bill Gates and Steve Case, exert inordinate control of the development of cyberspace. But I suspect that many adults who grew up without computers will always share the sense that they are aliens or, at best, naturalized citizens in cyberspace, while children are its natives.

Precisely because they are technologically sophisticated but sexually naïve, minors are considered easy prey for pornographers and sex offenders rumored to be stalking cyberspace. It's worth noting that the introduction of computers into homes, public schools, and libraries coincided with an intense preoccupation with child abuse engendered by feminism and the late-twentieth-century recovery movement. It was bad luck for free speech advocates that the digital culture, with its vast new networks of information and entertainment, emerged at a time of intense concern about the effects of sexually explicit material on both children and adults. Campaigns against sexual expression became identified with crusades against child abuse, and the enjoyment of sexually explicit material was labeled an addiction—along with excessive use of computers.

But there is an even more insidious link between recent censorship campaigns and pop psychologies: The therapeutic culture promoted a xxxii   FOREWORD TO THE SECOND EDITION

preoccupation with self-esteem and psychic safety or comfort that practically compelled the censorship of speech considered offensive or abusive. (Sexual harassment is "making someone feel uncomfortable," students have explained to me.) "If you can't say something nice, don't say anything," my grandmother used to say, and popular victimist therapies, embraced by some regressive therapeutic feminists, reflected this very traditional feminine ideal. Argument, critical inquiry, and the raucous exchange of ideas, as well as presumptively offensive speech, were discouraged because, as my grandmother might have said, they're not "nice."

Neither is pornography, so it has been particularly vulnerable to attack in this overly solicitous culture that values inoffensiveness more than the right to speak. The notion that free expression has only instrumental value—that speech must be "good" or useful, or at the very least not bad, to be protected by the First Amendment—is the underlying rationale of censorship. Speech shouldn't have to justify itself as nice, socially constructive, or inoffensive in order to be protected. Civil liberty is shaped, in part, by the belief that free expression has normative or inherent value, which means that you have a right to speak regardless of the merits of what you say.

Unfortunately, the Supreme Court disagrees and has required that sexually explicit speech exhibit redeeming social value in order to avoid being prohibited as obscene. Meanwhile, relying on ideology rather than evidence, censors exaggerate the presumed harm of speech by focusing on its instrumental value or effects: Antiporn feminists accuse pornography of causing rape; denizens of the therapeutic culture (including advocates of political correctness) view words as actual weapons that inflict actual wounds and ought to be regulated; cybercensors claim that children are traumatized or forever corrupted by encountering sexually explicit speech and images on the Net.

Free speech advocates often find themselves trying to demonstrate the social value of sexual explicitness, in order to keep the censors at bay. Judges and juries are drawn into highly subjective discussions about what constitutes art (or politics), which ought to be legally irrelevant. You don't need to know anything about art—you don't even need to know what you like—in order to defend speech deemed hateful, sick, or pornographic. All you need is a commitment to liberty. It is just such a commitment that invigorates this book.

Introduction to the Second Edition

Eternal vigilance is the price of liberty.
—THOMAS JEFFERSON

No fight for civil liberties ever stays won.
—ROGER BALDWIN

The Same Old Suspect: Sexual Expression

Defending Pornography: Free Speech, Sex, and the Fight for Women's Rights documents battles that the American Civil Liberties Union (ACLU) and other activists have fought over and over in defending freedom for sexually oriented expression, and also for the advocates of women's rights, reproductive freedom, and lesbian and gay rights who are the disproportionate targets of efforts to suppress such expression. Since I wrote the book in 1994, we have continued to fight these very same battles, in the very same arenas, including school and public libraries, college and university courses and conferences, and art exhibits in public museums. Under continuing assault are all types of expression—words and images—with any sexual content, no matter how valuable, including rigorous academic programs, critically acclaimed art works, and every form of popular culture.

Since 1994, the major change in the attacks on sexual expression has been in form, not in substance. Hard as it now seems to believe, until the mid-1990s, most politicians, citizens, and even journalists were not paying much attention to the Internet or cyberspace. As soon as this new medium did make a big splash in the media, politics, and public consciousness, in 1995,[1] it prompted immediate cries for censorship—and, in particular, for censorship of sexually oriented expression. Once again, Thomas Jefferson and Roger Baldwin have proven prescient.

Since 1995, many of the high-profile struggles to defend freedom of expression have involved online expression.[2] In that sense, these struggles are new in form. In substance, however, these recent and ongoing struggles are "the same old, same old." For one thing, as I already indicated, almost all of the many cybercensorship measures that have been adopted or considered by lawmakers across the United States, mirroring media discussion, have focused on sexually oriented expression. This is true despite the fact that public concerns also have been provoked by many other types of online expression, ranging from racist "hate speech," to militaristic antigovernment sites, to Holocaust "revisionism" disinformation, to bomb-making instructions. By singling out sexual expression online, the new cybercensorship laws follow a longstanding American tradition, reflected in all efforts to restrict all media.

True to America's puritanical heritage, online sexual expression was the target of the two federal cybercensorship laws that had been enacted as of the turn of the millennium—the 1996 Communications Decency Act (CDA)[3] and the 1998 Child Online Protection Act (COPA).[4] Sexual expression also has been the target of all but one of the five state laws that single out particular types of online content for criminalization. And it has been the preeminent target of the many proposed policies to block access to certain online content, through filtering software, in public schools and libraries.

Just as the new cybercensors are carrying forward the old tradition of focusing on sexual expression, cyberlibertarians have been responding by carrying forward another old tradition—what the distinguished First Amendment scholar Harry Kalven, Jr. called "a worthy tradition: freedom of speech in America."[5] Specifically, the ACLU and other cyberlibertarians have been arguing that the tried-and-true First Amendment principles and precedents that the Supreme Court has enforced to provide a high degree of protection to traditional print publications should be carried forward into cyberspace. And the courts consistently have agreed; most significantly, the Supreme Court unanimously concurred with that central point in its landmark 1997 decision striking down the CDA, *Reno v. ACLU*.[6]

Despite our essentially unbroken string of victories in challenging cybercensorship laws at all levels of government, politicians continue to advocate and enact these laws. "Cyberporn" continues to serve as a popular scapegoat for a host of societal problems, such as the tragic school shooting incidents, and for an ideologically diverse array of cultural critics. Thus, the unholy alliance between the "Religious Right" and "radical feminists," described in this book, continues concerning cyberspace.

The cybercensorship laws all have sought to expand the boundaries of the sexually oriented expression that the Supreme Court has deemed unprotected in traditional media—notably, obscenity, child pornography, and sexual solicitation of a minor. To the extent that these laws simply have extended to cyberspace the limits on protected expression that the Supreme Court has upheld for print media, the ACLU has not challenged them. Rather, we have challenged the cybercensorship laws only to the extent that they also have sought to criminalize vague, broad categories of sexual expression that would be perfectly lawful—indeed, constitutionally protected—in print. For example, the CDA would have criminalized all expression that might be deemed "indecent" or "patently offensive" in any community, no matter how valuable that expression might be.

As *Defending Pornography* explains, the sole category of sexually oriented expression that the Supreme Court has held to be beyond the First Amendment pale only because of the (allegedly) offensive nature of its content* is obscenity, and that category has been relatively limited, thanks in substantial measure to the Court's requirement that it lack any serious literary, artistic, political, or scientific value, as determined by national standards.[7] In short, no matter how offensive a judge or jury may deem certain material under local community standards, it will still be constitutionally protected so long as it has serious value according to national standards. Therefore, people in any part of the United States cannot be reduced to seeing only what is deemed acceptable in every other part of the country. If the cybercensors had their way, this approach would be turned on its head, and the global medium

---

*In contrast, other sexually oriented expression may be regulated because of actual or threatened physical harm it causes—for example, the exploitation or abuse of a minor in producing child pornography or soliciting sexual contact.

of cyberspace would be reduced to the lowest common denominator that would not offend any local community.

As *Defending Pornography* details, the epithet "pornography" has demonized everything from the Bible to *Our Bodies, Ourselves*. Likewise, contemporary politicians and citizen activists crusade against "cyberporn" and then pass laws criminalizing everything from the ACLU's own website to those of the mainstream news organizations that posted the Starr Report online. In light of the dangers that the CDA and other sweeping cybercensorship laws pose for sexually oriented expression of particular value to women and women's rights causes, I am especially disheartened that some feminists have supported these laws. As has been true of all measures targeting sexual expression in any media throughout history, these virtual variations on the same old theme are especially threatening to relatively disempowered groups and relatively unpopular causes.

The Same Old Targets

Alas, it is still true, at the dawn of the new millennium, that women and sexual-orientation minorities are relatively disempowered, and that their rights are relatively unpopular causes. Moreover, there is reason to fear that these groups and causes will remain embattled. Consider, for example, the most comprehensive assessment of student attitudes, the annual survey of incoming college students conducted by UCLA's Higher Education Research Institute and the American Council on Education. Since the early 1990s, that survey has shown decreasing support for reproductive freedom and gay rights. Among students who entered college in 1999, only 52.7 percent believe that abortion should be legal and 30.3 percent said that "it is important to have laws prohibiting homosexual relationships."[8]

In Cyberspace . . .

These antichoice and antigay rights attitudes are manifest in the many antichoice and antigay actions by government officials and citizens all over the country, ranging from legislative assaults on rights to literal assaults on individuals who seek to exercise them. Therefore, it is not surprising that courts have concurred with the ACLU that prime targets of all the cybercensorship laws would include any expression concerning women's sexual and reproductive health and options, as well as any concerning lesbian and gay sexuality. This sad-but-true fact is illustrated by the clients that the ACLU has represented in our challenges to cybercensorship laws.

I find it particularly striking, for instance, that one of our clients in *Reno v. ACLU* was Planned Parenthood Federation of America. As *Defending Pornography* recounts, during the ACLU's first decade of existence, one of our clients was Margaret Sanger. She was repeatedly harassed and prosecuted under the Victorian-era Comstock Act, the first federal anti-obscenity law, which criminalized the information she conveyed about women's reproductive health and options. Sadly, more than three-quarters of a century later, we had to defend the organization that Sanger founded against the Internet era's first federal cybercensorship law, which criminalized the very same information.

Consider, also, just a few of the ACLU's other clients in challenges to cybercensorship measures that endangered their expression:

- American Association of University Women: Maryland, which promotes equity, education, self-development over the life span, and positive societal change, for all women and girls, and works to remove barriers and to develop opportunities to enable women and girls to reach their full potential
- Books for Gay and Lesbian Teens/Youth Page, which has a website operated by a high school student listing books that may be of interest to gay and lesbian youth
- Critical Path AIDS Project, an AIDS treatment and prevention information project that offers AIDS treatment and safer sex information specifically geared toward young people
- Full Circle Books, one of the oldest and largest feminist bookstores in North America
- Human Rights Watch, the largest U.S-based international human rights organization, which documents and challenges human rights abuses around the world, many of which involve sexual abuse against women

- Obgyn.net, a comprehensive international online resource center for professionals in obstetrics and gynecology and the women they serve, offering up-to-the-minute information, clinical reference collections, and discussion forums
- *Philadelphia Gay News,* an award-winning weekly
- PlanetOut, a website that serves as an online community for gay, lesbian, bisexual, and transgendered people and is a valuable resource for "closeted" people who do not voluntarily disclose their sexual orientation due to fear of other's reactions
- Queer Resources Directory, one of the largest online distributors of gay, lesbian, and bisexual resources on the Internet
- *Riotgrrl,* a magazine aimed at young feminists
- The Safer Sex Page, which maintains a large archive of information about minimizing the risks of sexually transmitted diseases
- *Salon Magazine,* a leading general-interest online magazine, whose feature articles address sexuality, among other topics, and which also includes a regular column entitled "Sexpert Opinion" by feminist author and sex therapist Susie Bright
- Sexual Health Network, which provides information about sexuality geared toward individuals with disabilities, including articles on erectile dysfunction, the use of sex toys, and sexual surrogacy as a form of sexual therapy
- Stop Prisoner Rape, which is dedicated to combating sexual abuse in our nation's prisons, including among the fastest growing segment of our nation's prison population—women[9]
- Jeff Walsh, editor of *Oasis Magazine,* a monthly online magazine for lesbian, gay, bisexual, and questioning youth, which includes news, reviews, and safer sex advice columns written by and for gay and lesbian youth.

The courts have agreed with us that the online expression of these individuals and organizations is subject to prosecution under the various cybercensorship laws that have been touted as "protecting children" from "cyberporn"—no matter how much serious value that expression has in general, and no matter how much serious value it has for the causes of women's rights, reproductive freedom, and lesbian/gay rights in particular. Thus, *Defending Pornography's* bottom-line conclusion—that

defending freedom of sexual expression is especially essential for advocates of women's rights, as well as of equality rights more broadly—
remains as true in cyberspace as it has been in other contexts. Far from
promoting equality, as procensorship feminists claim, suppressing sexually oriented expression undermines the equality cause.

This conclusion is captured visually by the frontispiece to this book:
Second Child Coming—a lovely, moving image, of a woman, by a woman,
for all women (and men). It is one of the many online images that celebrate the beauty and power of women's bodies and sexuality, but that
are nonetheless—or even, perhaps, for that very reason—imperiled by
cybercensorship laws. The artist, Saelon Renkes, is one of the more than
125 artists who maintain their own online studios or gallery spaces on
the Art on the Net website, which is yet another client in three ACLU
lawsuits challenging state cybercensorship laws (in Michigan, New
Mexico, and New York).[10] These statutes threatened any online display
of nudity, even in fine art.

Moreover, the model antipornography law drafted by Andrea Dworkin and Catharine MacKinnon would also jeopardize *Second Child Coming*. That law's dangerously vague, broad terms encompass any "pictures
and/or words" in which "women's body parts—including . . . breasts—
are exhibited such that women are reduced to those parts."[11] Renkes has
a very different view of her nude works, explaining: "In my nudes I am
often trying to capture just one of the many moods that make up a whole
person. The nudes are all collaborations with my models and I am very
much indebted to the women and men who have modeled for me."[12] The
MacDworkin law does not take account of the artist's—or model's—
intent. It holds all depictions of women's bodies—not just nudes or
semi-nudes—hostage to the (mis)perceptions of particular viewers. As
Andrea Dworkin herself said about a photograph of the writer Ntozake
Shange wearing a shoulder-baring bustier (which is reproduced following page 160 in this book), "It's very hard to look at a picture of a woman's
body and not see it with the perception that her body is being exploited."[13]

In Saelon Renkes' own words, *Second Child Coming* depicts a friend who

enjoys sharing her beauty and . . . being a part of the artist's efforts at
representing a healthy sensuality. She was about 8.5 months pregnant
in this photo, and she was giving her 2-year-old daughter a little extra

attention and making her a part of this exciting thing that was happening. To me the image is about all of those things: sexuality, fertility, family relationships and love, and our need for reassurance.[14]

While I am as uplifted by Renkes's words as by her image, I know from actual experience that other citizens and government officials have demonized similar images as illegal pornography, both online and off. For example, the expert witness who testified for the U.S. government in *ACLU v. Reno* condemned another photograph of the essentially identical subject matter—the nude torso of a woman in her last month of pregnancy—as precisely the type of "patently offensive" or "indecent" expression that would have been outlawed in cyberspace under the CDA, subjecting anyone who posted it online to two years in prison and $250,000 in fines. Specifically, the government witness decried such a photograph of the actress Demi Moore, even though she was discreetly posed so as not to reveal breast, buttock cleavage, or pubic area.[15]

In contrast, Renkes's stirring photograph of her friend does show frontal nudity, and moreover includes a provocative title and a child's bare arm, which will surely inflame the imaginations and the ire of those who are quick to spot that ultimate demon, "child porn," in any nude or semi-nude image of a child.[16]

Renkes herself has had repeated experiences with offline exhibits that banned any and all nudes because of the proprietors' concerns that viewers might consider them pornographic, and Renkes has received some similar email complaints about her online nudes.[17] To be sure, those complaints have been rare, and Renkes has received far more email praising and thanking her for her online work. These disparate reactions underscore the core problem with the CDA and other sexual censorship schemes: No matter how highly valued a work is, among no matter how large a majority of the viewing public, it can still be banished; all that takes is one prosecutor or judge who considers the work to fall afoul of his or her personal, subjective view of material that is "offensive," "indecent," or "harmful to minors." Likewise, under the model antipornography law promoted by procensorship feminists Andrea Dworkin and Catharine MacKinnon, all it takes is one person who considers the work to be "subordinating" or "degrading" to women.

. . . *And in Meatspace*

I would like to cite one example of an attack on sexual expression, subsequent to the original publication of *Defending Pornography,* that underscores how these attacks erode equal rights and foster discrimination against relatively disempowered groups—in this instance, sexual-orientation minorities. This particular attack was a relatively little known aspect of the otherwise widely publicized controversy about President Clinton's nomination of James Hormel, the distinguished San Francisco philanthropist, to serve as U.S. Ambassador to Luxembourg. As an openly gay man, Hormel saw his nomination stonewalled (pun intended!) for almost two years by Senate Majority Leader Trent Lott, acting at the behest of the "Religious Right."[18] Although Hormel's nomination was widely endorsed by respected leaders from across the political spectrum, influential senators expressed concern that he would promote the "gay agenda" in Luxembourg.[19] What is less well known is that one of the accusations in the vicious attack against Hormel was that he promoted pornography—because he gave a generous gift to help establish the Gay and Lesbian Center at the new San Francisco Public Library. Anti-gay-rights activists pored through materials at the Center and compiled a collection of works that they condemned as "pro-pedophilia, anti-Christian, and pornographic."[20] It would be bad enough to attack the professional library staff for deciding to acquire these materials; it adds insult to injury to attack the donor who had no role in the acquisition decisions. Still, Hormel's well-organized, influential opponents demanded that he explicitly denounce each of the challenged works.

As advocates of Hormel's ambassadorial appointment pointed out, these supposedly pornographic, supposedly disqualifying works are also included in the Library of Congress's collection. But I always get nervous when this kind of comparative argument is offered up in an attempt to placate censors. Chances are, rather than diverting the censors from one target, this argument will *also* channel their suppressive efforts toward a second target. Sure enough, the Traditional Values Coalition indicated an interest in investigating the "pornography" that is polluting the Library of Congress's collection.[21]

The Same Old Double Standard

Fascination . . .

Americans' attitudes toward sexual expression—not to mention toward sex itself—continue to reflect inconsistency at best, and hypocrisy at worst. While deploring the dangers of sex and sexual expression—especially for other people and their children—Americans are major consumers of all manner of such expression. Again continuing patterns in other media, among the first and most popular uses of cyberspace by John Q. Public—and Jane—has been for purveying and procuring sexually oriented words and images. (The fact that sexually oriented online sites are relatively popular should be distinguished from the fiction—purveyed by cybercensors[22]—that the Net is dominated by pornographic sites. A comprehensive 1999 survey of publicly indexable websites concluded that only 1.5 percent contain pornographic content.[23])

In the late 1990s, online sex merchants were the major Internet content providers who were making a profit,[24] prompting one observer to dub them "Web commerce's dirty little secret."[25] According to Media Metrix, the PC Meter Co., which monitors consumer activity online, in nearly one-fourth of households with Internet access, adult sites are visited at least once monthly. Industry sources say that sex-related Web searches account for up to 20 percent of search engine requests.[26] A March, 2000 *U.S. News & World* Report cover feature on "porn dot com" documented the continued burgeoning of the cyberporn business after the turn of the millennium and the maturing of e-commerce:

> Just a few years ago, Web pundits predicted that erotica would recede into the shadows once "legitimate" E-commerce blossomed. But with the dot-comming of America near complete, salacious fare remains a huge—and growing—cyberspace draw. According to Nielsen NetRatings, 17.5 million surfers visited porn sites from their homes in January, a 40 percent increase compared with four months earlier. The top E-porn site—PornCity.net—boasted more unique visitors in January than ESPN.com, CDNOW, or barnesandnoble.com.[27]

Women are active purveyors, as well as consumers, of online sexual expression. For example, an article about "cybermistresses" concludes that "in the rapidly exploding world of cyberporn, some of the most successful entrepreneurs are women."[28]

Our fellow—and sister—Americans are also consuming more traditional forms of pornography on a massive, and growing, scale. Total annual porn sales in *fin-de-siècle* America topped $8 billion per year,[29] and at least a quarter of these sales were directly generated by women.[30] More than 80 percent of college women report having used some kind of adult material.[31]

The porn industry is large, not only in absolute terms, but also relative to its nonpornographic counterparts, and it is on an upward trajectory. For example, in 1998 the production of porn videos was a $4-billion-per-year business,[32] up from $1.6 billion in 1992.[33] This was nearly half the total revenues of the major Hollywood studios combined, and accounts for about a quarter of all video sales in the United States.[34] As of mid-1999, feature filmmaking had declined by 13 percent since the previous year, while porn videomaking had grown by 25 percent.[35] Likewise, as *U.S. News & World Report* detailed in a 1997 cover story, "The Business of Pornography," the revenues from strip clubs outstripped—so to speak—those of "Broadway, off-Broadway, regional, and non-profit theaters," as well as "the opera, the ballet, and jazz and classical music performances—combined."[36] When one considers the whole panoply of adult entertainment—"hard-core videos, peep shows, live sex acts, adult cable programming, sexual vices, computer porn, and sex magazines"—Americans spend a total amount "much larger than Hollywood's domestic box office receipts and larger than all the revenues generated by rock and country music recordings."[37] As *U.S. News's* then editor, James Fallows, noted in an essay introducing the cover story, "the pornography boom" constitutes "one of the most rapidly growing [businesses] in the modern American economy."[38]

Not only is the adult entertainment industry flourishing, but it is doing so in the open, and around the country—a phenomenon that has been described as "the mainstreaming of pornography."[39] Approximately 25,000 video stores rent and sell hard-core films, and "mom and pop" video shops derive substantial income from porn.[40] Additionally, recent hit movies such as *The People vs. Larry Flynt* and *Boogie Nights* cast the adult entertainment industry in a relatively positive light.[41] According to the Free Speech Coalition, the nation's largest adult industry trade association,[42] "The barrier separating adult entertainment from the rest of the entertainment world is crumbling." In support of that conclusion it noted, for example, that "cable television has embraced explicit sexual series, often depending on adult industry talent, from both sides of the camera."[43]

There is another indication that most Americans at least tolerate pornography, even if they do not personally participate in its burgeoning market. Although there has been much clamoring for technological devices and other measures to limit access to sexually oriented expression, once these are available they are not used by most members of the public, or even by most parents. That has been true, for example, of lockboxes on cable TV, procedures to block dial-a-porn services on telephones, and—most recently—the vaunted V-chip on TV.[44] If these patterns continue to hold true in cyberspace, then we should expect relatively few parents to avail themselves of the access that Internet service providers routinely offer, free of charge, to blocking software that aims to shield children from materials that are deemed inappropriate for them—including, preeminently, sexual materials.[45]

If these devices could operate in a way that truly facilitated individual choices, they would be fully consistent with freedom of speech, as well as with parents' fundamental, constitutionally protected right to shape the education and values of their own young children. But when these devices have the practical effect, for technological or economic reasons, of reducing freedom of choice for mature adults, they undermine free expression and should be held unconstitutional. In the one litigated case involving mandatory filtering software on computers in public libraries, this was precisely the court's conclusion.[46]

To allow a noisy minority that chooses not to partake of sexual expression themselves to censor it for everyone else would be to turn the First Amendment upside down. Along with other fundamental rights, the free speech guarantee is intentionally countermajoritarian, designed to protect the rights of even small, unpopular minorities against what has been called the "tyranny of the majority."[47] As Justice William Brennan wrote for the majority of the Supreme Court in invalidating the very popular laws that criminalized the very unpopular expression of flag burning, the "bedrock principle" of our free speech jurisprudence is that "government may not prohibit the expression of an idea simply because society finds the idea offensive or disagreeable."[48] Accordingly, it should be unconstitutional to suppress sexual expression just because it is offensive to the majority of the community; worse yet is suppressing sexual expression that is not offensive to most members of the community.

. . . And Fear

Notwithstanding the widespread and growing consumption of sexually oriented expression, popular opinion on the whole appears at least to profess support for censoring sexual expression, particularly in media that are widely accessible. For example, in a comprehensive survey that the Freedom Forum conducted in 1999, only 24 percent of respondents said that sexually explicit material should be permitted online, and for basic cable and magazines the corresponding numbers were 26 and 45 percent, respectively.[49]

This apparent inconsistency between actions and attitudes no doubt reflects in part a double standard—wanting sexual expression to be available for oneself but not for other people. It likely also is partly attributable to embarrassment or hypocrisy—an unwillingness to admit, or even a false denial, that one wishes to have access to sexual expression. This apparent inconsistency may well also reflect the fact that most people contemplate some category of sexually oriented expression that they would sincerely choose not to see themselves. Whatever that type of expression might be for any particular woman, it quite likely springs to mind when she hears such stigmatizing terms as "pornography" or "cyberporn."

In my experience, most people are genuinely surprised—and shocked—when they learn that laws that have been billed as "protecting children" from "cyberporn" in fact endanger adult access to sexually oriented expression that is not connoted by this epithet. And most people who have not personally wrestled with the intractable problem even of defining the category of sexual expression they choose not to see—let alone the category of sexual expression (if any) that should be illegal—cannot fully appreciate the significance of Justice Potter Stewart's famous dictum: "I shall not today attempt further to define [obscenity] . . . ; and perhaps I could never succeed in intelligibly doing so. But I know it when I see it."[50]

The general popular support for restricting sexual expression is reflected in the votes of our so-called political "leaders," who too often simply follow the latest public opinion polls. Almost no one in Congress, on either side of the aisle, has had the political courage to vote against measures touted as "protecting children" against "cyberporn." With legislation bearing labels such as the "Child Online Protection Act," it is hardly surprising that most politicians dare not oppose it. Therefore, these measures typically have passed by overwhelming majorities in Congress and state legislatures, and also have been championed by the White House and by governors across the country.

Shifting Cultural Sands

Measures suppressing sexual expression online and elsewhere continue to garner especially strong support from particular segments of the public—notably, cultural or religious conservatives and procensorship feminists. Since the early 1990s, however, cultural shifts seem to indicate a decline in influence on the part of both factions. Admittedly, these trends are difficult to measure. Still, many observers have commented that these movements appear to have lost some influence in what had been their respective strongholds—for the "Religious Right," the Republican Party,[51] and for "radical feminists," academia in general and women's studies programs in particular. Indeed, so far has the Republican Party distanced itself from the cultural and religious right that this was cited by one of the party's own stalwarts, Pat Buchanan, as the reason why he jumped ship.[52]

Journalists have chronicled the rise of a new breed of feminists, increasingly prominent both in women's studies programs and in academia more generally, as well as on the wider cultural scene, who hardly eschew sexuality and sexual expression. To the contrary, this group of female, feminist scholars, artists, and activists not only defend sexuality and sexual expression against repression; what's more, they proactively celebrate and even create it.[53] From their perspective, the title of my book conveys a posture that is overly—well—defensive.

One manifestation of this new feminist prosex movement is the nationwide success of Eve Ensler's award-winning play, *The Vagina Monologues*.[54] Its graphic treatment of not only female sexual organs but also female sexual pleasure extends beyond simulation to stimulation. In short, it satisfies the dictionary denotation of "pornography" as sexually arousing expression. As one (male) reviewer observed:

> All around the country, men are dialing those 900 numbers and paying several bucks a minute for this kind of performance. And the show has the feel of male pornography, from the stupid puns on the posters ("Think Outside the Box"), to the structure (a series of unrelated sexual encounters), to the worldview (women want to have sex all the time), to the underlying message of each episode (great sex is possible between people who have absolutely no emotional commitment to each other).[55]

In February 2000, *The Vagina Monologues* was attacked by a conservative taxpayers' group in New York, which objected to the play's planned performances at state colleges and universities and said, "This show should be kicked off the campuses."[56] That *The Vagina Monologues* would be criticized by cultural and religious conservatives is not surprising. After all, it celebrates not only women's sexuality, but also women's freedom to explore and enjoy that sexuality outside the "traditional nuclear family." What is surprising, though, is that this wise and witty work has escaped the wrath of antiporn feminists. To the contrary, it has been produced and attended all over the country, including on hundreds of campuses, with the strong support of the feminist community. I doubt this could have happened in the heyday of Mac-Dworkinism; procensorship feminists likely would have tried to block the production or would have attended it only for purposes of picketing and protesting. Recall that the Dworkin-MacKinnon model antipornography statute condemns any sexually explicit material in which "women's body parts—including . . . vaginas . . . —are exhibited such that women are reduced to those parts."[57] A recurrent theme in *The Vagina Monologues* is precisely that women do or should see themselves as their sexual body parts. The author and the actresses clearly intend this process of sexual self-discovery to serve an expansive function—opening women up to new pleasures, possibilities, and powers. Yet, viewed through the antiporn prism (speculum?), the work could well be attacked as reductionist.

Nor would the play's antisexual violence theme save it from procensorship feminists. On the contrary, the Dworkin-MacKinnon model law expressly proscribes descriptions or depictions in which "women are presented in scenarios of degradation, humiliation, injury, torture, shown as . . . bleeding, bruised, or hurt in a context that makes these conditions sexual."[58] One of the most powerful, vivid *Vagina* monologues was a Bosnian Muslim woman graphically recounting—and visibly reliving—the savage gang rapes and other forms of sexual torture and disfigurement she endured during the Balkan conflict. In a 1993 *Ms. Magazine* cover story, Catharine MacKinnon denounced descriptions or depictions of the mass rapes in the Balkans as themselves pornographic.[59]

Another measure of the mark that the new proporn and prosex movement has made is that it already has triggered its own backlash—a neo-antisex movement.[60] As this development indicates, the debates within feminism, as well as within society at large, will predictably continue in cyclical fashion, which is why the arguments in *Defending Pornography* will continue to be relevant, no matter which viewpoint happens to be in the ascendancy at any particular moment or in any particular segment of society. For one thing, there are distinct geographical differences in the prevailing debate—reflecting, in part, differences in timing. Movements and views that at one time reflect the avant-garde in one region or country may be adopted as such in other regions or countries only after those movements and views have become passé in their places of origin. For example, feminists in Britain and New Zealand have told me that their women's movements are several years "behind" those in the United States in terms of debates about pornography and free expression.

While the procensorship position is increasingly recognized as not being "the"—or even the most important—feminist perspective on sexual expression, it certainly continues to be disturbingly dominant in many important quarters. There are still too many individuals and institutions, including within the academic elite, inclined to accept uncritically the procensorship perspective. Moreover, there are important areas of the law—notably, concerning sexual harassment—that continue too reflexively to mirror MacDworkinism, falsely equating any sexual expression with sexist harassment.

There's More to Sex than Harassment

Defending Pornography contains one of the earliest discussions about the dangerously diversionary nature of this distorted concept of sexual harassment, which deflects attention away from nonsexual expression or conduct that *does* constitute gender-discriminatory harassment, at the same time that it demonizes sexual expression or conduct even if it does *not* constitute gender-discriminatory harassment. Since then, a number of articles and books—including by feminist scholars—have echoed and amplified this critique.[61] Additionally, the U.S. Supreme Court has issued a series of decisions that have provided more guidance in this area of the law,[62] including a welcome—and needed—clarification that not every remark or action with sexual connotations should be treated as sexual harassment.[63]

Despite these encouraging developments, situations continue to abound in which even serious discussions with some sexual dimensions are automatically deemed to be punishable sexual harassment, even in the academic settings where such discussions are especially important. For example, in 1992 Dean Cohen, a professor of English and film studies at San Bernardino Valley College in California, was punished for sexual harassment after a student complained because Cohen required his class to write essays defining pornography—yes, that was de*fin*ing pornography, not de*fend*ing it. Worse yet, the federal trial court actually upheld the college's disciplinary actions against Cohen; he was not finally vindicated until the appellate court ruled on his case in 1996.[64] Even then, four years after Cohen had been charged with and punished for sexual harassment, an after-the-fact ruling by appellate judges was hardly vindication; nothing could be. Under these circumstances, it is not surprising that many professors say they avoid discussing any topic with sexual connotations, no matter how relevant it might be to the subject they are teaching.

Chilly as the climate concerning sexual expression is on public campuses, at least there the Constitution's free speech guarantee constitutes
a potential safety net for such expression. In contrast, the Constitution
does not extend, even in theory, to the private sector. Accordingly, professors at private universities engage in any expression with any sexual
connotations or implications—even attenuated ones—at their peril.

Consider one situation that occurred at Columbia Law School in
1999.[65] A prominent criminal law professor, George Fletcher, was accused
by some students of creating a "hostile environment for women" and was
castigated by the law school dean, David Leebron, in memoranda to the
faculty and second-year students, for violating "the standards of respect
for all students that we expect and encourage in members of the Columbia Law School community."[66] Why? Because a question on Fletcher's
forty-eight-hour take-home examination for the required introductory
criminal law course, based on important actual cases that had been discussed in the class, graphically described brutal attacks on fetuses in
utero, and hence on the pregnant women who were carrying them.

The contested question focused on the problem of feticide, the mali-
cious killing of a fetus against the woman's will, surely a matter of grave
concern to advocates of women's rights and women's safety. Yet various students and faculty members denounced the question as "offensive," "insensitive" to women, "misogynistic," "coercive," and an "abuse
of power." While no official sanction was imposed against Fletcher,
Dean Leebron's letter to students conveyed official disapprobation: "On
behalf of the law school, I want to express my regret for the offense and
distress that many of you . . . experienced."

While some complaints focused on the exam's "tone," rather than the
issues it presented, some also opined that any issues of particular concern to women, such as abortion or bias crimes against women, should
be off-limits as examination subjects. By this standard, I would have to
plead guilty to creating a hostile environment for my female students
by including a question in the final exam for my fall 1999 constitutional
law course about the Violence Against Women Act,[67] whose (un)con-
stitutionality was argued before the Supreme Court in January 2000.
The lower court opinions[68] and the lawyers' briefs, portions of which
I required my students to read, were replete with graphic details about
sexist and sexual violence and abuse against a woman.

I have discussed the Fletcher exam controversy with colleagues at Columbia Law School and elsewhere—including colleagues who are committed to free speech and women's rights—who believe that Fletcher was appropriately censured for this exam question. They stress that he remained free to address the issues presented in the exam in other fora, including the classroom. From their perspective, though, an exam is a unique setting, in which students are especially vulnerable and professors must be especially careful to avoid treating any student(s) unfairly or unequally. While I certainly share these principles, I do not share the view that they are violated whenever an exam question involves sexual abuse, violence against women, abortion, or other matters specific to women.

At stake in this situation are not only free speech and academic freedom, but also women's dignity and equality. How can female law students be trained to follow in the footsteps of Linda Fairstein and other leading prosecutors of those who attack women—including pregnant women—if they are deemed too fragile to confront even abbreviated verbal descriptions of these crimes? How, then, can they confront the assailants directly in court? And does this mean that women are presumptively even less capable of becoming police officers and confronting actual and would-be assailants even more directly, at street level? Indeed, one female student informed Professor Fletcher that the process of wrestling with the issues presented by his exam question was a valuable preparation for her summer job, which required her to analyze numerous files on rape prosecutions.

The position advocated by some of Fletcher's critics smacks of a paternalistic—or maternalistic—protectionism that is antithetical to women's equality and empowerment more broadly. This point was forcefully made by two female Columbia Law School students in a letter to the school's newspaper about the Fletcher exam controversy:

> There is an insidious implication, when asking for special sensitivity in dealing with women, that women are fragile little things who can't hear anything unpleasant, much less meet the challenges that are regularly doled out to men. Now that's offensive to women. . . . The best way to prepare women for the inevitable sexism permeating the legal community is to treat them as full equals, unflinchingly handing out the burdens of equality as well as the benefits.[69]

The false equation between expression touching on sexuality and sexist harassment has also been extended into cyberspace. Worse yet, government officials have cited concerns with avoiding sexual harassment as a purported justification for banning online sexual expression from workplaces or other facilities, such as libraries, where there are computers with Internet access. Their sweepingly censorial contention is that the mere availability of sexually explicit materials on those computers somehow creates a hostile environment for women employees, students, or others who are in the vicinity of the computers.

This was an asserted justification for a 1997 policy adopted by the Loudoun County, Virginia public library system, requiring filtering software to block sexually oriented material in all library computers.[70] (This law was held unconstitutional for several reasons, including that it was not narrowly tailored to promote the asserted government interests.)

Protecting women from sexual harassment was also an asserted justification for a 1996 Virginia law that effectively barred any government employees from using workplace computers to access any sexually oriented material, no matter how relevant to their work. The ACLU challenged the law on behalf of state university professors who were thus prevented from using their office computers to do research in their fields, including women's studies and lesbian/gay studies.[71]

George Mason University cited this sexual harassment rationale (rationalization?) in ordering a professor to remove from his own website sexually explicit images he had posted as examples of censorship. Paul Smith, then a professor of English and cultural studies at George Mason, had researched and published extensively on the relations among gender, sexuality, and visual representations, including the ways in which pornography shapes gender roles and sexual identity. Smith maintained his own website as part of his academic work. Although no university employees were required to look at this website, university officials said that they had received complaints about it from some employees, and cited these complaints as a purported justification not only for censoring Smith's website, but also for the restrictive law in general. Fortunately, the lower court judge rejected the government's breathtakingly suppressive "contention that a female employee's voluntary decision to access sexual material not on display in the workplace can be construed as sexual hostility directed against that employee."[72]

It is important to understand that the doubly distorted approach undergirding the attacks on these professors—treating all expression with sexual dimensions as creating a hostile environment—is not a misinterpretation of the MacDworkinite philosophy. On the contrary, MacKinnon has expressly advocated precisely this result.[73] This misguided approach has been accepted too uncritically, not only in media and public notions of sexual harassment or "hostile environments," but also in legal and institutional rules. Therefore, we tend too readily to conflate sex with sexism.

As University of Massachusetts women's studies professor Daphne Patai has trenchantly observed, "'[H]arassment' threatens to become the predominant word associated with 'sexual.'"[74] Tellingly, the title of her book critiquing sexual harassment doctrine is *Heterophobia*. In the same vein, Joan Kennedy Taylor laments that "the very mechanisms that have been instituted . . . with such high hopes to revolutionize society and create better relationships, are instead sowing anger and mistrust."[75]

The unfortunate excesses and distortions concerning sexual harassment not only threaten free speech, but also fail to effectively promote—and may well subvert—the very gender equality, and positive working and educational environments that this legal concept aims to promote. Therefore, it is especially important that Patai, Taylor, and other feminists continue to raise concerns about these trends and to try to redirect our focus away from the "sexual" and back toward the "harassment." This theme has been developed in the greatest detail by Yale Law School professor Vicki Schultz. She summarized the analysis she presents in her exhaustive law review article on the topic as follows:

The prevailing paradigm for understanding sex-based harassment places sexuality . . . at the center of the problem. . . . It is time for a reconceptualization of sex-based harassment—and harassment law—along more comprehensive lines. It is time to focus on gender along with sexuality, on the monopolization of work competence along with sexual abuse. . . . That task involves returning to Title VII's original purpose, which was to empower everyone—whatever their sex or gender—to pursue their life's work on equal terms.[76]

Despite the increasing critiques of and alternatives to MacKinnon's dangerously capacious notion of sexual harassment, it still tends to be viewed as "the" feminist perspective on this issue, and as such is accepted too uncritically in too many quarters. For example, during the spring of 1998, no less prestigious a law school than Yale hosted a conference on MacKinnon's contributions to sexual harassment law and policy that was essentially a lovefest. Only a few speakers were invited who had anything critical or even skeptical to say about her ideas—and those were, by design, white males.[77] Not only were any free speech concerns cavalierly brushed aside as, to quote one speaker, "frivolous,"[78] worse yet, it was suggested that only sexist men could possibly have any such concerns. Dworkin denounced those who dare to raise First Amendment (or other) criticisms of the MacDworkin orthodoxy on sexual harassment as "millions of men [who] want to have a young woman at work to suck their cock."[79]

Not All Feminists Think Alike

Both the exclusion of female, feminist critics and the male-bashing at the Yale Law School conference reflect an ongoing strategy of MacKinnon, Dworkin, and their acolytes, as described in *Defending Pornography*, they want to convey the misimpression that they speak for all women, and perhaps even for all members of traditionally disempowered groups, including racial minorities. If you disagree with their views, you must be a man—or a lackey of the male power establishment. Accordingly, MacKinnon and Dworkin continue to refuse to share public platforms with me and other women who have different perspectives on pornography, sexual harassment, and other issues concerning equality and free speech. Let me cite just one such incident subsequent to those I describe in this book.

David M. O'Brien, professor of political science at the University of Virginia, was editing a textbook on various civil liberties issues, including the censorship of pornography.[80] He wanted to include excerpts from some of my writings and some of MacKinnon's. When she heard that some of my words would be included—heaven forefend—in the same book as some of hers, she had a tantrum and told the publisher that he would have to choose—her words or mine. The publisher refused to withdraw my piece, so MacKinnon pulled hers—even though the book was in galleys. In the end, MacKinnon was hoisted by her own petard; my piece got published and hers did not. Yet for each such incident that comes to my attention, I am sure there are many others that do not, and in which the outcome is quite different.

Mind you, in selecting or designing a particular forum, both the speaker and the forum organizer are exercising free speech rights. The ACLU and I would have defended the Yale conference organizers against any attempt to interfere with their agenda, which would have violated academic freedom principles. Likewise, I am exercising my own free speech rights to criticize such forums and the ideas they showcase on their (de)merits. No draconian Dworkinian hyperbole can camouflage the fact that she is just plain wrong in denying the existence of female, feminist "heretics" from Mac-Dworthodoxy. And it is intellectually shoddy at best, and dishonest at worst, to dismiss dissenting views as mere sexist, misogynist prejudices, not ideas to be discussed and debated.

While none of the growing number of female, feminist critics of the MacDworkinite approach to sexual harassment law was invited to speak at the Yale Law School symposium, they have found other forums for their important message, including some in which MacDworkinites do not participate. In short, if one looks beyond any particular forum to discussions about sexual harassment and sexual expression more generally, a healthy range of feminist perspectives is represented.

These specific situations in which the perspectives of anticensorship feminists are—or are sought to be—stifled underscore the ongoing importance of airing those perspectives in other situations that do provide such an opportunity. The call for "eternal vigilance" cannot be repeated too often.

Media and Political Attacks against Sexually Oriented Campus Expression

The speech-threatening incidents I have described reflect the deep-rooted, pervasive, persistent hostility to sexual expression in America, which descends from our puritanical heritage and extends to some of the very precincts where we would expect sexual expression to be most protected, such as academia. As many commentators have noted, some of these suppressive efforts emanate from within the campus communities themselves, including from faculty and administrators with left-leaning views.[81] MacKinnon is a prime case in point.

Important as it is to criticize and resist any attacks of this ilk on campus free speech, it is also important to keep them in perspective. We must not lose sight of the fact that many if not most attacks on campus free speech continue to come from other sources, including conservative commentators and politicians who attack professors and campus officials for engaging in or defending expression about sex.

Some of the attacks on campus expression with sexual themes, including feminist and lesbian/gay expression, are well-publicized. One prominent example is the crusade by New York governor George Pataki and some of his appointees to the New York Board of Regents against the faculty and administration of the State University of New York (SUNY) at New Paltz because of the November 1997 women's studies conference "Revolting Behavior: The Challenges of Women's Sexual Freedom," which included workshops on some sexually oriented themes.[82] Governor Pataki denounced the university's president, Roger W. Bowen, for defending the academic freedom rights at stake, and SUNY trustee Candace de Russy was one of many vitriolic critics who called for Bowen's resignation.

Bowen earned a rare award from the American Association of University Professors for his stalwart support of First Amendment values against enormous pressures.[83] Even five months after the controverted conference, when I visited SUNY–New Paltz to address a symposium on academic freedom that Bowen had convened in response to the furor, the censorial, political pressures remained palpable.

Other incidents do not receive much, if any, publicity beyond the campus concerned, thus increasing the chilling effect there. Let me mention two such incidents, of which I happen to know only because I had some personal contact with the programs at the center of the controversies.

The first took place at California State University–Northridge (CSU-Northridge), arising from a 1998 symposium that was organized by the

University's Center for Sex Research, with the provocative title "World Pornography Conference: Eroticism and the First Amendment." This global gathering included some representatives from the adult entertainment industry—for example, porn movie performers and producers—who provided fascinating perspectives on their work. Most participants and presenters, though, were far more typical of an academic conference, engaged in providing stimulation of only the intellectual sort. The majority of symposium participants were professors who had examined pornography from a wide range of disciplines, including anthropology, comparative literature, film studies, history, law, philosophy, psychology, and sociology; and lawyers who had advocated constitutional protection for sexually oriented expression. I had the honor of delivering the keynote address at the conference, and I was dazzled by the diverse array of scholars and lawyers it brought together, from various countries, engaged in the serious study of sexually oriented expression, and making intellectually challenging, thought-provoking presentations about their research and reflections.[84]

In light of the constant scapegoating of sexually oriented expression, it was predictable that the conference and its organizers would come under attack. Indeed, just in my limited role as a speaker at the conference, I was immediately excoriated in two New York City tabloids.[85] Those salvos were nothing, though, compared to what was endured by the director of CSU-Northridge's Center for Sex Research, and the chief conference organizer, Professor James Elias. He and his whole Center became targets of a witchhunt by certain California politicians, who repeatedly questioned him, called him and other university officials before legislative committees, and launched a full-scale official audit by the California Bureau of State Audits. The government auditors subjected Professor Elias and his academic colleagues not only to verbal inquisitions, but also to a culling through their offices and papers. The asserted justification for this massive invasion of academic freedom was an allegation that the Center had somehow misused state university resources. Despite persistent, punitive probes, however, the Center's political persecutors were unable to find any evidence to substantiate any charge.[86]

As if the unjustified political inquisition were not punishment enough, the Center still suffered additional penalties, despite its exoneration on all allegations. The Center's charter, which it had initially received in the mid-1970s, and which had been periodically renewed since then, was put on hold in 1998 when it came up for another renewal. Furthermore, the Center's proposed 1999 conference—"Queer Activisms for a New Millennium: Lesbian, Bisexual, Gay, and Transgender Politics in California"—was dropped. After the controversial 1998 conference, the CSU-Northridge Provost instructed Professor Elias not to plan any conferences for 1999.

Even more chillingly, the California State Auditor suggested that California universities take steps "to protect . . . the State from objections arising over future conferences dealing with controversial subjects."[87] Note that the potential future objections that are of concern to this government official do not have to do with the absence of academic merit, but rather, merely with the presence of controversial subjects—no matter how important, and no matter how valuable a conference's examination of them.

Both the goals and the tactics aimed against Professor Elias were, in a word, McCarthyite (or, as one of my colleagues suggested, "MacKarthyite"!), violating constitutional rights, academic freedom, and human dignity in an effort to taint him as a subversive force, an "enemy of the state." Now that the Communist bogeyman is no longer here to haunt us, some politicians seek to demonize sexuality more than ever.

This tendency is illustrated by another similar situation, of which I also happened to learn because of my personal contact with some members of the campus community in question. This controversy erupted in 1999 at Wesleyan University in Middletown, Connecticut. Since the 1997–98 academic year, one of the many challenging, diverse courses that Wesleyan offered, "Pornography: Writing of Prostitutes," involved an in-depth study of pornography as a social and cultural artifact. It was designed and taught by a respected senior faculty member who was one of the founders of Wesleyan's Women's Studies Department, Professor Hope Weissman. The course description stressed that the reading materials would be difficult for all, and even offensive to some. The readings included classic works of literature and literary criticism. Students were held to rigorous standards and required to produce several in-depth papers and projects.

In contrast to the caricatured depiction of this course that swirled through the media when it somehow captured a commentator's attention in 1999, it was hardly a mindless celebration of commercial erotica. To the contrary, it adopted an intensely intellectual, highly critical stance, focusing on pornography that "depict[s] the extreme states of sexuality and aggression," and that "can be considered a . . . disease of the psychological and social human organism, much as tuberculosis . . . is a disease of the physical human organism."[88] Indeed, when I read this portion of Professor Weissman's description, I was initially concerned that, if anything, the course's focus on the violent aspects of pornography might encourage students to adopt a censorial perspective. This concern was allayed by the remainder of the course description, though, with its overall emphasis on open intellectual inquiry and expression.

I also had the opportunity to discuss the course with Professor Weissman and her students at a fall 1999 campus-wide forum, arising from the controversy, which I had been invited to address. They stressed that the course challenged students to examine the senses in which certain violent pornography reveals individual and societal "dis-ease" or disturbances, and to grapple with root causes of such societal problems as sexual violence. While certainly not advocating censorship, the course also was worlds apart from the pro-pornography pandering that the media concocted.

Given how provocative the topic of pornography always is—under siege by everyone from procensorship feminists to proponents of "traditional family values"—it is an extraordinary testament to Professor Weissman and her course that, during the two years it was taught, it garnered not a single complaint by a Wesleyan student, parent, faculty member, member of the administration, alumnus, or alumna.

Then, in 1999, the media got wind of the course and all hell broke loose! Dr. Laura Schlessinger launched the attack on her radio show and in her syndicated column,[89] and Rush Limbaugh and other conservative media mouthpieces also jumped on the bashing bandwagon.[90] The course they lampooned was a parody of the intellectually serious, demanding one that was actually taught. Schlessinger "condemned" Wesleyan "for this vile offering under the guise of education."[91] An editorial in the *Hartford Courant* denounced the entire university as "that bastion of liberal and libertine thought in Middletown" and the particular course as "trash."[92]

All of this hoopla apparently led some Wesleyan alumni and potential donors to raise some questions with the administration. President Douglas Bennet received such a glut of critical letters that he had to reroute his email account. In response to the uproar, Bennet undertook an unprecedented review of the course, contrary to Wesleyan's standard procedures, under which such reviews are initiated only by the faculty. Worse yet, he proposed a new procedure of special "screening" for any course that contains "sensitive" material that "could offend," citing race or gender issues as examples.[93] But subjects that are especially "sensitive" are also especially important. Therefore, we must be free on campus to explore and discuss matters of sex, gender, and race candidly, without fear of being denounced as pornographers, sexists or racists, not to mention without fear of being denied tenure or disciplined.

Unfortunately, there are many situations in which faculty members and students alike have been silenced and punished precisely for exercising their free speech rights on these sensitive and significant topics. Sometimes this has happened through the type of media and political pressure that occurred at CSU-Northridge, SUNY–New Paltz, and Wesleyan. Sometimes this has happened thanks to exaggerated, distorted concepts of sexual harassment, as in the San Bernardino Valley College, Columbia Law School, and George Mason University situations.

The episodes that garner some publicity are only the tip of the iceberg. No doubt there are many more that go unreported—and, hence, even uncriticized, not to mention unredressed—because the victims are unaware of their rights or unwilling to attract the adverse publicity, as well as the economic and psychological harms, that accrue even to someone who is ultimately vindicated as a matter of law.

Censorship of My Anticensorship Message

Not only do sexually oriented expression and those who engage in it continue to be vilified; the same is true for those who merely defend the First Amendment rights of such expression. Here I'll cite yours truly as Exhibit A.

As I noted earlier, one such incident occurred after I delivered the keynote address at the CSU-Northridge-sponsored international conference on pornography, in which I stressed the ACLU's ongoing efforts to defend sexually oriented expression in cyberspace and elsewhere. Notably, the ACLU has an essentially unbroken winning streak in these cases.[94] In short, we are simply vindicating existing, established First Amendment rights, consistent with longstanding Supreme Court precedents. Yet, as far as some of the vitriolic, hyperbolic criticism is concerned, we are not championing free speech, but rather, fetishes.

For example, a *New York Post* editorial castigated not only the CSU-Northridge conference, but also my participation in it, making the completely unfounded assertion that I was defending "bestiality videos."[95] Significantly, the editorial's title, "More Revolting Academic Behavior," alluded to the embattled SUNY–New Paltz women's studies conference, which the *Post* had also condemned, and which had the double-entendre title, "Revolting Behavior: The Challenges of Women's Sexual Freedom." As these censorial incidents underscore, to engage in expression that some view as "revolting" in the sense of being offensive, is to engage in behavior that is also "revolting" in the sense of rebelling against and challenging conventional mores and beliefs.

That sexual expression is a lightning rod for political attacks illustrates that "the sexual is political" and that no coherent line can be drawn between "political speech," which now receives the most full-fledged First Amendment protection, and sexual speech, which the Supreme Court has relegated to second-class status under the First Amendment.

My address at the CSU-Northridge conference became an issue in a political controversy of the most core kind: an election campaign. The incumbent governor of Hawaii, Ben Cayetano, was attacked during the November 1998 election by his opponent, Linda Lingle, for being a "card-carrying member" of an organization whose president would dare to address the World Pornography Conference. Governor Cayetano was reelected despite this tactic, or perhaps because of it!

The attacks I faced for addressing the World Pornography Conference were hardly the first I had experienced as a defender of free speech for pornography. Indeed, no sooner had *Defending Pornography* been published (in 1995) than I heard that the managers of a major bookstore chain had made a corporate decision that I would not be permitted to do any readings at any of its stores, anywhere in the country—not even in that den of iniquity where I live, Manhattan—because the topic was deemed too controversial and provocative. This reported reluctance certainly was consistent with realistic concerns about the negative reactions that the book, predictably, provoked in some quarters, which did lead to some protests and even attempts to scuttle scheduled readings.

Fortunately, all that these actions accomplished was to stimulate speech, rather than to squelch it. For example, David Unowsky, owner of the Hungry Mind bookstore in St. Paul, Minnesota, credits the presence and participation of protestors with helping to make my appearance at his store such "a great event" that he wrote it up in the American Booksellers Association's newsletter. In his words:

> Over 300 people attended . . . representing all sides of the debate, from Dworkin/McKinnon [*sic*] supporters on one side, to someone carrying a sign that said "God Bless Nadine Strossen and the ACLU" on the other. The question and answer period was heated but respectful; Strossen's appearance resulted in [many] sales; First Amendment issues were raised on local radio and in the local press; and our staff, particularly the younger ones, gained an awareness of what book-selling can be about.[96]

I am indebted to David Unowsky and the many other courageous bookstore owners who graciously hosted not only me, but also those who were demonstrating for and against my ideas, during my memorable nationwide 1995 book tour. I came away from that experience with more respect than ever for the booksellers, librarians, teachers, and other citizens, all across the country, who are on the frontlines of fights for free speech—and for feminism.

One especially noteworthy example is Ed Elrod, owner of the Ventura Bookstore in Ventura, California. To advertise my reading and booksigning at his store, Ed put a poster-sized copy of the book's cover on an easel at his store's entrance. No sooner had he done this than some irate citizens stormed into his store, complaining that the very presence of the sign endangered the safety and welfare of women and children in their community and demanding that he take it down. When he refused, some of them announced that they would organize protests at my reading and boycotts of the bookstore. A number of them also filed complaints with the city government.[97]

In fairness, I must admit that the book's title and the cover of the original hardback edition are rather provocative. Having previously written only academic works, I was myself quite startled when the trade press publisher of the original hardback edition first presented the cover design to me. With its flamboyant neon colors and in-your-face title, it was a far cry from, say, the *Harvard Law Review*. (And also from the cover of subsequent editions of the book, including this one.)

It is one thing to find the cover arresting, but another altogether to find yourself in danger of being arrested just for displaying it. And that is in fact what faced the Ventura Bookstore owner, Ed Elrod. Shortly after he had displayed that cover poster, a local fire department official came into Ed's store and asked him to remove the sign, noting that it had been the target of citizen complaints. While this official cited certain obscure local ordinances with which the sign allegedly did not comply, Ed routinely had used exactly the same type of sign to advertise readings and other events at his bookstore for the previous seventeen years, and never once had a city official suggested that this practice posed any legal problems.[98] With the backing of the local ACLU, Ed Elrod stood his ground. I was able to give my talk, complete with a lively audience discussion. And the women and children of Ventura County managed to survive this event.

Since this Ventura episode, as national ACLU president I have had to rely on the advocacy efforts of ACLU lawyers and activists on one other occasion—in 1998, in that city many of us think of as "Censor-nati." In the wake of the then latest wave of attacks on erotic expression there, triggered by Larry Flynt's opening of a store,[99] the local ACLU chapter and other free speech groups[100] banded together to bring me out to give a public lecture presenting the anticensorship perspective. They gave the lecture the same title as the book: "Defending Pornography."

For the Cincinnati event, my hosts rented the lecture hall at the city's Museum Center, which is open to the public on a first-come, first-served basis. A couple days before my lecture, however, the Museum Center suddenly decided to cancel my appearance, because my lecture topic was so "distasteful."[101] Fortunately, some dedicated Cincinnati lawyers,[102] working with the local ACLU, were able to defend my right to speak as scheduled.

Of all the many talks I have given since I became ACLU president in 1991, on so many hot-button issues where feelings run very high—from abortion, to affirmative action, to the death penalty, to gay rights, to separation of church and state—the only overt efforts to stop me from speaking consistently have been aimed at talks about sexually oriented expression. I have given more than two hundred talks per year, all over the United States, before many diverse audiences, ranging from the most liberal to the most conservative. So this experience is a telling indication of the unique, irrational, emotional antipathy toward sexual expression in our society.

Not Speechless in Salt Lake

The same hostility fueled the only death threat that has been issued either to me or to someone who has invited me to speak. In 1993, when A Woman's Place Bookstore in Salt Lake City, Utah, announced that I would be presenting my feminist anticensorship perspective there, the store's owner, Sally Smith, received a written death threat against herself, her employees, and her customers—not to mention against her invited speaker. Sally Smith bravely stood her ground, explaining to me that if she allowed herself to be intimidated by this kind of threat, she might as well close up shop. As indicated by the name of the store, Smith had founded it expressly to serve as a safe harbor for feminism and other perspectives that are outside the mainstream in Salt Lake City.

Even though I was inspired by Sally Smith to go forward with this speaking engagement, I must confess that I did not feel the courage that she displayed. I was encouraged, though—literally, endowed with courage—both by her moral support and by the tangible safety measures that federal and local law enforcement officials helpfully provided throughout my visit, including a bodyguard and police escort. This was an uplifting example of government personnel *defending*—in the most literal sense—freedom of speech about sex, rather than suppressing it.

Moreover, the Salt Lake City police actually provided positive publicity for my presentation. A number of audience members told me that they had not previously known about the talk, but as they happened to be driving past the bookstore, their interest was piqued by the massed police cars parked outside, complete with flashing red lights—inadvertently apt lures for a discussion of pornography! Of course, this is hardly the first time that efforts to suppress speech have backfired.

So I was not silenced in Salt Lake, after all. This episode thus exemplifies the good news/bad news theme that threads throughout this introduction. Yes, the attacks on sexually oriented expression are persistent—but not more so than the individuals who resist them. I dedicate this book to all the women and men who have fought for all the rights at stake, including freedom for women and for words. I salute and thank not only the many brave souls I have described in these pages, but also the countless other unsung heroines and heros who are maintaining the eternal vigil.

NADINE STROSSEN
New York, February 2000

NOTES

I am indebted to my outstanding Chief Aide, Amy L. Tenney, for multiple forms of invaluable assistance in preparing this edition of the book, including legal and factual research, drafting endnotes, and overseeing the innumerable administrative tasks involved. I am grateful to Mark Konkel for his superb assistance with most of the research and annotations required for the new introduction. Background research assistance was also provided by Joseph Molinari, as well as Maria Pedraza, Hannah Slan, and Elena Vournas. For administrative assistance, I thank Kathy Davis, Amy E. Fallon, and Jaci Flug. For insightful comments on earlier drafts of this introduction, I thank Ann Beeson, Cathy Crosson, Carlin Meyer, Eli Noam, and Loren Siegel. I am deeply grateful to Wendy Kaminer and Saelon Renkes for their valuable additions to this edition. Last, but far from least, I thank the two individuals who most literally made this edition possible: my literary agent par excellence, Carol Mann, and the inimitable director and editor-in-chief of New York University Press, Niko Pfund.

1. For example, see Philip Elmer-DeWitt, "On a Screen Near You: It's Popular, Pervasive and Surprisingly Perverse, According to the First Survey of Online Erotica. And There's No Way to Stamp It Out," *Time*, 3 July 1995.
2. For regularly updated information about these issues, see the ACLU's website, www.aclu.org.
3. 47 U.S.C. § 223.
4. 47 U.S.C. § 231.

5. Harry Kalven, *A Worthy Tradition: Freedom of Speech in America* (New York: Harper & Row, 1987).
6. 521 U.S. 844 (1997).
7. *Pope v. Illinois,* 481 U.S. 497, 500–01 (1987).
8. L. J. Sax et al., *The American Freshman: National Norms for Fall 1999* (Los Angeles: UCLA Higher Education Research Institute, 2000).
9. Brooke A. Masters, "Arlington to Pay Inmates Who Alleged Sex Abuse," *Washington Post,* 19 March 1999, sec. B, p. 1.
10. *ACLU v. Johnson,* 194 F.3d 1149 (10th Cir. 1999); *Cyberspace v. Engler,* 55 F. Supp. 2d 737 (E.D. Mich. 1999); *American Library Assoc. v. Pataki,* 969 F. Supp. 160 (S.D.N.Y. 1997).
11. Andrea Dworkin and Catharine MacKinnon, *Pornography and Civil Rights: A New Day for Women's Equality* (Minneapolis: Organizing Against Pornography, 1988), pp. 138–42.
12. Saelon Renkes, "Bodies of Nature: Artist's Statement," http://www.saelon.com /exhibits/serrastatement.html.
13. Andrea Dworkin, "Where Do We Stand on Pornography?" (Roundtable), *Ms.,* January/February 1994, pp. 32–41.
14. Saelon Renkes email to author, 25 January 2000.
15. For example, see Leslie Miller, "Decency Act Challenge: Trial Wrestling with New Net Law Nears End," *USA Today,* 9 May 1996, sec. D, p. 10.
16. For example, see Katha Pollitt, "Prosecuting Innocence," *Nation,* 13 December 1999, p. 10.
17. Renkes to Strossen.
18. David E. Rosenbaum, "Clinton Vow to Congress Ends a Threat to His Nominations," *New York Times,* 17 June 1999, sec. A, p. 24.
19. Frank Rich, "All in the Family," *New York Times,* 18 April 1998, sec. A, p. 13.
20. Jonathan Weisman, "Envoy's Nomination Fires Debate over 'Gay Agenda'; Hormel's Support for Homosexual Causes Attacked in Senate," *Baltimore Sun,* 23 June 1998, sec. A, p. 1.
21. Louis Freedberg, "Books Cited by Hormel Foes Found in D.C.; Gay Material in Library of Congress," *San Francisco Chronicle,* 27 February 1998, sec. A, p. 3.
22. U.S. House, *Child Online Protection Act,* 105th Cong., 2d sess., 105 H. Rept. 775 (citing 1996 "estimates that almost 50 percent of the content available on the Web was unsuitable for children" and suggesting that "as of 1998" that figure, for "adult-oriented material," had "increased to almost 70 percent").
23. Steve Lawrence and C. Lee Giles, "Accessibility of Information on the Web," *Nature* 400 (1999): 107; Larry Williams, "Net Search Engines May Need Tuneup," *Chicago Tribune,* 8 July 1999, p. 3.
24. Ron Russell, "On the Internet, Where Porn Means Mega-Profits, L.A.'s Cybermistresses Are in the Vanguard of a Boom Industry," *New Times Los Angeles,* 17 September 1998.
25. Paul Franson, "The Net's Dirty Little Secret: Sex Sells," *Upside,* April 1998, p. 78.
26. Russell, "On the Internet."
27. Brendan I. Koerner, "A Lust for Profits: Pornography Is a Huge and Growing Cyberspace Draw. But Will Salacious Web Sites Be a Hit on Wall Street?" *U.S. News & World Report,* 27 March 2000, p. 36.
28. Russell, "On the Internet."

29. Eric Schlosser, "The Business of Pornography," *U.S. News & World Report,* 10 February 1997, p. 42. See also "The Truth about California's Adult Entertainment Industry: White Paper 1999," submitted to California Legislature by Free Speech Coalition, p. 5 (noting that "industry professionals estimate that the figure is at least $2–3 billion higher than" the $8 billion cited by *U.S. News & World Report*).
30. Laurence O'Toole, "More Sex, Please, We're British: Film Censorship in Britain," *New Statesman* 128 (August 30, 1999): 29.
31. Ibid.
32. Thomas Korosec, "Tower Records and a Local Store Owner Learn the Hard Way What the City Wants to See," *Dallas Observer,* 7 October 1999.
33. Edward Helmore, "LA's Skin Flicks Boom Is Putting Hollywood in the Shade," *The Guardian,* 12 September 1999, p. 6.
34. Andrew Gumbel, "The Other Tinseltown," *The Independent* (London), 28 September 1999, p. 9.
35. Helmore, "LA's Skin Flicks."
36. Schlosser, "The Business of Pornography."
37. Ibid.
38. James Fallows, "Why Write about the Porn Industry?" *U.S. News & World Report,* 10 February 1997, p. 9.
39. Free Speech Coalition, "The Truth about California's Adult Entertainment Industry," p. 14.
40. Schlosser, "The Business of Pornography."
41. Free Speech Coalition, "The Truth about California's Adult Entertainment Industry," p. 14.
42. Solomon Moore, "CSUN Is Vindicated in the Staging of a 1998 Pornography Trade Show, But Clearer Policy Is Urged," *Los Angeles Times,* 10 November 1999, sec. B, p. 1.
43. Free Speech Coalition, "The Truth about California's Adult Entertainment Industry," p. 14.
44. Tara Weiss, "At Long Last, V-Chip (Yawn) Arrives," *Hartford (Conn.) Courant,* 30 June 1999, sec. F, p. 1.
45. Glenn Gamboa, "Internet, New Software Offer Many Protections against Pornography," *Akron (Ohio) Beacon Journal,* 26 February 1998.
46. *Mainstream Loudoun v. Board of Trustees of the Loudoun County Library,* 24 F. Supp. 2d 552 (E.D. Va. 1998).
47. For example, see Robert J. Morgan, *James Madison on the Constitution and the Bill of Rights* (New York: Greenwood Press, 1988), 199 (quoting Madison as stating that rule by a majority is "the most tyrannical and intolerable of all").
48. *Texas v. Johnson,* 491 U.S. 397, 414 (1989).
49. Paul McMasters, *State of the First Amendment: A Survey of Public Attitudes* (Washington, D.C.: Freedom Forum, 1999), p. 4.
50. *Jacobellis v. Ohio,* 378 U.S. 184, 197 (1964) (concurring).
51. David Wastell, "Pro-Life Groups Hit Bush's Hopes for White House," *Sunday Telegraph* (London), 4 April 1999, p. 30.
52. Francis X. Clines, "Buchanan Bolts G.O.P. for Reform Party Run," *New York Times,* 26 October 1999, sec. A, p. 1.
53. M. G. Lord, "Porn Utopia: How Feminist Scholars Learned to Love Dirty Pictures," *Lingua Franca,* April/May 1997, http://linguafranca.com/9704/porn.9704.html; James

Atlas, "The Loose Canon: Why Higher Learning Has Embraced Pornography," *New Yorker,* 29 March 1999, p. 60, 62 ("Nearly all the leading figures in the field of porn studies are women.").

54. For example, see Dottie Indyke, "Private Parts," *Santa Fe New Mexican,* 18 February 2000, p. 58; Fintan O'Toole, "Privates on Parade," *Daily News* (New York), 4 October 1999.

55. David Brooks, "Our Bodies, Our Surgeons: Feminism in the Age of Body Worship," *Weekly Standard,* 7 February 2000, p. 22.

56. Joe Mahoney, "Tax Group: Sez Play Too Risque; Wants It Banned at Colleges," *Daily News* (New York), 10 February 2000, p. 8.

57. Dworkin and MacKinnon, *Pornography and Civil Rights,* pp. 138–42.

58. Ibid.

59. Catharine MacKinnon, "Turning Rape into Pornography: Postmodern Genocide," *Ms.,* July/August 1993, pp. 24–30.

60. For example, see Pamela Johnson, "Sexless and Satisfied," *Essence,* July 1999, p. 52; Wendy Shalit, *A Return to Modesty: Discovering the Lost Virtue* (New York: Free Press, 1999).

61. For example, see Joan Kennedy Taylor, *What to Do When You Don't Want to Call the Cops: A Non-Adversarial Approach to Sexual Harassment* (New York: New York University Press, 1999); Daphne Patai, *Heterophobia: Sexual Harassment and the Future of Feminism* (Lanham, Md.: Rowman & Littlefield, 1998); Vicki Schultz, "Reconceptualizing Sexual Harassment," *Yale Law Journal* 107 (1998): 1683; Carlin Meyer, "Feminism, Work and Sex: Returning to the Gates" (1995) (unpublished manuscript).

62. For example, see *Burlington Industries v. Ellerth,* 524 U.S. 742 (1998); *Faragher v. City of Boca Raton,* 524 U.S. 775 (1998).

63. *Oncale v. Sundowner Offshore Services, Inc.,* 523 U.S. 75, 80 (1998) ("We have never held that workplace harassment . . . is automatically discrimination because of sex merely because the words used have sexual content or connotations.").

64. *Cohen v. San Bernardino Valley College,* 883 F. Supp. 1407 (C.D. Cal. 1995), *rev'd,* 92 F. 3d 968 (9th Cir. 1996).

65. David Cross, Letter to the Editor, "Fletcher Committed to Students," *Law School News* (Columbia University Law School), February 2000, p. 11; Beth Gunn and Margaret Garnett, Letter to the Editor, "Fletcher Committed to Students," *Law School News* (Columbia University Law School), February 2000, p. 11; Jeremy Pam, Letter to the Editor, "Fletcher Committed to Students," *Law School News* (Columbia University Law School), February 2000, p. 11; Glenn Harlan Reynolds, Letter to the Editor, "Law Exams Often 'Farfetched,'" *Chronicle of Higher Education,* 14 January 2000, sec. B, p. 11; "Excerpts from Fletcher's Nov. 22 Crim Exam Forum," *Law School News* (Columbia University Law School), December 1999, p. 4; Stephen Lee and George Rheault, "Fletcher Exam Forum Inspires Spirited Debate," *Law School News* (Columbia University Law School), December 1999, p. 1; Stephen Lee and George Rheault, "Scandal's Chronology Disputed," *Law School News* (Columbia University Law School), December 1999, p. 1; "Columbia U. Law Students and Dean Object to 'Offensive' Exam Question," *Chronicle of Higher Education,* 3 December 1999, sec. A, p. 16; Robyn Schwartz, "Prof. Defends Language in Final Exam," *Columbia Spectator,* 23 November 1999, pp. 1, 7. See also Editorial, "Waiting for Professor Fletcher's Apology," *Law School News* (Columbia University Law School), December 1999, p. 6.

66. Dean David Leebron, Columbia University Law School, to Full-time Faculty, Columbia University Law School, 18 November 1999; Dean David Leebron, Columbia University Law School, to Second Year Law Students, Columbia University Law School, 18 November 1999.
67. 42 U.S.C. §13981 (1999).
68. *Brzonkala v. Virginia Polytechnic Institute,* 169 F.3d 820 (4th Cir. 1999); *Brzonkala v. Virginia Polytechnic Institute,* 132 F.3d 949 (4th Cir. 1997); *Brzonkala v. Virginia Polytechnic Institute,* 935 F. Supp. 779 (W.D. Va. 1996).
69. Gunn and Garnett, "Fletcher Committed to Students."
70. *Mainstream Loudoun v. Loudoun County Library,* 24 F. Supp.2d 552, 565 (E.D. Va. 1998).
71. *Urofsky v. Gilmore,* 167 F.3d 191 (4th Cir. 1999).
72. *Urofsky v. Allen,* 995 F. Supp. 634, 641, n. 6 (E.D. Va. 1998), *rev'd on other grounds, Urofsky v. Gilmore,* 167 F. 3d 191 (4th Cir. 1999).
73. Catharine A. MacKinnon, *Sexual Harassment of Working Women: A Case of Sex Discrimination* (New Haven: Yale University Press, 1979); idem, Introduction to "Comment on Sexual Harassment," *Capital University Law Review* 10 (Spring 1981): 1; idem, "Not a Moral Issue," *Yale Law and Policy Review* 2 (1984): 321.
74. Patai, *Heterophobia,* p. 3.
75. Taylor, *What to Do When You Don't Want to Call the Cops,* p. 177.
76. Schultz, "Reconceptualizing," pp. 1686, 1692.
77. Ibid., pp. 4–7; Jeffrey Rosen, "In Defense of Gender-Blindness," *New Republic,* 29 June 1998, p. 39.
78. Ibid. (quoting Frederick Schauer, Frank Stanton Professor of the First Amendment at Harvard University).
79. Patai, *Heterophobia,* p. 6.
80. *Lanahan Readings in Civil Rights and Civil Liberties,* ed. David M. O'Brien (Baltimore: Lanahan Publishing, 1999).
81. For example, see Alan Charles Kors and Harvey A. Silverglate, *The Shadow University: The Betrayal of Liberty on America's Campuses* (New York: Free Press, 1998).
82. Catharine Stimpson, "Activist Trustees Wield Power Gone Awry," *Chronicle of Higher Education,* 16 January 1998, sec. B, p. 4; Meredith Tax, "Pataki's Army Goes Onward to SUNY," *Newsday* (New York), 16 November 1998, sec. A, p. 29; Jack Sirica, "Jitters on SUNY Sexuality Forum," *Newsday* (New York), 8 February 1998, sec. A, p. 25.
83. Eric Rich and Robert A. Frahm, "Porn, Professors and Purse Strings: Porn Course at Wesleyan Rekindles Debate," *Hartford (Conn.) Courant,* 28 May 1999.
84. Many of the conference papers and presentations were published in *Porn 101: Eroticism, Pornography, and the First Amendment,* ed. James Elias et al. (Amherst, N.Y.: Prometheus Books, 1999).
85. Editorial, "Biased Judge Tips Justice's Scales," *Daily News* (New York), 12 August 1998, p. 28 ("It is one thing for the ACLU to defend pornographers on First Amendment grounds, quite another to cheer them on."); Editorial, "More Revolting Academic Behavior," *New York Post,* 11 August 1998, p. 26 ("The Strossen . . . may believe the Founders intended the U.S. Constitution to defend bestiality videos.").
86. California State Auditor, California State University, Northridge, "Absent University Standards and Other Guidance, the World Pornography Conference Was Allowable

Under the Basic Tenets of Academic Freedom and Free Speech," November 1999, No. 99122.

87. Ibid., p. 19.

88. Hope Weissman, Associate Professor of Letters, Wesleyan University, to President Douglas Bennet, Wesleyan University, 24 May 1999, p. 2.

89. Laura Schlessinger, "College Course Rewards Skill in Writing Porn," *Washington Times,* 15 June 1999, sec. E, p. 1.

90. Eric Rich, "Wesleyan to Review Porn Course; Some Professors Critical of Inquiry," *Hartford (Conn.) Courant,* 22 May 1999, sec. B, p. 1.

91. Schlessinger, "College Course Rewards Skill in Writing Porn."

92. Editorial, "Over the Top at Wesleyan," *Hartford (Connecticut) Courant,* 11 May 1999, sec. A, p. 12.

93. Eric Rich, "Porn-Free Curriculum Returns to Wesleyan—for Now," *Hartford (Conn.) Courant,* 1 September 1999.

94. *ACLU v. Reno,* 929 F. Supp. 824 (E.D. Pa. 1996), aff'd by *ACLU v. Reno,* 521 U.S. 844 (1997); *ACLU v. Reno II,* 31 F. Supp. 2d 473 (E.D. Pa. 1999); *ACLU v. Johnson,* 4 F. Supp. 2d 1029 (D.N.M. 1998), aff'd by *ACLU v. Johnson,* 194 F.3d 1149 (10th Cir. 1999); *Cyberspace v. Engler,* 55 F. Supp. 2d 737 (E.D. Mich. 1999); *American Library Assoc. v. Patai,* 969 F. Supp. 160 (S.D.N.Y. 1997).

95. Editorial, "More Revolting Academic Behavior."

96. R. David Unowsky, "On My Mind," *Bookselling This Week,* 27 February 1995.

97. Robin Abcarian, "Chances Are, Women Can Decide for Themselves," *Los Angeles Times,* 15 February 1995, sec. E, p. 1; Catherine Saillant, "Bookseller Ends Dispute over Sign," *Los Angeles Times,* 3 February 1995, sec. B, p. 2.

98. Lisa See, "Ventura Bookstore Fights Censorship," *Publishers Weekly* 242, no. 7 (13 February 1995): 23.

99. Tim Bonfield, "'99 Year in Review," *Cincinnati Enquirer,* 26 December 1999, sec. B, p. 1.

100. The ACLU of Ohio, Campaign Against Censorship in the Arts, the Free Inquiry Group, and Stonewall Cincinnati.

101. Ben Kaufman, "Censorship Face-off Averted," *Cincinnati Enquirer,* 19 March 1998.

102. I gratefully acknowledge the excellent work of Scott Greenwood, General Counsel of the ACLU of Ohio, Steven Stuhlbarg, Bernard Wong, and Daniel Zavon. I would also like to acknowledge William Messer, Founder of the Campaign Against Censorship in the Arts, for organizing this event and for resisting the pressure to withdraw it from the Museum Center.

DEFENDING
PORNOGRAPHY

Acknowledgments

This book builds upon the words and work of many other people too numerous to name individually. Therefore, I express my deep gratitude, collectively, to the many women and men who have spoken, written, organized, and acted to defend liberty *and* equality, free speech *and* feminism, words *and* women, including all those who are quoted or cited in these pages and all those who have supported the American Civil Liberties Union, Feminists Against Censorship, the Feminist Anti-Censorship Taskforce, Feminists for Free Expression, and the National Coalition Against Censorship's Working Group on Women, Censorship and "Pornography." Among the many people in this category, I'd like to single out for special, individualized thanks four women with whom I have had the privilege of working especially closely: Marjorie Heins, executive director of the ACLU's Arts Censorship Project; Leanne Katz, executive director of the National Coalition Against Censorship; Carlin Meyer, professor of law, New York Law School; and Marcia Pally, president of Feminists for Free Expression. I'd also like to extend a special thanks to the other women whose writings have been especially influential upon my own thinking: Varda Burstyn, Lisa Duggan, Nan Hunter, Wendy Kaminer, Sylvia Law, Thelma McCormack, Katha Pollitt, Ann Snitow, and Carole Vance.

Many other individuals made important contributions to my work on this book. The dean and associate dean of New York Law School, Harry Wellington and Ellen Ryerson, have consistently provided intellectual, moral, financial, and logistical support for my research and writing. Harry Wellington's leadership, inspiration, and support for scholarly activity at New York Law School have been particularly stimulating to my work. Cardozo Law School professor Michel Rosenfeld, by teaching one of my classes, made it possible for me to write this book in a timely fashion. The indefatigable staff of the New York Law School Library, including William Mills, Joelle Lemmons, and Joyce Saltalamachia,

1

helped me to locate even the most arcane, elusive sources. In particular, Joseph Molinari, the library's head of public services, provided invaluable assistance with both the text and the images. Other NYLS staff members to whom I am especially grateful are our resident computer whiz, Dorothea Perry-Coleman, Claire (Knows Everything) Voulgarelis, and Carmen Frazier.

Thomas Hilbink, my outstanding assistant, himself provided skilled and thorough research assistance, oversaw the work of all other researchers, including finalizing the endnotes—herculean tasks—and held the fort in my hectic office. Tom's conscientious attention to all other areas of my work allowed me to devote the time required to write this book. The lionesses' share of the wide-ranging legal and factual research underlying the book was carried out by Karen Shelton and Carolyn Richmond, with principal support from Stephen Hendricks, Carmen Tausik, and Dolly Voorhees. Additional, valued research assistance was provided by Martin Adler, Nina Carpiniello, I-Jung Chiang, Gabriel Falcon, Tyler Kandel, Debra Klinek, Ronak Kordestani, Stephanie Landess, Nancy Meyers, Vinit Parmar, Tara Phelan, Tony Ross, Helen Ullrich, and Donna Wasserman.

Many people have provided information, documents, and other materials to me and my research assistants. Although we have tried to keep detailed records of all these individuals, for the purpose of acknowledging them here, I fear that—given the scope of the project and the number of people involved—some omissions are probably inevitable. If you did help and are not listed here, please accept our apologies for the omission and, more important, our sincere gratitude. Thanks, then, to the following individuals and organizations: Nancy Abraham, Floyd Abrams, Michelle Adams, Shoshanna Addley, Alternative Tentacles Records (especially Jello Biafra and Greg Werckman), the American Association of University Professors, Art Resource (including Paul Evans and Ita Gross), Peter Awn, *Bad Attitude* magazine (especially Jasmine Sterling), Leslie Barany, Marianna Beck, Floyd Beckford, Kevin Beigel, Zoravia Bettiol, Toni Blake, Boston Women's Health Book Collective (especially Judy Norsigian), Anne Boudreau, Bradley Smith Productions, Susie Bright, Mimi Brown, Ken Burrows, Karen Busby, Jamie Cameron, the Canadian Civil Liberties Association (especially Alan Borovoy and Danielle McLaughlin), Dennis Cauchon,

Rebecca Chalker, M. Chemiakin, Roberta Cohen, David Cole, Columbia University's "Draw the Line" Project (including Alex Davis, Molly Eagan, James Stoterau, and John Vagelatos), Carol Connolly, Sandra Corti, Cathy Crosson, Marsha Cummings, Nicole Cummings, Dorit Cypis, Josh Dare, Edward de Grazia, Harriette and Norman Dorsen, Carol Downer, Claudia Dreifus, Mark Duran, Susan Fall, Femme Productions (especially Candida Royalle), Patricia Flynn, Allison Foster, Lisa Frank, Jessica Fredericks, Jill Frisch, Andrew Frothingham, Gemini Smith, Inc., Michael Greve, Barry Gross, Gerald Gunther, Shona Gupta, Randy Hecht, Jack Hafferkamp, Nat Hentoff, Paul Hoffman, Peter Holtberg, Jenny Holzer, Penn Jillette, Burt Joseph, Fred Kallister, Leslie Kantor, Steve Kass, Sam Kerson, Paula Klaw, Michael Krauss, Robert Kreiser, Bill Kuntz, Gara LaMarche, Judith Levine, Doris Linneman, Lacey Logan, Bill Love, Jennifer Maguire, Adál Maldonado, Sally Mann, Mary Ellen Mark, Kimberly McCollum, Wendy McElroy, *Michigan Journal of Law & Gender* (especially Elise Bruhl), Frank Miller, Julia Molinder, John Morris, David Moshman, Liza Mundy, the National Association of Scholars, National Campaign for Free Expression (including Steve Johnson and David Mendoza), National Coalition Against Censorship (including Max Cartagena, Jamie Katz, Jennifer Lopes, Stephen McCammon, Joanna Samuels, and Roz Udow), David Ogden, *On Our Backs* magazine (especially Melissa Murphy), Chris Penner, Niko Pfund, Naomi Pritchard, Debra Raskin, Nicole Rice, Roger Rosenblatt, Joanne Savio, Liana Scalettar, Mark Schapiro, David Schoenbrod, Maimon Schwarzschild, Ntozake Shange, Josh Shenk, Judith Singer, Elliott Sparkman, Christine Sperber, Lawrence Stanley, Jeff Stephenson, Laura Strauss, Hudson Talbott, Douglas Tausik, Marcia Teronas, John Thompson, William Tourtillote, Suzanna Turman, Michelle Urry, Veronica Vera, Sam Walker, Liz Weisberg, Joel Peter Witkin, and Roger Worsham.

Many staff members of the ACLU and its state affiliates have been very helpful; in particular, I'd like to thank Steve Bates, Robyn Blumner, Jean Bond, Harv Dean, Lynn Decker, Dorothy Ehrlich, Arthur Eisenberg, John Fahs, Ira Glasser, Edward Gomez, Florence Green, Phil Gutis, Douglas Honig, Deborah Leavy, Kenia Olivera, Kevin O'Neill, Kathy Parrent, Robert Peck, Bill Saks, Steve Shapiro, Loren Siegel, Barry Steinhardt, Vic Walczak, Diane Weiss, and Jane Whicher. I also wish to acknowledge my debt to the ACLU in general, which has given me the opportunity to develop many of the ideas in this book. However, this book is a personal statement, not an organizational one, for which I alone bear responsibility.

Vital to the development of this book were my literary agent, Carol Mann, and her assistant, Deborah Clifford. Essential encouragement and superb editorial assistance were also provided by my editor, Bill Goldstein; Billy was the first person who asked me to think seriously about writing a book, several years ago, and I'm delighted that he was also the first to propose a subject that compelled me to carve out the time to write my first book. Copy editors Carole McCurdy and Kristine Larson Vesley combined meticulous technical skills with gifted facilities with words and ideas; the title "copy editor" doesn't do justice to their contribution. For helpful comments on my manuscript, I thank Cathy Crosson, Marjorie Heins, Gara LaMarche, Joan Mahoney, Eli Noam, and Marcia Pally.

For their constant companionship throughout my work on this book, pets go to my purring paperweights, Winnie and Squeaky 2.1. Finally, my deepest thanks go to my beloved husband, Eli M. Noam, whose manifold contributions would take another book—a love story—to describe.

Introduction

Pornography, in the feminist view, is a form of forced sex, . . .
an institution of gender inequality. . . . [P]ornography, with
the rape and prostitution in which it participates, institutionalizes the sexuality of male supremacy.
                                    —CATHARINE MACKINNON[1]

Feminist women are especially keen to the harms of censorship. . . . Historically, information about sex, sexual orientation, reproduction and birth control has been banned
under the guise of . . . the "protection" of women. Such
restrictions have never reduced violence. Instead, they
have led to the jailing of birth control advocate Margaret
Sanger, and the suppression of important works, from *Our
Bodies, Ourselves* to . . . the feminist plays of Karen Finley and Holly Hughes. Women do not require "protection"
from explicit sexual materials. . . . Women are as varied as
any citizens of a democracy; there is no agreement or feminist code as to what images are distasteful or even sexist.
It is the right and responsibility of each woman to read,
view or produce the sexual material she chooses without
the intervention of the state "for her own good." . . . This is
the great benefit of being feminists in a free society.
                                    —FEMINISTS FOR FREE EXPRESSION[2]

The strain of anti-pornologism is hardly what's distinctive
about feminism; whereas anti-anti-pomology—the critique of the anti-porn movement on grounds other than

5

constitutional formalism or First Amendment pietism—is a
distinctive feminist contribution.

—HENRY LOUIS GATES
W. E. B. Du Bois Professor
Harvard University[3]

In the past decade, some feminists have dramatically altered the
long-standing debate in this country about sex and sexually oriented expression. Liberals—including those who advocated women's
rights—had long sought increased individual freedom, and decreased
government control, in the realm of sexuality. Accordingly, liberals
had urged the repeal both of laws restricting consensual private sexual conduct between adults, and laws restricting the production of or
access to sexually oriented materials, including books, photographs,
and films.

Conversely, conservatives—including those who opposed women's
rights causes—had consistently advocated strict government controls
over both sexual conduct and sexual expression. With the 1980 election of Ronald Reagan and the growing mobilization of the so-called
Religious Right, what had become a conservative clamor gained enormous political clout. It led to the 1986 Report of the Meese Pornography Commission,[4] which in turn led to sweeping new law enforcement
crackdowns on all manner of sexual materials, including popular,
constitutionally protected works such as *The Joy of Sex*[5] and *Playboy*
magazine.

The startling new development is that, since the late 1970s, the traditional conservative and fundamentalist advocates of tighter legal
restrictions on sexual expression have been joined by an increasingly
vocal and influential segment of the feminist movement. Both groups
target the sexual material they would like to curb with the pejorative
label "pornography." Led by University of Michigan law professor
Catharine MacKinnon and writer Andrea Dworkin, this faction of
feminists—which I call "MacDworkinites"[6]—argues that pornography
should be suppressed because it leads to discrimination and violence
against women. Indeed, MacKinnon and Dworkin have maintained
that somehow pornography itself *is* discrimination and violence against

women; that its mere existence hurts women, even if it cannot be shown to cause some tangible harm.[7]

I share the fears, frustration, and fury about the ongoing problems of violence and discrimination against women, which no doubt have driven many to embrace the "quick fix" that censoring pornography is claimed to offer. Who wouldn't welcome an end to the threat of violence that so many women feel every time they venture out alone in the dark? But censoring pornography would not reduce misogynistic violence or discrimination; worse yet, as this book shows, it would likely aggravate those grave problems. In the words of feminist attorney Cathy Crosson, while the procensorship strategy may be superficially appealing, at bottom it reflects "the defeated, defeatist politics of those who have given up on really altering the basic institutions of women's oppression and instead have decided to slay the messenger."[8]

The pornophobic feminists have forged frighteningly effective alliances with traditional political and religious conservatives who staunchly oppose women's rights, but who also seek to suppress pornography. As noted by feminist anthropologist Carole Vance, "Every right-winger agrees that porn leads to women's inequality—an inequality that doesn't bother him in any other way."[9]

Under their joint antipornography banner, the allies in this feminist-fundamentalist axis have mounted increasing—and increasingly successful—campaigns against a wide range of sexually oriented expression, including not only art and literature, but also materials concerning such pressing public issues as AIDS and other sexually transmitted diseases, abortion, contraception, sexism, and sexual orientation.

So influential have the MacDworkinites become that all too many citizens and government officials believe that the suppression of sexually oriented materials is a high priority for all feminists, or even for all women. But nothing could be further from the truth.

An increasingly vocal cadre of feminist women who are dedicated to securing equal rights for women and to combating women's continuing second-class citizenship in our society strongly opposes any effort to censor sexual expression. We are as committed as any other feminists to eradicating violence and discrimination against women; indeed, many of us work directly for these goals every day of our lives. But we believe that suppressing sexual words and images will not advance these crucial causes. To the contrary, we are convinced that censoring sexual expression actually would do more harm than good to women's rights and safety. We adamantly oppose any effort to restrict sexual speech not only because it would violate our cherished First Amendment freedoms—our freedoms to read, think, speak, sing, write, paint, dance, dream, photograph, film, and fantasize as we wish—but also because it would undermine our equality, our status, our dignity, and our autonomy.

Women should not have to choose between freedom and safety, between speech and equality, between dignity and sexuality. Women can be sexual beings without forsaking other aspects of our identities. We are entitled to enjoy the thrills of sex and sexual expression without giving up our personal security. We can exercise our free speech and our equal rights to denounce any sexist expressions of any sort—including sexist expressions that are also sexual—rather than seek to suppress anyone else's rights.

Women's rights are far more endangered by censoring sexual images than they are by the sexual images themselves. Women do not need the government's protection from words and pictures. We *do* need, rather, to protect ourselves from any governmental infringement upon our freedom and autonomy, even—indeed, especially—when it is allegedly "for our own good." As former Supreme Court Justice Louis Brandeis cautioned: "Experience should teach us to be most on our guard to protect liberty when the government's purposes are beneficent. . . . The greatest dangers to liberty lurk in insidious encroachment by men of zeal, well-meaning but without understanding."[10] Or *women* of zeal.

The feminist procensorship movement* is a far greater threat to women's rights than is the sexual expression it condemns with the epithet "pornography." For women who cherish liberty and equality, Big Sister is as unwelcome in our lives as Big Brother. Defending the sexual expression that some feminists condemn with the dread *P* word is thus

---

*Dworkin, MacKinnon, and others have protested that their proposals for suppressing pornography should not be labeled "censorship." To borrow the title of MacKinnon's latest book, such a protest is "only words." The reasons why the Mac-Dworkinites' antipornography scheme is fairly considered censorship, no matter what euphemism they might prefer, are discussed in chapter 3.

a critical element in our support of free speech, sexual and reproductive autonomy, and women's equality.

Traditional explanations of why pornography must be defended from would-be censors have concentrated on censorship's adverse impacts on free speech and sexual autonomy. This book supports the anticensorship position from an important different perspective, which is not as widely understood. In light of the increasingly influential women's rights–centered rationale for *censoring* pornography, this book focuses on the women's rights–centered rationale for *defending* pornography. It explains why the procensorship faction of feminism poses a serious threat not only to human rights in general but also to women's rights in particular.

CHAPTER 1

The Sex Panic
and the Feminist Split

The American feminist movement's battle over censorship—
those who favor legal limits on pornography versus those
who oppose them—has escalated dramatically in the past
year [1993]. . . . Anti-porn feminists have won significant
courtroom, campus, and public-relations victories in the
past year. . . . Anticensorship feminists—who've long maintained that it is people, not books or pictures, that harm
women, and that women have historically been targets of
censure when censorship is condoned—find their ideological opponents' growing influence alarming.

—MAUREEN DEZELL, journalist[1]

"Pornography" Is a Dirty Word

The term "pornography" is ordinarily reserved for sexually
explicit words and images whose sole purpose is sexual arousal.
However, literature, art, sex education and information about
women's sexuality are often attacked—and suppressed—as "pornography." Recently, "pornography" has been employed by certain feminists as though sexually explicit expression is inherently
"subordinating" or "degrading" to women (and as though these
terms are themselves not subject to disagreement).

—LEANNE KATZ, Executive Director
National Coalition Against Censorship[2]

11

People have very different definitions of the term "pornography," but it has become a convenient weapon, just as "communism" was during the McCarthy era, to brand any person
or work with whose ideas the censor disagrees.

—MARJORIE HEINS, Director
American Civil Liberties Union
Arts Censorship Project[3]

"Pornography" is a vague term, which *Webster's International Dictionary* defines as "a depiction (as in writing or painting) ... of erotic
behavior designed to cause sexual excitement."[4] In short, it is sexual
expression that is meant to, or does, provoke sexual arousal or desire.

The term has no legal definition or significance. The category of sexually oriented expression that the Supreme Court has held to be subject
to restriction is labeled "obscenity." In recent times, the word "pornography" has assumed such negative connotations that it tends to be used
as an epithet to describe—and condemn—whatever sexually oriented
expression the person using it dislikes. As one wit put it, "What turns
me on is 'erotica,' but what turns *you* on is 'pornography'"! Likewise,
Walter Kendrick's comprehensive 1987 study of the subject, *The Secret
Museum: Pornography in Modern Culture,* makes clear that the term
"pornography" consistently has been applied to whatever sexual representations a particular dominant class or group does not want in the
hands of another, less dominant class or group.[5]

Indeed, the dread *P* word has been used still more loosely and
pejoratively, to tar *any* disfavored idea or expression. A striking—
and ironic—example of this phenomenon is contained on the jacket
of Catharine MacKinnon's 1993 book *Only Words.* Reinforcing fears
about the vague, expansive bounds of the "pornography" that MacK-
innon and her allies seek to suppress, the book jacket blurb by law professor Patricia Williams castigates criticism of MacKinnon's ideas as
"intellectual pornography."

Even the so-called Meese Pornography Commission, which issued
its controversial report in 1986, did not attempt to define the term.
In contrast, the procensorship feminists use this stigmatized word to
underscore that they seek to suppress a category of sexual expression

that is, in theory, distinguishable from the category banned under traditional "obscenity" laws. Essentially, "obscene" speech is sexual speech that the community deems "immoral," whereas in model legislation drafted by MacKinnon and Dworkin, "pornography" is defined as the "sexually explicit subordination of women through pictures and/or words."[6]

Although various supporters of the feminist procensorship faction have proposed slight variations on the MacKinnon-Dworkin definition of pornography, the core concept is always the same—sexual expression that allegedly demeans women. In 1992, for example, the Canadian Supreme Court issued a decision that Catharine MacKinnon hailed as a victory for women (it apparently was influenced by a brief she had coauthored). In that case, entitled *Butler v. the Queen,*[7] Canada's high court interpreted the Canadian obscenity laws as embodying the Mac-Dworkin concept of pornography and hence outlawed materials that are "degrading" or "dehumanizing" to women.

Throughout this book, I use the term "pornography" to refer to the sexually oriented expression that MacKinnon, Dworkin, and their supporters have targeted for suppression. As I show, though, this definition is so amorphous that it can well encompass any and all sexual speech.

"Sex" Is Also a Dirty Word

This culture always treats sex with suspicion. . . . Sex is presumed guilty until proven innocent.
                    —GAYLE RUBIN, anthropologist[8]

Although the strange bedfellows in the current campaign against sexual speech—Meese, MacKinnon, and their respective allies—employ some differing rhetoric in their unified call for censoring sexually oriented expression, they sound many common chords, notably that sex and materials that depict or describe it inevitably degrade and endanger women. In short, the war on sexual expression is, at bottom, a war on sex itself, at least as far as women are concerned. Because the philosophy of leading antipornography, procensorship feminists reflects a deep distrust of sex for women, such feminists are, in my view and in the view of others, aptly labeled "antisex" (see chapter 5).

Taken together, the traditional and feminist antipornography, antisex crusaders appeal to a broad gamut of the ideological spectrum in both the government and the public. They pose an unprecedented danger to sexual expression, which has always been uniquely vulnerable in the United States, as well as to the concept that the First Amendment protects such expression. Moreover, their attacks have been alarmingly successful.

We are in the midst of a full-fledged "sex panic," in which seemingly all descriptions and depictions of human sexuality are becoming embattled. Right-wing senators have attacked National Endowment for the Arts grants for art whose sexual themes—such as homoeroticism or feminism—are allegedly inconsistent with "traditional family values." At the opposite end of the political spectrum, students and faculty have attacked myriad words and images on campus as purportedly constituting sexual harassment. Any expression about sex is now seen as especially dangerous, and hence is especially endangered. The pornophobic feminists have played a very significant role in fomenting this sex panic, especially among liberals and on campuses across the country.

The fear of sexual expression has become so high-pitched lately that it even has deterred an AIDS clinic from giving out information about combating the deadly spread of the virus. In Oklahoma City, the American Civil Liberties Union (ACLU) represented a doctor who was prosecuted for displaying a safe-sex poster on the windows of his AIDS clinic, which was located in an area frequented by gay men. Yet public health experts maintain that the allegedly illegal and offensive image in the poster—a man wearing a condom—is an important instrument in the life-or-death campaign to halt the spread of HIV. Although the charges were dismissed, the city has threatened further prosecutions, thus deterring the clinic from mounting similarly explicit educational displays in the future.[9]

Society's wariness toward sex is highlighted by contrasting it with the greater societal tolerance toward violence. This dichotomy is especially vivid in the media and mass culture, where violent depictions are far more accepted than sexual ones. The contrast was aptly capsulized by Martin Shafer, a top executive at a film production company, when he noted, "If a man touches a woman's breast in a movie, it's an R rating, but if he cuts off a limb with a chain saw, it's a PG-13."[10]

Because the domain of sexual expression, always a difficult terrain, has lately been laced with land mines placed by diverse enemies, it has become more treacherous than ever. Not surprisingly, artists, academics, and others are increasingly deterred from entering and exploring this potentially explosive—but also rich, wonderful, and important—territory.

All over the country, artists say that they dare not pursue sexual themes for fear that their work will be perceived as too controversial to be funded or displayed. Indeed, outraged officials and citizens alike have indignantly demanded the defunding and deposing from display of art with a wide range of sexual themes; lately it seems that even a mere sexual connotation, no matter how subtle, is vulnerable.

In our current epidemic of erotophobia, even images of nude or seminude bodies in wholly nonsexual contexts have been attacked. For example, in 1993, Vermont officials hung bedsheets over a mural that artist Sam Kerson had painted in a state building's conference room. One press account described the mural, which was commissioned to mark the five-hundredth anniversary of Christopher Columbus's voyage, as "a politically correct rendition of Columbus and his men arriving in the New World, battle-axes and crucifix raised, ready to oppress the natives."[11] But the painting was not politically correct enough for a number of female employees, who complained that its depictions of bare-breasted native women constituted sexual harassment. Because the mural could not be removed without destroying it, the state resorted to the bedsheet "solution."

In 1992, a painting of the classical seminude statue the Venus de Milo was removed from a store in a Springfield, Missouri, shopping mall because mall managers considered the topless masterpiece "too shocking."[12] The painting of the ancient Greek sculpture, which was carved about 150 , and which stands in a place of honor in Paris's Louvre museum, was replaced by a painting of a woman wearing a long, frilly dress.

Another example of a famous artistic masterpiece that has been suppressed in the current sex panic is *The Nude Maja*, or *Maja Desnuda*, by the celebrated Spanish painter Francisco de Goya. In 1992, Pennsylvania State University officials removed a reproduction of this acclaimed work from the front wall of a classroom following a complaint by English professor Nancy Stumhofer that it embarrassed her and made her female students "uncomfortable."[13]

No matter that the reproduction hung, along with reproductions of other masterpieces, in a room used for art history classes. No matter that university officials offered to move the painting to a less prominent position in the classroom, such as the back wall. No matter that they also offered to remove the Goya from the classroom altogether whenever Professor Stumhofer taught there, or even to relocate her classes to another classroom. No. Apparently, nothing short of extirpating the work from all campus classrooms would purge its taint, from her perspective.[14] And the university capitulated. As writer Nat Hentoff commented, at that Penn State campus the administration defines sexual harassment as "anything that makes people uncomfortable about sexual issues."[15]

Moving even beyond nudity or partial nudity, the sex panic has engulfed certain forms of clothing that some observers might deem provocative. In a 1994 *Ms.* magazine discussion on pornography, writer Ntozake Shange described one such situation that she said was "very heavy on my heart":

> I was on the cover of *Poets & Writers* and I wore a pretty lace top. In the next two issues, there were letters asking if *Poets & Writers* is now a flesh magazine—why was I appearing in my underwear? Bare shoulders are exploitation now?[16]

In response, Andrea Dworkin, another participant in the *Ms.* discussion, confirmed that she would indeed see Shange's photograph as exploitation: "It's very hard to look at a picture of a woman's body and not see it with the perception that her body is being exploited."

Whether the stigmatizing epithet of choice for particular protesters happens to be "pornography" or "sexual harassment," the result is the same: the conclusory label intimidates campus officials and others who should defend artistic expression, so they instead suppress it. Objecting to another such suppressive incident, which occurred at Vanderbilt University in 1993 (and is described in the next section of this chapter), Vanderbilt art professor Marilyn Murphy said: "Human sexuality has been a recurring theme in art since antiquity. Visual arts is the most misunderstood discipline on this campus and on college campuses everywhere."[17]

Liza Mundy, a writer who has chronicled campus attacks on art with sexual themes, has concluded that "MacKinnonite ideas underlie many" such attacks, noting the irony that many of these battles "pit feminist students against feminist artists." At the University of Arizona in Tucson, students physically attacked a group of photographic self-portraits by graduate student Laurie Blakeslee, which were displayed in the student union. The alleged offense? Blakeslee had photographed herself in her underwear. In Mundy's words, "Young women and men influenced by crusading law professor Catharine MacKinnon—and these are in the ascendance on many campuses—believe that . . . sexually explicit imagery create[s] an atmosphere in which rape is tolerated and even encouraged."[18]

An essential aspect of women's right to equal opportunity in employment and education is the right to be free from sexual harassment. What is troubling, though, is the spreading sense—perpetuated by the feminist antipornography movement—that *any* sexual expression about a woman, or in her presence, *necessarily* constitutes such harassment. This presumption is stated expressly as the basis for the sweeping sexual harassment codes that are becoming increasingly common on campuses.

Syracuse University, for example, adopted a sexual harassment code in 1993 that prohibits not only "requests for sexual relations combined with threats of adverse consequences" if refused, and assaultive acts such as "pinching or fondling," but also nonassaultive, vaguely described acts such as "leering, ogling and physical gestures conveying a sexual meaning," and loosely described expressions including "sexual innuendoes, suggestive remarks, [and] sexually derogatory jokes." What all of these seemingly disparate behaviors have in common, the code informs us, "is that they focus on men and women's sexuality, rather than on their contributions as students or employees in the University."[19]

But this should not be an either-or choice, should it? Are women not—along with men—sexual beings, as well as students or employees? Is women's sexuality really incompatible with their professional roles?

Is it really increasing women's autonomy, options, and full-fledged societal participation to posit such an incompatibility? Have we not learned from history, and from other cultures, that the suppression of women's sexuality tends to coincide with the suppression of women's equality? And that when women's sexuality has been banished from the public sphere, women themselves are also banished from key roles in that sphere?

Far from advancing women's equality, this growing tendency to equate any sexual expression with gender discrimination undermines women's equality. Women are, in effect, told that we have to choose between sexuality and equality, between sexual liberation and other aspects of "women's liberation," between sexual freedom and economic, social, and political freedom. This dangerous equation of sexual expression with gender discrimination, which is at the heart of the feminist antipornography movement, is a central reason that movement is so threatening to the women's rights cause.

The misguided zeal to strip all sexual expression from workplaces and campuses, in an alleged effort to strip those places of gender-based discrimination, now has reached even to subtle interpersonal expressions, prone to subjective perceptions and interpretations, such as looks and glances. A growing number of campus policies, including the one at Syracuse University already quoted, extend the concept of harassment to "sexually suggestive looks." Likewise, a survey about the sexual harassment of female doctors by their patients, published in the prestigious *New England Journal of Medicine* in December 1993, included "suggestive looks" among the "offenses" reported.[20] In fact, though newspaper headlines trumpeted the dramatic conclusion that 75 percent of the female doctors surveyed said that they had been sexually harassed by patients, further reading revealed that "most of the offenses involved suggestive looks and sexual remarks."[21]

Are women doctors, faculty, and students to be relegated to a figurative equivalent of the purdah of traditional Hindus and Muslims, or the clothing and segregation requirements of orthodox Jews—designed to prevent men from looking at women, and to "protect" women from men's looks? While these traditional religious practices shield women from the eyes of anyone outside their domestic circles, they also imprison women within those domestic circles. The outside world cannot see women, and women cannot see the outside world.

To be sure, "sexual looks," as well as the other nonassaultive conduct proscribed in the Syracuse code, could constitute sexual harassment if they were sufficiently severe or pervasive—for example, if a professor repeatedly subjected a young student to such behavior. In contrast, isolated incidents where the behavior is not targeted at someone who has less authority or status should not be deemed harassment.

No Classroom Talk about Sex Is Safe— Not Even Talk about Safe Sex

The sex panic that antiporn feminists have helped to spark and to spread has had another adverse effect that should be of particular concern to those who are committed to women's rights: on college and university campuses around the United States, students and faculty have been penalized for seemingly any sexually related expression, even in class discussion and other academic settings in which freedom of speech should be especially cherished and safe. The list of such incidents is long and rapidly expanding. Let me describe just a few of them here.

- At Vanderbilt University in 1993, associate fine arts professor Don Evans, a recognized photographer, was charged with sexual harassment and subjected to restrictions on his future teaching following the university's secretive, individual questioning of each of his students, without informing him. This furtive inquiry was launched by one female student's complaint about the display and discussion of nude and sexually oriented photographs in Evans's course on photography and design. The offended student complained that the sexually explicit photographs, which included some by Robert Mapplethorpe and some by Evans himself, "degraded women."[22]

  In response, the university ordered Evans to warn future students in advance about the "potential nature and content of material shown" in his courses.[23] As Evans noted, the same "logic" that would force him to warn students about what they might see in a photography class would also require English literature professors to warn students that they might be offended by some writings of Chaucer. (Indeed, Chaucer's writings have repeatedly provoked objections; to cite one incident of particular relevance here, in 1987, the Columbia County, Florida, school board barred students from reading a widely used humanities textbook because it contained Chaucer's "The Miller's Tale," which community members denounced as "pornography and women's lib.")[24] "I find it sad a professor has to warn adult students their sensibilities might be offended by course material," Evans said. "I guess we'll have to put a sign over the entrance of the university that says, 'Danger: some of the information you receive here might offend you.'"[25] Sadly, Evans's prediction proved prophetic. Several months later, Vanderbilt student leaders, at the request of other students, asked every faculty member to announce at the beginning of any course whether or not it would include any sexually explicit material.

- In 1993, the Iowa Board of Regents ordered all faculty members to warn students before presenting any materials that include "explicit representations of human sexual acts that could reasonably be expected to be offensive to some students."[26] Students had to be excused from those classes without penalty and allowed to complete an alternative assignment or to drop the course. Even beyond the paternalistic attitude toward students that this policy reflects— and its enormous chilling effect on faculty and student speech—it deprives students of information and ideas that are vitally important to themselves and others. Under the Iowa rules, for example, medical students could be exempted from learning about sexually transmitted diseases.

- In 1993, the University of New Hampshire suspended English professor J. Donald Silva from teaching for at least one year (without pay), and required him to undergo counseling at his own expense with a counselor selected by the university, after students complained that some of his in-class statements created a sexually intimidating atmosphere. His offenses? During a writing class covering rhetorical devices, Silva (who is also the longtime pastor at the Great Island, New Hampshire, Congregational Church) had given an example of a simile that came from an old record his wife had about belly dancing: "Belly dancing is like Jell-O on a plate, with a vibrator under the plate." In addition, in trying to explain the concept of focus in a way that would grab the students' attention, he said:

> Focus is like sex. You seek a target. You zero in on your subject. You move from side to side. You close in on the subject. You bracket the subject and center on it. Focus connects experience and language. You and the subject become one.[27]

(Silva sued the university for violating his constitutional rights to free speech and due process of law, and in September 1994 a federal judge issued a preliminary ruling in his favor.)

- In 1994, Chicago Theological Seminary professor Graydon Snyder, an ordained minister, was severely disciplined merely for reciting a lesson from the Talmud, the compendium of Jewish law, during a religion class. The lesson centers around a story about a man who falls off a roof, lands on a woman, and accidentally has intercourse with her; the Talmud comments that the man is innocent, because the act was unintentional. For thirty years, Snyder had used this lesson as a springboard for discussing Jewish and Christian concepts of responsibility, guilt, and sin. But when he did so in 1994, a female student filed a sexual harassment charge against him. In response, the seminary issued a formal reprimand and put notices in the mailboxes of every student and teacher at the school, telling them that Dr. Snyder had engaged in sexual harassment. Although Snyder was allowed to continue teaching, he has had to endure the further indignity of being visibly monitored by a school official, who sits near him in the classroom with a tape recorder—"a kind of word cop," according to *The New York Times*.[28]
- At the University of Nebraska-Lincoln in 1993, a male student accused female graduate instructor Toni Blake of sexual harassment because of her actions and statements in teaching a class about contraception and sexually transmitted diseases. In instructing her students about the appropriate use of condoms, she demonstrated how to put them on by using a banana. Moreover, to make a point about the timing of

putting on condoms, she quoted to her class the old joke that men, like basketball players, "dribble before they shoot." Blake was trying to to give her students a memorable lesson on the crucially important subjects of contraception and safer sex. According to the male student who filed the complaint against her, though, she had "objectified" the penis and thereby created a hostile academic environment for men.

Toni Blake's experience demonstrates the long-range adverse effects of complaints by sex police in deterring students and faculty from any discussion of sexuality or, indeed, of any topic with any sexual connotations. In response to the complaint against her, Blake concluded that it would be prudent to delete material on human sexuality from her future courses to avoid further problems, and her department chair also advised her to do this. In short, there is no safe expression about safe sex.

Given statistics indicating that at least 80 percent of young people in the United States are sexually active by age twenty,[29] the alleged "protectionism" of shielding students from sexually oriented information and ideas is surely exactly the opposite. Our colleges and universities do not (and should not) protect the students from sex itself, with its attendant physical risks and emotional and psychological complications, but they do "protect" the students from learning about sex, including about safer-sex practices.

It is essential to derail the traditionalist–feminist antisex juggernaut before its impact on public perceptions and public policy becomes even more devastating. This juggernaut poses a great danger to free speech about sex, which is central to a range of urgent current concerns—abortion, contraception, other aspects of reproduction, gender roles, sexism, sexual orientation (and the legal status of homosexual or bisexual people), and sexually transmitted diseases. In addition, the conservative–feminist drive to suppress sexual expression threatens the movement for women's equality, since that movement depends on robust free expression, particularly in the realm of sexuality, which historically has been a focal point in defining—and limiting—women's societal and legal status.

Women Having It All: Free Speech *and* Equality

From a feminist perspective, there is no choice between
equality and freedom of expression; they are two sides of the
same coin, and cannot be played off against each other any
more than we can separate mind and body.
—THELMA MCCORMACK, Director
York University Centre for Feminist Studies[30]

Since free expression about sexual issues is critically important to the
women's rights cause, it is ironic that those feminists who advocate
curbing such expression say they do so out of concern for women's
rights. They define as pornography, and seek to suppress, sexually
explicit expression that "subordinates" or "degrades" women, on the
theory that this expression causes discrimination and violence against
women. They argue that free speech protection for pornography is antithetical to women's rights, and therefore that we have to compromise
the constitutional free speech guarantee to advance the constitutional
equality guarantee. This was the major theme, for example, of Catharine MacKinnon's 1993 book *Only Words*. She declares: "The law of
equality and the law of freedom of speech are on a collision course in
this country."[31]

In fact, though, this line of argument is pernicious and wrongheaded.
In our society, founded on the interlinked goals of liberty and equality,
we all are entitled to both freedom of speech and equal opportunity
under the law. Moreover, these two ideals are mutually reinforcing.

In the women's rights context, freedom of speech consistently has
been the strongest weapon for countering misogynistic discrimination and violence, and censorship consistently has been a potent tool
for curbing women's rights and interests. Freedom of sexually oriented
expression is integrally connected with women's freedom, since women
traditionally have been straitjacketed precisely in the sexual domain,
notably in our ability to control our sexual and reproductive options.
Accordingly, during the first wave of feminism in this century, Margaret Sanger, Mary Ware Dennett, and other pioneering birth control

advocates were prosecuted (and, in some cases, convicted, fined, and imprisoned) for disseminating birth control information. Significantly, this information was held to violate *antiobscenity* statutes. Such laws were used not to promote women's equality, but rather, to erode it (see chapter 11).

Because the American Civil Liberties Union, since its founding, has represented many women's rights activists whose free speech has been throttled—including Sanger and Dennett—its opposition to the antipornography laws endorsed by some feminists is grounded in the organization's long-standing commitment to women's rights, as well as in its consistent defense of free speech. In opposing an antipornography ordinance that Indianapolis enacted in 1984, modeled on one drafted by Dworkin and MacKinnon,[32] the ACLU argued that the law "unconstitutionally introduced gender-based discrimination into the First Amendment." As the ACLU's brief explained:

> The ordinance . . . presumes a natural and inevitable vulnerability of (weaker) women to the unbridled and voracious sexual appetites of (stronger) men and accordingly promises to "protect" all women. As in the past, the cost of "protection" is the perpetuation of gender-based stereotypes and the denial to women of sexually explicit material which may itself benefit women by providing information about sexuality, sexual functions, or reproduction. . . . While it is undoubtedly true that many women are victims of male violence . . . the attempt to [justify] widespread censorship on the false stereotypical assumption that all women are unable to resist male domination . . . is precisely the type of sex-based protectionism that inhibits the evolution of genuine equality between the sexes.[33]

All censorship measures throughout history have been used disproportionately to silence those who are relatively disempowered and who seek to challenge the status quo. Since women and feminists are in that category, it is predictable that any censorship scheme—even one purportedly designed to further their interests—would in fact be used to suppress expression that is especially important to their interests.

That prediction has proven accurate in our neighboring country of Canada, which in 1992 adopted the definition of pornography advocated by MacKinnon, Dworkin, and other procensorship feminists: sexually explicit expression that is "dehumanizing" or "degrading" to women.[34] The Canadian authorities have seized upon this powerful tool to suppress lesbian and gay publications and feminist works, and to harass lesbian and gay bookstores and women's bookstores (see chapter 11).

With Friends Like These, Who Needs Enemies?

The widespread misperception that Dworkin and MacKinnon speak for feminists generally concerning sexual speech is fostered by their own divisive rhetoric, which suggests that their censorship campaign is the one and only feminist position. Catharine MacKinnon has stated that "Pornography, in *the* feminist view, is a form of forced sex . . . an institution of gender inequality" (emphasis added).[35] Moreover, Dworkin and MacKinnon have charged that those who disagree with them are not true, but "liberal, so-called" feminists.[36] MacKinnon has compared feminists who oppose censorship to "house niggers who sided with the masters," and has denounced a leading feminist anticensorship group, the Feminist Anti-Censorship Taskforce (FACT): "The labor movement had its scabs, the slavery movement had its Uncle Toms and Oreo cookies, and we have FACT."[37] In the same vein, Dworkin has condemned feminists who maintain that the constitutional free speech guarantee extends to sexual speech as "politically self-righteous fellow travelers of the pornographers."[38]

Leanne Katz, executive director of the National Coalition Against Censorship, recently described "the extraordinary name-calling tactics" that the procensorship feminists brandish against anticensorship feminists:

> Opposition to their activities is called "slander," and "hate campaigns";
> we are charged with being manipulated by "pimps," with being mouthpieces of pornographers. We are accused of being indifferent to violence against women, the Uncle Toms of patriarchy. It is apparently unthinkable that one might care about women and *therefore* oppose censorship.[39]

The procensorship feminists' views that women who disagree with them are being manipulated as tools of "pimps" or "pornographers," and are not thinking for ourselves, conveys at least as subordinating or degrading a view of women as does the pornography they decry. One example of the procensorship feminists' patronizing, "maternalistic" view of their anticensorship counterparts was provided by Norma Ramos, general counsel of Women Against Pornography. Commenting about me in a *Vogue* magazine article in 1992, Ramos said, "The ACLU . . . uses its women to further its antifeminist agenda. When Strossen became an apologist for the pornographers, she passed their litmus test to become president."[40]

In a letter to the editor of *Vogue,* writer Marcia Pally, founder and president of Feminists for Free Expression, responded to Ramos's remarks:

> I was especially edified by comments from Norma Ramos, of Women Against Pornography. Without them, I might never have known that Strossen, a Phi Beta Kappa Radcliffe graduate and editor of the *Harvard Law Review* . . . was a puppet—"used" by ACLU men. . . . Ramos is right: any woman who disagrees with Ramos's own views on sexual material must be a stooge. How foolish to believe that Strossen, a professor at New York Law School, could think for herself, or that her contributions to [various scholarly journals] were anything but sad efforts to pass the "litmus test" of male colleagues. How silly, when it has so long been known that women are muddle-minded pawns. I wonder only that Ramos failed to report that Strossen slept her way to the top.[41]

The Anticensorship, Prosex Feminists

If you love freedom and like sex, censorship is bad news.
—KATHLEEN PERATIS
women's rights attorney[42]

Contrary to the MacDworkinites' image of a unified front, many feminist women disagree with their implacably negative analysis of sexual expression, and reject their calls for censoring it. Moreover, contrary to the MacKinnon-Dworkin line that to dissent from their views reflects an elevation of free speech principles over principles of women's equality, many feminist women oppose censoring sexually oriented speech specifically from a feminist perspective; we believe that censorship would not promote women's rights, but, to the contrary, would undermine them. Therefore, the proposed feminist antipornography laws are doubly flawed: they would undermine both free speech and equality.

Because anticensorship feminists reject the procensorship feminists' negative views that sex inherently degrades women, we often are called "prosex" feminists by partisans on both sides of this debate.

Feminist opponents of censorship include leading activists, artists, psychologists, scholars, writers, and women (and men) from all other walks of life. Among the best known are Betty Friedan, founding president of the National Organization for Women (NOW); Faye Wattleton, longtime president of Planned Parenthood; Karen DeCrow, another former NOW president; and writers Anne Bernays, Judy Blume, Barbara Ehrenreich, Nora Ephron, Nancy Friday, Mary Gordon, Susan Isaacs, Molly Ivins, Erica Jong, Jamaica Kincaid, Kate Millett, Katha Pollitt, Anne Rice, Adrienne Rich, Alix Kates Shulman, and Wendy Wasserstein.

In the United States, organizations that oppose censoring pornography specifically from a feminist perspective include the Feminist Anti-Censorship Taskforce; Feminists for Free Expression; and the National Coalition Against Censorship's Working Group on Women, Censorship, and "Pornography." (As indicated by its name, the Working Group consistently puts the word "pornography" in quotation marks to underscore the word's inherent ambiguity and subjectiveness.) Although these organizations have slightly different emphases, they and their supporters all share a commitment to both free speech and equality, and a belief that suppressing pornography would subvert, rather than promote, efforts to counter misogynistic violence and discrimination. Feminists have also banded together in other countries—including Canada and Great Britain—to oppose MacDworkinite proposals from a women's rights perspective.

This book focuses on the reasons so many feminists have concluded that censorship would in fact undermine important women's rights goals. Before turning directly to those reasons, though, I will address some related issues to provide a legal and factual context for the feminist anticensorship, prosex position.

First, I will outline the current law governing sexual expression. It is this tired body of law that procensorship feminists seek to resuscitate, and that anticensorship feminists seek to retire. After that, I will sketch the early history of what have been dubbed the feminist "sex wars"—showing how the feminist antipornography movement has sought to change the current law concerning sexual expression, and how its initial efforts were soundly rebuffed by the Supreme Court. Then I will chronicle the alarming recent renaissance of the feminist procensorship faction, and its increasing influence on popular attitudes, public policy, and law.

CHAPTER 2

Sexual Speech and the Law

Martin Luther King, Malcolm X,
Freedom of speech is as good as sex.
　　　　　　　　　　　　　—MADONNA, performer[1]

Since Christianity . . . concentrated on sexual behavior as
the root of virtue, everything pertaining to sex has been a
"special case" in our culture, evoking peculiarly inconsistent
attitudes.
　　　　　　　　　　　　　—SUSAN SONTAG, writer[2]

While Madonna believes that free speech and sex are equally good,
many other Americans believe that they are equally bad—at least when
the speech is *about* sex. Therefore, just as the American legal system has
outlawed certain types of sexual activity—even by consenting adults
in private—it has outlawed certain types of sexual expression—again,
even by or for consenting adults in private.

This sexual prudery in American law reflects our Puritan heritage.
Garrison Keillor made this point with characteristic humor in his
1990 congressional testimony supporting the National Endowment for
the Arts, which was embattled because it had funded certain sexually
oriented works, including Robert Mapplethorpe's homoerotic photographs. Keillor said: "My ancestors were Puritans from England, [who]
arrived here in 1648 in the hope of finding greater restrictions than
were permissible under English law at the time."[3]

The First Amendment's broadly phrased free speech guarantee—
"Congress shall make no law . . . abridging the freedom of

29

speech"—contains no exception for sexual expression.* Nevertheless, the Supreme Court has consistently read such an exception into the First Amendment, allowing sexual speech to be restricted or even banned under circumstances in which it would not allow other types of speech to be limited. While American law is, overall, the most speech-protective in the world, it is far less protective of sexual speech than the law in some other countries. Our First Amendment jurisprudence, along with everything else in our culture, as Susan Sontag suggests, treats sex as a "special case."[4]

The very change in current law that procensorship feminists advocate—that it target sexual expression that "subordinates" or "degrades" women—highlights the important ideas that such speech conveys about significant public issues, notably, gender roles and gender-based discrimination. Consequently, the courts have recognized that the subset of sexual speech that the Dworkin-MacKinnon faction seeks to suppress, as distinct from the subset of sexual speech that is unprotected under current obscenity doctrine, is really "political" speech, which has traditionally received the highest level of legal protection.

The MacDworkinite concept of pornography, in focusing expressly on the political ideas conveyed by sexual expression, would necessarily threaten other forms of political expression, too. In contrast, the Court's concept of obscene expression focuses specifically on the alleged lack of ideas conveyed by such speech. At least in theory, then, obscenity is a self-contained category of sexual expression whose unprotected status does not directly threaten other speech. As I will explain, in practice the concept of obscenity cannot be cabined, and does threaten valuable expression. But the alternative, more expansive notion of pornography-as-discrimination even more directly threatens a broader range of speech, as well as many core free speech principles.

If we should restrict sexually explicit speech because it purveys sexist ideas, as the feminist antipornography faction argues, then why

---

*Although the First Amendment expressly prohibits only congressional laws that abridge free speech, the Supreme Court has interpreted it as implicitly prohibiting any government action that abridges free speech. Moreover, the Court has held that the First Amendment bars private citizens from invoking the legal system—for example, through private lawsuits—to suppress free speech.

shouldn't we restrict non–sexually explicit speech when it purveys sexist ideas? And if speech conveying sexist ideas can be restricted, then why shouldn't speech be restricted when it conveys racist, heterosexist, and other biased ideas? These logically indistinguishable applications of the feminist antipornography analysis lead many in the Dworkin-MacKinnon camp, including Dworkin and MacKinnon themselves, to advocate restricting racist and other forms of "hate" speech.[5]

Yet the Supreme Court has repeatedly held that the First Amendment protects not only speech that is *full of hate* on the speaker's part, but also speech that is *hateful* to its audience. As former justice Oliver Wendell Holmes declared, "[I]f there is any principle of the Constitution that more imperatively calls for attachment than any other it is the principle of free thought—not free thought for those who agree with us but freedom for the thought we hate."[6]

Furthermore, the Supreme Court has consistently rejected calls for censoring (nonobscene) speech when there is no demonstrable, direct causal link between the speech and immediate harm. But this is the feminist procensorship argument in a nutshell—that pornography should be suppressed based on speculation that it may lead to discrimination or violence against women in the long run, despite the lack of evidence to substantiate these fears (see chapter 12). If we should restrict pornography on this basis, then why shouldn't we suppress any expression that might ultimately have a negative effect?

If MacDworkinism should prevail in the courts, it would jeopardize all of the foregoing free speech precedents and principles. The government could outlaw flag burning and the teaching of Marxist doctrine because they might lead to the erosion of patriotism and our capitalist system; white supremacist and black nationalist speeches could be criminalized because they might lead to racial segregation; peaceful demonstrations for (or against) civil rights, women's rights, gay rights, and, indeed, any other potentially controversial causes could be banned because they might provoke violent counterdemonstrations; advertising for alcohol, tobacco, and innumerable other products could be prohibited because it might cause adverse health effects; feminist expression could be stifled because it might threaten "traditional family values" and the attendant domestic order and tranquillity; abortion clinic advertising and other prochoice expression could be suppressed because it might lead to the termination of potential life; indeed, feminist antipornography advocacy could itself be suppressed because it could endanger cherished constitutional rights! The list is literally endless.

Make no mistake: if accepted, the feminist procensorship analysis would lead inevitably to the suppression of far more than pornography. At stake is all sexually oriented speech, any expression that allegedly subordinates or undermines the equality of any group, and any speech that may have a tendency to lead to any kind of harm. One might well ask about the feminist procensorship philosophy, not what expression would be stifled, but rather, what expression would be safe.

The "Preferred" Status of Speech in Our Hierarchy of Constitutional Rights

As noted above, the U.S. Supreme Court has relegated sexual expression to second-class status. To understand the significance of this disparity, we need first to consider the Court's rules concerning freedom of expression in general, and then to consider how the Court has refused to extend these speech-protective general rules to sexually oriented speech.

At the heart of the Supreme Court's extensive free speech jurisprudence are two cardinal principles. The first specifies what is *not* a sufficient justification for restricting speech, and the second prescribes what *is* a sufficient justification. A Dworkin-MacKinnon–style antipornography law violates both of these core principles. Accordingly, for such a law to be upheld, the very foundations of our free speech structure would have to be torn up.

The first of these basic principles requires "content neutrality" or "viewpoint neutrality." It holds that government may never limit speech just because any listener—or even, indeed, the majority of the community—disagrees with or is offended by its content or the viewpoint it conveys. The Supreme Court has called this the "bedrock principle" of our proud free speech tradition under American law.[7] In recent years, the Court has steadfastly enforced this fundamental principle to protect speech that conveys ideas that are deeply unpopular with or offensive to many, if not most, Americans: for example, burning an

American flag in a political demonstration against national policies,[8] and burning a cross near the home of an African-American family that had recently moved into a previously all-white neighborhood.[9]

The viewpoint-neutrality principle reflects the philosophy that, as first stated in pathbreaking opinions by former Supreme Court justices Oliver Wendell Holmes and Louis Brandeis, the appropriate response to speech with which one disagrees in a free society is not censorship but counterspeech—*more* speech, not *less*. Persuasion, not coercion, is the solution.

Rejecting this philosophy, the feminist procensorship position targets for suppression a category of sexual expression precisely because of its viewpoint—specifically, a gender-discriminatory viewpoint. Because of this fatal constitutional flaw, all Dworkin-MacKinnon–style antipornography laws will continue to be ruled unconstitutional, as were the two such laws that courts have reviewed to date, as long as our courts continue to enforce the viewpoint-neutrality principle.

The feminist antipornography laws also violate the second cardinal principle that is central to free speech law—that a restriction on speech can be justified only when necessary to prevent actual or imminent harm to an interest of "compelling" importance, such as violence or injury to others. This is often summarized as the "clear and present danger" requirement. As Justice Oliver Wendell Holmes observed in a much-quoted opinion, the First Amendment would not protect someone who falsely shouted "Fire!" in a theater and caused a panic.[10]

This second core free speech principle entails two essential prerequisites for justifying any speech restriction: that the expression will cause direct, imminent harm to a very important interest, and that only by suppressing it can we avert such harm. Each of these requirements is crucial for preserving free expression, and neither is satisfied by advocates of suppressing pornography.

The restricted speech must pose an imminent danger, not an alleged "bad tendency." Allowing speech to be curtailed on the speculative basis that it might indirectly lead to possible harm would inevitably unravel free speech protection. *All* speech might lead to potential danger at some future point. Justice Holmes recognized this fact in an important 1925 opinion. Holmes rejected the argument that pacifist and socialist ideas should be repressed because they might incite young men to resist the draft or to oppose the U.S. system of government—actions and views that many thought might ultimately undermine national interests. As Holmes noted, "Every idea is an incitement."[11]

If we banned the expression of all ideas that might lead individuals to actions that might have an adverse impact even on important interests such as national security or public safety, then scarcely any idea would be safe, and surely no idea that challenged the status quo would be. Judge Frank Easterbrook made precisely this point in holding the Indianapolis version of the Dworkin-MacKinnon model antipornography law unconstitutional. Accepting for the sake of argument the law's cornerstone assumption that "depictions of subordination tend to perpetuate subordination," Easterbrook explained:

> If pornography is what pornography does, so is other speech. . . . Efforts to suppress communist speech in the United States were based on the belief that the public acceptability of such ideas would increase the likelihood of totalitarian government. Religions affect socialization in the most pervasive way. . . . The Alien and Sedition Acts passed during the administration of John Adams rested on a sincerely held belief that disrespect for the government leads to social collapse and revolution—a belief with support in the history of many nations. . . .
>
> Racial bigotry, anti-Semitism, violence on television, reporters' biases—these and many more influence the culture and shape our socialization. . . . Yet all is protected as speech, however insidious. Any other answer leaves the government in control of all of the institutions of culture, the great censor and director of which thoughts are good for us.
>
> Sexual responses often are unthinking responses, and the association of sexual arousal with the subordination of women therefore may have a substantial effect. But almost all cultural stimuli provoke unconscious responses. Religious ceremonies condition their participants. Teachers convey messages by selecting what not to cover; the implicit message about what is off limits or unthinkable may be more powerful than the messages for which they present rational argument. . . . If the fact that speech plays a role in a process of conditioning were enough to permit governmental regulation, that would be the end of freedom of speech.[12]

While Justice Holmes rejected the so-called bad tendency argument—namely, that speech could be suppressed if it might have a tendency to bring about future harm—his Supreme Court brethren accepted that argument in a series of cases during the World War I era and the ensuing "Red Scare." In one of the low points for free speech in this country, they allowed the imprisonment of thousands of political leaders and other citizens who did nothing more than peacefully express views critical of U.S. participation in World War I and other government policies.

The Supreme Court has since repudiated the bad tendency argument in the context of what it calls "political speech," or speech about issues of public policy. But it continues to accept that argument in the context of sexual speech. The Court allows certain sexual expression—"obscenity"—to be restricted merely because of its alleged tendency to undermine community morality, without any evidence of any direct or immediate harm.

The feminist antipornography activists seek to expand the bad tendency rationale to allow suppression of even more sexual speech than is currently restricted under traditional obscenity laws. In 1992, the Canadian Supreme Court adopted the MacDworkinite bad tendency approach. The Canadian court acknowledged that no evidence establishes a direct causal connection between pornography and discrimination or violence against women (as detailed in chapter 12), but it nevertheless ruled that the mere *belief* that such a connection exists is enough to justify suppressing the speech.[13]

In contrast, the U.S. Supreme Court has rejected this censorial notion, maintaining the crucial distinction between *advocacy* of violent or unlawful conduct, which is protected, and intentional, imminent *incitement* of such conduct, which is not. The classic free speech dissents of justices Holmes and Brandeis earlier in this century endorsed this critical distinction as an essential aspect of the "clear and present danger" requirement that they also launched. The Court enshrined the distinction as a cornerstone of contemporary free speech law in a 1969 case, *Brandenburg v. Ohio*.[14] *Brandenburg* upheld the First Amendment rights of a Ku Klux Klan leader who addressed a rally of supporters, some of whom brandished firearms, and advocated violence and discrimination against Jews and blacks. The Court held that this

generalized advocacy was neither intended nor likely to cause immediate violent or unlawful conduct, and therefore could not be punished.

The Supreme Court has consistently applied *Brandenburg's* critical
distinction between protected advocacy and unprotected incitement
to protect incendiary expression of every stripe. In 1982, it relied on
this distinction to protect expression whose thrust was diametrically
opposite that of the expression that had been protected in the *Brandenburg* case. The Court held that officials of the National Association for
the Advancement of Colored People (NAACP) had a First Amendment
right to make speeches advocating violent reprisals against individuals who violated an NAACP-organized boycott of white merchants
who had allegedly engaged in racial discrimination. Even though some
violence was subsequently committed against blacks who patronized
white merchants, it occurred weeks or months after the inflammatory
addresses. Accordingly, in a major victory for the civil rights cause,
as well as for free speech principles, the Supreme Court overturned a
lower-court ruling that had declared the boycott unlawful and held the
NAACP responsible for white merchants' large financial losses. The
Court explained the fundamental free speech principles at stake:

> The [NAACP leaders'] addresses generally contained an impassioned
> plea for black citizens to unify, to support and respect each other, and
> to realize the political and economic power available to them. In the
> course of those pleas, strong language was used. . . . Strong and effec-
> tive extemporaneous rhetoric cannot be nicely channeled in purely dul-
> cet phrases. An advocate must be free to stimulate his audience with
> spontaneous and emotional appeals for unity and action in a common
> cause. . . . To rule otherwise would ignore the "profound national com-
> mitment" that "debate on public issues should be uninhibited, robust,
> and wide-open."[15]

Procensorship feminists seek to eliminate the fundamental distinction between protected advocacy and unprotected incitement, arguing
that sexual expression should be suppressed even if it does not expressly
advocate, let alone *intentionally incite,* violence or discrimination
against women. They want to suppress sexual words or images they
interpret as consistent with views that accept violence or discrimination

against women, and which might reinforce such views on the part of some audience members.

It has become fashionable among some law professors, of whom Catharine MacKinnon is a prominent example, to question the ongoing relevance of classic First Amendment principles, and I certainly endorse and engage in the constant critical reexamination of all established legal principles. Reexamining the landmark Holmes and Brandeis free speech opinions that I have cited has left me more impressed than ever with their universal, timeless force. They remain relevant and persuasive, specifically in the context of the current pornography debate. Further, the majority rulings that these dissents so powerfully criticize stand as sobering reminders of how much freedom we would lose should we accept the procensorship feminists' call to revive the now discredited "bad tendency" approach that these rulings reflect.

Heed the following passage from Justice Holmes's 1916 dissent in *Abrams v. United States,* in which the majority had upheld prison sentences of up to twenty years for a group of Russian immigrants who had expressed their support for the Russian Revolution and called for a general strike in the United States. It reads as if it were Justice Holmes's answer to contemporary feminists' pleas for censoring pornography— an answer that is understanding of, and even sympathetic to, their reasons for urging such censorship, but that also explains why those reasons are fundamentally at odds with a sustainable constitutional philosophy:

Persecution for the expression of opinions seems to me perfectly logical. If you have no doubt of your premises or your power and want a certain result with all your heart you naturally express your wishes in law and sweep away all opposition. To allow opposition by speech seems to indicate that you think the speech impotent. . . . But when men have realized that time has upset many fighting faiths, they may come to believe even more than they believe the very foundations of their own conduct that the ultimate good desired is better reached by free trade in ideas—that the best test of truth is the power of the thought to get itself accepted in the competition of the market, and that truth is the only ground upon which their wishes safely can be carried out. That at any rate is the theory of our Constitution. It is an experiment, as all life is an experiment. Every year if not every day we have to wager our

salvation upon some prophecy based upon imperfect knowledge. While
that experiment is part of our system I think that we should be eternally
vigilant against attempts to check the expression of opinions that we
loathe and believe to be fraught with death, unless they so imminently
threaten immediate interference with the lawful and pressing purposes
of the law that an immediate check is required to save the country. . . .
Only the emergency that makes it immediately dangerous to leave the
correction of evil counsels to time warrants making any exception to
the sweeping command, "Congress shall make no law . . . abridging the
freedom of speech."[16]

Next, listen to Justice Brandeis's powerful opinion in *Whitney v. California,* a 1927 case in which the majority upheld a one- to fourteen-
year prison sentence that had been imposed on Anita Whitney merely
because she was a member of the Communist Labor Party, whose plat-
form advocated the violent overthrow of the U.S. government. Although
Whitney herself unsuccessfully opposed this position, and had called
upon the party to pursue its goals through the political process, the
Supreme Court majority held that Whitney's mere party membership
warranted her criminal punishment.

While Brandeis, like Holmes, is sympathetic to fears about potential speech-induced harms, he eloquently reminds us that our constitutional philosophy reflects and requires not fear, but rather courage, in
the realm of ideas. Moreover, directly responsive to the procensorship
feminists' concerns about women's relatively powerless status, Brandeis
presciently warns that it is precisely those who are relatively weak who
will be victimized, not protected, by any fear-based repression:

> Those who won our independence . . . believed liberty to be the secret
> of happiness and courage to be the secret of liberty. . . . They recognized
> the risks to which all human institutions are subject. But they knew
> that order cannot be secured merely through fear of punishment for its
> infraction; that it is hazardous to discourage thought, hope and imagi-
> nation; that fear breeds repression; that repression breeds hate; that hate
> menaces stable government; that the path of safety lies in the opportu-
> nity to discuss freely supposed grievances and proposed remedies; and
> that the fitting remedy for evil counsels is good ones. . . .

Fear of serious injury cannot alone justify suppression of free speech and assembly. Men feared witches and burned women. . . .

Those who won our independence by revolution were not cowards. . . . They did not exalt order at the cost of liberty. To courageous, self-reliant men, with confidence in the power of free and fearless reasoning applied through the processes of popular government, no danger flowing from speech can be deemed clear and present, unless the incidence of the evil apprehended is so imminent that it may befall before there is opportunity for full discussion. If there be time to expose through discussion the falsehood and fallacies, to avert the evil by the processes of education, the remedy to be applied is more speech, not enforced silence. Only an emergency can justify repression.[17]

In urging "courageous, self-reliant" individuals to have "confidence" in their own speech as an effective response to "evil counsels," rather than asking the government to protect them by suppressing such evil counsels, Justice Brandeis anticipates an important theme in the current feminist anticensorship movement. Rejecting the procensorship faction's emphasis on women as victims in need of governmental protection through censorship, anticensorship feminists are willing to trust our own voices—as well as those of our antipornography sister feminists—to effectively counter misogynist expression, including misogynist sexual expression. Ironically, the feminist procensorship faction apparently does not view women as capable of such self-help, but instead sees us as helpless.

Speech May Be Restricted Only as a Last Resort

As stated earlier, before the government may restrict expression, it must show not only that the expression threatens imminent serious harm but also that the restriction is *necessary* to avert the harm. This requirement is often described as the "least restrictive alternative" concept: even when a limitation on speech would promote an extremely important goal, if the government could advance that goal by methods that restrict speech less, then it must use those alternative measures.

Undeniably, the interests that procensorship feminists seek to promote, women's equality and safety, are compellingly important. But just as pornography poses no imminent harm to those interests, its suppression is not necessary to promote them. Advocates of MacDworkinite laws cannot even show that these laws would effectively promote women's safety and equality, let alone that they are the necessary and least speech-restrictive means for doing so (see chapters 12 and 13).

In enforcing the preceding principles, which generally permit government to restrict speech only under tightly limited circumstances, American law no doubt provides more protection for speech about most subjects than does the law of any other country. Our legal system protects all manner of controversial, inflammatory, and subversive expression, including speech that is harshly critical of political leaders and policies; speech that is highly provocative or offensive to those who hear it; speech that advocates the overthrow of the existing form of government; and speech that advocates violence or crimes against certain people.

   In stark contrast, American law provides far less protection for sexually oriented expression.

The Second-Class Status of Sexual Speech under First Amendment Law

I will not criticize the power of pictures and words to arouse; to arouse passion or ideas, erections or damp panties, fears, curiosities, unarticulated yearnings and odd realizations. Sexual speech, not MacKinnon's speech, is the most repressed and disdained kind of expression in our world, and MacKinnon is no rebel or radical to attack it.

—SUSIE BRIGHT, writer[18]

Nor is pornography's purported aim or effect—to excite the reader sexually—a defect. . . . The physical sensations involuntarily produced in the reader carry with them something that touches upon the reader's whole experience of his humanity.

—SUSAN SONTAG, writer[19]

Pornography is, again, "designed to cause sexual excitement."[20] Yet the fact that expression arouses feelings and passions does not justify giving it less First Amendment protection than expression that is likely to arouse a more intellectual response. If that were the case, then much literature and art would surely have to join sexually oriented speech as second-class citizens under the First Amendment. But the Supreme Court long has held that the First Amendment extends to all forms of art and entertainment, and has rejected attempts to construe it more narrowly as applying only to ideas or information.[21] Indeed, if all emotion-provoking discourse were relegated to a less protected status, then much political speech—which is at the apex of First Amendment protection—would have to be similarly demoted.

Notwithstanding the Court's appropriate protection of expression that arouses all manner of nonsexual passions and inflames all manner of nonsexual senses, it has consistently given scant protection to sexually oriented expression, without ever offering a coherent explanation of why it is either less important or more dangerous than other kinds of expression. The Court has allowed government to restrict sexually oriented expression on the basis of mere assertions or assumptions about its alleged lack of importance or the purported harms associated with it.

Where sexual speech is concerned, the Court simply fails, without explanation, to enforce its generally applicable, stringent preconditions for restricting expression. The Court never has demanded that the government justify restrictions on sexual speech by showing that they were necessary to avert a "clear and present danger," or to prevent the intentional incitement of imminent violence or illegal conduct, or to promote another goal of compelling importance; if it had, the government would not have been able to satisfy such standards. Instead, the Court allows sexual speech to be suppressed based on vague, unsubstantiated allegations that it is dangerous. Just as our society tends to view sex itself as inherently dangerous, so too our courts view words or images that describe or depict sex.

The "sexual revolution" of the 1960s and 1970s called this view into question, as it ushered in greater societal tolerance for various modes of sexual activity and expression. In 1970, the President's Commission on Obscenity and Pornography (which had been appointed by President

Johnson, and submitted its report to President Nixon) recommended the repeal of all laws prohibiting the distribution of sexually explicit materials to consenting adults and advocated a massive sex education program.[22] In the decade that followed, the "women's liberation" movement advocated women's sexual liberation, demanding that women be given information and options that would allow them to break beyond traditional sexual roles. Accordingly, as central aspects of the reenergized women's rights movement, women opened feminist health clinics, provided information and training on women's sexuality, and worked for accessible, safe contraception and abortion.

Although the Supreme Court aided the movement for increased freedom in the sexual arena by invalidating laws restricting contraception and abortion, the Court did not increase freedom for sexual expression. Ironically, in 1973, the very year that the Court issued its landmark *Roe v. Wade* ruling,[23] which recognized that women have a constitutional right to choose to have an abortion, it also adopted a broader definition of "obscenity," the legal term for sexually oriented speech that the Court deems to be beyond the First Amendment pale and thus subject to prohibition and criminal punishment.

Before its 1973 rulings in *Miller v. California*[24] and the companion case of *Paris Adult Theatre I v. Slaton*,[25] the Supreme Court had held that sexually oriented expression would be constitutionally unprotected only if it were "utterly without redeeming social value."[26] In *Miller,* though, the Court altered that standard so that material could be banned unless it had "*serious* literary, artistic, political, or scientific value"[27]—a standard that lawyers refer to as the "SLAPS" test. Until the *Miller* ruling, *any* literary or other value was enough to redeem a sexually oriented work, whereas after that, only *serious* value would suffice.

In 1973, then, the Court decreased the government's power to curb sexual *conduct,* but it increased the government's power to curb sexual *expression.* In so doing, the Court's majority completely ignored the recommendation of the President's Commission on Obscenity and Pornography that sexually oriented expression should be legalized (for consenting adults) because there is no link between it and criminal or violent conduct. Indeed, the majority acknowledged that "there are no scientific data which conclusively demonstrate that exposure to obscene material adversely affects men and women or their society." Nonetheless, contrary to general First Amendment principles, the Court asserted that such material could be banned based on "unprovable assumptions" about its negative impacts on the moral "tone" of "a decent society."[28]

The Supreme Court's 1973 decisions, as well as its earlier obscenity rulings, failed to provide a clear, objective definition of proscribable obscenity. The justices have wrestled with various definitions over the years, but never have been able to craft one that did not simply call for subjective value judgments. This intractable problem is highlighted by former justice Potter Stewart's well-known statement in a 1964 obscenity case: "I shall not today attempt further to define [obscenity] . . . ; and perhaps I could never succeed in intelligibly doing so. But I know it when I see it."[29]

Justice Stewart's candid statement underscores the inevitably subjective judgment at the heart of any determination that a particular sexually oriented expression is or is not obscene. While none of us could intelligibly articulate a neutral standard for judging sexually oriented works in general, each of us no doubt can recognize particular works that we find less appealing, and more offensive, to our own personal tastes and sensibilities. Each of us, though, including each judge and each juror, sees a different "it."

In its 1973 *Miller* decision, the Supreme Court laid out three criteria for assessing whether any work is obscene, all inescapably vague: (1) the "average person, applying contemporary community standards, would find that the work, taken as a whole, appeals to the prurient interest" in sex; (2) "the work depicts or describes, in a patently offensive way, sexual conduct specifically defined by the applicable state law"; and (3) "the work, taken as a whole, lacks serious literary, artistic, political, or scientific value."[30]

The inherent ambiguity and subjectivity of the *Miller* criteria are underscored by the Court's attempted clarification of the term "prurient," which raised more questions than it answered. The Court explained that a "prurient" interest in sex is a "sick and morbid" one, as opposed to a "normal and healthy" one.[31] Imagine yourself sitting as a judge or a juror attempting to determine whether a particular sexually oriented work appeals to a "sick" interest or a "healthy" one. Can you honestly imagine doing anything other than invoking your own tastes and preferences? Do you want other individuals to judge by their own standards a work that you find exciting?

As Stanford law professor Kathleen Sullivan memorably paraphrased *Miller's* first two requirements, "prurient" means that the expression "turns you on," whereas "patently offensive" means that it "grosses you out."[32] More specifically, Sullivan pointed out, the definition essentially means that material that "turns on" *some* people—namely, those who created, distributed, or viewed it—"grosses out" *other* people—namely, the police, prosecutors, judges, and jurors who found it obscene.

The unpredictability of whether a given work will be determined "obscene" is heightened by the Supreme Court's ruling that the "prurient interest" and "patently offensive" criteria are to be weighed in light of "community standards" in each particular locale where the work might be prosecuted. Consequently, even if the work might not be deemed "prurient" or "patently offensive" in one place, it could well be found to satisfy these criteria in another place.

In reality, the obscenity definition functions more as a Rorschach test for judges and jurors than as an objective legal standard for protecting sexual speech against unwarranted prosecutions or convictions.

Second-Class Speech Gets Second-Class Law Enforcement Treatment

As with any law whose definition entails subjective determinations, the obscenity criteria give vast discretionary power to law enforcement officials. Such power invites officials to wield it in an arbitrary or discriminatory fashion. Accordingly, obscenity laws can easily become instruments for suppressing the expression of those who are relatively unpopular or disempowered, whether because of their ideas or perspectives, or because of their membership in particular societal groups. Recent major obscenity prosecutions, in fact, have targeted expressions by or about members of groups that traditionally have been victims of discrimination.

The 1991 prosecutions in Broward County, Florida, of 2 Live Crew's song "As Nasty as They Wanna Be" marked the first time in U.S. history that any work of music had been criminally prosecuted under an obscenity law. Likewise, the 1991 prosecutions of the Cincinnati Contemporary Art Center and its director, Dennis Barrie, marked the first time in U.S. history that any art museum or art museum director had been criminally prosecuted under an obscenity law. In the 2 Live Crew case, the targeted musicians and record store owner were African Americans, and in the Cincinnati case, the works of art that triggered the prosecution were homoerotic photographs by the gay photographer Robert Mapplethorpe.

Because of their subjectivity, current obscenity laws offer a license to the police and prosecutors in any community, or the members of any jury, to punish sexual expression that they find distasteful. White middle-class, middle-aged jurors might well be "turned off" by the erotic rap lyrics that "turn on" poor, inner-city black youth. And heterosexual jurors might well be "grossed out" by Robert Mapplethorpe's gay erotica. In our racially polarized society, many jurors might find Mapplethorpe's arresting images of interracial sexuality frightening, and hence also a "turn-off." Indeed, when Senator Jesse Helms attacked the National Endowment for the Arts for having funded Mapplethorpe's photographs, he singled out their interracial, as well as homoerotic, themes, stating: "There's a big difference between 'The Merchant of Venice' and a photograph of two males of different races on a marble table top. . . . This Mapplethorpe fellow was an acknowledged homosexual . . . the theme goes throughout his work."[33]

Because the obscenity laws allow—indeed, *direct*—the majority in any community, and the members of any jury, to criminally punish sexual depictions that they dislike or disapprove, these laws squarely violate the viewpoint neutrality principle that the Supreme Court has called the "bedrock" of our proud American free speech tradition. If the expression concerned any other subject, First Amendment law would protect it against majoritarian sanctions, no matter how hated it might be. This fact is underscored by the Court's recent decisions upholding the First Amendment right to burn both the American flag and a Ku Klux Klan–style cross.[34]

Sexual Prosecution as Political Persecution

The First Amendment's free speech clause refers unqualifiedly to "the freedom of speech," indicating that *all* speech should be protected equally. Nonetheless, the Supreme Court has deemed some kinds of speech "more equal" than others, creating categories and hierarchies of speech. Sexually oriented expression long has been relegated to the bottom of the Court's First Amendment pecking order. But sex is a vitally important subject, of as much concern to many people as the classically "political" subjects that the Court has placed at the First Amendment apex. The Court itself recognized this in 1957 in *Roth v. United States*: "Sex, a great and mysterious motive force in human life, has indisputably been a subject of absorbing interest to mankind through the ages; it is one of the vital problems of human interest and public concern."[35]

The fact is (and here I agree with procensorship feminists), the sexual *is* political. The Court's bright-line distinction between political and sexual speech, for First Amendment purposes, ignores the significant overlap between those categories made clear by the many major recent political controversies that have centered on sexual issues: the legal rights to be accorded to lesbians and gay men; the protection to be granted to individuals' choices concerning contraception and abortion; the legal, public health, and scientific responses to AIDS and other sexually transmitted diseases; the availability and nature of sex education in public schools; the public funding and display of art with sexual themes; and the legal protection available to women and men from discrimination based on traditional sex roles.

Throughout history, obscenity prosecutions have in fact targeted individuals who have expressed controversial or disfavored ideas about political or religious subjects. One of the earliest British obscenity prosecutions, in the eighteenth century, was instituted by the Tory government to imprison its leading Whig opponent, John Wilkes.[36] In early American experience, antiobscenity laws targeted expression offensive to the prevailing religious orthodoxy and deemed blasphemous or sacrilegious.

The pattern holds today. The so-called NEA Four, performance artists whose NEA grants were denied because of their works' alleged obscenity or indecency, explored themes of domestic violence, the feminization of poverty, homophobia, male dominance, the oppressiveness of traditional gender roles, sexism, and sexual harassment. In the words of one of their lawyers, Marjorie Heins of the ACLU, their work deals with "the politics of sex."[37]

Although a majority of the Supreme Court continues to enforce the *Miller* definition of obscenity, six justices who have sat on the Court during the past quarter century have argued that this definition violates free speech principles. Most recently, in a 1987 dissent, Justice John Paul Stevens, joined by Justices William Brennan and Thurgood Marshall, concluded that all criminal obscenity statutes are unconstitutional, at least as applied to consenting adults.[38] In that same case, moreover, even archconservative justice Antonin Scalia urged the Court to reconsider its *Miller* holding, stating:

> [I]t is quite impossible to come to an objective assessment of (at least) literary or artistic value, there being many accomplished people who have found literature in Dada, and art in the replication of a soup can. Since ratiocination has little to do with esthetics, the fabled "reasonable man" . . . would have to be replaced with, perhaps, the "man of tolerably good taste"—a description that betrays the lack of an ascertainable standard. . . . Just as there is no use arguing about taste, there is no use litigating about it.[39]

The critiques of obscenity law that have been advanced by individual justices on the United States Supreme Court have been adopted unanimously by two state supreme courts: those in Hawaii and Oregon. These courts have invalidated obscenity laws under the free speech guarantees in their state constitutions.[40] Moreover, a number of state legislatures have refused to adopt, or have repealed, antiobscenity laws.

As even the Meese Pornography Commission was forced to recognize, "the bulk of scholarly commentary" has criticized the Supreme Court's obscenity rulings for transgressing First Amendment values.[41] In his authoritative constitutional law treatise, Harvard law professor Laurence Tribe states that the Court's treatment of certain sexual expression as constitutionally unprotected is "incompatible with the First Amendment premise that awareness can never be deemed harmful in itself." He eloquently explains why:

> [I]n the last analysis, suppression of the obscene persists because it tells us something about ourselves that some of us . . . would prefer not to know. It threatens to explode our uneasy accommodation between

sexual impulse and social custom—to destroy the carefully-spun social web holding sexuality in its place. . . . [T]he desire to preserve that web by shutting out the thoughts and impressions that challenge it cannot be squared with a constitutional commitment to openness of mind.[42]

Dangerous as the suppression of obscenity under traditional law is to open minds and a free society, the suppression of pornography under MacDworkinite laws poses even greater dangers, as we see in the next chapter.

CHAPTER 3

The Fatally Flawed Feminist Antipornography Laws

Because of the important respects in which antiobscenity laws endanger free expression, advocates of free speech, including anticensorship feminists, oppose those laws. That should not be surprising. What may be surprising, though, is that this is one issue on which procensorship feminists agree with anticensorship feminists: MacKinnon, Dworkin, and their allies also oppose the concept of obscenity.[1]

Here the agreement quickly ends. Procensorship feminists do not seek freedom for all sexually oriented expression; rather, they would have the law suppress a new and broader category of sexually oriented expression, distinct from the speech that is targeted under the obscenity laws—namely, the ill-defined category for which they have appropriated the term "pornography." (The term "pornography" has no legal significance in the Supreme Court's First Amendment jurisprudence. While the Court has upheld two state statutes that prohibited what each defined as "child pornography," the Court has not itself defined a constitutionally unprotected category of "child pornography." Both state statutes defined the prohibited expression relatively narrowly, as encompassing photographs or films that show actual children either engaging in sexual activities or in a state of nudity.)[2]

As previously noted, the crux of the procensorship feminists' definition of pornography, as set out in a model law drafted by MacKinnon and Dworkin, is "the sexually explicit subordination of women through pictures and/or words."[3] Obscenity laws, then, do not focus on what procensorship feminists see as the harm that results from certain sexually oriented expression, and they believe that these laws therefore do not target the appropriate subset of such expression. Their own definition of the speech they would censor, however, is so broad as to permit

49

the suppression of virtually all sexually explicit materials, including those encompassed by the obscenity concept.

First Amendment Infirmities

Ironically, the procensorship feminists' revisionist definition of prohibited sexually oriented expression as speech that conveys a misogynistic message reveals the constitutional Achilles' heel of their antipornography law: its focus on the political dimension of sexual expression. Whatever one's views about what the status of women should be in our society, it is indisputable that such status is a matter of great public and political concern. Therefore, to suppress speech because it depicts the subordination of women would be as antithetical to central First Amendment principles as suppressing speech that depicts—or, indeed, even advocates—the subordination of racial minorities, as in the *Brandenburg* Ku Klux Klan case or the more recent cross-burning case, both referred to in chapter 2. Likewise, suppressing speech that depicts the subordination of women, or any other group, would be as contrary to the First Amendment as suppressing speech that depicts the *equality* or *superiority* of women or others.

In brief, traditional antiobscenity laws differ from the newer antipornography laws some feminists advocate primarily in that the former seek to suppress certain *sexual* expression, whereas the latter seek to suppress certain *sexist* expression. The feminist antipornography laws are another example of the "hate speech" laws that the Supreme Court consistently has held to violate the First Amendment. In accordance with the fundamental viewpoint neutrality principle, the Court long has held that expression may not be restricted simply because it expresses bigoted or discriminatory ideas concerning any individual or group, no matter how offensive, incorrect, or dangerous those ideas may appear to anyone, including even the majority in the community.

The 1992 cross-burning case is the most recent example of the Supreme Court's long-standing refusal to allow society to punish even the most odious, dramatic expressions of group-based hatred—in that case, racism toward African Americans. As Justice Scalia concluded the Court's opinion: "Let there be no mistake about our belief that burning a cross in someone's front yard is reprehensible. But [the government] has sufficient means at its disposal to prevent such behavior without adding the First Amendment to the fire."[4] The Court's unanimous ruling in that case underscores the secure status of the basic principle that expression conveying discriminatory ideas, including sexist ideas, is constitutionally protected. Consistent with this principle, the lower courts have uniformly stricken the "hate speech codes" recently adopted or considered on many college and university campuses, holding that such codes violate the First Amendment. These courts have ruled that the schools' attempts to punish expression that might be offensive or demeaning to members of various groups, including women, breach the free speech guarantee.[5]

Governments have no more constitutional power to restrict speech that advocates *unequal* treatment of certain societal groups, on the ground that it is deemed incorrect or unpopular, than they have to restrict speech that advocates *equal* treatment of those groups on such a ground. If the protectibility of expression about equality issues turned on its acceptance or popularity, then various communities throughout the South and elsewhere would have been allowed to silence the voices of pro–civil rights activists during the 1960s and 1970s. Likewise, the women who advocated the federal Equal Rights Amendment (ERA) during the 1970s and early 1980s could have been silenced because that amendment went down to defeat. Indeed, advocates of women's equal constitutional rights could still be stifled around the country, because voters continue to reject proposed women's equal rights amendments to their state constitutions. In November 1992, Iowa voters became the latest group to do so.

Further cautionary illustrations against allowing views about equality issues to be suppressed based on their unpopularity are provided by the recent epidemic of votes at the city, county, and state levels rejecting legal protections against discrimination on the basis of sexual orientation. If the majority in any community could suppress views about equality issues that they deem incorrect or unacceptable, then advocacy of equal rights for lesbians and gay men would be widely censored around the United States.

In fact, all laws restricting speech—including traditional obscenity laws, laws curbing sexist and other hate speech, and Canada's version of the feminist antipornography law—have consistently been used to suppress speech by members of unpopular or disempowered groups, including political dissidents, feminists, and racial and sexual minorities (see chapter 11). It shouldn't be surprising that government officials and legal institutions would enforce censorship measures in ways that reflect majoritarian biases.

While "tyranny by the majority" is surely to be resisted, as our constitutional framers recognized, tyranny by a minority is hardly more palatable. Thus, the dangers of viewpoint-based speech suppression, which are inherent in MacDworkinite laws, could not be allayed by procensorship feminists' assurances that they would "only" limit speech that conveys "incorrect" ideas about sex, gender, and equality, no matter how (un)popular those ideas might be. Such a "dictatorship of virtue" (in writer Richard Bernstein's apt phrase[6]) is frightening both in the abstract and when we consider the broad range of important expression—including speech by feminist women—that procensorship feminists have actually assailed (see chapter 10).

Beyond suppressing expression because of its viewpoint, the feminist antipornography law's definition of suppressible sexual speech differs from the traditional obscenity concept in two additional respects that make it even more plainly inconsistent with First Amendment values.

First, remember that the Supreme Court's definition of obscenity excludes any material that has serious literary, artistic, political, or scientific value, as discussed in chapter 2. Under the MacDworkin model law, though, there is no such limitation. Sexually explicit material that is "subordinating" to women would be banned no matter how significant its overall literary, artistic, or other value.

Second and relatedly, the Court has held that, to be deemed obscene, works must be considered as a whole. Therefore, isolated passages that meet the obscenity definition will not justify suppressing a work if, overall, it is not obscene. This important qualification is absent from the Dworkin-MacKinnon model law, under which even an isolated sexually explicit, "subordinating" depiction would warrant suppressing an entire work. As MacKinnon has asked, "If a woman is subjected, why should it matter that the work has other value?"[7]

By suppressing works without regard to their overall value, the MacDworkin law reverts to an archaic nineteenth-century obscenity definition that twentieth-century courts have emphatically rejected. For example, in a 1936 ruling, which was subsequently followed by the United States Supreme Court, the great appellate judge Learned Hand explained:

> This earlier doctrine necessarily presupposed that the devil against which the [obscenity] statute is directed so much outweighs all interests of art, letters or science, that they must yield to the mere possibility that some prurient person may get a sensual gratification from reading or seeing what to most people is innocent and may be delightful or enlightening. No civilized community not fanatically puritanical would tolerate such an imposition.[8]

The Concept of Civil Censorship

MacDworkinite antipornography laws differ from traditional antiobscenity laws in more than content or focus. While the latter are criminal laws, enforced by police and prosecutors (sometimes in response to private citizens' complaints), the former are civil laws, whose enforcement is initiated directly by private citizens. Under the model law drafted by Dworkin and MacKinnon, anyone could bring a lawsuit that could lead ultimately to a court order prohibiting the production, sale, exhibition, or distribution of pornographic works. In addition, individuals who claimed that they had been injured by pornography could seek damages. Under a proposed federal antipornography law that was inspired and supported by the feminist procensorship faction, the Pornography Victims' Compensation Act (the Senate Judiciary Committee reported favorably on this bill in 1992, but it died when the full Senate failed to consider it before recessing), any victim of a sexual assault could sue those involved in the production or distribution of certain sexual materials for unlimited damages and could recover if the jury found the materials to be a "substantial cause" of the assault.[9]

No doubt recognizing the stigma that is, appropriately, associated with the term "censorship," Dworkin, MacKinnon, and other advocates of feminist antipornography laws protest that these laws do not constitute censorship because they are civil in nature and do not involve any "prior restraint" on expression. In seeking to explain away the draconian censorial impact of the Canadian Supreme Court's 1992 adoption of her pornography concept in construing its antiobscenity law, Catharine MacKinnon has stressed that the Canadian law is enforced through criminal prosecutions rather than civil lawsuits.[10] (In redefining the targeted speech, the Canadian Supreme Court substituted the MacDworkinite focus on degrading expression for the traditional obscenity law's focus on immoral expression; the court incorporated that new definition into its preexisting criminal obscenity law.) In short, MacKinnon would have us believe that if pornography were subject to civil sanctions, rather than criminal, our free speech concerns should disappear. Andrea Dworkin has revealed similarly constricted concepts of free speech and censorship. In a 1994 *Ms.* magazine article, Dworkin asserted, "In legal terms censorship has always meant prior restraint: you pass a law that stops something from being made or being done."[11]

Not surprisingly, Dworkin's and MacKinnon's notions of speech that should be protected and censorship that should be prohibited are unduly narrow. Their protests that their model law does not constitute censorship that violates the First Amendment's free speech guarantee is doubly flawed. First, as the Supreme Court has consistently held, unconstitutional censorship may assume many forms and is not confined either to criminal laws or to formal pre-publication restraints. Indeed, the Court has expressly recognized that civil lawsuits may well have a more devastating censorial impact, as a practical matter, than criminal prosecutions.[12] Second, in any event, the feminist-style antipornography laws do in fact restrain the publication and distribution of many sexually oriented materials; one of the reasons why the trial court judge held the Indianapolis version of the MacDworkin law unconstitutional was her conclusion that it constituted a prohibited prior restraint.[13]

Government-imposed prior restraints violate First Amendment principles in an especially dramatic fashion, as in the U.S. government's attempt to prevent publication of the Pentagon Papers in 1970.[14] But direct, governmental prior restraint is not the only form of censorship that violates the First Amendment. To the contrary, the Supreme Court has recognized that constitutionally prohibited censorship includes any use of government authority—or any threatened use of such authority—to limit the flow of ideas, information, or expression based on their content. Accordingly, the Court has correctly struck down many different types of measures that have prohibited, restricted, regulated, punished, deterred, or threatened expression, regardless of the particular nature or form of such measures. Contrary to the MacDworkinites' semantic quibbling about "criminal" versus "civil" vehicles for suppressing speech, the Court has recognized that censorship in civilian garb is still censorship. In fact, the Court has expressly recognized that "[t]he fear of damage awards" in civil liability actions "may be markedly more inhibiting" upon free expression "than the fear of prosecution under a criminal statute."[15]

In focusing on the actual adverse impact that any particular measure has on expression, the Court correctly refuses to elevate form over substance. Whether the government directly bars the publication of a work through either a criminal conviction or a civil injunction, or whether the work's publication is deterred by the threat or the actuality of damages in a civil lawsuit, the end result is the same.

Of course, private pressure through such vehicles as speaking, writing, and demonstrating may also have the practical impact of deterring a work's publication. Nevertheless, such private pressure not only is not unconstitutional; to the contrary, it is itself a protected exercise of cherished First Amendment rights, precisely the counterspeech that justices Holmes and Brandeis urged as the appropriate response to expression with which we disagree.

The crucial distinction between the constitutionally protected speech-retarding activity of private pressure groups and the constitutionally prohibited speech-retarding lawsuits that would result under Dworkin-MacKinnon–type laws, turns on the role of the government. Thus, those of us who defend free speech rights concerning pornography agree that individuals may raise their voices to denounce it, and may seek to persuade their sister citizens not to produce, pose for, sell, buy, or look at it. (We may, in turn, raise our own voices to counter and criticize such advocacy; see chapter 10.) In contrast, we resist any efforts, through governmental fiat, to remove these choices from individuals. *Private persuasion and counterpersuasion* embody and promote essential human rights values, whereas *governmental coercion* is antithetical to them. This fundamental distinction is recognized even by anticensorship feminists who are critical of pornography—indeed, even by those who believe that pornography may encourage misogynistic discrimination or violence. Writer Molly Ivins, for instance, put it this way, in her inimitable style:

> I do not like pornography. In fact, I think it probably does harm people. . . . [P]robably, all those ugly pictures do encourage violence against women. What should we do about it? Well, my answer is: not a goddamn thing. The cure for every excess of freedom of speech is more freedom of speech. . . . I need the First Amendment so that I'll be able to say to people who say things I do not agree with, "Look, you yellow-bellied son of a bitch—you run on all fours, you molest small children, you have the mind of an adolescent tyrant." I need to . . . be able to answer them back. That's what this whole fuss is about.[16]

The MacDworkin model law authorizes civil lawsuits that trespass beyond the permitted realm of private persuasion into the forbidden territory of governmental coercion. Although the government plays a less direct role in civil lawsuits than in criminal prosecutions, that role is still substantial. Most important, judges, as government officials, have a significant impact on the outcome of civil lawsuits through their rulings about the legal contours of such suits—for example, what evidence should be admitted and how the jury should be instructed. Additionally, civil injunctions can be enforced by police, prosecutors, and sheriffs, and can lead to imprisonment when judges hold defendants in criminal contempt of court.

One of the Supreme Court's landmark free speech rulings, its 1964 decision in *New York Times v. Sullivan*,[17] clearly demonstrates the equivalency between criminal prosecutions and civil damage actions as vehicles for unconstitutional censorship, and how they differ from constitutionally protected private pressure activities. The *Sullivan* decision struck down not a criminal law that barred speech, but rather a civil cause of action that—like MacDworkinite laws—allowed individuals allegedly harmed by the speech to recover damages for it. In the *Sullivan* case, the lawsuit was for libel. Noting that the damages that the jury had awarded dwarfed the maximum fine that the *Times* would have faced in a criminal libel prosecution, the Court held the state's civil libel law unconstitutional because of its "chilling" effect on free speech. In other words, to avoid the economic cost of damages, as well as the economic and intangible costs of defending against a civil damage action, many people would be deterred from saying anything that might result in a successful lawsuit. Indeed, the tangible and intangible costs of defending against a civil damage action—even if the defense is ultimately successful—are so enormous that many prudent people would be deterred from saying anything that might result in a lawsuit, regardless of whether any such lawsuit would be likely to succeed.

In fact, publishers and booksellers have consistently stressed that the only rational response to the threat of expensive litigation and enormous damage awards under Dworkin-MacKinnon–style antipornography laws might well be to avoid creating or distributing any sexually explicit material. Testifying against the proposed Pornography Victims' Compensation Act in 1991, Joyce Meskis, president of the American Booksellers Association, noted that with 700,000 books in print, and about 27,000 book publishers producing more than 50,000 new titles every year, booksellers have no economical way to review all works. Accordingly, she stated, a bookseller's "only real option" under the Act would be "to inform publishers that the store will no longer receive any works with sexual content." Not surprisingly, Meskis therefore concluded that the Act would "produce the most pervasive censorship the U.S. has ever experienced."[18]

In addition to their enormous adverse economic impact, the civil lawsuits that are authorized by feminist-style antipornography laws would be more burdensome on free speech than criminal prosecutions in significant legal respects. Under our legal system, defendants in criminal actions have the benefit of certain constitutionally mandated procedural safeguards. Most important, defendants have the benefit of a presumption of innocence, and cannot be convicted unless the government satisfies a very heavy burden of proof, convincing the jury of their guilt "beyond a reasonable doubt." The standard for establishing civil liability is much lower, requiring only a "preponderance of the evidence." Additional important procedural safeguards in a criminal prosecution are that an indictment must be made by an impartial grand jury, and be carried forward by a prosecutor, whose legal responsibility is to serve the cause of justice neutrally. In contrast, the feminist-style antipornography laws authorize lawsuits to be brought by self-interested parties who hope to secure substantial financial benefits. Yet another important procedural protection available only in the criminal context is the pro-hibition on "double jeopardy," which means that any publication could produce only one criminal conviction. In contrast, a single publication could lead to an unlimited number of civil actions and damage awards.

Protecting Endangered Spaces: "Forced" Public Exposure

Feminists who want to restrict sexual expression argue that no one should be forced to see such expression against his or her will. The Dworkin-MacKinnon model antipornography law makes it illegal to "force pornography on a person in any place of employment, education, home, or any public place."

The Supreme Court has recognized that one's right to privacy in one's home affords shelter against being subjected to certain unwanted expression there.[19] But the feminist antipornography law's comprehensive prohibition upon any "forced" exposure, not only in the privacy of one's home but even in "any public place," sweeps far beyond legitimate privacy concerns and intrudes far too deeply into important free speech rights in the public arena. Even in cases concerning private homes, the Supreme Court has been appropriately reluctant to infringe on freedom of expression in order to protect householders' privacy. The Court has held that although some recipients might object to the contents of unwanted mailings to their homes concerning public policy issues, the intrusion was too minimal to warrant curtailing the senders' First Amendment rights. In the Court's words, the involuntary recipients could "escape exposure to the objectionable material simply by transferring [it] from envelope to wastebasket."[20]

As in so many other contexts, the Supreme Court has treated sexually oriented materials less protectively here too, holding that individuals may prohibit erotic mailings they deem objectionable from being sent to their homes, thereby avoiding even the minimal intrusion that would be involved in disposing of these materials.[21] Even concerning sexually oriented materials, though, the Court has stressed that decisions about which items should not be mailed must be left to the potentially offended individuals, and cannot be made categorically by the government "on their behalf."[22] Accordingly, Judge Frank Easterbrook concluded that the "forced exposure" provision of the MacDworkin law would be unconstitutional even in the context of the home unless it added "a definition of 'forcing' that removes the government from the role of censor."[23]

While certain limitations on expression might be warranted to maintain privacy in the home, there is no sufficiently compelling justification for imposing similar limitations in public places. Therefore, unless the Dworkin-MacKinnon law's prohibition on "forced" public exposure were construed very narrowly, to apply only to intentional, individually targeted, sustained exposure, it would be unconstitutional. To the extent that it purports to outlaw even passing exposure to sexual imagery such as displays outside movie theaters, in bookstore windows, or on newsstands, it violates the First Amendment without sufficient countervailing justification in terms of promoting privacy, gender equality, or other equivalently important interests.

Certainly no one should have to tolerate any unwanted words or images thrust directly at her unwilling eyes and ears repeatedly or for a sustained period, in a deliberate attempt to annoy or upset her; this would constitute harassing or assaultive behavior, which is prohibited under both criminal and civil law. But the situation is different when our contact with unwanted words or images is fleeting. Our fellow and sister citizens' free speech rights to express themselves and to hear or see the expression of others, which is especially important in public places, necessarily means that each of us will occasionally encounter words or images that we may find offensive, obnoxious, and otherwise unpleasant. In a 1975 decision, the Supreme Court recognized this critical distinction and therefore struck down a Jacksonville, Florida, ordinance that barred any nudity from drive-in movie theater screens. Although the law's purpose was to protect those who were driving or walking past the theater from being confronted with images that they might find offensive, the Court held that the fleeting glimpse they might have to endure before realizing they did not want to continue to look, and hence turning away, was only a minor imposition. To bar those images from all who chose to see them, the Court ruled, would be a severe deprivation of First Amendment rights.[24]

We obviously cannot suppress any expression that any passersby might find objectionable, because that would plainly leave us with no free speech in public at all. As Andrea Dworkin walks through the

Times Square area in New York, she no doubt is offended by the displays in front of the many "adult" movie theaters, bookstores, and strip joints—not to mention the billboards advertising underwear, jeans, and other merchandise with gigantic seminude, sexually provocative photographs. Some reproductive freedom and gay rights activists who are walking to the ACLU's national headquarters building, which is in that same general area, might well be offended by the rantings against abortion and homosexuality by a soapbox orator who regularly holds forth a few yards away. Others are probably offended by the incendiary messages of African-American men in the vicinity who regularly inveigh against white and Jewish "devils." And, as public opinion polls demonstrate, increasing numbers of passersby are offended by the written or spoken messages of the poor, jobless, and homeless people in Times Square and elsewhere, who describe their dire straits and ask for money, food, or work.

Rather than denude our public square of the diverse, provocative messages that will inevitably offend some who pass through, we have two other remedies, which accord with both common sense and constitutional law. First, we can simply walk on by, averting our eyes, ears, and attention. Second, we can engage in counterspeech. In sum, when confronted in public with speech we find offensive, we should not shut it up; rather, we should either ignore it or answer back.

Procensorship feminists themselves have vividly demonstrated how effective the counterspeech, or "more speech," approach is. By denouncing the misogynistic messages conveyed by some sexual expression, they have made important contributions toward the goal of countering misogynistic attitudes and behavior. But ironically, an essential element of the procensorship feminists' message is conveyed by their own public displays of sexually explicit work that is graphic, violent, and hateful toward women—examples of the very pornography that they seek to ban. Women Against Pornography has compiled a slide show of such images, and its members lead interested observers on tours of the Times Square area and equivalent "red light districts" in other cities. Similarly, Feminists Fighting Pornography (FFP) maintains tables on sidewalks and in other public areas on which members display what they consider to be particularly horrific, violent, misogynistic pornography.

The irony in the procensorship feminists' graphic public exhibitions, aggressively thrusting before passersby the most outrageous examples of the sexual materials they seek to banish from precisely such public displays (as well as from private consumption), was especially acute during an incident in New York City several years ago. When FFP was ordered to remove its display from Grand Central Terminal, on the ground that such material was "disgusting" to commuters, this anti-pornography, procensorship group promptly sought the assistance of the New York Civil Liberties Union (NYCLU)! Feminists Fighting Pornography asked the NYCLU to champion its free speech right to display pornography—yet the purpose of the display was to persuade viewers that pornography should not be protected speech! Of course, the NYCLU unhesitatingly (and, it should be noted, successfully) sprang to FFP's defense, consistent with the ACLU's policy of defending any private expression, even that which seeks to "constrain the marketplace of ideas," as long as there is no "governmental complicity."[25]

MacDworkinite antipornography laws pose an even greater threat to First Amendment values than do traditional obscenity laws. Accordingly, though the Supreme Court has held that obscenity is not entitled to First Amendment protection, it has held that pornography is entitled to such protection. Before looking further at that 1986 ruling, I will briefly outline the events that led to it—the development and enactment of the MacDworkin antipornography law.

History of the MacKinnon-Dworkin Model Law

In its initial phase in the late 1970s, the feminist critique of sexist, violent imagery in sexual expression was simply a part of a broader critique of sexist, violent imagery throughout our culture and media. The goal was only to mobilize public opinion to persuade the media to revamp their depictions; the feminist cultural and media critics expressly rejected any legal restrictions on expression. In 1979, Women Against Pornography (WAP) was formed in New York. Although WAP advocated education about and protest against pornography, it specifically disavowed censorship: "We . . . are not carving out any new exceptions to the First Amendment."[26]

By the early 1980s, though, a growing faction of feminists began to focus on pornography to the exclusion of other forms of expression that conveyed sexist or violent images, and also began to call for legal restrictions on it. The so-called sex wars within the feminist movement became more polarized, as women who shared other feminist goals became bitterly divided over the pornography issue. This development was described as follows by Columbia University professor Carole Vance, who from the beginning has been a leader of the anticensorship forces and was a founding member of the Feminist Anti-Censorship Taskforce (FACT):

> Initially, most feminists could certainly agree with the contention that pornography was often sexist; but before long it became clear that the claims and characterizations of the antiporn groups and leaders were becoming grandiose and overstated. . . . Sexism in sex, or in its substitute, sexually explicit material, was apparently worse than sexism anywhere else. According to its critics, pornography was now the central engine of women's oppression, the major socializer of men, the chief agent of violence against women.[27]

The increasing focus by some feminists on pornography as the preeminent cause of discrimination and violence against women, and on censorship as the corresponding solution, is no doubt linked to frustrations at setbacks in the women's rights cause that began in the late 1970s. Marcia Pally wrote in *The Nation* in 1985:

> Few feminists were prepared for the E.R.A. debacle . . . or for Reaganism, with its . . . social service cutbacks. Pro-choice activists found themselves again fighting battles they thought they'd won; women athletes in colleges lost the equal facilities and funding newly guaranteed under Title IX; pregnant women on public assistance could no longer count on supplemental food allowances. . . . Our despair increased and we became desperate for solutions. . . .
>
> Here "cultural feminism" came into play. A strain of the movement since the early 1970s, cultural feminism holds that there exists a

benevolent, nurturant female way of being and an aggressive, conquering male approach to life. . . .

By the time feminist politics began to flag, cultural feminism had laid the ground for a new campaign: get at the source of men's mayhem, attack their sexuality and the culture that forms it. Yet it's hard to organize against something as amorphous as sexuality or culture. A focus was needed, a target, a Bastille. Pornography. The changing names of feminist organizations tell the story. Early on, there was Women Against Violence Against Women; then, later, Women Against Violence and Pornography in the Media; and then Women Against Pornography.[28]

In 1983, Andrea Dworkin and Catharine MacKinnon, who were then teaching at the University of Minnesota, drafted a model antipornography law that was passed by the Minneapolis City Council.[29] Declaring that pornography "is a practice of sex discrimination," the law authorizes civil lawsuits for damages and injunctive relief for four offenses: "trafficking in pornography," "coercion into pornography," "forcing pornography on a person," and "assault or physical attack due to pornography." All four offenses are linked by the common—and hopelessly vague—definition of pornography as "graphic sexually explicit subordination of women through pictures and/or words." The definition also lists eight additional criteria purporting to give further specificity to the central notion of "subordination," but these just compound its inherent, intractable vagueness and subjectiveness:

a. women are presented as dehumanized sexual objects, things or commodities; or
b. women are presented as sexual objects who enjoy humiliation or pain; or
c. women are presented as sexual objects experiencing sexual pleasure in rape, incest, or other sexual assault; or
d. women are presented as sexual objects tied up or cut up or mutilated or bruised or physically hurt; or
e. women are presented in postures or positions of sexual submission, servility, or display; or

f. women's body parts—including but not limited to vaginas, breasts and buttocks—are exhibited such that women are reduced to those parts; or

g. women are presented being penetrated by objects or animals; or

h. women are presented in scenarios of degradation, humiliation, injury, torture, shown as filthy or inferior, bleeding, bruised, or hurt in a context that makes these conditions sexual.[30]

Beyond the model law's pervasive chill—if not deep freeze—of free speech resulting from its ambiguous "definition" of pornography, each of the specific offenses that it creates also raises philosophical, practical, and constitutional problems of its own (as treated in more detail elsewhere in this book).

The prohibition on "coercion into pornography" reflects an all-encompassing concept of coercion, effectively decreeing that no woman may ever volunteer or consent to perform in sexually explicit productions, and thus treating women like children, as discussed in chapter 9.

The prohibition on "forcing pornography on a person" reflects a similarly sweeping concept of force. In addition, as discussed earlier in this chapter, this section of the model law purports to limit sexual expression not only in settings such as "a home" or "a place of employment [or] education," where important privacy and equality rights may limit free speech rights, but also "in any public place," where free expression must receive its maximal protection.

The cause of action for "assault or physical attack due to pornography" effectively makes anyone who participates in producing or distributing a sexually explicit work responsible for any assault that might be committed by any individual who happened to see that work, thus deterring the production or distribution of any sexually oriented materials, while displacing legal and moral responsibility from the actual assailant (as explained in chapter 13).

The section of the law that proscribes "trafficking in pornography" is the most frontal attack on constitutional freedoms, because it essentially makes it illegal "to produce, sell, exhibit, or distribute" the targeted sexual speech, decreeing that it constitutes "discrimination against women." This "trafficking" proscription is essentially old-fashioned, moralistic prior restraint dressed in the modern, progressive garb of a private antidiscrimination action, an "empress's new clothes." It can be enforced by "any woman . . . acting against the subordination of women," as well as "[a]ny man or transsexual who alleges injury by pornography in the way women are injured by it." Behind its rhetorical facade, the law empowers *anyone* to bring a lawsuit to halt *any* production or distribution of sexual materials. Even libraries, including college and university libraries, may be sued under this breathtakingly broad provision, for any "special display presentations."

Laws based on this model have been considered in the following locations throughout the United States: Bellingham, Washington; Cambridge, Massachusetts; Indianapolis, Indiana; Los Angeles County, California; Madison, Wisconsin; the State of Massachusetts; Minneapolis, Minnesota; and Suffolk County, New York. As already noted, in 1992 the Senate Judiciary Committee approved the Pornography Victims' Compensation Act (which died when the full Senate failed to consider it before recessing), and the Canadian Supreme Court has incorporated the Dworkin-MacKinnon concept of pornography into Canadian obscenity law. According to a letter MacKinnon wrote to *The New York Times* in 1994, versions of her antipornography legislation also have been introduced in Germany, the Philippines, and Sweden.[31] In addition, feminist antipornography activists have advocated these laws in Great Britain and New Zealand.

The Minneapolis City Council, the first government body to consider a MacDworkin-style law, adopted it twice in 1983. On both occasions, however, Minneapolis's liberal Democratic mayor Donald Fraser vetoed the law on the ground that it violated the First Amendment. Significantly, Fraser had championed women's rights throughout his distinguished government career, and his wife, Arvonne Fraser, long had been an internationally recognized leader of the women's rights movement. (After serving many years as mayor of Minneapolis, Fraser did not run for reelection in 1993. Shortly after his successor took office, an antipornography feminist issued a call for the city's renewed consideration of the MacDworkin law.)[32]

In 1984 (in an appropriately Orwellian twist), the same law was enacted in Indianapolis with the support of conservative Republican politicians and right-wing groups that had consistently opposed women's rights. One leading supporter, Baptist minister Greg Dixon, had been an official in the Moral Majority. Every Democratic member of the Indianapolis City Council voted against the law, while every Republican member voted for it. This ostensibly feminist law received no support from local feminist groups; the local chapter of the National Organization for Women (NOW) opposed it, while it was endorsed by the prominent antifeminist Phyllis Schlafly. Catharine MacKinnon's closest ally in securing the law's passage was a conservative Republican woman who had been a leader of the Stop ERA movement, former Indianapolis City Council member Beulah Coughenour.[33]

Testifying in support of her antipornography law before the Indianapolis City Council, MacKinnon described Indianapolis as "a place that takes seriously the rights of women and the rights of all people. . . ."[34] This description came as a shock to the Indiana women who had lobbied unsuccessfully for the ERA, as well as to the gay men who had been beaten by Indianapolis police only weeks before MacKinnon's testimony, in an ugly episode that happened to be caught on videotape. Sheila Suess Kennedy, a Republican feminist attorney whom MacKinnon's antipornography ally Coughenour had attacked in a 1980 political race specifically for her pro-ERA and other feminist positions, stated in her written testimony to the council:

> As a woman who has been publicly supportive of equal rights for women, I frankly find it offensive when an attempt to regulate expression is cloaked in the rhetoric of feminism. Many supporters of this proposal have been conspicuously indifferent to previous attempts to gain equal rights for women.[35]

As Kathy Sarris, president of an Indiana lesbian and gay rights organization, asked, "It has not occurred to Mayor Hudnut to put women in leadership positions in city-county government; why is he now so concerned with the subordination of women in pornography?"[36]

These key aspects of the Indianapolis situation—MacKinnon's unholy alliance with opponents of women's rights, and her disregard for both the local political reality and the views of local feminist leaders—presaged what have since become patterns in the feminist antipornography movement. From its support of the 1986 Meese Pornography Commission, which was dominated by right-wing opponents of women's rights, to its support for the 1992 Canadian Supreme Court decision that has wreaked havoc on feminist bookstores and lesbian literature, the feminist procensorship movement has repeatedly overlooked the actual concerns of the real women who are most directly affected by its initiatives. These tendencies are at best politically naive and at worst cynically opportunistic.

Less than ninety minutes after the Indianapolis version of the Dworkin-MacKinnon law was signed by Mayor William Hudnut (a conservative Republican who was also a minister), it was challenged in federal court by a coalition of booksellers, publishers, and others involved in creating, distributing, and reading or viewing the types of materials that the law targeted. This coalition argued, and in a case entitled *American Booksellers Association v. Hudnut*,[37] the courts agreed, that the feminist antipornography law violated the First Amendment's free speech guarantee.

The Courts Call It Censorship

The law was struck down originally by the federal trial court judge in *Hudnut*; her ruling was affirmed by a panel of the U.S. Court of Appeals for the Seventh Circuit; and the U.S. Supreme Court affirmed that ruling. Indeed, the law so plainly violated fundamental free speech principles that the Supreme Court affirmed the Seventh Circuit's holding through a procedure called "summary affirmance," under which the Court did not even receive briefs, hear oral arguments, or issue an opinion.

The Seventh Circuit's ruling stressed that, by singling out only depictions or descriptions that subordinate women, the feminist antipornography law violates the cardinal free speech principle of content or viewpoint neutrality (discussed in chapter 2). In an opinion by Judge Frank Easterbrook, who was a law professor at the University of Chicago before President Ronald Reagan nominated him to the Seventh Circuit, the court explained:

The ordinance discriminates on the ground of the content of the speech. Speech treating women in the approved way—in sexual encounters "premised on equality"—is lawful no matter how sexually explicit. Speech treating women in the disapproved way—as submissive in matters sexual or as enjoying humiliation—is unlawful no matter how significant the literary, artistic, or political qualities of the work taken as a whole. The state may not ordain preferred viewpoints in this way. The Constitution forbids the state to declare one perspective right and silence opponents.[38]

Both the American Civil Liberties Union and the Feminist Anti-Censorship Taskforce (FACT) filed briefs in the *Hudnut* case arguing that the Indianapolis antipornography law violated women's constitutional equality rights, as well as free speech rights. Because the trial and appellate courts invalidated the law on First Amendment grounds, they did not need to address the other issues raised in these briefs. Nevertheless, the opinion of the trial judge—who happened to be a woman, Sara Evans Barker—referred to a defect in the law that was one of the bases for the conclusion by both the ACLU and FACT that it undermined women's equality. Judge Barker observed:

It ought to be remembered by . . . all . . . who would support such a legislative initiative that, in terms of altering sociological patterns, much as alteration may be necessary and desirable, free speech, rather than being the enemy, is a long-tested and worthy ally. To deny free speech in order to engineer social change in the name of accomplishing a greater good for one sector of our society erodes the freedoms of all and . . . threatens tyranny and injustice for those subjected to the rule of such laws.[39]

Although MacKinnon has decried the *Hudnut* case as "the *Dred Scott* of the women's movement,"[40] referring to the Supreme Court's justly maligned 1856 decision upholding slavery and racial discrimination,[41] *Hudnut* is in fact more like the *Brown v. Board of Education*[42] of the women's movement. Just as *Brown* recognized that racially separate schools are inherently unequal, *Hudnut* recognized that any separate concept of free speech for expression by or about women or sexuality is also inherently unequal.

The Supreme Court's 1986 summary affirmance in the *Hudnut* case seemed to seal the constitutional doom of any attempt to embody the feminist antipornography analysis in law. Following *Hudnut,* a federal court struck down another version of the MacDworkin model law, which had been enacted by voter referendum in Bellingham, Washington, in 1988 and was promptly challenged by the ACLU.[43] Likewise, in 1989, the U.S. Court of Appeals for the Ninth Circuit rejected an argument by Andrea Dworkin (in a lawsuit she had brought against *Hustler* magazine, based on unflattering statements it had published about her) that it should hold pornography to be constitutionally unprotected expression; the court stated that this argument was "contrary to fundamental First Amendment principles."[44]

In the wake of this string of judicial defeats for the feminist procensorship position, the feminist anticensorship advocates relaxed their organized efforts. A 1986 news story about the Supreme Court's ruling in the Indianapolis case quoted New York University law professor Sylvia Law, a founder of FACT and coauthor of FACT's brief in that case, as stating, "It's over. We've won."[45] Indeed, FACT became inactive shortly after this ruling, but reorganized in 1992, in response to the Pornography Victims' Compensation Act and other signs of the resurgence of the feminist procensorship forces, which I discuss in the next chapter; these developments also prompted the 1992 formation of two new feminist anticensorship organizations, Feminists for Free Expression and the National Coalition Against Censorship's Working Group on Women, Censorship and "Pornography."

Strange Bedfellows Make Gains

Just as the Supreme Court's 1973 abortion rights ruling in *Roe v. Wade*[46] galvanized the antiabortion movement, so the Court's 1986 ruling in the Indianapolis case motivated the feminist antipornography faction. For the time stymied in the courts, the procensorship feminists redoubled their efforts in other forums.

Even during the year of its Supreme Court setback, the MacDworkinite movement was given a second wind when the Meese Pornography Commission co-opted its feminist rhetoric to camouflage the reactionary nature of its report. Following the pattern that had been set in Indianapolis, the feminist antipornography faction worked closely with, and provided strategically important support for, the right-wing conservatives and fundamentalist Christians who spearheaded the report.

Feminist opponents of pornography recently have secured new restrictions on sexual speech, even beyond such speech in the traditionally unprotected category of obscenity. Here in the United States, they have persuaded courts, as well as other decision makers, that a wide range of sexually oriented expression may constitutionally be banned from workplaces and campuses, on the pretext of protecting women from sexual harassment.

Buoyed by the acceptance of its doctrine in the Canadian Supreme Court in 1992, the feminist antipornography faction recently has introduced and supported various versions of the Dworkin-MacKinnon law in the U.S. Congress and in state legislatures. Although these laws will be held unconstitutional as long as the Supreme Court continues to adhere to its 1986 ruling in the *Hudnut* (Indianapolis) case, it cannot be taken for granted that the Court will do so, given the appointment of new members and some *post-Hudnut* rulings that indicate an unwillingness to protect sexual speech even outside the traditional obscenity category.[47] Alarmingly, *The New York Times Magazine* reported in 1991 that "a few leading constitutional theorists now predict that, within a decade, [MacKinnon] will have carved out a new exception in constitutional protection of speech."[48]

As a result of the renewed efforts by the feminist-fundamentalist alliance against sexual speech, we recently have witnessed an all-out—and increasingly successful—war on sexually oriented expression, an across-the-board suppression of "sexpression." In the next chapter, we take a closer look at each front in this war.

CHAPTER 4

The Growing Suppression
of "Sexpression"

The Dworkin-MacKinnon approach to pornography enjoys an enormous intuitive appeal to many feminists and liberals, as well as to many conservatives and moderates; it offers political advantages to a wide spectrum of government officials and politicians; it is disproportionately covered, and hence strengthened, by the media; it has dominated many segments of academia, including elite law schools and women's studies programs; and it accordingly exerts a significant impact on public opinion.

It is not surprising that proposals to censor words and images that are claimed to foster discrimination and violence against women would meet with broad acceptance. After all, proposals to censor words and images that are associated with any troubling societal issue are always popular, for they hold out the alluring promise of a cheap "quick fix" for seemingly intractable problems. It also is no wonder that such proposals inevitably meet with broad support among politicians, who then can tell their constituents that they are "doing something" about pressing problems but not causing attendant tax increases.

Public Perception, Public Permission

We might expect that feminist proposals to suppress pornography would be supported by the many conservative and moderate members of the public who often are enticed by what Marcia Pally has termed "the great soothing appeal of censorship."[1] But it is disturbing that these proposals have been sympathetically received among sectors of the public that traditionally have resisted calls for censorship, including liberals, the

71

media, and academia. The reason so many individuals in these groups are willing to overcome their normal predisposition against censorship in this context no doubt stems from their well-intentioned desire to support measures that would advance women's rights and interests, and to be aligned with the feminist movement. Consequently, the widespread misconception that feminists generally support censorship of pornography is very influential—and very damaging—among these groups. As writer Anne Rice has noted:

> I think they're [MacKinnon and Dworkin] absolute fools. If two Baptist ministers from Oklahoma came up with their arguments, they would have been immediately laughed out of the public arena. They got away with their nonsensical arguments because they were feminists, and because they confused well-meaning liberals everywhere.[2]

The media magnification of MacDworkinism has done its share to perpetuate the misperception that most or all feminists consider pornography harmful and want it to be censored. A statement by a female *New York Times* reporter in a 1993 article is symptomatic. She simply asserted, without explanation, that "virtually all feminists agree that pornography is detrimental to women."[3] Yet this statement is patently untrue, as this book demonstrates.

Also symptomatic is the fact that, while MacKinnon's 1993 book *Only Words* received many critical reviews, most mainstream publications carried reviews either by men or by women who are not associated with the feminist anticensorship movement. Noted Alice Echols, a women's studies professor and one of the few anticensorship feminists to write such a review (in the *Voice Literary Supplement*): "Most reviews of *Only Words* fail to register that MacKinnon's views on pornography are by no means gospel among feminists."[4]

The media give disproportionately extensive coverage to the procensorship faction of feminism. As one commentator wrote in 1992:

> Catharine MacKinnon is on a roll. A cover story [about her] in *The New York Times Sunday Magazine* coincided with the Thomas confirmation debacle. Suddenly she is everywhere, identified as "a national expert on sexual abuse," "a brilliant political strategist," or "the Meese

Commission's favorite feminist." Peter Jennings anointed her as "the country's most prominent legal theorist in behalf of women, whose dedication to laws which serve men and women equally has made it better."[5]

The common misperception that MacKinnon, Dworkin, and other leading procensorship feminists speak for women's rights advocates generally has been fueled by their refusal to debate feminist women who disagree with them about pornography. Catharine MacKinnon has said, "I do not allow myself to be used to orchestrate and legitimate a so-called 'debate within feminism' over whether pornography harms women. It is my analysis that that is the pimps' current strategy for legitimizing a slave trade in women. I do not need to be sucked into the pornographers' strategy, period."[6]

Leading feminist anticensorship advocates repeatedly have been invited to participate in such debates, only to have the invitations rescinded because of MacKinnon's and Dworkin's refusal to share the podium with them. By accepting similar invitations when the anticensorship position is presented by men, though, or by traditional First Amendment advocates, the feminist censorship proponents perpetuate the misconception that women and feminists support censorship, with the opposition coming only from men and nonfeminists. The media, as well as other institutions that arrange for speakers, too often abet this strategy by capitulating to the procensorship feminists' dictates about whom they will or will not debate.

This tactic is vividly illustrated by MacKinnon's diametrically different responses to two invitations for debates on the same day in the same city. She was invited to debate me on NBC's *Today* show in New York City on December 20, 1993, but declined. She accepted, however, an invitation for another debate on that very same date, also in New York City, against a male First Amendment champion and opponent of censoring pornography, Floyd Abrams. (Portions of this debate were published in *The New York Times Magazine*.[7])

When MacKinnon refused to debate me on the *Today* show, the show simply tabled its plans to cover the important pornography debate within feminism. Disappointing as that was, it was less disappointing than the decisions that others have made to stage completely one-sided presentations on the issue, showcasing only the procensorship view.

Although MacKinnon does not expressly acknowledge that she has a policy of refusing to debate feminists in the anticensorship camp, her apparent practice has been so consistent that it is now well known; many people simply assume that she would be unwilling to participate in such a debate, and hence do not even seek to arrange one. As noted by *New York Times* legal columnist David Margolick in 1993, "So eager are interviewers and conference organizers to mollify [MacKinnon] that feminists who consider her views censorious and harmful to women have grown used to being unceremoniously dropped from programs at which she is scheduled to appear."[8]

This type of capitulation to MacKinnon's often unspoken, but still widely understood, practice of not sharing the podium with anticensorship feminists apparently afflicted the women judges who organized the 1993 conference of the National Association of Women Judges (NAWJ)—an especially influential audience, and one that should particularly value the exchange of ideas on a legal issue as important as the First Amendment status of sexual expression.

In early 1993, a federal district court judge, on behalf of NAWJ, wrote me a letter inviting me to address the Association's annual convention in November on the pornography issue. I gladly accepted the invitation. When my assistant called several months later to finalize travel plans, though, she was told that I would no longer be needed. This summary disinvitation was hardly the height of professional courtesy, but I attributed it to an administrative error and dismissed the incident from my mind.

It rudely resurfaced in November 1993. At that time, an ACLU colleague of mine, Deborah Leavy—who knew nothing about my retracted speaking invitation—told me that she had attended the NAWJ convention and that Catharine MacKinnon had addressed it for almost an hour. There was no opposing speaker, and only a few minutes were allowed for audience questions. I suddenly had a very strong hunch as to why my invitation to address the convention had been rescinded, and why that development had been communicated to my assistant with a great deal of embarrassment and apology, but with no explanation.

Although MacKinnon apparently did not tell the women judges who were organizing the convention that she refused to debate me or another anticensorship feminist, they evidently understood this to be

her position, and acted on it. One of the judges who organized the conference admitted as much to the *Times's* David Margolick: "I had heard
[MacKinnon] was not very receptive to be with women who disagree
with her. The general feeling was that MacKinnon would be less than
pleased to be on the program with Strossen, so we had no choice."[9]
MacKinnon, in answer to Margolick's question about whether she
would have accepted an invitation to debate me or another anticensorship feminist, commented that participating in such debates played
into what she called "a pimp strategy to hide behind feminist women."[10]
(She elaborated on that "analysis" in the statement I quoted earlier.)

Similarly, when arguing against including anticensorship voices
in another discussion of pornography, MacKinnon asked, "When
world hunger is discussed, is it necessary to have the pro-hunger side
present?"[11]

(Thanks to the intervention of some prominent female judges, who
were upset about the 1993 NAWJ incident, I was invited to address the
1994 NAWJ convention. In contrast with MacKinnon's invitation, mine
was to debate women with differing viewpoints, something I am always
happy to do.)

One-Sided Legal Forums

Recently, two leading law schools hosted conferences that featured *only*
the procensorship perspective in the feminist debate over pornography.
In March 1993, the University of Chicago Law School hosted a conference that brought together advocates of censoring pornography and
advocates of censoring racist, sexist, and other forms of biased speech,
in an effort to forge a common strategy for overturning traditional
constitutional protections for both types of expression. The conference
attracted a very large and enthusiastic group of participants, including many law students from all over the country. Notwithstanding the
conference's relatively neutral, academic title—"Feminist Legal Perspectives on Pornography and Hate Propaganda" (although the term
"propaganda," along with the term "pornography," has pronounced
negative connotations)—it included only a single feminist perspective
on pornography and eschewed rational, academic discourse. As the

National Coalition Against Censorship's executive director, Leanne Katz, commented: "Feminists who disagreed were brushed aside and insulted away."[12]

New York Times correspondent Isabel Wilkerson, who attended the event, reported that the atmosphere was at times more appropriate for a "revivalist meeting" than an academic conference.[13] Feminists who disagreed with the procensorship perspective were constantly and viciously reviled by speakers throughout the proceedings. One conference attendee, who left reprints of an article criticizing the procensorship feminist position on an information table, was spat upon by conference participants, who ripped up the reprints. Madonna's book *Sex*[14] was also ritually torn to shreds, and speakers trumpeted—to cheering crowds— that no evidence that pornography harms women was needed as a prerequisite for censoring it, since "*we know* it causes harm." A lawyer who works for the ACLU of Illinois, Jane Whicher, likened her attendance at the conference to "combat duty," saying she feared physical violence if other conference participants discovered her ACLU affiliation.[15]

One flier that was produced and distributed to conference participants by a procensorship feminist group showed a picture of a woman in panties and bra, with nipples clearly visible, who was bound, gagged, and lashed to a chair with multiple straps, her arms pinioned behind her. The caption read: "A free speech message brought to you by the American Civil Liberties Union." Ironically, this flier would fall squarely within the procensorship feminists' conception of proscribable pornography and hence could well be subject to suppression should their own views prevail. Of course, though, the ACLU would defend the conferees' right to produce and distribute this flier (notwithstanding its defamatory nature), should it be challenged under MacDworkinite laws or any others; in that sense, the flier does indeed convey an ACLU free speech message.

As journalist Maureen Dezell noted, the Chicago conference, as the first official gathering of leaders from both the antipornography and the anti–hate speech movements, was widely perceived as "mark[ing] a turning point in the feminist anti-porn movement, increasing its respectibility by dint of its association with scholars" such as University of Chicago law professor Cass Sunstein and Stanford University law professor Charles Lawrence, its being hosted by the prestigious University of Chicago Law School, and its funding from the MacArthur Foundation.[16]

Another conference, held at the University of Michigan Law School during the fall of 1992, further demonstrates the extent to which feminist proponents of censoring sexual expression have silenced those who disagree with them within the legal academy. (For the details of that episode, see chapter 10.)

Just as some feminists' attempts to censor sexually oriented expression have dominated law school conferences, such views have dominated academic law journals in recent years. A survey of all law review articles about the feminist controversy over this issue, which law students conducted under my supervision in 1994, revealed both that a majority of these writings advocated censorship, and that almost all that were written from a feminist viewpoint did so. Because most of the law review literature that refutes the MacKinnon-Dworkin analysis does not do so from an acknowledged feminist perspective, it does not counter the misperception that feminist values necessarily weigh in favor of censoring pornography.[17]

Strength in Numbers:
The Feminist-Fundamentalist Axis

The persistent conservative, fundamentalist sentiment in favor of censoring sexually explicit work that propelled the Meese Pornography Commission also has fueled the feminist censorship movement. Traditionalist crusaders against sexual speech such as Jesse Helms, Ed Meese, Phyllis Schlafly, and Donald Wildmon seek on one level to distance themselves from what they describe as "radical feminists," and the pro-censorship feminists likewise seek distance from such conservatives. Yet these feminists, fundamentalists, and conservatives all reinforce each others' mutual pursuit of largely overlapping goals concerning sexual speech. Underscoring this point, writer Susie Bright calls MacDworkinites "fundamentalist feminists,"[18] and others have aptly labeled them "reactionary" or "right-wing" feminists. Political scientist Jean Bethke Elshtain elaborates:

> Feminist antipornographers vehemently deny any mutual interest with conservative campaigners. In their view . . . conservative groups have

the heaviest interest of all in maintaining male dominance. . . . But if, as feminists claim, the explicit intent of pornography is to keep women in a subordinate position . . . it is hard to figure out why "right-wing men" wouldn't . . . favor pornography. . . . Despite disavowals from both sides, the right-wing and radical feminist efforts do converge. The rationales may differ, but the ends sought—the elimination of pornography as defined by each group—are identical.[19]

The mutually reinforcing relationship between the Dworkin-MacKinnon attacks on pornography and those of extreme conservatives undermines women's equality because it strengthens the right wing, with its antifeminist agenda.

The mutuality of interest between "traditional family values" conservatives and antipornography feminists is illustrated by a 1992 campaign against sexual expression. The National Coalition Against Pornography undertook this well-publicized campaign under the slogan "Enough Is Enough." Although the program's leaders were mostly conservative women with ties to such right-wing organizations as Phyllis Schlafly's Eagle Forum and Beverly LaHaye's Concerned Women for America, the group's promotional materials, including billboards throughout the Midwest, prominently featured quotes from Andrea Dworkin.[20]

As feminist anthropologist Carole Vance has shown, right-wing and fundamentalist organizations around the country "have mastered the sound bite that pornography 'degrades women' and contributes to an 'inequality' that they otherwise favor."[21]

The allies in the feminist–fundamentalist axis are united by many substantive, as well as strategic, bonds—most importantly, their use of the stigmatizing term "pornography" to condemn an increasingly broad range of sexual expression, extending far beyond the scope of constitutionally unprotected obscenity to encompass virtually all sexual imagery. As Vance says, "Both groups are skilled in deploying demagogic charges of 'pornography' and mobilizing sex panics in order to eliminate expression, images and perspectives that counter their own agendas."[22]

History shows that when women's rights advocates form alliances with conservatives over an issue such as pornography, prostitution, or temperance, they promote the conservatives' antifeminist goals, relegating women to traditional sexual and gender roles. Historian Judith

Walkowitz emphasized this conclusion in her 1980 book *Prostitution and Victorian Society: Women, Class and the State,* which documented the antifeminist impacts of such a misalliance in Victorian England: "As late as 1914, feminists were rediscovering once again that the state 'protection' of young women inevitably led to coercive and repressive measures against those same women."[23] Yet, eighty years later, the procensorship feminists still have not learned this historical lesson.

Government Assaults on Sexually Explicit Speech

Beginning with the 1980 Reagan election, the conservative censorship forces have had the necessary political power to implement their views—and, indirectly, those of their procensorship feminist sister travelers—through increased government efforts to curtail or punish sexually explicit speech. The climate of hostility to sexual expression—especially any branded with the inflammatory epithet "pornography"—which the feminist antipornography movement had played a key role in creating, was exploited by reactionary right activists and their representatives in the Reagan and Bush administrations, as well as in local and state governments around the country. In turn, their stepped-up assaults on sexual expression contributed to the recent resurgence of the procensorship feminists.

Because these government assaults were influenced by, and reflect, the feminist procensorship rhetoric, and because the targeted works could all be pursued under the capacious MacDworkinite concept of pornography, these government attacks provide strong indications of the actual impact that a MacDworkin-style antipornography law would have if it were directly adopted. Therefore, it is important to examine them in some detail. They include both direct law enforcement actions and indirect government pressures—notably, through the power of the purse.

The Justice Department's National Obscenity Enforcement Unit was formed in 1986 in response to the Meese Commission's call for renewed enforcement of obscenity laws. This Unit has done lasting, irreparable damage by forcing many sellers of sexually oriented materials out of business.

The activities of this zealous Justice Department operation were not widely known prior to the 1991 publication of *Above the Law: The Justice Department's War against the First Amendment*,[24] an exposé by the ACLU Arts Censorship Project. That report documented the unlawful, improper tactics that the Obscenity Unit deployed in its concerted campaign to drive constitutionally protected sexual expression from the market. Several courts held that these tactics did indeed violate constitutional guarantees, strongly criticizing the Unit's abuse of prosecutorial powers.

Under the Unit's direction, government agents raided businesses, entrapped previously law-abiding individuals into violating the law, and instituted multiple prosecutions against distributors of sexually oriented work in carefully selected forums where the juries were expected to be less tolerant and the defense to be more expensive and burdensome. Even if the defendants ultimately were likely to win these legal battles on the ground that the targeted material was not constitutionally unprotected obscenity, many could not afford the economic, psychological, and other costs involved in mounting defenses, especially in multiple cases and in courts far from their homes and places of business.

To short-circuit the Unit's harassing law enforcement strategies, distributors of sexually oriented works were forced to enter into settlements that imposed sweeping limitations on their future activities. Under the coercive pressure of avoiding the Unit's heavy-handed prosecutorial tactics, some distributors agreed not to distribute even works that are clearly eligible for constitutional protection, including popular materials such as *Playboy* and *The Joy of Sex*.

Even some law enforcement agents with experience in combating obscenity denounced the extremist goals and tactics of the Obscenity Unit. Robert Marinaro, who ran the FBI's antiobscenity operations, denounced the Unit's leaders as religious zealots who suppressed much constitutionally protected material: "[T]hey became zealots about . . . pornography, and their religious beliefs overstepped good judgment."[25]

The Obscenity Unit's misplaced zealotry fomented an atmosphere in which all sexual expression was suspect, even works by respected artists. One of the best-known victims of this sexual hysteria is the San Francisco-based, internationally renowned photographer Jock Sturges.

The *Los Angeles Times* vividly described his nightmarish ordeal at the hands of the Obscenity Unit, which began in 1990, as follows:

> The doorbell rings. You open the door. Standing on your front porch are six FBI agents and plainclothes police officers with guns and badges. They force their way into your apartment and begin canvassing the place, observing everything you own. Your address books. Your clothes. The art on your walls. Every page of your personal diaries.[26]

That is what happened to Sturges, whose portraits of nude families appear in the permanent collections of many museums, including the Metropolitan Museum of Art and the Museum of Modern Art in New York, and the Bibliothèque Nationale in Paris. Claiming that photographs of "partially disrobed juveniles" in Sturges's possession might violate child pornography laws, the agents turned his apartment upside down; seized all his photographic prints, negatives, equipment, and business records; and drove off. Moreover, according to Sturges, about six dozen of his clients, friends, and family members across the United States and Europe were telephoned or visited by law enforcement authorities. Agents demanded that art galleries representing Sturges turn over their customer lists.

It took Sturges almost two years to get his property back after a grand jury that the Justice Department had impaneled to investigate his case failed to find evidence that he had committed any crime. Sturges and his associates were made to suffer through this prolonged nightmare simply because he had taken nude photographs of children, many in nudist colonies or on nude beaches in Europe. As indicated by the grand jury's refusal to indict Sturges, the children had not been abused or exploited. Sturges had releases from their parents, and the resulting photographs, characteristic of Sturges's portfolio, were works of art, not "child porn."

Abusive prosecutorial efforts, allegedly directed at child pornography, even resulted in a reversed conviction at the hands of the Rehnquist Supreme Court, despite that Court's strong pro-prosecutorial leaning and routine affirmances of criminal convictions. The federal government's antipornography tactics went too far even for the

Rehnquist Court, which in 1992 held that the U.S. Postal and Customs Services (which worked with the Obscenity Unit) had unconstitutionally "entrapped" a Nebraska farmer, Keith Jacobson, into buying sexually explicit photographs of minors through a concerted campaign to lure him into making the purchase.[27] As the Court ruled, Jacobson had not been "independently predisposed to commit the crime" of buying the photographs. Moreover, there was no evidence that Jacobson had any pedophiliac interests, let alone that he had ever had any sexual contact with minors.

The kind of relentless sting operations that U.S. officials aimed at Jacobson and thousands of other individuals who had never displayed any interest in such materials made the federal government one of the major marketing forces of child porn in the U.S., according to one commentator.[28] Invalidating some of these operations, the U.S. Court of Appeals for the Ninth Circuit noted that the government authorities were seeking to entrap "individuals possessing . . . a broad range of legal sexual and non-sexual interests."[29]

Tragically, these stings led at least five targeted individuals to commit suicide. One was thirty-four-year-old Robert Brase, another Nebraska farmer. There was no evidence that he had ever molested a child. But, after his arrest for receiving a "kid-porn" videotape in the mail, in response to the government's sustained solicitations, Brase parked his pickup truck on a country road and shot himself. He left a widow and two sons.

The court rulings denouncing the Obscenity Unit's overzealous attacks on sexual expression came too late to protect Brase and countless other victims. Given the stigma that is now associated with the term "pornography," the mere charge that someone has produced or distributed an allegedly pornographic work could lead to more unfortunate and tragic consequences—including some individuals being driven out of business and others being driven to commit suicide. If that charge carried with it the threat of a lawsuit for potentially unlimited damages, as under MacDworkinite laws, the resulting fear and pressure would no doubt increase the desperate responses.

Seizing upon the porn panic inspired by Meese and MacKinnon in recent years, state and local governments also have increased the number of arrests and prosecutions under obscenity laws, protection-of-minor laws, and newly enacted laws designed to impose additional restrictions on sexually oriented expression. In 1992, for example, the legislature in the State of Washington passed a law banning the sale to minors of recordings containing "erotic" lyrics. In our erotophobic era, almost no members of the Washington legislature dared to vote against this sweeping censorial measure, whose vague terms barred minors from purchasing an enormously broad spectrum of vocal music. Dealers who violated the law could be fined up to five hundred dollars and sentenced to six-month jail terms.[30]

Frightening as it is to contemplate the wide-ranging "erotic" lyrics—from country western to opera—that would be off-limits to young people under a law such as Washington's, it is yet more frightening to contemplate the devastating impact on music that might result from the antipornography feminist philosophy. Susan McClary, a musicologist at the University of Minnesota, has described some classical music masterpieces as conveying the sort of sexually violent messages that would run afoul of the Dworkin-MacKinnon model law were they transmitted through words or images. Given that many believe music to be an even more powerful medium in influencing our emotions and impulses, it is not unthinkable that antipornography activists might seek to control it as well. If so, Professor McClary's description of Beethoven's symphonies affords a somber warning of the works that would be embattled:

Beethoven's symphonies add two other dimensions to the history of style: assaultive pelvic pounding . . . and sexual violence. The point of the recapitulation in the first movement of the Ninth is one of the most horrifying moments in music, as the carefully prepared cadence is frustrated, damming up energy which finally explodes in the throttling, murderous rage of a rapist incapable of attaining release.[31]

In another type of assault on sexual expression by state and local governments, law enforcement authorities have sent out lists of "suspect," purportedly obscene videotapes to video store owners, strongly hinting that they might well face criminal charges if they continued to sell or rent these tapes.[32] In some cases, police and prosecutors had obtained the videotape blacklists from right-wing, fundamentalist organizations. Perhaps because neither the citizens' organizations nor the law enforcement officials wanted to actually look at these allegedly "dirty" videotapes, they seemed to conclude rather casually that the tapes should be off-limits. In a variation on Justice Stewart's famous dictum, "I know it when I see it," these law enforcement officials and their citizen-informants "knew it when they *heard* it"—they claimed to be able to ascertain a work's obscenity from its title!

The flaw in this overly aggressive approach is illustrated by the fact that one of the tapes that was blacklisted in some Ohio communities, *Doing It Debbie's Way*, turned out to be not a sequel to the erotic video-tape *Debbie Does Dallas*,[33] but rather an exercise video featuring Debbie Reynolds, icon of traditional, "all-American" femininity.

Feminist antipornography activists might well concur with the right-wing organization that attempted to suppress Debbie Reynolds's exercise videotape, Citizens for Community Values. In a 1987 study, University of Southern California professor Margaret Morse, taking a feminist perspective, criticized many aerobics videos for depicting women as sexual objects and for their allegedly "soft-porn" content. Morse cited heavy breathing; revealing exercise clothing; sexy stares; close-up shots of breasts, legs, and thighs; and "camera action that seems to simulate sexual activity." According to Morse, even Debbie Reynolds's video, which was aimed at the over-forty audience, pre-sented her as a sex object. Under feminist-style antipornography laws, all these tapes could be suppressed as "subordinating" or "degrading" to women. Even the popular exercise tapes of Jane Fonda, a prominent spokeswoman on women's rights issues, might well be vulnerable under the MacDworkin regime. As Morse commented:

> I see poses of Jane Fonda sitting on her buttocks with her legs raised in the air in a V On the one hand, that looks powerful. But on the other, it completely immobilizes her and forces her into a submissive posture. The message clearly is, "I'm powerful but I'm still a woman who needs a man."[34]

Some of these attacks on sexual expression have been successfully challenged by the ACLU and others.[35] But they and the many other, similar attacks that they typify still have an ongoing adverse effect on free speech. Many individuals and organizations are unwilling to endure the controversy, let alone the more tangible costs, associated with even a successful resistance to threatened criminal charges or civil sanctions against sexual speech. For each record, video, or book dealer who defends against accusations of handling suppressible sexually oriented materials, there are many others who respond to such accusations—or even the possibility of such accusations—by refraining from handling sexually oriented materials.

The many recent attacks on sexual expression that have been carried out under current law are only a mild foretaste of the wide-ranging assaults that would be launched under feminist-style antipornography laws, given their more open-ended definition of sanctionable sexual speech. Therefore, recent efforts to pass such laws are cause for alarm.

Although the U.S. Congress has not—yet, at least—passed the Pornography Victims' Compensation Act, in 1990 the State of Illinois enacted a similar law.[36] Moreover, other laws based on the MacDworkin model are also being considered in other states and localities. For example, the Massachusetts legislature considered such a law in 1992. Underscoring the infantilizing outlook of all these feminist antipornography laws, the Massachusetts bill was tellingly entitled *An Act to Protect the Civil Rights of Women and Children*.[37]

The feminist procensorhip perspective, blaming books and images for misogynistic violence, also has infiltrated federal and state legislation in more subtle guises. For example, both House and Senate versions of the Violence Against Women Act, which was considered in 1993–1994, originally allocated funds to train state court judges and other personnel about misogynistic violence, including "current information on the impact of pornography on crimes against women, or data on other activities that tend to degrade women"; concerted lobbying by anticensorship feminists led to the deletion of this language from the final law.[38] Similarly, a bill filed in the Oregon legislature in 1993 would impose a 30 percent "sin tax" on sales and rentals of X-rated videos, with proceeds going to rape and child sexual abuse counseling programs. As anticensorship feminists have noted, such bills reflect the unproven—and counterproductive—procensorship feminist assumption that erotic material can be blamed for sexual violence, thereby exonerating the flesh-and-blood men who actually assault women (see chapters 12 and 13).

Indirect Pressure: The Power of the Purse

In addition to direct threats and prosecutions, the government recently has used funding cutbacks and other limitations on grants from the National Endowment for the Arts (NEA) to curb sexual expression. The procensorship feminists did not explicitly endorse these efforts; nonetheless, their antipornography crusade and their collaboration with the Meese Pornography Commission and other right-wing censorship initiatives had laid the groundwork for the vicious—and in key respects victorious—attack on the hitherto respected NEA.

Of course, no artist has a First Amendment right to government funding, so the government's denial of an NEA grant would not ordinarily implicate constitutional rights. If, though, the government uses its funding policies to exert impermissible pressure on the content of an applicant's work, the courts have rightly recognized that this is unconstitutional censorship. Just as the Supreme Court has been alert to curb other indirect governmental restraints on speech, such as the civil lawsuits discussed in chapter 3, it has said that the government may not use the funding "carrot" to silence certain messages any more than it may use the prior restraint "stick" to achieve such a result.

Obviously, the government has some legitimate concern with the content of artwork for which NEA funding is sought, to the extent that it reasonably seeks to fund only work that has artistic merit. Accordingly, since the NEA's inception, "peer review" panels of recognized artists have made recommendations about which grant applications reflect artistic quality. Such a limited, ideologically neutral consideration of a work's content raises no First Amendment problems.

But if the government seeks to impose limitations on the content of a work that go beyond a politically neutral concern with its artistic quality, and if the government funds only works that conform to some prescribed ideological or moral agenda, it transgresses free speech rights. Specifically, it violates the core First Amendment requirement of content or viewpoint neutrality, discussed in chapter 2. To take an extreme example, the government clearly could not decide to fund only art with a political message supportive of the current administration, or of the party that currently has a congressional majority.

Although the recent restrictions on NEA funding are not so bla-tantly partisan, they do in fact seek to impose an ideological and moral orthodoxy, deterring sexually oriented works that are not obscene, and therefore are constitutionally protected. The special targets of the new NEA funding restrictions have been artists who explore sexually related themes that challenge "traditional family values"—in particu-lar, themes of homosexuality and of feminism. Several lower federal courts have held that these restrictions violate the First Amendment (the Supreme Court has not yet ruled on this issue).[39]

As with the direct government crackdowns on sexually oriented expression already discussed, these indirect assaults reflect the exten-sive influence that the procensorship feminists have already exerted. The NEA experience also highlights the types of sexual speech that would be even more endangered should the procensorship feminists' own laws be enacted. The feminist antipornography leaders have nei-ther disavowed the onslaught against the NEA nor supported its many female, feminist victims. As performance artist Holly Hughes, who (with the ACLU's assistance) sued the NEA over an ideologically moti-vated grant denial, remarked:

> In this, the most censorious period since McCarthy, when the term "por-nographer" is being used to silence people as "Communist" was then, I hoped that prominent feminists . . . might protest. . . . Instead there has been a huge deafening silence that I have found not only painful but complicitous.[40]

The attacks on the NEA were spearheaded by North Carolina senator Jesse Helms and by citizens' groups from the far right, including Donald Wildmon's American Family Association and Pat Robertson's Christian Coalition. They targeted grants that supported art concerning mainly homosexual or feminist themes, but any sexual themes or references—indeed, even any nudity—came under suspicion. One lightning rod for the right-wing, fundamentalist NEA bashing was the work of photographer Robert Mapplethorpe. The attacks against Mapplethorpe's work extended not only to explicit homoerotic images but also to works whose sexual con-notations were, at most, subtle and implicit, including studies of calla lilies.

The NEAs entire annual budget has always been less than the Pentagon's yearly allotment for military bands, and in 1994, at the level of $170.2 million,[41] it amounted to a trifling two one-hundredths of 1 percent of the national budget, an expenditure of about sixty-five cents per American. Moreover, only a handful of the more than 100,000 grants that the NEA has given have ever raised questions of "decency."[42] Nevertheless, shell-shocked by recent right-wing attacks on a few such grants, Congress has repeatedly subjected the agency to difficult reauthorization struggles and further trimmed its budget. As NEA chair Jane Alexander has noted, the combined impact of congressional cutbacks and inflation made the NEA budget effectively 46 percent lower in 1994 than it had been in 1979.[43]

Despite Alexander's entreaties, in 1994 Congress voted to slash the NEA's budget still further, yet again in response to protests over a grant for a sexually and politically controversial work—this time, a $150 grant that indirectly supported a performance by Ron Athey, a gay, HIV-positive man, whose piece dealt with public anxiety about AIDS.[44] Significantly, the epithet "pornography" was hurled against this disfavored work during the congressional debate about the NEA's budget. Referring to Athey, Representative Robert K. Dornan exclaimed, "I can't comprehend . . . how these porno freaks keep getting this money."[45]

In 1989, Congress further hamstrung the NEA and its grantees (as well as would-be grantees) by imposing unprecedented restrictions on the content of funded art, aiming at certain sexually oriented art. It barred the NEA from supporting any art that it "may consider obscene," including "depictions of . . . homoeroticism." In 1990, Congress attached another unprecedented restriction on NEA funding, requiring all grant applications to be evaluated in light of "general standards of decency and respect for the diverse beliefs and values of the American people." In a 1992 ruling in a case brought by the so-called NEA Four—four performance artists whose grants had been denied (and who were represented by the ACLU, the Center for Constitutional Rights, and the National Campaign for Freedom of Expression)—a federal trial court held that these kinds of restrictions violated the First Amendment. Noting the "close relationship between academic freedom and artistic expression," Judge A. Wallace Tashima commented:

[T]he fact that the exercise of professional judgment is inescapable in arts funding does not mean that the government has free rein to impose whatever content restrictions it chooses, just as the fact that academic judgment is inescapable in the university does not free public universities of First Amendment scrutiny. The right of artists to challenge conventional wisdom and values is a cornerstone of artistic and academic freedom. . . .[46]

Unfortunately, these controversies are not remote relics of the Reagan-Bush era. While campaigning for the presidency, Bill Clinton said he opposed conditioning NEA grants on criteria unrelated to artistic merit. He vowed to depoliticize the agency; criticized the Bush administration's defense of the vague, open-ended decency standard; and specifically praised Judge Tashima's First Amendment ruling in the NEA Four case. However, in March of 1993, in a dramatic about-face, the Clinton Justice Department filed a brief asking a federal appellate court to overturn that very ruling. As noted by an attorney for an artist whose NEA grant had been withheld under the decency standard, the Clinton administration's position in the brief is "indistinguishable from the arguments by the Bush administration."[47]

Whether or not the executive branch continues to advocate politically and ideologically driven restrictions on NEA grants, influential members of Congress no doubt will. Even absent future attempts to impose limitations on NEA grantees, the persistent criticism of certain controversial NEA grants in the past has already created a chilly artistic climate that cannot quickly be thawed. Ellen Stewart, founder of the La Mama Experimental Theatre in New York City, told the press that in response to the attacks on the NEA, she had instructed her troupe members "to clean up their acts."[48] In the words of performance artist Karen Finley, one of the NEA Four: "It's the biggest form of censorship, where you question yourself When people are attacked it stops the creativity from growing."[49]

The sustained attack on sexual content in works for which artists are seeking NEA grants has had a spillover effect far beyond the government funding context. Support from the NEA has served as a seal of approval for art, which in the past had been seen as a "safe" investment or contribution for conservative corporate and individual donors.

Accordingly, NEA grants had a catalytic effect, spurring private sector funding of the arts. Now, would-be patrons recognize that art, no matter how dimly or subtly touching on sexual themes, is hardly a noncontroversial object of support.

Just as there is no longer any safe sex, there is no longer any safe art about sex. Artists all over the country are suffering from decreased financial support from the private sector as well as from the government. Judy Blume, whose candid novels about adolescent sexuality have made her beloved among young readers but also one of the most widely banned writers in school and public libraries around the country, made a poignant observation. If she were starting out as a writer today, she said, "I might find it impossible to write honestly about kids in this climate of fear."[50] The tragic overall consequence of this fearful sex panic, in the words of theater director and critic Robert Brustein, is that art in the United States is "inadequately evaluated, published, produced, [and] disseminated."[51]

Art would be even more embattled if the procensorship feminists had their way. For example, the performance art of Karen Finley involves exhibition of her own body, smearing food on herself, and inserting objects into herself. Although Finley's performance pieces are angry protests against sexual abuse, violence, and discrimination against women, they could well be regarded as in themselves sexually degrading under the Mac-Dworkin model law. Nor would other, less daring art be any less endangered. Not only would all depictions of women be threatened—recall the protests over Goya's *Nude Maja* and the *Venus de Milo* described in chapter 1—but so would even abstract works, as indicated by the following passage in Marilyn French's 1992 book *The War against Women*: "Visiting galleries and museums (especially the Pompidou Center in Paris) I feel assaulted by twentieth-century abstract sculpture that resembles exaggerated female body parts, mainly breasts."[52]

Targeting Lesbian and Gay Expression

Almost all of the recent anti-NEA initiatives have targeted works that are by or about gay men, lesbians, and feminists. As Judge Tashima

noted in upholding the NEA Four challenge to the "decency" requirement for all funded art, "At least since 1989 . . . the NEA has been the
target of congressional critics . . . for funding works . . . that express
women's anger over male dominance in the realm of sexuality or which
endorse equal legitimacy for homosexual and heterosexual practices."[53]

The actual and threatened NEA cutbacks for art exploring feminist or homoerotic themes demonstrate a major danger of any restrictions on free expression: they will be enforced against the ideas and
expressions that are least popular with the community at large and
with the political establishment. Unfortunately, in many communities
and political bodies, such unpopular themes include feminism and
homosexuality.

As this book was going to press, yet another government attack on
sexual speech dramatically displayed the usual hallmarks of all such
attacks, including the singling out of expression with an unpopular
political message and the persecution of gays and lesbians. During
the summer of 1994, the City of Cincinnati brought obscenity charges
against a gay and lesbian bookstore, the Pink Pyramid, and its owner,
manager, and clerk. These individuals, who were arrested and hand-
cuffed, face sentences of up to six months' imprisonment and fines up
to $1,000. Their "crime"? They had rented out a video of the film *Salò,
120 Days of Sodom,* by Pier Paolo Pasolini, a world-renowned Italian
filmmaker, novelist, and poet. The film's sexual-political subject is the
dark aspect of sexuality that had served Italian fascism. In the words of
American film critic Peter Bondanella, *Salò* "is a desperate . . . attack
against . . . a society dominated by manipulative and sadistic power."[54]

Just as the allegedly obscene video itself had a deeply political message, so too did the charges against those who rented it out. These
prosecutions were announced on the opening day of a federal lawsuit
(brought by the ACLU and Lambda Legal Defense & Education Fund,
Inc.) challenging a referendum that had overturned gay and lesbian
civil rights legislation. As the National Coalition Against Censorship
commented: "At best, the timing suggests indifference to the possibility
that these prosecutions would exacerbate already existing prejudices
and intolerance."[55] At worst, given the frivolous nature of obscenity
charges based on a film of such indisputably serious value (see chapter 2), the prosecution was a calculated act of harassment. Accordingly,

the ACLU filed a brief on behalf of an impressive array of individuals and organizations from the worlds of film, art, and academia, urging the court to dismiss these charges before subjecting the defendants to a pointless and chilling criminal trial. On October 3, 1994, though, the municipal court judge rejected this argument.

The feminist procensorship movement provides still further tools and tactics that can—and, given our society's persistent homophobia, inevitably will—be seized upon to suppress the already embattled writings and artworks of lesbians and gay men. (This danger, which has been both clear and present in Canada since it adopted the procensorship feminists' concept of pornography, is detailed in chapter 11.)

Although the Dworkin-MacKinnon model law defines pornography as the "sexually explicit subordination of *women* through pictures and/ or words" (emphasis added), it expressly stipulates that even images of men could be interpreted as portraying the subordination of women: "The use of men, children, or transsexuals in the place of women . . . is pornography for purposes of this law." Moreover, prominent procensorship feminists have made clear that they view depictions of lesbian and gay sexuality as indistinguishable from heterosexual depictions in their alleged subordination of women (see chapter 8). In a statement that sounds frighteningly similar to some homophobic rhetoric—and is also a wholesale condemnation of all forms of intercourse—Andrea Dworkin has written: "Fucking requires that the male act on one who has less power. . . . [T]he one who is fucked is stigmatized as feminine during the act even when not anatomically female."[56]

Alongside the recently growing suppression of "sexpression" is an attack on sexuality on another front: "sexistence," the sexuality that is part of being alive and human in public, at work, and in school. To fathom this attack, which I describe in chapter 6, you first must understand the antisex attitudes behind it. These attitudes, which Andrea Dworkin has expressed in particularly vivid language, underlie the entire feminist campaign against sexual expression. It is important to air the procensorship feminists' negative views toward sex, which is the purpose of the next chapter, precisely because these views are not as well publicized as the antipornography theory and laws to which they have given rise.

CHAPTER 5

Revealing Views of Women, Men, and Sex

Unambiguous conventional heterosexual behavior is the worst betrayal of our common humanity.

—ANDREA DWORKIN[1]

The procensorship feminists' effort to extirpate sexually explicit expression that, in their view, perpetuates demeaning stereotypes about women, itself perpetuates such demeaning stereotypes. The most important such subordinating stereotype, which is central to the feminist antipornography movement, is that sex is inherently degrading to women. Of course, this is the very same conclusion that long has been advocated by traditional conservatives and right-wing fundamentalists, although for somewhat different reasons.

To emphasize that the feminist procensorship position rests upon traditional, stereotypical views disapproving sex and denying women's sexuality, many have characterized the procensorship feminists as being antisex, while labeling anticensorship feminists as prosex. The basic contours of these opposing positions are delineated by feminists Lisa Duggan, Nan Hunter, and Carole Vance as follows:

Embedded in [the feminist procensorship] view are several . . . familiar themes: that sex is degrading to women, but not to men; that men are raving beasts; that sex is dangerous for women; that sexuality is male, not female; that women are victims, not sexual actors; that men inflict "it" on women; that penetration is submission; that heterosexual sexuality, rather than the institution of heterosexuality, is sexist. . . . It's ironic

93

that a feminist position on pornography incorporates most of the myths about sexuality that feminism has struggled to displace. . . .[2]

While the procensorship feminists' negative, traditional attitudes toward sex are on one level ironic—as noted by Duggan, Hunter, and Vance—on another level, these attitudes are completely expected. After all, it should not be surprising that advocates of banning sexual expression would view sexuality itself with such suspicion.

The Antisex Thrust of the Procensorship Position

Intercourse with men as we know them is increasingly impossible. It requires an aborting of creativity and strength, a refusal of responsibility and freedom: a bitter personal death. It means remaining the victim, forever annihilating all self-respect. It means acting out the female role, incorporating the masochism, self-hatred, and passivity which are central to it.

—ANDREA DWORKIN[3]

Compare victims' reports of rape with women's reports of sex. They look a lot alike. . . . [T]he major distinction between intercourse (normal) and rape (abnormal) is that the normal happens so often that one cannot get anyone to see anything wrong with it.

—CATHARINE MACKINNON[4]

I am inclined to worry that . . . after the feminist revolution, "approved" sex will consist of everyone joining hands and circling round until we all simultaneously fall asleep.

—CARLIN MEYER, professor
New York Law School[5]

If I can't dance, I don't want your revolution.

—EMMA GOLDMAN[6]

The antisex position of the procensorship feminists essentially posits a mutual inconsistency between a woman's freedom and her participation in sexual relations with men. Both Dworkin and MacKinnon, for example, have argued that, in light of society's pervasive sexism, women cannot freely consent to sexual relations with men. Accordingly, as Cardozo Law School professor Jeanne Schroeder has observed, their analysis of pornography "functions as a critique of sexuality as such, not of violence, violent sex or sexualized violence."[7]

The equation of all heterosexual intercourse and rape, which underlies the feminist antipornography analysis, is articulated in especially dramatic terms in Dworkin's 1987 book *Intercourse*. According to that book, "[I]ntercourse remains a means or the means of physiologically making a woman inferior."[8] The book argues that the physical "invasion" of a woman's body, which is the essential, physiological aspect of heterosexual genital intercourse, inevitably entails the same kind of loss of freedom and subjugation that occurs when the armed forces of one country invade and occupy another: "The political meaning of intercourse for women is the fundamental question of feminism and freedom: can an occupied people—physically occupied inside, internally invaded—be free?"[9]

In *Pornography: Men Possessing Women* (1979), Dworkin states:

> The penis causes pain, but the pain enhances the pleasure. It is as if the ability of the penis to cause pain were an intrinsic quality of the penis, not a use to which the penis is put.... As a result, fucking is inherently sadistic because it is necessarily both pain and pleasure; and when penile pain is supplemented by purposeful cruelty, it occasions the highest sexual ecstasy, emotional love, or both.[10]

In her 1988 book *Letters from a War Zone*, Dworkin essentially equates marriage and romance with prostitution and rape, in the following pithy phrases: "One of the differences between marriage and prostitution is that in marriage you only have to make a deal with one man," and "Romance ... is rape embellished with meaningful looks." Likewise, "Marriage ... is a legal license to rape" and "In seduction, the rapist bothers to buy a bottle of wine."[11] In Dworkin's novel *Ice and Fire* (1987), she writes: "Coitus is the punishment for the fear of being alone. . . . [C]oitus is the punishment for being a woman: afraid to be alone."[12]

As for those poor benighted women who believe that they actually choose to engage in intercourse with men and that they enjoy doing so, Dworkin has not only pity, but outright contempt. According to Dworkin, women who say they enjoy heterosexual lovemaking are "collaborators, more base in their collaboration than other collaborators have ever been, experiencing pleasure in their own inferiority, calling intercourse freedom."[13]

Catharine MacKinnon's writings offer ample variations on this same antisex theme. According to MacKinnon, feminism "sees sexuality as a social sphere of male power of which forced sex is paradigmatic."[14] Her observations about heterosexual intercourse include the following: "If there is no inequality, no violation, no dominance, no force, there is no sexual arousal";[15] "Women share . . . degradation in intimacy";[16] "[T]hey just want to hurt us, dominate us and control us, and that is fucking us";[17] "To be about to be raped is to be gender female in the process of going about life as usual";[18] rape and intercourse "express the same power relation";[19] "sexuality is itself violating";[20] "[H]eterosexuality . . . institutionalizes male sexual dominance and female sexual submission";[21] "[T]he degradation and violation and domination of women . . . defines the social meaning of female sexuality in societies of sex inequality";[22] "[A] women [sic] is . . . one whose sexuality exists for someone else";[23] and "Women's sexuality is, socially, a thing to be stolen, sold, bought, bartered or exchanged by others."[24]

As the foregoing statements indicate, MacKinnon views even nonviolent, consensual sex as inherently degrading to women; it isn't surprising, then, that she apparently considers any depiction of sex—not just images of violent, forced sex—to be oppressive. Indeed, she is at least as eager to suppress images suggesting that women welcome and enjoy sex as images showing women resisting and suffering from it. One of the specific indicia of subordination under the MacDworkin model law is that "women are presented as . . . inviting penetration."[25] MacKinnon has condemned pornography specifically because it shows that women "desire to be fucked."[26] One of the most popular sex manuals in our country, *The Joy of Sex*, which has been suppressed in right-wing antisex campaigns, would clearly be just as vulnerable under a MacDworkinite regime; the book not only shows that women, in MacKinnon's condemnatory phrase, "desire to be fucked," but, worse yet, it attempts to stimulate that desire in them.

MacKinnon also echoes Dworkin's thesis that women who believe they voluntarily engage in, and enjoy, heterosexual sex are victims of "false consciousness." She has said that women who believe in their sexual agency are merely denying the "unspeakable humiliation" of having been "cajoled, pressured, tricked, blackmailed, or outright forced into sex."[27] In the same vein, she has written: "Faced with no alternatives, the strategy to acquire self-respect and pride is: I chose it."[28] Denying that women can give meaningful consent to sex, MacKinnon asks: "If you feel that you are going to be raped when you say no, how do you know that you really want . . . sex when you say yes?"[29] According to MacKinnon, women who believe they are free sexual agents are, instead, the dupes of men: "The so-called sexual agency people insult women by assuming that living out a role men have assigned women in sex—the 'wallow in filth' whore as opposed to the 'violate the pure' madonna—amounts to sexual freedom."[30]

The condemnation of sex, or at least heterosexual sex, by Dworkin and MacKinnon is also expressed by other procensorship feminists. Dorchen Leidholdt, a founder of Women Against Pornography, has stated that "under male supremacy . . . women's . . . denigration and abuse is sexual pleasure," and that male "sexual pleasure . . . is usually achieved through women's subordination and violation." Likewise, Leidholdt has denounced the "prosexism" among anticensorship feminists as "embrac[ing] pleasure in our degradation and pacifying lies."[31]

Since the pornophobic feminists' negative views of heterosexual sex flow from their critique of pervasive societal sexism, it would seem to follow that heterosexual sex is verboten until that sexism is eliminated. This presents a serious dilemma for those who deplore sexism but not sex. As New York Law School professor Carlin Meyer asked:

Even if it were desirable, can we eliminate inequality in the realm of the intimate? Can we do so before we eliminate pervasive economic and social inequality? And if not, what do we do in the meantime? Eschew all sex? Heterosex only?[32]

The only "solution" consistent with the antipornography feminists' worldview was aptly summarized by one group of such feminists who participated in a conference at New York University in the early 1980s; the group's acronym, WAS, stood for Women Against Sex. This same "solution" to the challenge of fulfilling female sexuality in a sexist world was offered by Sally Cline's 1993 book *Women, Passion, and Celibacy.* Cline argues that sexual intercourse, and even female orgasm, are essentially forced on women through media manipulation in order to please men. She therefore concludes that genuine female liberation can be found through celibacy. Cline decries women's orgasms as "a form of manipulated emotional labour which women worked at in order to reflect men and to maintain male values." In the same spirit, she disparagingly dismisses sexual intimacy by declaring, "Like militarism today, fur coats the day before, sexual intercourse and general genital thrashing about, are things a woman is expected to purchase—if she can afford the price."[33]

The Anti-Male Angle
in the Feminist Procensorship Position

An integral element of the procensorship feminists' hostility toward both heterosexual sex and pornography is their view that men are essentially bestial, like the attack dogs to which MacKinnon has compared them. (In *Only Words,* she argues that showing pornography to men is less like protected speech and "more like saying 'kill' to a trained guard dog, and the training process itself."[34]) For this reason, Katie Roiphe refers to MacDworkinism as the "zookeeper school of feminism—training the beasts to behave within 'acceptable parameters.'"[35]

In this respect, too, the procensorship feminist philosophy is a carbon copy of the right-wing view of sexuality and gender roles. An important theme in sex education materials that the extreme right has been pushing in many public schools around the country is that, by nature, females are nonsexual, whereas males are sexually aggressive and manipulative. When such ideas are touted by conservatives, liberals appropriately denounce them as retrograde sexist stereotypes, but when such ideas are touted by so-called radical feminists, too many liberals do not respond, at best, or acquiesce, at worst.

That men are innately violent, and that they instinctively use sex as an instrument of violence, was repeatedly emphasized in Dworkin's book *Pornography: Men Possessing Women.* Here's one illustrative passage:

> Force—the violence of the male confirming his masculinity—is seen as the essential purpose of the penis, its animating principle as it were. . . . This penis must embody the violence of the male in order for him to be male. Violence is male; the male is the penis. . . . What the penis can do it must do forcibly for a man to be a man.[36]

In *Letters from a War Zone,* Dworkin added to this invective, "For fun they rape us or have other men or sometimes animals, rape us and film the rapes and show the rapes in movie theaters or publish them in magazines."[37] Echoes MacKinnon: "[W]hat men want is: women bound, women battered, women tortured, women humiliated, women degraded . . . women killed."[38]

Ironically, since the feminist antipornography law is written in gender-neutral terms, many of the writings of those who advocate the law would be subject to censorship under it, because of their dehumanizing depictions of men. (As noted in chapter 11, the Canadian version of the MacDworkinite law has in fact been used to suppress feminist works, including nonsexual works, because of their critical views about men.)

Two Steps Backward

For those who view feminism as an inclusive movement to end all gender-based discrimination and all gender stereotyping, the feminist antipornography movement is doubly distressing: it perpetuates negative, demeaning, disempowering stereotypes of both men and women, and hence deeply damages the cause of gender equality. In the words of the ACLU brief challenging Indianapolis's antipornography law: "A statute that formally equates women with children and men with satyrs is hardly a step toward sexual equality."[39]

In asserting that sex and sexual expression degrade women, procensorship feminists not only repudiate central tenets of 1970s-era feminism, but also revive traditional, patriarchal, subordinating stereotypes that the feminism of the 1970s had in turn sought to repudiate. In this respect, the feminist antipornography movement is a throwback to the archaic stereotypes that underlay nineteenth-century-vintage laws prohibiting "vulgar" or sexually suggestive language from being used in the presence of women and girls, as well as statutes and judicial decisions "protecting" women from exposure to such language in the courtroom by barring them from practicing law or serving on juries. These stereotypes—not pornography—have traditionally been used to subjugate women.

In *The Female Eunuch,* published in 1971, Germaine Greer emphasized that the repression of women's sexuality was integrally bound up with women's second-class political and economic status, and thus that reclaiming women's sexuality was an essential aspect of advancing women's societal status more generally. In words that are at least as relevant today as they were in 1971, Greer powerfully rebutted the antisex feminist position:

> It is often falsely assumed, even by feminists, that sexuality is the enemy of the female who really wants to develop . . . her personality. . . . It was not the insistence on her sex that weakened the American woman student's desire to make something of her education, but the insistence upon a *passive* sexual *role.* In fact, the chief instrument in the deflection and perversion of female energy is the denial of female sexuality for the substitution of femininity or sexlessness.[40]

Learning how to derive greater sexual pleasure in a greater variety of situations was a major theme of the women's movement during the early 1970s, as indicated by the following events of central importance to the then-new second wave of feminism:

- In 1971, the Boston Women's Health Book Collective published the first edition of *Our Bodies, Ourselves,* a guide to women's sexuality and sexual health;

- In 1972, Shere Hite embarked on her study of women's sexuality, sending detailed questionnaires on sexual practices and preferences to thousands of women;
- In 1973, prostitutes formed COYOTE (Call Off Your Old Tired Ethics), an organization advocating the decriminalization of prostitution and seeking to end the stigma attached to working in the sex business;
- In 1974, Betty Dodson self-published *Liberating Masturbation* after five thousand women responded to a notice in *Ms.* magazine offering a booklet on women and masturbation.

At its outset, then, the modern women's movement considered sexual liberation to be an essential aspect of what was then commonly called "women's liberation." Just as feminists then sought to be freed from confining social stereotypes and legal restrictions concerning other aspects of their personal and professional lives, they sought to be freed from limiting, conventional stereotypes concerning their sexuality. Aptly capsulizing the contrast between her prosex, anticensorship perspective and MacDworkinite views, writer Ann Snitow stated: "Ti Grace Atkinson [a procensorship feminist] says, 'I do not know any feminist worthy of that name who, if forced to choose between freedom and sex, would choose sex.' While women are forced to make such a choice we cannot consider ourselves free."[41]

The misogynistic stereotypes to which contemporary procensorship feminists revert, and which they perpetuate, are throwbacks to earlier eras and their archaic, repressive views about women, men, and sexuality. While commentators have aptly compared MacDworkinism to nineteenth-century Victorianism and seventeenth-century Puritanism, Cardozo Law School professor Jeanne Schroeder has unearthed the even deeper historical roots of this contemporary antisex movement. Comparing MacKinnon's writings to those of St. Augustine and other early Christian philosophers, Schroeder observed:

> Catharine MacKinnon is widely considered to be one of the most radical . . . feminist theorists writing today. . . . [T]hat perception is incorrect. In her antipornography analysis, MacKinnon . . . embraces a deeply reactionary theory of the flesh—the very approach to sexuality

that has served to underpin American gender roles. What at first blush appears to be a postmodern sociological theory . . . is actually a modern liberal theory of the individual grafted onto a premodern Christian concept of the body. MacKinnon's. . . . analysis devolves into a conservative paean to the potency of masculinity as traditionally conceived.[42]

MacKinnon's views, Schroeder concludes, are "radically traditional."[43] It is not surprising, then, that these theories closely parallel those of contemporary Christian fundamentalists, as mentioned previously. Marcia Pally has noted the substantial overlap between the views of the "Religious Right" and those of procensorship feminists, whom she accordingly labels "right-wing" feminists:

> Both groups propose that ridding society of sexual words and images will reduce rape, incest, and battery. Right-wing feminists would add sexual harassment to the list; religious fundamentalists would add interracial sex, homosexuality, AIDS and feminism.[44]

Just as the procensorship feminist faction views women as inevitably being victims in sexual matters, that faction also perpetuates the stereotype that women are victims in a more general sense. This constitutes a fundamental reorientation from the conception of women that animated feminism in the 1960s and 1970s, when "assertiveness" was the watchword.

As writer Cathy Young has observed, from some perspectives it is considered strategically advantageous to depict women as victims: "Victimhood is powerful. Both feminists and antifeminists see advantages in keeping women down."[45]

On the other hand, though, growing numbers of feminists are recognizing that purveying the view of women as victims can backfire against gender equality. This is the theme, for example, of two 1993 books: Katie Roiphe's *The Morning After: Sex, Fear, and Feminism on Campus,* and Naomi Wolf's *Fire with Fire: The New Female Power and How It Will Change the 21st Century,* in which she criticizes what she calls "victim feminism" and advocates instead "power feminism."[46]

The growing rejection of the victim-centric view of women among many feminists is now being mirrored in some feminist art and fiction, with depictions of women as aggressive avengers against male violence and sexism. Ironically, many of these works could well fall prey to the MacDworkinite antipornography law. Consider, for example, a comic strip from a 1993 issue of an underground feminist magazine called *Frighten the Horses,* described in Wolf's book. Entitled "Penis Envy II," the strip shows a man reading violent erotica until he turns into a gigantic penis that devours women he picks up in bars. After destroying several women, though, the penis-man gets his comeuppance: he meets a woman who becomes a huge vagina dentata, completely consuming him.[47] Recall that the MacDworkin law prohibits "women's body parts—including . . . vaginas" from being "exhibited such that women are reduced to those parts." The law contains no exception for depictions of women's body parts that, as in this strip, in turn reduce men to *less* than *their* body parts!

The courageous "vagina-woman"—whose sexuality is synonymous with her strength—contrasts dramatically with the procensorship feminists' image of the cowering, cringing female whose sexuality is synonymous with her weakness. The procensorship feminists' archetype of the chronically vulnerable, victimized woman is further perpetuated through their views on sexual harassment, as described in the next chapter.

CHAPTER 6

Defining Sexual Harassment

SEXUALITY DOES NOT EQUAL SEXISM

Although pornophobic feminists have not succeeded in purging pornography from our public sphere, as the Dworkin-MacKinnon model law would do directly, they recently have made significant strides toward that goal through an alternative strategy. They have used the concept of sexual harassment as a Trojan horse for smuggling their views on sexual expression into our law and culture. By influencing the legal and societal understandings of this concept, procensorship feminists have been alarmingly successful in effectively outlawing *all* sexual expression in many sectors of our society, even without any claim that the particular expression is subordinating or degrading.

The serious problem of sexual harassment, and how it should be defined, recently has been at the forefront of public consciousness and public policy. Building on the theory that sexual speech necessarily degrades women, antipornography feminists have argued that it should be deemed sexual harassment and accordingly prohibited, at least in workplaces and on campuses.

This distorted concept of sexual harassment reflects two false assumptions: first, that all sexually oriented expression is gender discriminatory; and second, that all such expression is harassing. The false equation of sexuality and sexism, which lies at the core of the procensorship feminist philosophy, is as dangerous to women's rights as it is to free speech. As discussed in the previous chapter, the notion that women are inherently demeaned by sex and sexual expression reflects archaic, infantilizing stereotypes that long have been used to deny women full equality, not only in employment and education, but also in our society at large.

The second MacDworkinite false equation—of sexual expression and sexual harassment—has unfortunately been widely accepted by employers, employees, campus officials, students, and policy makers, too often without any serious examination. Given the special importance of free expression in an academic setting, this stifling of sex-related speech on campus is particularly frightening.

Even more ominously, as explained later in this chapter, the procensorship feminists have also experienced some success in attempting to leverage their malleable, expansive harassment concept into a general proscription on sexual expression not only in all public spaces, but worse yet, in some private spaces too.

It is not surprising that the concept of sexual harassment has proven a fast-lane vehicle for transporting the feminist antipornography analysis into our law, since Catharine MacKinnon has been a leading theorist and activist in both areas. Her 1979 book *Sexual Harassment of Working Women: A Case of Sex Discrimination*[1] is widely credited with having pioneered the notion that sexual harassment constitutes a form of gender-based employment discrimination. She also successfully argued the first sexual harassment case that the Supreme Court decided, in which the Court unanimously adopted this notion.[2]

Our society's recent concern about promoting gender-based equality in education and employment by preventing actual sexual harassment in those settings is commendable. However, in the wake of such widely publicized events as the Anita Hill–Clarence Thomas confrontation and the Tailhook scandal, thoughtful concern too often has degenerated into unthinking overreaction. Too many policy makers and citizens have uncritically accepted the overly expansive MacDworkinite conception of harassment, to the detriment of women's rights as well as free expression.

To date, the procensorship feminists' notion that pornography *is*—not just causes, but *is,* in and of itself—gender-based discrimination,[3] has been universally dismissed by the courts as the hyperbolic rhetoric it is. But, as just noted, the Supreme Court has unanimously accepted the argument that sexual harassment is gender-based discrimination. Therefore, when employers, campus officials, judges, and other policy makers accept the argument that pornography, in turn, *is* sexual harassment—as distressingly many have done—then, in effect, they have accepted the claim that pornography is gender-based discrimination. This is a backdoor way into the procensorship feminist camp. It illustrates the most insidious threat posed by MacDworkinite ideas, to which Katie Roiphe astutely pointed in her 1993 book: "The threat is that MacKinnon's radical premises are absorbed into our culture: her pure, crystalline politics is distilled into other, less strident forms."[4] But only slightly less strident.

Although the Supreme Court has not yet ruled on the burgeoning claims, reflecting the antipornography feminist world-view, that virtually all sexually oriented expression may be deemed proscribable sexual harassment, some lower courts have upheld these claims. Furthermore, many employers and campus officials have accepted and enforced these claims in situations that are not subject to judicial review.

Once again, I want to stress that eliminating gender-based discrimination in employment and education, and promoting equality of opportunity in those important spheres, are critically important goals, and that eliminating sexual harassment is an essential element of these goals. The incorporation of the antipornography feminist analysis into the concept of sexual harassment, however, has severely undermined not only free speech, but also the very gender equality concerns that the procensorship (and anticensorship) feminists seek to advance. The misguided emphasis on sexually oriented expression has diverted the attention of policy makers from *sexist conduct* to *sexual speech*, and has shifted their focus from gender-based discrimination to sexual expression. By presuming that all sexual expression constitutes or leads to gender-based discrimination, this distorted approach also has revived outmoded, confining stereotypes about women's alleged sexual purity and vulnerability that will perpetuate rather than eradicate gender-based discrimination in employment and education.

As Feminists for Free Expression stated in a brief challenging a workplace rule that treated *all* sexually oriented expression as sexual harassment:

> It is ironic that just as women are finally making inroads into such male-exclusive venues as handling a skyscraper construction crane, a hostile corporate takeover attempt, and an Air Force fighter plane, we are being

told we cannot handle dirty pictures, and certainly that we would never enjoy them.[5]

In chapter 1, I described some examples of the proliferating situations in which any sexual reference to a woman has been deemed to be proscribable harassment and therefore subject to banishment from work, school, and other settings. Now I will outline the legal standards governing sexual harassment, explain how these standards and actual current practices reflect and perpetuate the feminist antipornography philosophy, and elaborate on the resulting dangers to both free speech and equality.

The Legal Definition of Sexual Harassment

The concept of sexual harassment has mushroomed—in both its legal elaboration and its practical implications—since the Supreme Court's 1986 ruling on the Indianapolis version of the MacDworkin antipornography law. When the Court issued that decision, it had not yet decided any case concerning sexual harassment. Since then, it has ruled in two such cases—the first in 1986, and the second in 1993.

In 1986, the Supreme Court held that sexual harassment in the workplace violates Title VII of the 1964 Civil Rights Act, which prohibits various types of employment discrimination, including discriminatory "terms" or "conditions" of employment, because of an employee's "sex."[6] The Court endorsed guidelines that the Equal Employment Opportunity Commission (EEOC) had issued in interpreting Title VII, which recognized two types of sexual harassment: first, "quid pro quo" harassment, which occurs when an employment opportunity or benefit is conditioned on an employee's granting sexual favors to a supervisor; and second, "hostile environment" harassment, which occurs when "verbal or physical conduct of a *sexual* nature has the purpose or effect of unreasonably interfering with an individual's job performance or creating an intimidating, hostile or offensive work environment"[7] (emphasis added).

The EEOC's definition of "hostile environment" harassment, consistent with MacKinnon's writings on the subject,[8] targets conduct that is sex*ual* rather than *sexist*. Yet since Title VII's goal, appropriately, is to protect women from gender-based discrimination, this EEOC focus is misplaced; in legal terminology, it is both "underinclusive" and "overinclusive." It is underinclusive insofar as it does *not* encompass nonsexual conduct that *is* gender discriminatory. It is overinclusive insofar as it *does* encompass *sexual* conduct that is *not* gender discriminatory.[9]

Discussion and controversy concerning the appropriate scope of prohibited sexual harassment have focused on the "hostile environment" branch of harassment, given its relatively vague, subjective contours. It was this aspect of harassment that the Court revisited in its second decision on the subject, its 1993 ruling in *Harris v. Forklift Systems, Inc.*,[10] in which Justice Sandra Day O'Connor wrote an opinion for a unanimous bench. Specifically, the Court rejected the employer's argument that no conduct could rise to the level of hostile environment harassment unless it caused a demonstrable psychological injury to the employee. The Court likewise rejected the employee's argument that any conduct that she found "offensive" should be deemed hostile environment harassment.

Beyond rejecting these two extreme positions, though, the Court provided scant additional guidance. It said only that, to constitute hostile environment harassment, conduct has to be "severe or pervasive enough" that it would be perceived as abusive or hostile by both a hypothetical "reasonable person" and the actually affected employee.[11] This leaves enormous discretion to the corporate and academic officials who implement harassment policies.

The Court acknowledged in *Harris* that the standard it had adopted was imprecise, and emphasized the necessarily fact-bound nature of the determination in any particular case:

[W]hether an environment is "hostile" or "abusive" can be determined only by looking at all the circumstances. These may include the frequency of the discriminatory conduct; its severity; whether it is physically threatening or humiliating, or a mere offensive utterance; and whether it unreasonably interferes with an employee's work performance. . . . [W]hile psychological harm, like any other relevant factor, may be taken into account, no single factor is required.

As Justice Scalia commented in his separate concurring opinion, the Court's unclear standard, "[a]s a practical matter . . . lets virtually unguided juries decide whether sex-related conduct" in the workplace constitutes prohibited sexual harassment. He confessed, however, that he was unable to formulate an alternative, more precise, standard. Accordingly, he endorsed the open-ended, contextual approach laid out in O'Connor's opinion. I also believe that whether conduct is sexually harassing must be determined on a case-by-case basis, as Justice O'Connor's majority opinion stipulates. Consistent with this approach, Justice Ginsburg suggested a helpful definition of hostile environment harassment in her concurring opinion: "The critical issue . . . is whether members of one sex are exposed to disadvantageous terms or conditions of employment to which members of the other sex are not exposed."

The difficulty of constructing a precise legal definition of sexual harassment is compounded when the alleged harassing behavior consists of expression that would be entitled to First Amendment protection in other contexts. The Supreme Court's two sexual harassment decisions did not discuss such expression. But extrapolating from those cases, as well as from free speech rulings, it is clear that protected expression can be distinguished from proscribable harassment only on an ad hoc basis, turning on all the facts and circumstances of each particular case.

When employees work for a government agency, or when faculty or students are at a public educational institution, their expression is constitutionally protected. In private sector workplaces and campuses, the First Amendment does not literally bar employers and academic officials from regulating expression.* Nevertheless, consistent with our society's general commitment to First Amendment values, employers and campus officials should respect free expression even in the private sector. Given the importance of free speech and academic freedom in any educational setting, many experts and groups of experts, including the American Association of University Professors, persuasively argue

---

*The First Amendment provides that "Congress shall make no law . . . abridging the freedom of speech. . . ." Although the Supreme Court has interpreted this language to bar any action by the government (or with significant government involvement) that infringes on free speech—not just congressional enactments—the Court has never extended this provision to nongovernment actions.

that the First Amendment should be honored in spirit on all campuses, even if it is not literally binding. Likewise, given the central role that work plays in the lives of so many Americans, advocates of workers' rights, including the American Civil Liberties Union, maintain that all employees should enjoy freedom of expression while at work, as long as that expression does not substantially interfere with workplace operations. In any event, when private employers or campus officials adopt censorial policies to comply with antidiscrimination laws, then such government-mandated policies should be subject to First Amendment constraints.

The Practical Definition of Sexual Harassment

The process of distinguishing workplace or campus expression that constitutes punishable sexual harassment from workplace or campus expression that constitutes protected free speech—parallel to the process of defining hostile environment sexual harassment generally—turns on no precise, generally applicable formula; rather, it requires a fact-specific examination of each particular situation. In some cases it might be difficult to draw this line, so that even two individuals who are equally committed to both free speech and gender equality might well disagree about the proper outcome. For purposes of the present discussion, though, it is not necessary to address such potentially problematic situations, because so many employers, universities, courts, and other policy makers have drawn the line far beyond any legitimately proscribable harassment—and thus have egregiously violated not only free speech principles but also equality principles.

The many sexual harassment rules in place in America today that have too broadly condemned sexual expression have done so because they have not complied with the Court's essential requirement, sensibly emphasized in its unanimous 1993 *Harris* decision, that *any* expression or conduct must be evaluated in its overall context. Too many rules have treated sexually oriented expression in an acontextual fashion, concluding that, no matter what the surrounding facts and circumstances, such expression automatically constitutes sexual harassment. Worse yet, some lower courts have endorsed this approach.

Sexual expression—along with all other expression or conduct—might well constitute sexual harassment, *if*—but only if—it is used in a certain way. A case that is being litigated (and, as of fall 1994, has not been finally decided) under the name of *Robinson v. Jacksonville Shipyards, Inc.*[12] makes this point. In that case, there was some evidence that male coworkers had forced sexually explicit photographs upon a female welder, Lois Robinson, in situations designed to make it more difficult for her to work, with apparent gender-discriminatory intent.

For example, a picture of a nude woman, with her knees drawn up to her chest and exposing her genitals, was left on a toolbox where Robinson had to return her tools. Several male coworkers were present when she did so and laughed at her when she became visibly upset by the picture. Similarly, one of Robinson's coworkers waved around a picture of a nude woman with long blond hair holding a whip, in an enclosed area where he and Robinson were working with about five other men. Robinson said she felt particularly targeted by this action, because she has long blond hair and worked with a welding tool known as a "whip."

The foregoing treatment was appropriately deemed sexual harassment. But Robinson's complaint, as well as the federal trial judge's order, went much further. Robinson sought, and the judge issued, a total ban on *all* "sexually suggestive" pictures, regardless of how they were used. Thus, the court banished from the workplace not only the sexually oriented images that some employees used to harass Lois Robinson, but also sexually oriented images that employees used for their own private enjoyment, in places and at times that interfered with neither their own work nor that of any coworkers. Under the court's sweeping order, no employees could bring any sexually suggestive pictures to work, even if they only kept the pictures in their own lockers, or discreetly looked at them during their lunch breaks, without showing them to any other employees.

The *Robinson* judge's expansive definition of proscribed images included any picture of a woman "who is not fully clothed or in clothes that are not suited to . . . routine work in and around the shipyard and who is posed for the obvious purpose of . . . drawing attention to private portions of . . . her body."[13] The appellate brief that the ACLU filed in the *Robinson* case in 1992, challenging the trial judge's overbroad purge of sexually oriented expression, noted that this prohibition could well encompass fashion magazines, family photographs, and classic works of art. Defenders of the *Robinson* order pooh-poohed these fears as speculative. But they proved sadly prophetic in 1993, when officials of the University of Nebraska at Lincoln ordered a graduate teaching assistant to remove from his desktop a photograph of his wife in a bathing suit. They claimed that this photo constituted hostile environment sexual harassment of female faculty, students, and staff.[14] Although overbroad, the *Robinson* order at least was predicated on the court's conclusions that there had been some intentionally harassing acts, and that there was a pervasively gender-discriminatory atmosphere, in the Jacksonville Shipyards; in contrast, neither factor was found to be present in the University of Nebraska situation.

Because the Supreme Court has not yet ruled on *Robinson* (or any other case involving similar facts), we do not know whether the Court would accept the procensorship feminists' equation of sexual expression and sexual harassment. In any event, this false equation has inspired rules in many workplaces and campuses that are not subject to judicial review, because there are no legally enforceable free speech rights on many campuses and most workplaces. As previously pointed out, the First Amendment protects speech only from government-imposed restrictions. While some employees are covered by collective bargaining agreements negotiated by their unions that may extend some protection to their expression, only a small and shrinking percentage of America's workforce is in this category. Though most private employers and universities have no legal obligation to respect the free speech rights of their employees, faculty, or students, they do have legal obligations to protect these individuals from sexual harassment under civil rights laws. Employers and campus officials thus have legal and practical incentives to err in favor of overbroadly defining sexual harassment and overzealously enforcing antiharassment policies, rather than the opposite. (As I noted above, speech-restricting harassment policies that are adopted in order to comply with antidiscrimination laws could fairly be viewed as government-imposed and hence subject to First Amendment challenge. As of the time this is being written, though— the fall of 1994—I am unaware of any such challenge.)

As Nat Hentoff remarked when Penn State officials removed a reproduction of Goya's *Nude Maja* from a classroom in response to Professor

Nancy Stumhofer's complaint (as recounted in chapter 1), "It was either Goya or Stumhofer. And Title VII does not protect dead Spanish painters."[15] Ironically, shortly after this incident, and as a direct result of it, Professor Stumhofer herself was accused of sexual harassment because of the false equation between sexual expression and harassment. Here's her own account of what happened:

> In an effort to explain some nontraditional ways of seeing art to the faculty . . . I distributed a portion of John Berger's book *Ways of Seeing,* and invited people to read the article and discuss it with me. . . . Berger looks at representations of the female figure as the eternal object of the male gaze, and shows various paintings of naked or nude females. My attempts to increase people's awareness of how women are represented in art had an unexpected result. Two men on campus—one faculty member and one maintenance person—filed a complaint of sexual harassment with the Affirmative Action Office. They claimed I was harassing them with pictures of nude women.[16]

Referring to the burgeoning attacks on campus art inspired by Mac-Dworkinite perspectives, Marjorie Heins, director of the ACLU's Arts Censorship Project, has said: "Students are increasingly seduced by these code-word excuses. There's a tendency to describe anything you don't like in a work of art as sexual harassment, so that it becomes a civil rights violation."[17]

The all-purpose epithet "pornography" has been joined by a functional synonym, "sexual harassment," to stigmatize, and hence suppress, seemingly any expression that even hints at sexual themes. This decontextualized, demonized approach to art and expression betrays a fundamental misunderstanding of images and words. As Columbia University professor Carole Vance has noted:

> [T]he idea that an image per se is harassing . . . is totally incompatible with how we normally think about images. Context matters, so does interpretive frame, and viewers differ in how they interpret an image. If the question is posed as, Which images are sexually harassing? half of an important question has already been ceded to those who have a reductionist, simplified view of art and culture.[18]

A growing body of sexual harassment rules are expressly barring much, if not all, sexual expression from workplaces and campuses, even when such expression is not targeted at, or even seen by, any objecting female employees, students, or faculty members. Many workplaces have now been declared off-limits for materials with any sexual content. In 1992 the Los Angeles County Fire Department issued a sweeping sexual harassment policy that bans all "sexually-oriented magazines, particularly those containing nude pictures . . . posters or calendars which display nudity or are overtly sexual, [and] . . . [a]ll other material . . . of a clear sexual connotation"[19] from the entire workplace, including dormitories, restrooms, and lockers. All firefighters are forbidden to read these materials or even just to bring them to the firehouse. Similarly, the Ventura County Fire Department in California has banned the Playboy Channel at fire stations.

These total bans on sexual speech are especially onerous for firefighters, whose workplace functionally doubles as a home for long periods. Firefighters, for all intents and purposes, often live at their stations, serving many round-the-clock shifts each month, and regularly staying there for several days in a row. They have individual rooms or privately partitioned sleeping quarters in the dormitory section of the firehouse, and unless there is an emergency, are considered to be on "personal time" after the normal working day.

Given the extent to which the firehouse serves as their "home away from home," to forbid firefighters from looking at certain materials there, when they are on personal time and in their private quarters, is tantamount to prohibiting them from enjoying these materials alone in the privacy of their homes. As former justice Thurgood Marshall wrote in a Supreme Court opinion upholding the right to read or view obscene materials in one's home, "If the First Amendment means anything, it means that the State has no business telling a man, sitting alone in his own house, what books he may read or what films he may watch."[20] Accordingly, on behalf of Captain Steven W. Johnson, the ACLU challenged the Los Angeles County Fire Department's sweeping restraints as violating the firefighters' rights of free speech and privacy.

In June 1994, the trial court held that the rules were unconstitutional,[21] and Los Angeles officials said they would appeal. The ACLU's challenge has been supported by Feminists for Free Expression, which has emphasized that the mere possession of any materials, including sexually oriented materials, should never be deemed sexual harassment unless, at the very least, such expression was intended to discriminate. The Feminists for Free Expression brief, written by Cathy Crosson, also made the important point that overly broad sexual harassment rules undermine privacy principles that are pillars of the women's rights cause, with no countervailing gain for that cause:

> This case critically implicates the privacy rights which have been a fountainhead of protections for women's sexual and reproductive freedom. Without the privacy doctrine . . . women's access to abortion and contraceptives today could be dramatically curtailed at the whim of local legislators. . . . The [Los Angeles Fire Department] rules are entirely antithetical to this line of cases so crucial to women's interests, because they assail the basic premise that government has no business intruding into one's bedroom and into intimate personal decisions such as the choice to read or view sexual materials. . . . The defense of [privacy] rights should be high on the feminist agenda; the notion that women should be willing to trade them away for empty gestures like these repressive workplace rules is pure folly.[22]

Employers' moves toward broadly banning sexual expression as sexual harassment have been matched by similar moves on campuses. Author and Princeton graduate student Katie Roiphe reports, "Like most common definitions Princeton's definition of sexual harassment includes 'leering and ogling, whistling, sexual innuendo, and other suggestive or offensive or derogatory comments, humor and jokes about sex.'" Likewise, an American College Health Association pamphlet characterizes "unwanted sexual comments, jokes or gestures" as "a form of sexual assault."[23] As previously noted, these types of behavior could be deemed sexually harassing if they were part of a sufficiently severe or pervasive pattern of conduct, but isolated incidents of such behavior should not be considered sexual harassment.

In its 1993 statement on "Sexual Harassment and Academic Freedom," the National Association of Scholars (NAS), while recognizing that sexual harassment "constitutes a serious violation of an educator's responsibilities and is morally wrong," also warns that "[t]oo many [higher educational] institutions have adopted vague definitions of harassment that may all too easily be applied to attitudes or even to a scholar's professional views," thus inducing "a chill . . . on academic discussions of sensitive but legitimate topics, such as human sexuality, sex differences, and sexual roles." For example, the NAS statement points out that the University of Minnesota's official definition of sexual harassment provides that it "often consists of a callous insensitivity to the experience of women."[24]

The notion that sexual harassment extends to all manner of expression with any sexual connotation has reached the high school and grade school levels, too. In collaboration with the National Organization for Women's Legal Defense and Education Fund, researchers at Wellesley College's Center for Research on Women designed a survey on sexual harassment in schools, which included within the definition of sexual harassment student-to-student sexual "comments" or "gestures." In the same vein, the State of Minnesota recently adopted guidelines defining the student-to-student conduct that will be deemed sexual harassment. Students from kindergarten onward may now face expulsion for virtually every imaginable expression with any iota of sexual connotation or innuendo, including: "students 'rating' other students"; "sexually descriptive notes and letters"; "dirty jokes"; "spreading sexual rumors about other students"; "teasing students about their sexual activities or lack of sexual activity"; "students giving other students the finger"; and "displays of affection between students."[25]

The Expanding Definition of Sexual Harassment

Sweeping as the foregoing rules are in banning sexual expression from employment or educational settings, an even more capacious concept of sexual harassment is emerging that would make sexual expression unavailable to members of the general public. The charge has been made in both the United States and Canada that the sale of sexually oriented magazines such as *Playboy, Penthouse,* and *Playgirl* constitutes sexual harassment of female employees and customers. Such complaints have been leveled against a variety of outlets, including convenience stores and campus bookstores.

Since 1985, the Ontario Human Rights Commission has been investigating claims by antipornography feminists that the availability of such magazines in any stores other than "adult" bookstores creates an environment that is "hostile and discriminatory against women."[26] The complainants were not satisfied by the fact that, in accordance with local laws, all erotic magazines are displayed unobtrusively, behind opaque barriers that reveal little more than titles.

Similarly, in 1991, when Dolores Stanley was promoted to manager of the Ohio Dairy Mart C-Store where she worked, she yanked copies of *Playboy* and other adult magazines, even though they were covered in sleeves and concealed behind counters. Although Dairy Mart offered Stanley a job at the same pay in a store that did not sell these magazines, she sued for the "right" to run a "pornography-free store."[27] Stanley's objections to sexually oriented magazines were based on her Christian beliefs; other employees might well make the same claim based on their adherence to MacDworkinism. For instance, in 1992, with the support of antipornography feminists, some female students at Carleton College filed a complaint under the college's sexual harassment code against the campus bookstore because of its sale of sexually oriented magazines.[28]

If complaints of this sort prevail, sexually explicit material will be available only in specialty, "adult" stores. This development would not only make sexual material much less accessible to many would-be purchasers, but it also would allow the sex police to operate more effectively—there would be just a few retailers in any given locale for them to harass.

Procensorship feminist theories have engendered efforts to ban sexually oriented expression from the entire spectrum of public places—including the streets, sidewalks, and parks that the Supreme Court has deemed "traditional public forums" where free speech should be especially safe.[29]

In 1991, a waitress at Bette's Oceanview Diner in Berkeley, California, refused to serve a journalist who was reading an article in *Playboy* magazine on the ground that this constituted "sexual harassment in the workplace and a threat to women's self-esteem," hence violating Title VII of the 1964 Civil Rights Act. Ironically, the article he happened to be reading was about the Bill of Rights.[30] Suppose a customer had been reading a newsletter from the National Organization for

Women or from Planned Parenthood, and the waitress was a Catholic who believed that abortion is murder. Should she be permitted to deny service to the customer on the ground that this reading material constituted religious harassment, in violation of Title VII's prohibition on religious discrimination in employment? The 1964 Civil Rights Act barred discrimination not only in employment, but also in access to public accommodations.[31] What a setback that this Act should be invoked to deny equal access to public accommodations!

Harassment rules such as those adopted by the Los Angeles and Ventura County Fire Departments essentially assume that free speech need not be protected in workplaces. As previously noted, though, employees should indeed have free speech rights at work. Moreover, the Bette's Oceanview Diner scenario raises an additional reason for protecting expression in workplaces, even beyond a concern for employee free speech: one person's workplace is another person's public accommodation. And in the case of streets, sidewalks, and parks, one person's workplace may be another person's traditional "public forum," where free speech receives the greatest protection. As Cathy Crosson explained in the Feminists for Free Expression brief in the Los Angeles firefighters case:

> [T]he argument that the workplace can be simply excised from free speech protection ignores the reality that *every conceivable location* constitutes the workplace for some group of workers. . . . [E]ven these quintessential public fora [streets and parks] are workplaces for maintenance crews, garbage collectors, postal carriers, and an endless array of other employees. These workers surely have an equal claim to protection from a "hostile work environment." . . . In short, we cannot afford to exclude so pervasive a realm of life as the workplace from First Amendment protection, without rendering free speech a nullity.[32]

Crosson's warnings are realistic. As journalist Mark Schapiro reported in 1994, "In more than a dozen recent cases, allegations of sexual harassment have been used to force removal of artwork from classrooms, municipal buildings, and public art galleries."[33] To add insult to injury, some of these incidents have involved works by women artists and with feminist themes.

One such victim of this misconceived notion of sexual harassment was Brazilian artist Zoravia Bettiol, an outspoken proponent of artistic freedom under that country's former military dictatorship. How sad that her artistic freedom has now been stifled by government officials right here in the United States! In 1993, the Menlo Park, California, City Hall presented an exhibit of Bettiol's woodcuts that featured Greek gods and goddesses and scenes from *Romeo and Juliet*. City officials abruptly terminated the exhibit a few weeks after it opened in response to a female worker's complaint that the nude bodies portrayed in some of these works made her feel "violated." Alluding to the liberal bent of the Menlo Park area, an editorial in the conservative *Washington Times* offered the following sarcastic, but sobering, comment:

> [O]ne wonders what would have happened had [the employee's] protest been made on the grounds of public decency? The response would no doubt have been very different. Now, if someone could please make a case that the "performance art" of [lesbian and feminist artists] Holly Hughes and Karen Finley are a form of sexual harassment, too.[34]

Alas, Hughes's and Finley's work, as well as much other art, *will* apparently be off-limits in the public spaces of Menlo Park from now on. In the wake of the Bettiol imbroglio, Menlo Park City Attorney William McClure said that in the future the city planned to display only "pleasant, non-controversial art," such as "landscapes, holiday pictures, and children's handiwork."[35]

The campus sexual harassment codes that expansively prohibit sexual "looks" and "gestures" would also be extended to public streets and sidewalks if the feminist antipornography activists and their supporters have their way. In an article published in the prestigious *Harvard Law Review* in 1993, Northwestern University law professor Cynthia Grant Bowman urged cities to pass ordinances that would treat sexual harassment on public streets as a misdemeanor, punishable by a fine of up to $250.[36] Her proposed ordinance sweepingly defines punishable harassment as any intrusion upon a woman's attention "in a manner that is unwelcome to [her] with language or action that is explicitly or implicitly sexual." It proscribes "wolf-whistles, sucking noises and cat-calls," as well as comments that range from "Hello baby" to "vulgar" suggestions. Bowman's idea has been incorporated into a proposed sexual harassment bill that California state senator Tom Hayden has sponsored in the California legislature. He commented that her proposal was "on the cutting edge of a problem that needs to be addressed."[37]

The notion that *all* expressions, looks, or gestures that recognize a woman's sexuality are somehow antithetical to her personhood and equality, is *itself* inconsistent with personhood and equality. Surely men can be *sexual* beings at the same time that they are *human* beings with other attributes and potentialities. Why not women too? Marcia Pally, founder and president of Feminists for Free Expression, refutes the notion that viewing women as "sexual objects" necessarily undermines their full humanity:

> As a political condition, objectification is a frightful state. . . . In the realms of art, games, and sex, objectification is one of life's charms. . . . At times, one wants to be appreciated for all one's aspects by those who know one thoroughly. At times, one wants to be desired by total strangers, to grab the attention of a room. . . . Without the distinction between the worlds of money and power and those of art, games, and sex, image-blamers will deny women the thrill of admiration in a bogus bargain for safety. Women will deny themselves admiration in a mistaken ploy for respect. . . . One wants to be the author of one's life, its subject, but one also wants to be the object of irrepressible lust. . . . It cannot be the goal of feminism to eliminate moments during the day when a heterosexual man considers a woman . . . to be sexually desirable. Feminism seeks to expand the roles accessible to women, including the role of voyeur and sexual subject.[38]

Beyond Victorian Views

The growing presumption that a woman is demeaned or harassed by any sexual reference to her, or in her presence, hardly advances women's rights. To the contrary, it has the opposite effect, for three important reasons. First, when women, employers, or campus officials cry "sexual harassment!" at any passing reference to sex, they trivialize the issue, make it a laughingstock, and deflect attention and resources from the serious ongoing problems of gender discrimination in employment and education, including the many instances of quid pro quo harassment and the many instances of intentionally discriminatory, targeted, and persistent sexist conduct, which clearly give rise to legitimate claims of hostile environment harassment.

Second, and more fundamentally, the accelerating presumption that the mere presence of sexual words or pictures in the workplace or on campus is somehow inherently incompatible with women's full and equal participation in those arenas, resurrects the very traditional, and very disempowering, notion that sex is intrinsically demeaning to women.

Under this same rationale, nineteenth-century state laws prohibited "vulgar" and sexually suggestive language from being used in the presence of women; women, along with children, were deemed too fragile to be subjected to such language. Indeed, some of these laws relegated women to a status even below male children. Until recently, a South Carolina state law prohibited "any obscene, profane, indecent, vulgar, suggestive or immoral message" that was addressed to a "woman or woman child." At the behest of women's rights activists, in 1993 the South Carolina Supreme Court ruled:

> Statutes . . . that distinguish between males and females based on "old notions" such as a belief that females should be afforded special protection from "rough talk" because of their perceived "special sensitivities" can no longer withstand equal protection scrutiny.[39]

Likewise, in 1991, in a suit brought by the ACLU, a Michigan judge struck down that state's sixty-year-old law prohibiting the use of "indecent, immoral, obscene, vulgar or insulting language" in the presence of women or children. While the judge held that the law unconstitutionally infringed on free speech, Susan Fall, the ACLU attorney who challenged the law, noted that it was also a "discriminatory, paternalistic approach to protecting women."[40] Once again, suppression of sexual expression retarded, rather than advanced, gender equality.

Nineteenth- and early-twentieth-century judicial rulings—previous incarnations of the procensorship feminists' current view that women need to be protected from sexually oriented language—asserted that, in the words of former Supreme Court justice Joseph Bradley, women's "natural and proper timidity and delicacy" not only disabled them from entering into contracts, but also made them unfit "for many of the occupations of civil life."[41] In ruling that states could bar women from practicing law or serving on juries, for example, judges expressly cited the need to "protect" women from vulgar or sexual language. As recently as 1949, the Arkansas Supreme Court rejected a challenge to a statute that allowed women to serve on juries only if they specifically volunteered, on the ground that "[c]riminal court trials often involve testimony of the foulest kind, and . . . the use of filthy and loath-some words, references to intimate sex relationships, and other elements that would prove . . . degrading to a lady."[42]

Now procensorship feminists seem determined to reinstate such misguided protectionism through an overly expansive concept of sexual harassment. As Wayne State University law professor Kingsley Browne has commented: "The assumption that women as a group may be more offended by profanity than men as a group seems like just the sort of stereotype that Title VII was intended to erase."[43]

Third, procensorship feminists' concepts of sexual harassment subvert women's rights by making it harder for women to get jobs and to succeed in those jobs. The antipornography feminists seek to protect women from the rigors of the marketplace of ideas; numerous laws enacted during the nineteenth and early twentieth centuries sought to protect women from the rigors of the economic marketplace by limiting their hours and days of work, and the tasks that they would be allowed to perform on the job. Upholding one such piece of legislation, a 1908 Supreme Court decision compared women to children in their purported need for special government protection.[44] As a later Supreme Court recognized, though, in a 1973 decision that struck down a law reflecting such gender-based, ultimately incapacitating stereotypes, these allegedly protective laws "reflected an attitude of romantic paternalism that put women not on a pedestal, but in a cage."[45] (Ruth Bader Ginsburg, then director of the ACLU Women's Rights Project, successfully argued this case.)

Any doctrine resting upon the incomparability of women and men cannot be confined to circumstances that may at first appear "beneficial" to women; the principle can always then be used to "justify" denying rights to women. By invoking women's special reproductive role, some employers have excluded women from high-paying jobs that

involve exposure to certain substances that might impair their potential fetuses, even if the women do not intend to have children, and even
though there is evidence that these substances could damage the male
reproductive functions as well.

In occupations and professions that depend heavily on mentor relationships, women are being penalized, since the men who predominate
in the upper echelons are deterred from mentoring them by exaggerated concepts of sexual harassment; on campus, many female students
say they are especially hard-hit by this problem. I know from my own
involvement in professional legal organizations that many female
lawyers believe that, because of hyperbolic harassment charges, they
are being denied travel, social, and other opportunities for informal
interaction with male partners and clients that would help them to rise
to leadership positions at their firms.

Pittsburgh restaurateur Sarah J. McCarthy has said that the overly
broad concept of sexual harassment as all speech with sexual connotations has made even her, an avowed feminist, "fearful of hiring women."
Speaking both as the owner of a restaurant and bar who makes many
hiring decisions, and as a longtime women's rights advocate, McCarthy
berated proponents of the MacDworkinite sexual harassment concept:

> You do women a disservice. . . . You have made us ladies again. . . . [Y]ou
> are frightening managers into hiring men over women. . . . You have
> installed a double pane of glass on the glass ceiling. . . . Men and women
> who wanted to work shoulder to shoulder with you are now looking over
> their shoulders. You have made women into china dolls. . . . We women
> are not as delicate and powerless as you think. We do not want victim
> status in the workplace. Don't try to foist it on us.[46]

As the preceding discussion makes clear, in recent years the feminist
procensorship faction has enjoyed growing influence on many fronts in
the escalating war against sexual expression. It is past time to turn back
the troops that are trampling freedom of sexual speech. In the remainder of this book, I elaborate on the critical weaknesses in the feminist
procensorship analysis, beginning with its fatally flawed foundation:
simplistic demonization of sexual expression.

"Different Strokes for Different Folks"

The Panoply of Pornographic Imagination

I do not know what has caused MacKinnon to become, and, more surprisingly, to remain, so obsessed with pornography, and so zealous for censorship. But let us not sacrifice our civil liberties on the altar of her obsession.

—Judge Richard Posner

U.S. Court of Appeals for the Seventh Circuit[1]

In our pervasively sexist society, it should be expected that some expression in every genre, including sexually explicit speech, may convey, at least to some viewers, ideas about women (and men) that are antithetical to gender equality. By heightening public awareness of this dimension of some sexually oriented speech, the feminist antipornography movement has had a valuable educational impact. The American Civil Liberties Union's brief in the Indianapolis case lauded Dworkin, MacKinnon, and their allies for this contribution:

By emphasizing the degree to which sexually explicit speech glorifying humiliation and violence is fundamentally inconsistent with our national commitment to equality, proponents of the Indianapolis ordinance contribute to public understanding of the need to eradicate sex discrimination and violence against women from American life.[2]

What distinguishes the procensorship faction from other feminists, however, is its obsessive, oversimplified demonization of sexually explicit expression. This pornocentric tunnel vision distorts the reality of sexist imagery in our society in two important ways.

First, it ignores the many other words and images that reflect women's second-class status in our society, many of which are no doubt more important and influential because of their mainstream status. Based on her recent comprehensive survey of the views of women's sexuality and gender roles that are purveyed in nonpornographic media, New York Law School professor Carlin Meyer has concluded that the mainstream media—television, film, advertising, music, art, and popular literature—have a far greater impact in shaping these views than does pornography. As she explains, not only do we encounter mainstream language and imagery more often and at earlier ages than we do most sexual representation, but also, because mainstream imagery is ordinary and everyday, "it more powerfully convinces us that it depicts the world as it is or ought to be."[3]

Even if we could wave a magic wand and eliminate all sexually explicit sexist images from our culture, our social environment would still be pervaded by sexist and violent images. Thus, to end the purported "cause" of misogynistic discrimination and violence, we would have to ban virtually all communications. (And what, then, could be done to the sexist and violent *thought* that "caused" the communications?)

Second, the feminist antipornography movement's insistence that *all* pornography conveys misogynistic messages to *all* viewers—or at least to all male viewers—ignores the complex, variegated nature of sexually explicit expression and the subjective, nuanced nature of any viewer's interpretation of such expression. To categorically condemn all sexual expression is as inane as categorically condemning all nonsexual expression or all expression in any other category, as if responses to anything were uniform, rather than totally individualized and unique.

Those who pillory all sexually explicit expression promote another common misconception—that it appeals only to men, and that women, or at least feminists, find nothing of any redeeming value in such expression. These generalizations belie reality. In fact, many who categorically castigate sexually explicit magazines and films as misogynistic are unfamiliar with these materials, perhaps assuming that the overtly violent, sexist samples that are selectively presented in displays and slide shows mounted by feminist antipornography groups are typical. But the opposite is true, as writer Sallie Tisdale has concluded from her extensive viewing of commercial erotica: "Women who have seen little pornography seem to assume that the images in most films are primarily, obsessively, ones of rape. I find the opposite theme in American films: that of an adolescent rut, both male and female. Its obsession is virility, endurance, lust."[4] Consistent with Tisdale's account, surveys indicate that depictions of violent sexual encounters—rape or sadomasochism—account for only 3 to 8 percent of commercially available erotica.[5]

Lisa Palac, then editor of *Future Sex* magazine, recounted in a 1994 *Esquire* magazine interview how she had converted from a devout disciple of Catharine MacKinnon to an avid enjoyer of pornography simply by actually looking at some examples of this hitherto despised, but unseen, genre. Now, far from preaching against the perils of pornography, Palac proselytizes for the pleasures it can provide:

> When I was at the University of Minnesota in 1983, where Catharine MacKinnon taught in the law school, I was a devoted follower of hers and a real antiporn feminist. . . . One day at my boyfriend's house I opened his closet to get a sweater and *hundreds* of hardcore-porn magazines came tumbling out. I was disgusted, livid. I wanted him to burn them in a cleansing bonfire. . . . But a couple of days later he said, "Just watch one video, and if you still feel the same way, I'll get rid of them all." We watched *Sleepless Nights,* and it sparked some honest dialogue—I told him my "sick" sexual fantasies, and we rented more movies. The watershed event was when I was able to watch a movie—*Aerobisex Girls*— by myself and get so turned on I had to masturbate right away. Then I wanted to tell everyone how to use pornography. . . .[6]

The fact that many women find much that excites or otherwise pleases them in commercial erotica is indicated by their large and growing share of the burgeoning market for such imagery. Women, either singly or as part of a couple, constitute more than 40 percent of the adult videotape rental audience; to put this number in perspective, it should be noted that 410 million adult videos were rented in 1991 alone, and that adult video sales and rentals have soared since then.[7] In 1987 two social scientists conducting a survey of over 26,000 female readers of *Redbook* magazine found that nearly half the respondents said they regularly watch pornographic films.[8]

Women also make up a growing portion of those who produce erotic materials. Increasing numbers of women writers, filmmakers, and magazine editors have been producing sexually explicit materials, many expressly aimed at a female audience. These include Marianna Beck, copublisher of *Libido: The Journal of Sex and Sensibility*; author Susie Bright, whose many writings include the "Cliterati" column in the *San Francisco Review of Books* and three books entitled *Herotica*, annual collections of erotic writings by and for women; filmmaker Candida Royalle, who heads Femme Productions; the Kensington Ladies Erotic Society, which has published anthologies of women's erotica; and the editors of *Bad Attitude* and *On Our Backs*, two lesbian feminist erotic magazines. In the words of Marianna Beck, who estimates that *Libido*'s readership is 40 percent female, "We're . . . depicting sex as not just something that men engage in actively while the woman somehow endures while thinking of Catherine [*sic*] MacKinnon."[9]

Pornography also has literary value. In "The Pornographic Imagination," a 1967 essay, Susan Sontag analyzes and debunks the various assumptions underlying the view that pornography can be categorically distinguished from "authentic literature":

> The ratio of authentic literature to trash in pornography may be somewhat lower than the ratio of novels of genuine literary merit to the entire volume of subliterary fiction produced for mass taste. But I doubt that it's any lower than, for instance, that of another somewhat shady subgenre with a few first-rate books to its credit, science fiction. (As literary forms, pornography and science fiction resemble each other in several interesting ways.) Anyway, the quantitative measure supplies a trivial standard. Relatively uncommon as they may be, there are writings which it seems reasonable to call pornographic—assuming that the stale label has any use at all—which, at the same time, cannot be refused accreditation as serious literature.[10]

Procensorship feminists argue that they would ban only sexual materials that are violent or subordinating. But no consensus is possible concerning which pornography can be described with such reductionist, subjective labels. By ascribing to any sexually oriented work one meaning only, and by imposing that construct on the rest of us, the feminist antipornography movement is profoundly antithetical to individualism, denying autonomy both to all the people who create expressive works and to all the people who see their works.

As writer Sallie Tisdale has stated:

> Always, the [feminist] censors are concerned with how men *act* and how women are portrayed. Women cannot make free sexual choices in that world; they are too oppressed to know that only oppression could lead them to sell sex. And I, watching, am either too oppressed to know the harm that my watching has done to my sisters . . . or else I have become the Man. And it is the Man in me who watches and is aroused. (Shame.) What a misogynistic worldview this is, this claim that women who make such choices cannot be making free choices at all. . . . Feminists against pornography have done a sad and awful thing: *They* have made women into objects.[11]

The antipornography feminists rigidly presume that all viewers, or at least all male viewers, will interpret sexual speech as conveying misogynistic messages. But many other feminists view much such speech as conveying to many viewers messages that are at worst ambiguous and at best positive. Ambiguous and positive interpretations apply to the full range of sexual speech, including violent imagery and imagery that might well be labeled "subordinating" or "degrading," such as rape scenes and scenes dramatizing the so-called rape myth—namely, that women want to be raped. As I show below, women have found affirmations of eroticism and empowerment in all such images, and feminist women have seen them as exploring such pro-feminist themes as liberation from conventional sexual conduct and from traditional gender roles.

Pornography and Poststructuralism

The concept that no text or image has any objective, fixed meaning, but rather has a different meaning for each member of its audience, is an integral aspect of the poststructuralist, or deconstructionist, movement that has been so influential in the humanities and social sciences in recent years. Professor Thelma McCormack, director of the Centre for Feminist

Research at York University, notes that, under the influence of poststructuralism, "pornography began to slip quietly away as a younger generation of feminist literary critics deconstructed it, scooping out its literal meanings and leaving behind an empty shell with no fixed meaning."[12]

The reductionist approach of the procensorship feminists denies the existence of ambiguity, subtlety, and irony in the interactions between all individuals and a text or image. It overlooks the boundary between fantasy, imagination, and ideas, on one hand, and behavior, on the other. As writer Pete Hamill remarked, "In a way, the work of MacKinnon and Dworkin is some of the saddest writing I've ever read. . . . There is no fantasy or magic."[13]

The feminist antipornography faction disavows individual control over thoughts and actions, assuming that viewers of pornography will react to it in a simplistic, "monkey-see, monkey-do" fashion. This debased view of humanity is invoked to justify legal controls. Procensorship feminists "reject the distinction between thought and deed which is both the cornerstone of liberal democracy and the foundation of a humanistic model of human nature," writes Thelma McCormack. Elaborating on their error, she explains:

> Typically, [Dworkin and MacKinnon] disregard the work of social psychologists for whom the relationship between attitudes and behaviour, between what we think and what we do is the problematic. According to social psychologists, the relationship is . . . largely indeterminate; there is no way of specifying what the behavioral outcomes are of specific attitudes, especially when we live in a world of contradictory messages. . . .
>
> Our distinctively human capacity is to think, select, interpret and reinterpret content, to read texts on different levels and in different ways. The result is a broad spectrum of possible attitudes which loop back to shape how we read future texts. . . .
>
> Thus, when Dworkin-MacKinnon collapse the distinction between dream and deed, fantasy and act, thought and behavior they construct a Skinnerian model of human nature which, in turn, justifies an elaborate system of social control.[14]

The individualized interaction that viewers have with imagery and words in general certainly exists when the imagery and words concern sexual themes in particular. Just as sexuality and sexual relationships are themselves inherently individualized, tied to the most intimate, personal aspects of each human being's pysche and life, so one's interpretations of and reactions to sexually explicit expression are uniquely subjective and individualized. As observed by feminists Lisa Duggan, Nan Hunter, and Carole Vance:

> To some, *any* graphic sexual act violates women's dignity and therefore subordinates them. To others, consensual heterosexual lovemaking within the boundaries of procreation and marriage is acceptable, but heterosexual acts that do not have reproduction as their aim lower women's status and hence subordinate them. Still others accept a wide range of nonprocreative, perhaps even nonmarital, heterosexuality but draw the line at lesbian sex, which they view as degrading.[15]

An image that one woman views as misogynistic discrimination may for another reaffirm her desires and her equality; an image that one woman views as subordinating, another may view as liberating. Based on extensive discussions of sexual imagery with other women, as part of a sex and history study group, Columbia University anthropologist Carole Vance has formulated what she dubs "Vance's One-Third Rule": "Show any personally favored erotic image to a group of women, and one-third will find it disgusting, one-third will find it ridiculous, and one-third will find it hot."[16]

A 1992 editorial cartoon by Mike Mereu well captured the same idea by showing three different people's reactions as they all look at a sculpture of a naked female torso in an art museum; the thought-bubbles above each of their heads reveal the following responses, in order: "SMUT!," "*Art!*," and "An insult to headless quadruple amputees."

Life does indeed imitate art—or, depending on your perspective, smut or insults. Two years after the Mereu cartoon was published, it seemed to serve as the script for a real-life scenario, described as follows in the April 16, 1994, *San Francisco Chronicle*:

> Pulitzer-Prize-winning author Alice Walker was pleased to be named a "state treasure" by Governor Wilson, until she got a glimpse of the gilded statuette of a naked female torso that went with the prestigious award.

The hefty art piece, nearly a foot high, features the headless and limb-
less body of a woman mounted on a bronze base.

Walker's most recent work is "Warrior Marks," a film and companion book of the same title on female genital mutilation.

"Imagine my horror when, after four years of thinking about the mutilation of women, I was presented with a decapitated, armless, legless woman,
on which my name hung from a chain," said Walker earlier this week.

"Though these mutilated figures are prized by museums and considered 'art' by some, the message they deliver is of domination, violence
and destruction," she said.[17]

And, in the never-ending spiral of one person's art being another's
degradation or dirt, Walker's own work—while recognized as art by
those who awarded her the Pulitzer Prize and many others—has itself
been decried as pornographic and degrading. Even before she was presented with the sculpture she found so offensive, Walker had already
had hesitations about accepting the California "state treasure" award,
because California education officials had treated two of her own works
as offensive. In 1993, in response to complaints from religious conservatives, state educators had pulled two of Walker's stories from a pool of
writings used in state reading tests of public school students. (Following an ACLU protest, on behalf of Walker and various writers' groups,
the state restored Walker's stories to the testing pool.)[18]

Commenting on these two incidents, Los Angeles writer David Link
noted that the statue that Walker found so revolting—and which would
be considered taboo pornography under the MacDworkin law—"was
designed by one of the most gifted sculptors of our time, Robert Graham," whose work is in museums worldwide. Observing that "[t]he
paradox of Walker's offended sensibilities is breathtaking," Link underscored why we must never allow expression to be stifled—as it is under
antiobscenity and antipornography laws alike—because it is offensive
to someone's sensibilities: "Offense is a purely subjective experience, an
entirely solipsistic exercise."[19]

In 1993, one group of lesbian feminists sought to suppress the magazine
of another group of lesbian feminists because the first group saw the publication's cover photograph of a woman as degrading, whereas the second
saw it as empowering. The magazine in question was the May-June 1993

issue of *On Our Backs,* a San Francisco–based lesbian erotic magazine. The cover photograph showed model Dawn Wan, an Asian- American woman, fully covered in body paint portraying flames, with images of fire all around her. The caption says, "Dawn Wan in Flames."

A Seattle organization, Dykes Against Porn (DAP), ripped the covers off copies of this magazine in bookstores, spray painted protest messages on the sidewalks and walls of bookstores that carried it, and picketed outside one of the bookstores. Spokeswomen for DAP explained that they saw the Wan photograph as racist and as promoting violence against Asian women. A leader of the demonstration outside Red and Black Books—a leftist bookstore collective that specializes in multicultural and politically progressive titles—shouted: "*On Our Backs* glorifies and promotes violence against Asian women; what it basically says is that white dykes should be getting off on setting Asian girls on fire."[20]

Other feminists had very different, less literal, interpretations of the Wan photograph. Wan herself, who had had the idea for the body paint and the photograph, expressed "shock" that her choice was construed as racist and sexist, stressing that she had defined for herself how she wanted to look.[21] When informed that Wan had taken the lead in constructing this image, a DAP spokeswoman displayed the disrespect that procensorship feminists typically show toward anyone who chooses to pose for or look at images of which they disapprove: "I think she's a fucking sellout, and that's all I have to say about it."[22]

The editors of *On Our Backs* explained the positive associations that inspired the Wan cover photograph:

> When stripper Dawn Wan danced at the [*On Our Backs*] Christmas party last year, her body painted in flames, the room got so hot we decided that not sharing the heat with our readers would constitute cruel and unusual punishment. When she's all painted, says Dawn, she feels like she's in a wet suit. . . .[23]

And then–managing editor Heather Findlay explained her reaction to the end result:

> I *liked* how [the cover] portrayed an Asian-American woman complete with attitude and sexual assertiveness—a departure, in my opinion,

from the stereotype of the passive "oriental" lady—so I didn't feel we had any apologies to make to anyone, especially to Dawn, who came up with the cover concept herself.[24]

In the same spirit, Christine Wenz, editor of the Seattle-based *Stranger* magazine, said that she saw the photograph and its caption as "a metaphor for [Wan's] being really hot and turned on."[25]

Similarly, a letter to *Seattle Gay News* commented: "The woman looks empowered, for she has her head high with her hands on her hips. It is art! We interpret the fire-woman as a goddess, or a flame nymph. She is beautiful and strong."[26]

Antipornography feminists contend that women have historically and consistently been subjugated in the realm of sexuality, yet that view is contestable. In her book *Swept Away,* sex researcher Carol Cassell writes: "Sex has historically been a commodity. It's a valuable source of power. . . . Sexual power is . . . the female commodity."[27] In the same vein, author Nancy Friday has said that "women have always derived power from withholding sex."[28] Echoes former porn star Veronica Vera: "A dominant patriarchy? Wake up folks. . . . [A]s any good whore can tell you, it never existed in the bedroom."[29]

Even erotica that superficially depicts female subjugation can be understood as acknowledging, but seeking to overturn, women's greater power in the sexual arena and as advocating more equalized male-female sexual relationships. So, images that on their surface portray a sexually subordinate female may be interpreted as protesting *any* inequality in the sexual domain. Thus, men's rights activist Jack Kammer contends, "Ms. MacKinnon's efforts to suppress men's pictorial fantasies of reversing their sexual subjugation can be supported only by those who fail to acknowledge women's control of sex or by those who seek to preserve it."[30]

Wide-Ranging Reactions to Rape Scenes

Scenes of rape, which some viewers might well understand as showing a woman's subordination, nevertheless may be viewed by others, including some feminist women, very differently. For some women, scenes that would be real-life nightmares could be fantasy-life daydreams. Anaï's Nin's diary reveals her erotic excitement in fantasizing about violent, forced sex:

> Sometimes in the street, or in a cafe, I am hypnotized by the "pimp" face of a man, by a big workman with knee-high boots, by a brutal criminal head. I feel a sensual tremor of fear, an obscure attraction. The female in me trembles and is fascinated. . . . A desire to feel the brutality of a man, the force which can violate? To be violated is perhaps a need in women, a secret erotic need.[31]

As noted by feminist artist and writer Sara Diamond:

> [M]any women . . . fantasize about being ravished. It is not surprising that women daydream about being uncontrollably desired in a culture in which our value as human beings is based on our attractiveness, and in which we are constantly prevented from acting out our desires. If we fantasize a partner taking complete control of a sexual encounter, then we are absolved from responsibility for our abandoned behavior. In this way we can mentally break sexual taboos that still remain in place in practice.[32]

The impossibility of proscribing all overtly violent, sexist depictions, or of agreeing on which overtly violent, sexist depictions should be banned, is illustrated by the fierce debates that have swirled around *Swept Away*, Lina Wertmuller's provocative and artistically acclaimed 1975 film, released at precisely the historical moment when the then–newly revived women's movement had focused on rape and the rape myth (that women really want to be raped) as major symbols and instruments of women's oppression. With a story line that, on its surface, was a classic embodiment of the rape myth, the film set off an avalanche of controversy. *Swept Away* (its full title is *Swept Away by an Unusual Destiny in the Blue Sea of August*) would be a prime target for censorship under the MacKinnon-Dworkin model law. Yet consideration of both its story and the manifold reactions to it, including among feminists, underscores the hopelessly simplistic and surface-obsessed nature of the MacDworkin definition—and of any definition—of "sexually incorrect" expression.

The heroine of *Swept Away* is a wealthy socialite, haughty in general but particularly arrogant and condescending in her treatment of the members of the crew on her yacht. She taunts them with her sexual unattainability, prancing around in a tiny bikini while alternately completely ignoring them or treating them as near-animals or near-slaves—in either case, not as men who could possibly have any sexual response to her. After she is marooned on an uninhabited island with one of her former crew members, the tables are turned, as she becomes completely dependent on him, his virtual slave. He rapes her, beats her, and abuses her verbally. Nevertheless, she develops not only passion but also love for him.

Some feminists denounced *Swept Away* as a classic rape myth that allegedly perpetuated violence and discrimination against women. Others praised Wertmuller for spotlighting and exploding the false assumptions that have anchored women's second-class citizenship. Some thought the film propounded traditional and demeaning stereotypes about women's sexuality. Others thought it explored novel, liberating, alternative views. Some believed it celebrated the triumph of sexism. Others believed it celebrated the downfall of classism. Some considered it a glorification of violence. Others considered it a condemnation of violence. Some understood the film literally. Others viewed it symbolically. Some interpreted it straightforwardly; others construed it ironically. Some found its sex scenes aesthetically revolting; others disagreed. Some were turned off; others were turned on.

And so forth. The countless varying, even contradictory, reactions that the film engendered among its viewers—including its female, feminist viewers—simply mirrored the wonderfully infinite variety in the human mind, imagination, and emotions.

Degradation or Delight (or Both)

The inescapably individualized, and hence wildly divergent, interpretations that all persons bring to all sexual expression can be illustrated further by considering another type of such expression that, along with rape scenes, is commonly cited as a paradigmatic example of the subordinating imagery that would be banned under the antipornography feminist regime: the "come shot," in which a man ejaculates on a woman's body. In many such scenes, the woman then smears the sperm over her body and licks it. Although procensorship feminists routinely cite these as archetypal images of female degradation, this characterization is as oversimplified as every other aspect of their approach to sexual expression.

Canadian writer Wendy McElroy has suggested other interpretations of these scenes. She notes that makers of commercial erotic films often insert "come shots" simply to prove that the male *did* ejaculate, that he was "into" the sex. Likewise, the woman's response of spreading the sperm over her body or tasting it would simply demonstrate that she, too, was fully, enthusiastically involved in the sexual encounter.[33]

Many women viewers may be particularly interested in seeing come shots because men's ejaculations are usually hidden from them, occuring inside the woman's own body. As McElroy observes, to such women, the sight of male ejaculation "is as elusive as a glimpse of breast or lace panty must be to a pubescent boy. In this context, the come-shot can be interpreted in an almost romantic way: the woman wishes to share, as much as possible, in her lover's orgasm."[34]

In the introduction to *Perspectives on Pornography: Sexuality in Film and Literature,* Gary Day offers a more Freudian analysis of the come shot, which construes it as conveying pro-female messages:

> A feminist interpretation of this might be that it shows the subordination of a woman to a man's pleasure, thereby presenting him in a dominant role. However, if . . . pornography in part involves a realization of the incestuous phantasy, then the "come" shot takes on a very different meaning. For what the man does in ejaculating over the woman is in a sense to replicate the role of the mother giving milk to the infant. . . . If this analysis is accepted, then pornography does not show, as some feminists have claimed, a hatred of women but rather a desire to become like them.[35]

Accept these interpretations or don't, but my point is that they prove that when we look at sexually explicit depictions alleged to be misogynistic, violent, and subordinating—the quintessential examples of what procensorship feminists label as the pornography that should be banned—diverse interpretations are possible; *no* sexual imagery can be given one universal meaning. Each individual must make her—or his—own choices about what to read or view, and how to understand and respond to the material. To accept the MacDworkinite concept of "subordinating" sexual imagery would be, as Judge Richard Posner observed (see the epigraph at the beginning of this chapter), to elevate the "obsession" of some women above all other women's—and men's—civil liberties.[36] The procensorship feminist faction posits a false choice between free speech and women's equality. The true choice is between civil liberty and no liberty.

Do As They Say, Not As They Do

Procensorship feminists perforce must concede the oversimplified nature of their rhetoric denouncing the inherent dangers supposedly caused by exposure to pornography; their own experience proves that some individuals may survive exposure to pornography without any adverse impact on their attitudes and behavior toward women. Probably very few men have examined the volume of violent, misogynistic pornography with the attention that Dworkin, MacKinnon, and other procensorship advocates have lavished upon it. Katie Roiphe reports that when MacKinnon lectured at Princeton University in 1992, she "assure[d] the audience that she's seen more porn than any of us."[37] As Pete Hamill wrote:

> MacKinnon and Dworkin ... [have] obviously pored over more pornography than the ordinary man sees in a lifetime. ... If human beings are so weak and pornography so powerful, why aren't MacKinnon and Dworkin playing the Krafft-Ebing Music Hall with the rest of the perverts?[38]

Dworkin, MacKinnon, and their allies still maintain respect for women's equality, as they envision it, and for women's safety. Their proposed censorship regime thus is predicated on a double standard: that *they* can withstand the allegedly pernicious influence of exposure to pornography, but *others* cannot.

This double standard is typical of censorship advocates generally. Noting that "those who would suppress pornography often betray a mighty fascination with the subject of their condemnation," Marjorie Heins, director of the American Civil Liberties Union's Arts Censorship Project, pointed out:

> In 1990, Donald Wildmon's American Family Association [AFA] reproduced portions of artworks that it viewed as scandalously homoerotic, then mailed them by the truckload to its membership list, with a fund appeal letter noting that if contributions were sent, the AFA would supply more of this awful stuff. A 1992 Christian Coalition newsletter described in juicy detail a lesbian film that it simultaneously excoriated the NEA for having funded.[39]

Likewise, in a widely publicized television ad during his 1992 bid for the Republican Presidential nomination, Pat Buchanan's voice lambasted the NEA's funding of "filthy and blasphemous art, too shocking to show," while images from that very same, assertedly too-shocking art were simultaneously rolling across the screen! (The NEA-funded art that was pilloried in this case, true to the common pattern described in chapter 4, explored themes concerning sexual and racial minorities; it was a documentary film called *Tongues Untied,* about African-American gay men.)[40]

One of the most recent examples of crusaders against sexually explicit speech themselves perusing—and, moreover, purveying—such materials is the Meese Pornography Commission. Its voluminous report contained so many vivid descriptions of the sexual materials it ostensibly condemned that *Newsweek* labeled it "the Attorney General's dirty book."[41] Cardozo Law School professor Edward de Grazia reported that more than 300 of the report's 1,976 pages—a full 15 percent—were dedicated to "detailed descriptions of the plots, images, and ideas disseminated by 725 books, 2,325 magazines, and 2,370 films of the hard-core pornographic type."[42] No wonder "sexpert" Susie Bright exclaimed that she "came three times" while reading the Meese Commission Report![43]

In his thorough study of pornography in modern culture, Fordham University professor Walter Kendrick described the Meese Commission's report as "blatantly pornographic":

[T]he Commission provided three hundred pages of summaries and descriptions, some with dialogue: "I want to taste your cum. I want you to come in my mouth. I want to feel your hot cum squirt in my mouth," and much, much more in the same vein. No doubt this established a landmark in the history of government publications.[44]

Mirroring the Meese Commission in this respect, as in so many others, MacKinnon and Dworkin have published and distributed graphic, sexually explicit descriptions that fall squarely within their own definition of pornography, because it depicts the "subordination" of women. As Carole Vance has commented:

Ironically, in a culture where it was increasingly costly for feminists to present erotic images or speak in an erotic language, only the antipornography movement could publicly revel in the most graphic sexual images and lurid sexual language, all acceptable because their purpose was condemnation.[45]

Here, for example, is the opening passage of MacKinnon's 1993 book *Only Words*:

Imagine that for hundreds of years your most formative traumas, your daily suffering and pain, the abuse you live through, the terror you live with, are unspeakable—not the basis of literature. You grow up with your father holding you down and covering your mouth so another man can make a horrible searing pain between your legs. When you are older, your husband ties you to the bed and drips hot wax on your nipples and brings in other men to watch and makes you smile through it. Your doctor will not give you drugs he has addicted you to unless you suck his penis.[46]

As political scientist Walter Berns commented about MacKinnon: "Obsessed with pornography, yes, but does she really hate it? . . . As she puts it [in *Only Words*], talking sex is having sex, and the fact is, Catharine MacKinnon talks a lot of sex. She talks sex right off and never lets up. And some sex!"[47]

Dworkin's writings, too, are laced with passages that would violate her own concept of prohibited pornography. In a survey conducted by University of Pennsylvania professor James Lindgren, 63 percent of the respondents found that Dworkin's 1991 novel *Mercy* is "pornographic" under the criteria she and MacKinnon advocate.[48] Likewise, Dworkin's 1987 novel *Ice and Fire* contains much pornographic prose, as indicated by the following samplings:

She is lean and tough. She fucks like a gang of boys. . . . She fucks everyone eventually, with perfect simplicity and grace. She is a rough fuck. She grinds her hips in. She pushes her fingers in. She tears around inside. She is all muscle and jagged bones. She thrusts her hips so hard you can't remember who she is or how many of her there are. The first time she tore me apart. I bled and bled.

*   *   *

We are on the beach. Mister wants some sex. N whispers to me that she can't fuck, she is bleeding again. All summer she has this mysterious bleeding. . . . [S]he is bleeding, not menstruating, hemorrhaging; she can't be fucked. She and I make love for him on the beach. It is not enough. He is wired, tense, has spasms of violence, shows us his knife. N holds me down from behind, both arms. . . . She grins ear to ear. I try to get loose watching her grin. She is strong and I can't. She holds me down. He pulls down his pants. He fucks me.

*   *   *

He tears into me. He bites my clitoris and bites it and bites it until I wish I was dead. He fucks. He bites my clitoris more, over and over, for hours, I want to die. The pain is shooting through my brain. I am chewed and bitten and maimed. I am bleeding. He leaves. I hurt so bad I can't even crawl.

*   *   *

I teach him not to be afraid of causing pain. Not to be afraid of hurting me. . . . I teach him not to be afraid of piss and shit, human dirt. . . . I scratch, I bite, I tie him up, I hit him with my hand open, with my fist, with belts: he gets hard. He does each thing back to me. . . . I ended up cowering, caged, catatonic. . . . I wanted to help: but this was a hurricane of hate and rage let loose: I wanted to help: I saved him: not impotent, not suicidal, he beat me until I was a heap of collapsed bone, comatose, torn, bleeding, bruised so bad, so hard: how it will end, I don't know.[49]

With passages like these, it is hardly surprising that two of Dworkin's books have been seized at the Canadian border, where customs inspectors determined that they violated the Canadian version of the MacDworkin antipornography law.[50]

Simultaneously condemning pornography while engaging in pornographic expression themselves, procensorship advocates, from the Meese Commission members to Catharine MacKinnon, simply mirror the hypocrisy of much of the general public regarding sexually explicit material. In 1989, Americans bought 9 million copies of *Playboy, Penthouse,* and *Hustler* magazines *each month.*[51] Pornographic videos are widely credited with helping to make the VCR a household appliance; recent surveys indicate that "adult videos" constitute 30 percent of all rentals; adult video sales and rentals in general-interest video stores alone soared 75 percent between 1991 and 1993, when they reached $2.1 billion (adult-only outlets are estimated to take in hundreds of millions of dollars more).[52]

Now sexual words and images are burgeoning on the newer communications frontiers, in cyberspace, on computers.[53] Indeed, the human desire for sexually oriented words and images is so consistently strong that some experts see it as a major motivating factor behind the development and usage of all new communications media, throughout history. As John Tierney noted in a 1994 *New York Times* article aptly entitled "Porn, the Low-Slung Engine of Progress": "Sometimes the erotic has been a force driving technological innovation; virtually always, from Stone Age sculpture to computer bulletin boards, it has been one of the first uses for a new medium."[54]

In a 1994 interview, MacKinnon described the pornography business as a $10 billion annual enterprise,[55] and that figure is corroborated by the Justice Department.[56] This number underscores the fact that many members of the American public enjoy sexual materials. Yet public opinion surveys regarding such works indicate ambivalent attitudes; most people believe it's okay for People Like Us to see this material, just as long as we keep it away from People Like Them. In her essay "The Pornographic Imagination," Susan Sontag criticizes "this chronic mutual suspicion of our neighbor's capacities" to view sexual materials without sociopathic effects, because it "suggest[s], in effect, a hierarchy of competence with respect to human consciousness."[57]

In an important 1971 free speech decision (overturning the defendant's breach-of-peace conviction for wearing a jacket that said on its back, "Fuck the draft"), Supreme Court Justice John Marshall Harlan wrote, "One man's vulgarity is another man's lyric."[58] In the context of the feminist debate about pornography, Justice Harlan's famous epigram could be paraphrased as: "One woman's subordinating scene is another woman's liberating scene."

When writer Ntozake Shange posed for this photograph that appeared on the cover of *Poets & Writers* magazine, some readers complained that the publication was degenerating into a "flesh magazine." During a *Ms.* Magazine panel discussion on pornography in 1994, Shange described the incident, exclaiming, "Bare shoulders are exploitation now?" Andrea Dworkin responded, "It's very hard to look at a picture of a woman's body and not see it with the perception that her body is being exploited." [© ADÁL, 1993]

This ad for *Libido: The Journal of Sex and Sensibility*, copublished by Marianna Beck and Jack Hafferkamp, has been denounced as pornographic, and some magazines, including *The Atlantic Monthly*, have refused to run it (it has appeared in *Harper's* and *The Nation*). The photograph is of Beck herself, and the other hands are those of Hafferkamp (who is Beck's life partner, as well as her business partner) and the magazine's female art director. [Photograph by Jo Deitz]

In 1992, Pennsylvania State University officials removed a reproduction of the celebrated *Nude Maja* by Spanish painter Francisco de Goya from a classroom wall, and banished it from classrooms altogether, following professor Nancy Stumhofer's complaint that it made her and her female students "uncomfortable." In an effort to explain her stance to her faculty colleagues, Stumhofer circulated excerpts from a book that analyzes representations of the female figure as the eternal object of the male gaze. Because the circulated materials included pictures of nude women, two men on campus then filed a sexual harassment complaint against Stumhofer. [Prado, Madrid, Spain; courtesy Alinari/Art Resource, New York]

(*Opposite*) *Aphrodite* was included in an exhibit of woodcuts by Brazilian artist Zoravia Bettiol, which were on display in the Menlo Park, California, City Hall in 1993 until city officials shut down the exhibit in response to a female employee's complaint that the nude bodies portrayed in some of these works made her feel "violated." Bettiol, who was an outspoken proponent of artistic freedom under Brazil's former military dictatorship, has sued Menlo Park for violating her First Amendment rights. [Color woodcut, 51 × 81 cm, from Olympic God Series, 80 images by Zoravia Bettiol, 1976]

The image of Veronica Vera in an Indian temple appears in her video *Portrait of a Sexual Evolutionary*, an autobiographical account of her experiences as a porn actress, producer of female-oriented erotic films, and prostitutes' rights activist. This video, among others, was removed from an exhibit at a conference on prostitution at the University of Michigan Law School in 1992. Leading antiporn crusaders Dworkin and MacKinnon played influential roles in this episode.
[Photo by Robert Maxwell; courtesy Veronica Vera]

When Attorney General Edwin Meese announced the widely criticized report of his "Pornography Commission" in 1986, he stood in front of an enormous nude female statue of Justice in the U.S. Justice Department. News reporters gleefully snapped the ironic image of Ed Meese denouncing porn beneath the statue's pendulous breasts (from some angles, his head appeared to be nestled in her crotch). *Esquire*'s caption beneath the photo reads, "Tits and Ass." Both the statue itself, as well as the news photograph, would be "pornographic" under the Dworkin-MacKinnon law.
[© GRACE/SYGMA]

This work, *Le Viol*, by the French surrealist René Magritte, would be doubly damned under the model feminist antipornography law: it shows a woman "reduced to" her body parts and it at least suggests sexual violence, since its title means "the rape."
[Photograph © 1995 C. Herscovici, Brussels/Artists Rights Society (ARS), New York]

According to legend, the Christian saint and virgin martyr Agatha rejected the love of the Roman governor and was therefore thrown into a brothel and subjected to violent tortures, including the cutting off of her breasts. Any description or depiction of this legend, such as this painting, *The Martyrdom of St. Agatha*, by Sebastiano del Piombo, would fall afoul of the feminist antipornography law. The many other religious works that would also be imperiled include the Bible, which has often been blamed for instigating rapes and sexual abuse. [Palazzo Pitti, Florence, Italy; courtesy Giraudon/Art Resource, New York]

(*Opposite*) Roberta Cohen, whose works explore issues of domestic violence, explains that this drawing, entitled *Confronting Your Fears*, is about "the fact that four thousand U.S. women are beaten to death by their husbands each year." In 1994, in response to a complaint that this work was "pornographic," local officials in Baton Rouge, Louisiana, demanded that it (and another work by Cohen) be removed from an exhibit at a private gallery located on city property; the gallery doors were locked until the artworks were removed. (Cohen and the other artists are being represented by the ACLU's Arts Censorship Project.) [Charcoal, pastel, and chalk on paper; courtesy Roberta Cohen]

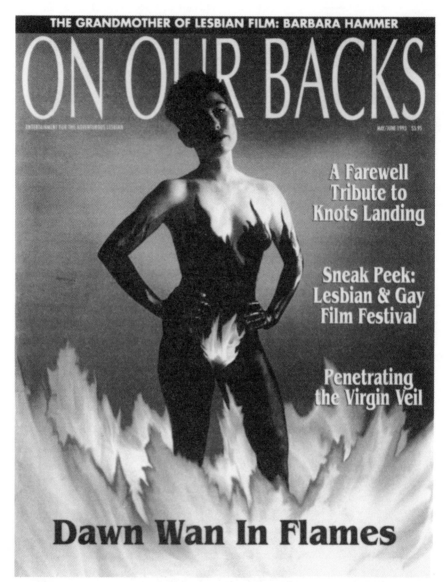

THE GRANDMOTHER OF LESBIAN FILM: BARBARA HAMMER

ON OUR BACKS

ENTERTAINMENT FOR THE ADVENTUROUS LESBIAN

MAY/JUNE 1993 $5.95

A Farewell
Tribute to
Knots Landing

Sneak Peek:
Lesbian & Gay
Film Festival

Penetrating
the Virgin Veil

Dawn Wan In Flames

This photo of model Dawn Wan, which was her idea, appeared on a 1993 cover of *On Our Backs*, a lesbian erotic magazine; many viewers saw it as countering stereotypes about the passivity of Asian women. But a lesbian feminist antipornography organization, Dykes Against Porn, denounced the image as racist pornography that promoted violence against Asian women, tore the covers off copies of the magazines in bookstores, and demonstrated against and vandalized feminist, lesbian/gay, and other bookstores that sold it. [Courtesy *On Our Backs*, 526 Castro, San Francisco, CA 94114]

CHAPTER 8

Positive Aspects
of Pornographic Imagery

> If pornography is part of your sexuality, then you have no
> right to your sexuality.
> —CATHARINE MACKINNON[1]

> I take this personally, the effort to repress material I enjoy—to
> tell me how wrong it is for me to enjoy it. Anti-pornography
> legislation is directed at me: as a user, as a writer. Catharine
> MacKinnon and Andrea Dworkin . . . are themselves pruri-
> ent, scurrying after sex in every corner. They look down on
> me and shake a finger: *Bad girl. Mustn't touch.* That branch
> of feminism tells me my very thoughts are bad. Pornography
> tells me the opposite: that *none* of my thoughts are bad, that
> anything goes. . . . The message of pornography . . . is that
> our sexual selves are real.
> —SALLIE TISDALE, writer[2]

Sexual Egalitarianism

Even if words and images could be interpreted literally, we would still
have to reject the pornophobic feminists' simplistic stance that pornography conveys unrelentingly negative messages about women. Much
commercial erotica depicts women in nonsubordinated roles, and contains images and ideas that may well be seen as positive for women and
feminists.

145

Although Catharine MacKinnon has described pornography with characteristic oversimplification as "man's boot on woman's neck,"[3] in many films and photos, the shoe is, literally, on the other foot—rather, the woman's boot is on the man's neck, if not on an even more vulnerable section of his anatomy. The female dominatrix and male slave are familiar characters in sexually explicit materials. Taking issue with the antipornography feminists' views that women are never on top sexually, either in the real world or in erotic materials, Norman Mailer observed with his typical saltiness, "I've seen any number of pornographic films where you have girls sitting on guys' heads."[4] And feminist aficionada of erotica Sallie Tisdale emphatically corroborates this perspective: "Women in modern films are often the initiators of sex; men in such films seem perfectly content for that to be so."[5]

Many sexual materials defy traditional stereotypes of both women and pornography by depicting females as voluntarily, joyfully participating in sexual encounters with men on an equal basis. Procensorship feminists may well view a woman's apparent welcoming of sex with a man as degrading, but this is because of their negative attitudes toward women's ability to make sexual choices. Other viewers are likely to see such a scene as positive and healthy. As feminist lawyer Nan Hunter asked, "What if a woman says to a man, 'fuck me'? Is that begging, or is it demanding? Is she submitting, or is she in control?"[6]

Men's rights activist Jack Kammer notes that "one of men's most enduring 'pornographic' fantasies is . . . about equalizing" sexual control between men and women, in a societal context in which women have often derived power from withholding sex. Accordingly, he notes:

> An archetype of male erotica is the woman who participates enthusiastically in sex, who loves male sexuality, who needs not to be cajoled, seduced or promised ulterior rewards. Erotica portraying such joyful, egalitarian sex does not demean women any more than men are denigrated by stories of women and men working cooperatively in an office where men no longer think it is their right to have women fetch them coffee.

Ironically, [MacKinnon's] greatest effect may be only to enhance men's need for what she wants to suppress. The more women accept arguments about the inherent cruelty, selfishness and danger of male sexuality, the more men will need to fantasize, possibly by resorting to pornography, about women who offer egalitarian, joyful, trusting sexual companionship.[7]

Sexual Opportunities and Options

Even the Meese Commission acknowledged "two areas in which sexually explicit materials have been used for positive ends: the treatment of sexual dysfunctions and the diagnosis and treatment of some paraphilias."[8] *(Webster's Third New International Dictionary* defines "paraphilia" as "a preference for or addiction to unusual sex practices.") Moreover, the Meese Commission recognized that pornography might have other beneficial effects, including providing entertainment, relieving people of the impulse to commit crimes (of course, this contradicts one of the Commission's other contentions, that pornography *causes* crime; see chapter 12 for more on this point), and improving marital relations by teaching about sexual techniques.

Popular sex manuals such as *The Joy of Sex* have recommended erotic pictures and videos as aphrodisiacs, and experts widely believe that it can improve the sex lives of many couples. In a 1992 letter to the Senate Judiciary Committee, opposing the then-pending Pornography Victims' Compensation Act, Patti Britton, Ph.D., wrote:

> As a board-certified clinical sexologist, I can tell you that it is common knowledge in my field that sexually explicit films and videos are often recommended as a mode of treatment for couples or individuals with clinical sexual problems. Such materials are viewed by professionals as helpful, not harmful, assets in the treatment process.[9]

Even for couples and individuals with no "clinical sexual problems," sexually explicit materials can spice up their sex lives, and hence solidify their relationships. At a conference at Columbia University, the eminent psychoanalyst Otto Kernberg said that inhibition too often

> limits a couple to conventional standards that stifle passion. Pornography, on the other hand, can stimulate an active fantasy life—can be an

antidote to stifled passion. A rebellious sex life within the bounds of a couple can be the cement of marriage.[10]

To the extent that erotic publications and videos offer an alternative sexual outlet for people who otherwise would be driven to engage in psychologically or physically risky sexual relations, they serve a positive public health function. This point was trumpeted by a banner that a Manhattan bookstore recently hung over a display of sexually oriented publications that had been threatened with censorship: "Enjoy some safe sex!" In the age of AIDS—to say nothing of the continuing rise of unwanted teenage pregnancies—sex itself is often fraught with risks. Yet sexually explicit materials *are* a safe alternative.

In addition, sexually explicit materials may well be the only source of sexual information or pleasure for many people who, for a host of reasons, do not have sexual contact with others—shy or inhibited people, people with mental or physical disabilities, people with emotional problems, gay people who are confused about their sexual orientation or are afraid to reveal or express it, people who are quite young or old, geographically isolated people, unattractive people. Disability rights activists protested Congress's attempt, in the mid-1980s, to prevent the Library of Congress from publishing *Playboy* in braille. Noting that this was "part of a long history of disabled people's sexual oppression," Barbara Faye Waxman, an expert in the sexual and reproductive health of disabled women, wrote, "[T]he last thing I'm going to do is call for any form of censorship that will inevitably have a backlash and reinforce the policies and practices that have kept disabled people sexually disempowered for so long."[11]

Even for individuals who generally have sexual relations with other people, pornography may well serve as a welcome alternative stimulus and outlet in situations where that is not possible, such as when travel separates them from their partners. Many hotels all over the United States, including some of the finest, now offer sexually explicit videos for in-room viewing.

Erotic publications and videos serve an egalitarian, pluralistic function beyond providing vicarious sexual experiences. Pornography depicts an enormous range of people and sexual practices, thus helping *all* viewers to explore and affirm their own sexuality, their own sexual practices and preferences, and their potential sexual relationships with all other human beings. As Paula Webster has written, "Pornography implies that we could find all races, genders, ages, and shapes sexually interesting, if only in our minds."[12]

This radically egalitarian premise that sex and sexual expression can break down any other barriers separating people is no doubt one of the reasons that they consistently have been viewed as threatening to established political, as well as moral and cultural, norms.

Instruction and Inspiration for Women's Sexual Pleasure

Contrary to the stereotypes of pornophobic feminists, many other feminists and many women in general say that porn has much to offer them. Let's now consider their views, so often drowned out by antiporn crusaders. Judith Kegan Gardiner, professor of English and Women's Studies at the University of Illinois, has cataloged some of pornography's positive aspects, specifically from a woman's perspective:

> For some women, pornography may actually de-objectify women because they can use it to validate their own desires and pleasures. They can also reinterpret or take control of the fantasy. For example, they may point out that a particular pictured position is not fun, but awkward and uncomfortable. Furthermore, women too can make comparisons between their lovers and the performers, for instance to the male stars' larger organs or more sustained erections, and they can use the pornography to encourage or instruct their partners how to please them. Pornography may also serve women to defamiliarize and romanticize the relationships in which they are already. For example, in a pornography sequence produced by the women of Femme Productions, a woman dressed in sexy finery is picked up by a man on the street who turns out to be her husband. The woman has left their child with her mother in preparation for their sexy night together.[13]

At the most basic level, porn provides information about women's bodies and techniques for facilitating female sexual pleasure, which is

otherwise sadly lacking in our society. Precisely to fill this gap, a growing number of women are becoming producers, as well as consumers,
of pornography. In a 1994 interview, erotica author Laurie Sue Brockway explains that she likes to write "really graphic stuff so people know
where the thing is and what to do with it," noting:

> A man friend of mine recently said to me, "I feel like I'm just doing fig-
> ure eights around a woman's clitoris [when giving oral sex]. Am I doing
> a good job? I don't know how to make her come." And I said, "Suck it."
> And he said, "*Suck* it?" And this is somebody who is fairly experienced.
> So, if you have a bunch of different characters in a bunch of different
> scenes, there's a lot of data in there.[14]

Pornography enhances women's ability to attain sexual pleasure on
their own, as well as with men. Recovered MacDworkinite Lisa Palac,
noting that many women do not masturbate, wrote that when she began
looking at "dirty pictures" and masturbating in response to them, she
"became sexually autonomous . . . in complete control of my own erotic
destiny."[15] In the same spirit, cartoonist Kris Kovic declared, "The First
Amendment is your most effective sex toy."[16]

As noted by Heather Findlay, editor of the lesbian erotic magazine
On Our Backs:

> [M]any women have come to appreciate their bodies through porn. . . .
> Betty Dodson's classic masturbation manifesto, *Sex for One,* tells the
> delightful story of how Dodson, who thought she'd deformed her pussy
> by jilling off too much, realized she was normal—and beautiful—by
> looking at split beavers in men's sex magazines. In 1973, Dodson put
> together a "cunt positive" slide show . . . took it on the road and inspired
> hundreds of women to feel proud of their equipment. One audi-
> ence member, Dodson relates, felt so puffed up by the slide show she
> demanded a raise from her boss the next morning—and got it. So much
> for porn degrading women![17]

Back in 1913, Dr. Howard Kelly said in the journal *Medical Gynecology*, "Good women possess no language and no terminology either
for their feelings or their anatomy." But Susie Bright, author of the

"Cliterati" column in the *San Francisco Review of Books,* says now, "In many years of teaching and talking sex, I have never had a man come up and say, 'I don't know where my penis is, and I've never had an orgasm.' . . . It's feminists who've put the Clitoris on the map."[18] Let's not let procensorship feminists take it off again.

Lesbian and Gay Images and Identity

As law professor Kathleen Sullivan has written, "In a world where sodomy may still be made a crime, gay pornography is the samizdat of the oppressed."[19] In light of the long-standing and ongoing legal and societal discrimination faced by lesbians and gay men, materials depicting and exploring their sexuality are especially important, serving to educate, liberate, and empower. The positive role that lesbian erotica played in her own life was described by the Canadian lesbian feminist writer and activist Chris Bearchell:

> My erotica "habit" began when I was coming out in a small Canadian city in the late '60s. It was hard admitting that I was sexually attracted to other women, but it got a lot easier when I saw pictures of women having sex. I squirreled away copies of soft-core men's magazines . . . I was vaguely disappointed by the lack of authenticity in much of what I saw, and by the meagerness of my collection, but I never gave up hope of finding more and better (juicier) images. Eventually, I moved to the big city—Toronto—and grew from a baby dyke into a gay activist and journalist. Then, what seemed to be a miracle happened. . . . [L]esbians began to make and distribute sexual imagery of our own.[20]

Referring to another beneficial aspect of porn from a lesbian and gay perspective, writer Pat Califia has noted that, should the antipornography feminists have their way, "homosexuals and other sexual minorities would lose a vital source of contact—the sex ads."[21]

The paucity of pornography produced specifically by and for lesbians, until recently, has led one lesbian feminist to put an amusing spin on the clichéd "excuse," in our porn-panicked society, for those "caught looking" at such magazines as *Playboy* and *Penthouse:* "I only read it for its articles." Noting that for lesbians who do not have access to lesbian porn, the only source of visual sexual stimulation is in straight-male-oriented magazines, Heather Findlay "confessed" that she occasionally bought them. Seeking to distance herself from what she described as the "male whining" in their texts, *her* defensive explanation, to *her* peers, was: "[B]ut, really, I only buy it for the pictorials!"[22]

If the procensorship feminists had their way, pornography would be equally unattainable for women and men, for gays and straights. Those concerned about the rights of lesbians, gays, and bisexuals should not delude themselves that the feminist antipornography juggernaut would not ride roughshod over their preferred sexual materials along with everyone else's. Such an exemption is available neither in theory nor in practice.

In theory, the feminist antipornography activists have made clear that homosexual, as well as heterosexual, materials are equally subject to censorship. Recall (from chapter 4) that the MacDworkin model law permits the suppression of any sexually oriented expression regardless of the genders (or the sexual orientations) of the individuals depicted. In this respect, the law reflects the procensorship feminists' equally condemnatory attitude toward all pornography—they certainly cannot be accused of discriminating on the basis of gender or sexual orientation!

The late John Preston, a gay activist and writer, illustrated Andrea Dworkin's long-standing antipathy toward *any* expression of male sexuality, including gay male sexuality, by recounting her actions during the early 1970s when he was director of the Gay House, Inc., in Minneapolis:

> Dworkin used to run a lesbian discussion group in the center. One of her favorite antics back then was to deface any poster or other material that promoted male homosexuality. "THIS OPPRESSES WOMEN!" she'd write all over the place.... I've come to understand that it's the expression of *any* male sexuality that she feels fuels the oppression of women in our society. That makes gay men not allies, but a big part of the problem.[23]

Further demonstrating her equal-opportunity loathing for all porn, Dworkin has also denounced lesbian pornography as "an expression of self-hatred."[24] This view has been echoed by other antipornography feminists. Norma Ramos, general counsel of Women Against Pornography, said in a 1994 *Ms.* magazine symposium:

> [T]here's no distinction between what lesbian pornographers are doing and what these women who are fronting for the [mainstream] pornography industry are doing. . . . They may package it as art, or say that they are introducing a new vision. But it is sexual exploitation.[25]

Likewise, the organization Dykes Against Porn, which has chapters in cities around the country, has stated that "[i]t was formed because of the need that many saw to fight pornography in the lesbian community, as well as heterosexual male porn."[26] *On Our Backs,* a lesbian erotic magazine published in San Francisco, has been repeatedly attacked by antipornography feminists, including Dykes Against Porn, as in the "Dawn Wan in Flames" incident described in the previous chapter.

Even more significant than the pornophobic feminists' nondiscriminatory denunciations of homosexual and heterosexual porn is the fact that any censorship measure would be enforced by government officials and legal systems that reflect society's pervasive homophobia and heterosexism. Thus, it is not surprising that *in the real world,* as under the first feminist antipornography scheme to go into operation, in Canada, lesbian and gay erotica has borne the brunt of the censorship.

Unreal Rape

Just as it is vitally important to enforce criminal and societal sanctions against *real* rape—defined by University of Southern California law professor Susan Estrich, in her book of that title, as all intentional nonconsensual sex[27]—it is also vitally important *not* to enforce sanctions against *unreal* rape—words or images *describing* or *depicting* nonconsensual sex.

The distinction between the imagined and the actual, between fantasy and reality, should be crystal clear. But the feminist antipornography movement has blurred it. For example, in her 1993 book, MacKinnon writes, "In pornography, pictures and words are sex"[28] and "[s]exual words and pictures . . . have sex."[29] Indeed, the title of that book, *Only Words,* conveys MacKinnon's sarcastic dismissal of the view that pornographic words are, in fact, only words.

This confusion between expression and action is yet another common bond between feminist censors and other censors. As writer Wendy Kaminer remarked, "[I]f pornography is sex discrimination, then an editorial criticizing the President is treason."[30] (Indeed, under English common law, it was a crime to "compass"—or imagine—the death of the king;[31] the law would be moving backward toward that long discredited notion were it to adopt the feminist procensorship philosophy.) And Thelma McCormack retorted to the MacDworkinite charge that pornography is rape by comparing it to "the Ayatollah Khomeini saying 'The Satanic Verses' is not a work of art but an act of heresy."[32]

To MacKinnon, there are apparently no distinctions between women who are raped by actual men in real life, and female actresses in erotic productions whose rapes are simulated by male actors. Moreover, MacKinnon apparently concedes no distinction between real-life rape victims and female models who are "raped" by the cameras that simply record their nude or sexual poses. In a 1993 article in *Ms.* magazine, MacKinnon wrote, "Pornography is made from rape in film studios, on sets, in private bedrooms, in basements, in alleys, in prison cells, and in brothels."[33]

Likewise, in *Only Words,* MacKinnon asserts that women are "gang raped," "hurt and penetrated, tied and gagged, undressed and genitally spread," and even "killed . . . to make pornography," and that these violent actions are "essential . . . to make pornography."[34] It should be emphasized that, since MacKinnon defines pornography as including verbal and visual representations—for example, stories and drawings—she is claiming not only that pornography necessitates harm to actual women who serve as models or actresses for photographs or films (this claim is itself inaccurate, as discussed in the following chapter); but further, she is claiming that pornography drawn solely from the writer's or artist's imagination inevitably harms women. Again, MacKinnon conflates imagination, acting, and actuality.

Precisely to dramatize and criticize MacKinnon's equation of words with actions, Carlin Romano—a former philosophy instructor and current president of the National Book Critics Circle—included in his

Nation magazine review of *Only Words* a fantasized, fictionalized rape of MacKinnon herself.[35] His strategy backfired, though, to the extent that MacKinnon and her allies reacted with all the ire that one would anticipate following a real-life assault. Indeed, MacKinnon declared that the review "was a public rape,"[36] and her publishers attacked *The Nation* for its "use of rape as a tool for the conduct of criticism."[37] Predictably, too, some procensorship feminists denounced the review as pornographic.[38]

In the MacDworkinites' virtual-reality universe, where "virtual rape" is seemingly identical with actual rape, it is hard to understand why their vicious verbal attacks against Romano would not likewise be deemed actual, punishable attacks. Romano's trenchant criticism of MacKinnon's *ideas* could not fairly be construed as "threatening MacKinnon" *herself* "with rape," as charged by Dexter Guerreri of a Brooklyn-based antiporn organization.[39] Ironically, though, as part of their verbal vendetta against Romano, both MacKinnon and her then-fiancé, Jeffrey Masson, made statements that could plausibly be viewed as the kind of "threat" that has long and appropriately been punishable under our legal system—namely, an utterance that is intended to, and does, instill a reasonable fear of impending personal harm. Masson wrote a letter to Romano stating:

> [W]hat you have done to Catharine . . . makes me so mad that I feel my blood start to boil, and I feel that if we were talking about it right now, I could not guarantee that I wouldn't hit you. I have never hit anybody, but I feel this rage rise up in me when I think of you that makes me want to grab you and shake you and hurt you in the same way that you thought of hurting Catharine. . . . I just want you to think for a minute about what you have done. And to recognize that there are so many people, more than you think, who are enraged by it. . . . I am not threatening you, but I want you to know, if there is ever anything I can do to hurt your career, I will do it.[40]

In short, while MacKinnon decrees a fictionalized rape to be an actual rape, Masson decrees an actual threat to be a non-threat! (Consistent with his vow to strive to damage Romano's career, Masson sent this letter not to Romano himself, but rather, to the editor of *The Philadelphia*

Inquirer, where Romano is the literary critic.) And MacKinnon herself echoed Masson's threatening words: "I do think Carlin Romano should be held accountable for what he did. There are a lot of people out there and a lot of ways that can be done."[41]

Many women can and do distinguish between real rape and descriptions or depictions of rape. By definition, no one wants to be raped; the very essence of this heinous crime is unwanted sex. That does not mean, though, that the unmitigatedly evil nature of real rape extends as well to unreal rape: rape fantasies, verbal descriptions of fictional rapes, paintings or sculpture depicting rape scenes, or photographs and films showing simulated rapes.

In her latest collection of women's sexual fantasies, the 1993 book *Women on Top,* Nancy Friday writes:

> The most popular guilt-avoiding device [in these fantasies] was the so-called rape fantasy—"so-called" because no rape, bodily harm, or humiliation took place in the fantasy. It simply had to be understood that what went on was against the woman's will. Saying she was "raped" was the most expedient way of getting past the big No to sex that had been imprinted on her mind since early childhood.[42]

And Jean MacKellar writes in her book *Rape: The Bait and the Trap:*

> [Rape fantasies] serve practical and healthy functions in human experience; they add *change.* And they do this without shattering the pattern of reality. This is important, for often a real change is neither desirable nor possible. The most important difference between a fantasy of rape and a desire for the real experience is the element of control. In the fantasy . . . the helpless victim actually controls the acts of the offender. . . . Real terror and uncontrolled pain are not experienced in these fantasies.[43]

Rape scenes in films or writing may also effectively galvanize constructive responses to the problem of actual rape in the real world. Feminists widely praised the gang rape scene in the movie *The Accused* and the attempted rape scene in the film *Thelma and Louise* because they dramatically decried sexual violence against women, despite the fact that, to some viewers, these rape scenes had strong erotic elements. As novelist Anne Rice commented about *Thelma and Louise:*

> I praise that movie because I think it showed how awful rape is. And it's hard to show it without its being sexy because it is sexy. And rape fantasies are part of our brain. They're part of our genetic heritage, and that's not going to go away if you ban pornography. It's an archetypal fantasy.[44]

Pornography, including pornographic rape scenes, may serve another, intensely political end for women who read or see them: they go against the grain, thus allowing viewers to express rebellion and individuality. In this sense, too, words or images that literally depict a woman's powerlessness may well have an empowering impact on female viewers. As journalist Ellen Willis has written:

> A woman who is raped is a victim; a woman who enjoys pornography (even if that means enjoying a rape fantasy) is in a sense a rebel, insisting on an aspect of her sexuality that has been defined as a male preserve. Insofar as pornography glorifies male supremacy and sexual alienation, it is deeply reactionary. But in rejecting sexual repression and hypocrisy—which have inflicted even more damage on women than on men—it expresses a radical impulse.[45]

Fantasies for Feminists and Other Freedom Fighters

[I]f social convention, backed by religion and law, confines sexuality to the heterosexual, monogamous, marital, familial, and reproductive, then the ambisexual, promiscuous, adulterous, selfish, and gratification-centered world of pornography is a charter of sexual revolution that is potentially liberating rather than confining for women.

—Kathleen Sullivan
Stanford University law professor[46]

Several anthologies of feminist writings illuminate the range of messages in pornography, specifically from the viewpoints of feminists and women in general.[47] Feminist writer and literature professor Ann Snitow, who coedited one such anthology, *Powers of Desire,* has described some of porn's positive facets:

> Pornography sometimes includes elements of play, as if the fear women feel toward men had evaporated and women were relaxed and willing at last. Such a fantasy—sexual revolution as *fait accompli* . . . can . . . be wishful, eager and utopian.
>
> Porn can depict thrilling (as opposed to threatening) danger. . . . [S]ome of its manic quality . . . seems propelled by fear and joy about breaching the always uncertain boundaries of flesh and personality. . . .
>
> Some pornography is defiant and thumbs a nose at death, at the limitations of the body and nature. . . .
>
> Porn offers . . . a private path to arousal, an arousal that may be all too easily routed by fear or shame. . . .
>
> [P]ornography also flouts authority, which no doubt in part explains its appeal to young boys.[48]

Feminist artist Myrna Kostash theorizes further positive, liberating aspects of pornography: "Until there is a revolution in the institutions that regulate sexual relations—the family, the school, the workplace— perhaps the pornographic fantasy is one of the few ways that women and men, captives together of those institutions, victims alike of their alienating procedures, are permitted connection."[49]

Pornography also contains many elements that are harmonious with feminist values. As the Feminist Anti-Censorship Taskforce brief noted in the Indianapolis case, it "may convey the message that sexuality need not be tied to reproduction, men or domesticity."[50] Feminists Lisa Duggan, Nan Hunter, and Carole Vance have suggested additional profeminist aspects of pornography:

> [P]ornography has served to flout conventional sexual mores, to ridicule sexual hypocrisy and to underscore the importance of sexual needs. Pornography carries many messages other than woman-hating: it advocates sexual adventure, sex outside of marriage, sex for no reason other

than pleasure, casual sex, anonymous sex, group sex, voyeuristic sex, illegal sex, public sex. Some of these ideas appeal to women reading or seeing pornography, who may interpret some images as legitimating their own sense of sexual urgency or desire to be sexually aggressive. Women's experience of pornography is not as universally victimizing as the [MacKinnon-Dworkin] ordinance would have it.[51]

Indeed, as feminist writer and video artist Sara Diamond has noted, "[F]eminism and porn have something in common. Both insist that women are sexual beings. Both have made sex an experience open to public examination and . . . debate."[52]

In response to the charge by procensorship feminists that pornography exploits women, Ann Snitow explains that its subversive quality challenges the entire status quo, including social structures that inhibit women's freedom:

Though pornography's critics are right—pornography *is* exploitation— it is exploitation of everything. Promiscuity by definition is a breakdown of barriers. . . .

It is a fantasy of an extreme state in which all social constraints are overwhelmed by a flood of sexual energy. Think, for example, of all the pornography about servants fucking mistresses, old men fucking young girls, guardians fucking wards. Class, age, custom—all are deliciously sacrificed, dissolved by sex.[53]

The fact that pornography always has rebelled against conventional constraints is precisely the reason it always has provoked such anxiety among moral traditionalists and political conservatives. Just as sex itself has enormous power to break down individual and social boundaries, so speech about sex threatens all manner of accepted bounds; the more unconventional the sexual expression is, the more revolutionary its social and political implications become.

The essays that were collected in the 1993 book edited by Lynn Hunt, *The Invention of Pornography: Obscenity and the Origins of Pornography, 1500–1800,* show that pornography was closely tied to democratic political movements during the period described. The essay by Margaret Jacob, for example, points to pornography's historic role in weakening state authority and strengthening democracy by mocking dogmatic religious credos.[54]

Walter Kendrick's 1987 history of pornography in modern culture, *The Secret Museum*, demonstrates that the zeal to restrict sexual expression consistently has reflected political anxiety, as well as moral or religious concern. He described America's leading crusader against sexual expression from the 1870s through the early years of this century, Anthony Comstock (whom we revisit in chapter 11) from this vantage point:

> Comstock represented . . . the urge to limit dissemination of all kinds, to control the availability of representations almost irrespective of their subjects. Like his more sophisticated contemporaries in France and England, Comstock at bottom feared nothing so much as the universal distribution of information. The prospect called up nightmarish images of a world without structure, where all barriers had been breached and all differences leveled. It was appropriate that sex should become the focus of such nightmares, since long before the modern threat arose, sex already stood for loss of control and the scattering of substance.[55]

When the U.S. Commission on Pornography and Obscenity submitted its report to President Nixon in 1970, recommending that all sexual expression be decriminalized for consenting adults, Nixon denounced the report in terms that expressly acknowledged the politically subversive implications of such expression. Nixon declared:

> Pornography is to freedom of expression what anarchy is to liberty; as free men willingly restrain a measure of their freedom to prevent anarchy, so must we draw the line against pornography to protect freedom of expression. Moreover, *if an attitude of permissiveness were to be adopted regarding pornography, this would contribute to an atmosphere condoning anarchy in every other field*—and would increase the threat to our social order as well as to our moral principles.[56] [emphasis added]

As Kendrick commented, "On the surface, pornography threatens nothing but the unleashing of sexuality; but that unleashing, as Nixon said, turns immediately into wantonness of every other kind, including the promiscuous redistribution of property."[57]

Just as *suppressing* sexual speech plays an essential role in *maintaining* the political, social, and economic status quo, conversely, *protecting* sexual speech plays an essential role in *challenging* the status quo. Accordingly, the women's rights cause should naturally be allied with the free speech cause for all expression, including sexual. Once again, the sexual *is* political.

CHAPTER 9

Posing for Pornography:
Coercion or Consent?

[M]any intelligent, self-confident women . . . have chosen to work in this lucrative industry. What sort of "feminism" is this that tells me I need "reforming" just because dancing buck naked on stage while people throw money at me is my idea of fun? By depicting sex workers as either too emotionally crippled or too stupid to escape a fate which apparently any decent woman would find unspeakably degrading, they help perpetuate the sorts of patronizing stereotypes a true women's liberation movement should strive to eradicate.

—"KAREN," stage name of a law student
who works as a nude dancer
at New York City clubs[1]

Antipornography feminists often seek to justify censorship by arguing that some women who pose for sexually explicit pictures or films have been forced into doing so, either through physical violence or through other types of coercion, such as fraud or duress. It is clearly illegal to coerce anyone into producing a sexual image, just as coercion is illegal in any setting. On that point, the procensorship and anticensorship feminists are united.

The two groups are sharply divided, though, on three related points. First, anticensorship feminists stress that the law already prohibits violence and other forms of coercion, and provides remedies when it occurs.

Second, anticensorship feminists reject the view of their procensorship counterparts that women who pose for sexual images are always and inevitably victims of coercion. Worse yet, the procensorship feminists' view that women cannot consent to pose for sexual pictures or films is antithetical to women's full and equal citizenship, relegating women to the subordinated legal status of children.

Third, anticensorship feminists stress that outlawing the production of any sexually explicit materials will decrease the protections available to women who participate in such productions. Rather than eliminating sexually explicit materials, Dworkin-MacKinnon–style laws would simply drive their production underground, where it would be impossible for models and actresses to invoke legal protections against violence and duress.

Any individuals responsible for physically assaulting women in the process of making sexually oriented materials can be criminally prosecuted as well as sued for damages. The law also provides civil and criminal remedies for fraud or duress. In addition, many states authorize damage actions for privacy-related torts, which could provide further avenues of redress for women who have been physically or psychologically forced into pornographic productions. Such tort actions allow recovery of damages for wrongfully disclosing private facts about someone in public and for wrongfully portraying someone in a false light in public. Another privacy-related tort action, for the wrongful appropriation of a person's image or identity, could also assist women who do not knowingly or voluntarily consent to pose for pornographic materials. Models have recovered damages for emotional distress when sexually oriented magazines wrongfully used nude photographs of them.[2]

Despite the existing panoply of criminal and civil remedies for women who have been physically or psychologically abused in the production of sexual materials, procensorship feminists insist that these measures are insufficient to counter the particular type of coercion that they believe to be inevitable whenever a woman poses for such materials. Procensorship feminists conclude that—at least in the realm of sexuality and sexual expression—women can never make free, voluntary, consensual choices, and that, rather, women are *always* coerced in this context, whether they realize it or not.

But women should not be treated like children or mentally disabled persons and deprived of the right to enter into contracts for the production of sexually explicit materials. That is the end result of the MacDworkin model antipornography law, which provides that a woman's decision to pose for a sexual image should be treated as the product of coercion even under circumstances where a man's decision would be treated as voluntary and consensual. Specifically, the model law provides that proof of any of the following will *not* disprove coercion:

> that the [allegedly coerced] person actually consented to a use of the performance that is changed into pornography; or ... that the person knew that the purpose of the acts or events in question was to make pornography; or ... that the person showed no resistance or appeared to cooperate actively in the photographic sessions or in the sexual events that produced pornography; or ... that the person signed a contract, or made statements affirming a willingness to cooperate in the production of pornography; or ... that no physical force, threats, or weapons were used in the making of the pornography; or ... that the person was paid or otherwise compensated.

This provision denies women our freedom of choice; indeed, consistent with the antisex aspect of the procensorship feminist philosophy, it presumes that women are incapable of exercising such freedom, at least as far as sex and sexual expression are concerned.

Even beyond its direct infantilization of women who voluntarily work in the sex business, this provision's "maternalistic" attitude toward women exemplifies the insultingly "matronizing" view that pervades the procensorship feminist critique of pornography. Indeed, Catharine MacKinnon and other supporters of feminist-style antipornography laws have expressly drawn analogies between women and children. MacKinnon has said: "Some of the same reasons children are granted some specific legal avenue for redress ... also hold true for the social position of women compared to men."[3] Likewise, the proposed Minneapolis antipornography ordinance, drafted by Dworkin and MacKinnon, stated:

> Children are incapable of consenting to engage in pornographic conduct, even absent physical coercion, and therefore require special protection.

By the same token, the physical and psychological well-being of women ought to be afforded comparable protection.[4]

Everyone's Looking at (Just) Linda

Some women who previously modeled or acted for pornographic publications or films have said that they were coerced to perform through physical violence. The most famous example, and one that Dworkin and MacKinnon consistently cite in an attempt to justify suppressing pornography, is Linda Marchiano, who starred in the movie *Deep Throat* under the stage name "Linda Lovelace." In her 1980 book *Ordeal,* Marchiano describes how she was raped and in other ways forced to make the film against her will.[5]

Although Linda Marchiano's *Ordeal* recounts deplorable physical and psychological abuse, which should be punished and prevented under the many existing laws that these acts clearly violated, Marchiano's ordeal provides no support for the conclusion that procensorship feminists repeatedly seek to draw from it—namely, that women who pose for pornographic materials are usually, if not inevitably, brutalized by the producers of such materials. Recently, in interviews published in *Ms.* and *The New York Times Magazine,* Dworkin and MacKinnon, respectively, cited Linda Marchiano as the sole "proof" that pornography is made by assaulting and abusing actual women.[6]

The violence and coercion that Marchiano suffered were outrageous. Yet her own account does not support the inference that producers of pornography generally inflict such violence and coercion upon the women who pose for them, for two reasons. First, in Marchiano's own case, it was not the participants in the porn industry who raped, beat, and forced her to take part in the movie, but rather, her own husband, Chuck Traynor, who had no other connection to the pornography business. Marchiano's autobiographical writings not only make clear that she experienced no abuse or force at the hands of participants in the porn industry; her writings also show that her career as a "porn star" gave her a welcome, if temporary, refuge from her husband's brutality. In *Ordeal,* Marchiano describes the sense of freedom she felt on the set of *Deep Throat,* and how she enjoyed the company of her costar,

Harry Reems. She wrote, "Something was happening to me, something strange. No one was treating me like garbage. . . . We laughed a lot that first day of shooting. . . . And no one was asking me to do anything I didn't want to do."[7] Evidently threatened by Marchiano's enjoyment of her participation in *Deep Throat,* her husband brutally beat her after that first day of shooting, throwing her against the wall and kicking her for hours.

Marchiano's autobiography underscores that her subsequent contacts with the pornography industry, after she had escaped from her abusive husband, were completely voluntary. Recounting the lucrative film offers she later received to reenact the *Deep Throat* sex scenes, Marchiano wrote in her 1986 book *Out of Bondage,* "[I]f I acted in a dirty movie, I would be doing it out of need and greed. . . . I had a choice."[8]

Procensorship feminists have distorted Linda Marchiano's actual experience in the pornography industry, manipulating it to suit their pornophobic agenda. As Dan Greenberg and Thomas H. Tobiason commented in a 1993 law review article:

> MacKinnon's view that women cannot authentically choose to be actors in pornographic films is not even true of the one woman she takes as a paradigm case of a coerced actor: Linda Lovelace. . . . Lovelace's autobiographical account of her life after the filming of *Deep Throat* unambiguously demonstrates that coercion is the exception, not the rule. . . . Although MacKinnon uses the life of Linda Lovelace to illuminate MacKinnon's reiterations that women who act in pornographic films have no choice but to do so, she does not explain why the experiences of Lovelace, the woman who is at the center of MacKinnon's accounts of coercion, are flatly irreconcilable with her theories.[9]

In the same vein, Leora Tanenbaum writes:

> Andrea Dworkin asks in *Ms.* magazine's recent roundtable discussion on pornography: "Why did a woman have to be brutalized to make that film [*Deep Throat*]?" The answer is: she didn't. *Ordeal* makes this clear.
>
> In the years following the publication of *Ordeal,* though, Marchiano has been all too willing to accommodate her antiporn sisters. When she appeared on *Geraldo* in 1988, Marchiano spoke of her experience

working on *Deep Throat* in a passive voice, obfuscating the source of her coercion: "I was beaten and I was forced into it, and I had a .45 pointed at me, an M-16 semiautomatic machine gun," she told the audience. . . . Not once did she mention that the abuser was her husband.[10]

The second reason Marchiano's experience does not provide proof of abusive working conditions within the porn industry is that she speaks only for herself. Therefore, even assuming for the sake of argument—directly contrary to what she herself has written—that Marchiano had been abused by members of the pornography industry, that still would provide no basis for concluding that other sex industry workers also suffered such abuse. Nor does the fact that Marchiano's then-husband forced her to perform in *Deep Throat* support the contention that other pornography models or actresses are also performing under duress.

It bears repeating that any instance of any form of physical or psychological abuse is deplorable whenever it occurs, including when it is inflicted to force a woman to pose for pornographic pictures or films (or to do anything else against her will). Instances of such abuse, however, cannot justify the complete prohibition of all posing for pornography. It is as illogical to leap to the conclusion that, because of Marchiano's ordeal, all women should be "protected" against performing in pornographic films, as it would be to conclude that, because numerous Navy women were sexually abused during the 1991 Tailhook convention, all women should be "protected" against joining the Navy.

For every Linda Lovelace who was coerced to perform for a pornographic work, there is a Nina Hartley, who proclaims herself to be an exhibitionist; a Veronica Vera, who celebrates the personal growth she experienced through performing in porn films; a Candida Royalle, who proudly declares that she produces pornography "from a woman's point of view"; and countless others. Royalle, who starred in over a dozen X-rated movies before she became a director, recently commented about the antipornography feminists who want to "protect" her: "I understand their desire to help women, but they are out of touch with women in the industry."[11] Many women who perform for pornography affirm that they do so voluntarily, and that their sister sex workers do likewise. Testifying before the Subcomittee on Juvenile Justice of the

Senate Judiciary Committee, Veronica Vera, who has decades of experience with porn films as an actress and director, said that she had "never met a woman who was coerced . . . into participating" in such works.[12] The recent increase of homemade pornographic films, in which unpaid women and men voluntarily perform for others' viewing, is telling. It should not be surprising that some women willingly do for money what others willingly do even for no money.

Women who voluntarily perform for pornography resent the procensorship feminists' attempts to outlaw their chosen occupation. When the MacDworkin law was passed in Indianapolis, deeming the production of pornography a civil rights violation, one actress who appears in porn films protested, "For them to tell me I can't make films about naked men and women making love is a grotesque violation of *my* civil rights."[13] And, underscoring the debilitating impact that antipornography laws would have on *all* women, not just those who choose to work in the pornography business, Veronica Vera said, "I don't think it would help women to beg the government to play Daddy and protect us from ourselves and then at the same time expect equality."[14]

Some sex industry workers affirm their occupational choice in explicitly feminist terms, stressing that they find it empowering as well as enjoyable. For example, Nina Hartley, who has worked in the porn business since 1983 and has hundreds of pornographic films to her credit, explains that the sex industry "provides a surprisingly flexible and supportive arena for me to grow in as a performer, both sexually and nonsexually." Proudly, she declares that "an intelligent, sexual woman could choose a job in the sex industry and not be a victim, but instead emerge even stronger and more self-confident, with a feeling, even, of self-actualization."[15]

Despite the fact that MacKinnon and Marchiano espouse views that many feminists and sex trade workers vehemently reject, both were celebrated by the Meese Commission as if their views and experiences were typical. The Commission unfairly stacked the deck even further by selectively hearing from a disproportionate number of other witnesses who endorsed the MacKinnon-Marchiano perspective. As law professor Edward de Grazia commented in his 1993 book *Girls Lean Back Everywhere: The Law of Obscenity and the Assault on Genius:*

The Meese Commission trundled out a parade of born-again basket-cases, antisex feminists and fun-hating fundamentalists. Their testimony was sad, misdirected—even pathetic. It was also inflammatory, misinformed scapegoating. In a court of law such witnesses would be dismissed for lack of credibility. Trial by headline—unsupported by evidence, unchallenged by cross-examination or witnesses for the defense—is a far cry from due process. But it was the method of the Meese Commission, with its fundamentalist foundation, as it had been for Joe McCarthy. This was nothing more nor less than sexual McCarthyism.[16]

One witness who powerfully countered the Meese-MacKinnon–Marchiano stereotypes—namely, the unmitigated evils of sexual materials and the inherent victimization of women who participate in producing those materials—was Dottie Meyer, a former fashion model, *Penthouse* centerfold, and "Pet of the Year," who went on to work at *Penthouse* as a promotion and circulation coordinator. Unlike the parade of self-described pornography victims, Meyer was subjected to scathing, skeptical cross-examination, and her views, along with those of Veronica Vera and other prosex, anticensorship feminists, were completely disregarded in the Commission's report and recommendations. Therefore, it is especially important to pay respect to her words here:

I was born in Saskatchewan, Canada, 38 years ago. My parents raised me, my brother and sister in a normal, healthy home. . . . I was encouraged to read the Bible and I joined many church organizations.

I consider myself sexually normal and healthy. I enjoy looking at erotic videotapes and reading erotic literature. Both my husband and I feel these sexual aids have enhanced the intimate part of our lives. As a policeman my husband is involved in the constant stress and threats of violence. I believe the fantasy of erotica helps him cope with those situations. We were married . . . before I posed for the centerfold, and for us it was just another modeling assignment. My involvement with *Penthouse* was one of my own choosing. They didn't come to me. I went to them. . . .

The term "Pet" is a term of endearment especially in England where the magazine originated. It is used affectionately. . . . And while I was growing up my mother being English often referred to me as Pet. . . .

In summary, I am a working woman. I work at a job that I like. I go home to my husband and my dog. I cook and clean my own house. . . . It hurts me when righteous so-called do-gooders assume anyone who has been a centerfold is an empty-headed bubble-brained idiot who's been led down the garden path into a life of moral decadence.[17]

While Dottie Meyer did not feel degraded by her modeling and other work for *Penthouse,* she *did* feel degraded by the questioning she underwent by members of the Meese Commission, including detailed questions about her sexual tastes and practices. She said:

You know, the Meese Commission complains about erotica being degrading to women, well, the Meese Commission was degrading to me. I walked out of there feeling . . . *horrible.* I think I felt more insulted about the questions they asked me than anything I've ever done in my life. . . .[18]

"No" Means "No," and "Yes" Means "Yes"

As grown-ups, we have won the right to say "no" and to be believed and taken seriously. As grown-ups, we also have the right to repeat, after Molly Bloom, "Yes I said yes I will Yes."
—KAREN DeCROW, former president
National Organization for Women[19]

Physically the woman in intercourse is a space invaded, a literal territory occupied literally; occupied even if there has been no resistance; even if the occupied person said, "Yes, please, yes, hurry, yes, more."
—ANDREA DWORKIN[20]

The 1992 Canadian Supreme Court decision endorsing the procensorship feminists' analysis in general also specifically adopted their position that a woman's consent to perform for sexually explicit photographs or films cannot prevent the works from being classified as "degrading" or "dehumanizing." To the contrary, in an Orwellian twist, the Court "reasoned" that a woman's consent may well "make the depicted acts even more degrading or dehumanizing."[21]

But what could be more degrading or dehumanizing to women than this view, espoused by the procensorship feminists, that woman are powerless to consent to pose for pornographic depictions, and that if they seek to do so, they are debasing themselves? This argument demeans all women. In accepting the MacDworkin theory that a woman's *consent* to perform for pornography should have no legal importance, the Canadian Supreme Court was showing precisely the same disregard for women's autonomy and dignity that previous courts showed when they ruled that a woman's *nonconsent* to sexual intercourse did not mean that she had been raped. The two views are flip sides of the same devalued coin.

The procensorship feminists' assumption that women cannot meaningfully consent to participate in producing sexual expression is one facet of their even broader, even more debasing, assumption that women cannot meaningfully consent to participate in sexual relations. The antisex aspect of the procensorship philosophy, as demonstrated throughout this book, is an important reason why it is profoundly inconsistent with women's equality.

Scarlet Collar Workers—Better Off in Pink?

Most people's work choices are constrained at least by economic pressures, and often by other pressures as well, including those exerted by peers or family members and internal psychological factors. All too many people find little self-fulfillment in their work but, to the contrary, find much that is self-abasing. From a corporate manager in a gray flannel suit to a porn star in her birthday suit, most working people do things they probably would not do were they independently wealthy.

Contrary to the claim of pornocentric feminists, though, choices are no more constrained for those who pose for sexually explicit materials than they are for other workers. Given the relatively high pay, many "scarlet collar workers" make an economically rational choice to enter the sex industry rather than to pursue more socially acceptable, but less remunerative, work.

Nor is there any reason to believe that force or violence are endemic in the sex industry, or more prevalent there than in other sectors of our society, including other workplaces and the home. Indeed, citing FBI reports about the prevalence of domestic violence, some experts maintain that "the home is the center of violence in twentieth-century America," in the words of women's rights lawyer Karen DeCrow;[22] Linda Marchiano's brutalization fits squarely into this general pattern.

Candida Royalle has said that she was never subjected to any violence or sexual harassment in the porn industry, but that she did experience both in "straight" jobs, recounting that, while she was working as a receptionist at a New York City health club, her boss sexually assaulted her, and that when she worked at Ticketron, her employer made her kiss him good night every night to keep her job.[23] In a 1994 interview with Leora Tanenbaum in *In These Times*, Royalle said:

> I was never forced to do anything in pornography. The closest I ever came to any attempt at coercion was during a film I made with a very famous director, about a guy who had abused prostitutes, who were now getting back at him. So the director was passing out beers. I was like, What is this? "This is the, uh, urination scene." I was like, Excuse me? I not only refused to do it, I organized all the other women and said, "We're not going to do anything we don't want to do." Four of the women did agree because they had no problem with it, but the rest of us didn't. The director was very angry, and said I would never work for him again, and that was fine.[24]

Although antipornography activists brandish accusations about the alleged prevalence of "snuff" films, in which women are purportedly actually murdered on camera, there is absolutely no evidence that *any* such film has *ever* been produced, let alone that it typifies the pornographic genre. To the contrary, as writer Susie Bright has noted, the original movie entitled *Snuff* "was long ago exposed as a fraud, a low-budget horror F/X [special effects] grossity with a helluva marketing angle."[25] The actress who was supposedly murdered on-screen later stepped forward to demonstrate that she was very much alive.

For many sex industry workers, working conditions are less dangerous and onerous than those experienced by the women who labor in
mills and on assembly lines. By some estimates, more than ten thousand workers die each year, or about thirty per day, from on-the-job
injuries; about seventy thousand more workers are permanently disabled annually. According to the National Institute for Occupational
Safety and Health, one in five poultry workers, who are mostly women,
have been seriously injured in the hands, wrists, or shoulders. And job-
related illnesses and crippling injuries are on the rise throughout the
workforce.[26]

A 1994 Justice Department report reveals that violence is a serious
problem in all workplaces: about one out of every six violent crimes
happens at work, including 8 percent of all rapes and 16 percent of all
assaults. Other data indicate that 4 percent of all homicides occur in the
workplace.[27]

These troubling facts should mobilize efforts to make all workplaces
safer for all working women and men. When we learn of hazards faced
by poultry workers, we do not call for closing down the poultry industry, but rather for requirements that it protect its workers' safety and
health; we should do likewise concerning the pornography industry.
Censoring pornography, though, would make it impossible to enforce
any such requirements.

Censorship Would Harm, Not Help,
Pornography Performers

By driving many pornography businesses out of existence, the censorship regime would deprive women of occupational options that many
now affirm they have freely chosen. Furthermore, as even procensorship feminists recognize, the practical impact of their approach would
not be to prevent the production of all pornography, but rather, to drive
that production underground. This development would also be devastating to the women who continued to work in the porn business. As
observed by federal Court of Appeals Judge Richard Posner, a leading
exponent of analyzing legal issues from an economic perspective:

When an economic activity is placed outside the protection of the law—as we know from Prohibition, prostitution, the campaign against drugs and the employment of illegal immigrants—the participants in that activity will resort to threats and violence in lieu of the contractual and other legal remedies denied them. The pimp is an artifact of the illegality of prostitution, and the exploitation of pornographic actresses and models by their employers is parallel to the exploitation of illegal immigrant labor by their employers. These women would be better off if all pornography were legal.[28]

Improved working terms and conditions for porn models and actresses could be achieved under a noncensorship regime through both private contracts (for either individual women or organized groups) and government regulation. If the sex industries were treated as legitimate businesses, they would be subject to a whole range of laws that would enhance the lives of the women who work in them. Conversely, if pornography were made illegal, the women who performed for pornographic materials would have no protection under a panoply of measures that can promote their welfare, including laws prohibiting coercion or duress, sanitation codes, wage and hour laws, the social security system, insurance and pension laws, laws protecting safety and health, and laws guaranteeing collective bargaining rights.

While MacDworkinite laws would not criminalize pornography, they would subject it to such crippling penalties that it would probably be produced by underworld-type operators, not likely to abide by applicable laws and regulations. As Judge Posner indicated, scarlet collar workers are already exploited because some sexual expression is now subject to legal sanctions; they would be even more exploited should more sexual expression be subject to legal sanctions.

For the foregoing reasons, it is not surprising that virtually all of the organizations representing sex trade workers have opposed schemes to censor pornography. Sex workers, including pornography models and actresses, have repeatedly lobbied the National Organization for Women to refrain from supporting the antipornography movement. Leonore Tiefer, a psychology professor who specializes in clinical and research work on sexuality, has written, "These women have appealed to feminists for support, not rejection. . . . Sex industry workers, like all women, are striving for economic survival and a decent life, and if feminism means anything it means sisterhood and solidarity with these women."[29]

Here is one such appeal, in the form of a letter written to me in 1993 by a woman who enjoys working in the scarlet collar industry—"Karen" (who is also quoted at the beginning of this chapter):

Dear Ms. Strossen:

After reading your interview in December's issue of *Vogue,* I feel compelled to thank you for your strong stand against antipornography/procensorship "feminists," and your rejection of the condescending images they propagate against women such as myself.

I am a "stripper" in a club here in New York. I am one of those women who consider nude dancing "a perfectly legitimate way to make a living."

I am also a first year law student at one of the top law schools in the country. No one coerced me into the sex industry. I had a good, although not terribly lucrative, job as an assistant editor when I first started dancing. I do not do drugs. I have not been brainwashed. As a student, I find dancing to be a dream job. I work once a week, and make enough money to support myself.

I find it sad and ironic that some of the loudest voices in feminism today perpetuate outmoded and patronizing stereotypes of women in the sex industry. Many of us are intelligent, well-educated women. Many of us are feminists, though we may feel torn and confused about what that means anymore.

Throughout college, I unequivocally considered myself a feminist, but since I started dancing I have begun to feel that the feminist "establishment" considers me, at best, an unenlightened victim, at worst, the enemy. In the current political climate, erotic dancing is now doubly stigmatized. Because I am also pursuing a "legitimate" career in law, my dancing career must remain my dark secret.

Rather than liberating us, the puritanical wing of contemporary feminism inhibits female sexual awareness and freedom. By painting all pornography or erotic dancing as a perverse and dangerous dark monster, inescapably degrading to women and responsible for violent sex crimes, the women's movement denies women's own sexuality. Women have sexual fantasies too—dirty, shocking, kinky fantasies. Many women are sexually aroused by a wide spectrum of erotic images and writing. Women rent porno movies; women read dirty books; a few women even come to watch us dance (much to my delight). Whereas everything the MacKinnon camp has to say about erotica implies that only men find erotica arousing. Their rhetoric is predicated on a false and repressive dichotomy between "perverse," "predatory" male sexuality and squeaky clean, politically correct female desire for intimacy. My grandmother's generation of young women was taught that lust was something only men felt. The 1960s were supposed to have changed all that.

Today increasing numbers of women direct pornographic movies, in which women play more interesting and aggressive roles than in traditional pornography. Their efforts should be applauded as an important contribution to *true women's liberation*. Instead, to the extent they are discussed at all by antipornography feminists (which isn't much), they are denounced as collaborators. As if sexual explicitness must always be exploitive of women.

Erotic dancing has been tremendously liberating for me. The first time I ever got up on stage and took off my clothes, I was terrified. But at some point I crossed a line after which I left behind forever a lifetime of feeling self-conscious about my naked body, left behind all the baggage of sexual inhibition civilized society had impressed upon me. Women who still cling to that baggage imagine the woman who dances or poses nude as vulnerable and degraded. They don't understand that for the woman who has crossed that line and embraced the taboo, she feels instead the thrill of empowerment.

I hope you will understand if I do not feel comfortable signing my full name. Thank you for taking the time to read my letter.

Sincerely,
Karen[30]

The Woman-as-Male-Pawn Worldview

As noted by writer Cathy Young, cofounder of the Women's Freedom Network, there is a striking parallel between the views of some abortion opponents that no woman could freely choose to have an abortion—or, as they would characterize it, to "kill her baby"—and the views of anti-pornography activists that no woman can freely choose to perform for sexually explicit materials. Both views presuppose an infantilized woman incapable of knowing what is in her own best interests, and needing the protection of the state, or of other women (or men) who invoke the state's legal apparatus, to make those determinations for her. In this respect, as in so many others, the procensorship feminists' alliance with the radical right is substantive, as well as strategic.

Young reports that Olivia Gans, the head of an organization called American Victims of Abortion, declared on a nationally televised panel discussion, "My child died because of *Roe v. Wade.*" When another panelist pointed out that Gans chose to have an abortion and that the Court's historic decision merely gave her the right to make that choice, Gans responded, "It was a choice I was forced to make, because of the pressure of the abortionist."[31]

This woman-as-male-pawn worldview echoes the common pro-censorship feminist theme that women who choose to pose for, look at, or defend pornography are really the dupes of the men for whom they are fronts. It must be stressed that Gans and others who contend that no woman could truly make a voluntary choice to terminate a pregnancy—some of whom call themselves "feminists for life"—believe they are protecting women's long-range interests in making the "right" decisions about their bodies and their lives. Of course, procensorship feminists share the identical belief. So we are faced with a through-the-looking-glass world in which antiabortion feminists believe that women's right to choose abortions really empowers only abortionists, and in which antiporn feminists believe that women's right to choose sexual expression really empowers only pornographers. Moreover, both groups ignore the fact that the occupations they respectively most despise, abortionist and pornographer, include many women as well as men.

Another unifying theme among Dworkin, Gans, and MacKinnon is that they all invoke the powerful, negative concept of rape to describe what they see as an inevitably involuntary act on the woman's part: Dworkin and MacKinnon analogize all heterosexual intercourse to rape; Gans and her allies describe abortion as "surgical rape."[32] Further reinforcing the commonality of the antiabortion and antiporn views, Dworkin has described childbirth through cesarean section as surgical rape. In her book *Pornography: Men Possessing Women*, Dworkin decries the "pornography of pregnancy" and condemns childbirth through C-section as a "surgical fuck" committed "by the new rapist, the surgeon." To be sure, there is much evidence that C-sections have been overused in the United States, but Dworkin's sensationalized, sexualized demonization of doctors may well redound to the disadvantage of the women at risk, by making it easy for readers to dismiss the serious problem buried beneath her hyperbolic harangue. Here is her horrific description:

> Pregnancy is confirmation that the woman has been fucked: it is confirmation that she is a cunt. . . . The display marks her as a whore. . . . Her belly is proof that she has been used. Her belly is his phallic triumph. . . . The pregnancy is punishment for her participation in sex. She will get sick, her body will go wrong in a thousand different ways, she will die. The sexual excitement is in her possible death. . . . And now, the doctors have added more sex—to birth itself. . . . They cut directly into the uterus with a knife—a surgical fuck. She is tied down—literally cuffed and tied, immobilized by bondage. . . . her legs spread; they pour drugs into her to induce labor; their bondage and their drugs cause intense and unbearable pain; . . . she is drugged and sliced into, surgically fucked. The epidemic of cesarean sections in this country is a sexual, not a medical, phenomenon. The doctors save the vagina—the birth canal of old— for the husband; they fuck the uterus directly, with a knife. Modern childbirth . . . comes from the metaphysics of male sexual domination; she is a whore, there to be used, the uterus of the whore entered directly by the new rapist, the surgeon, the vagina saved to serve the husband.[33]

Consistent with the procensorship feminists' view of women's nonagency in the sexual domain, MacKinnon has made statements specifically about abortion rights that are startlingly similar to statements by antiabortion activists. Looking at the world through the eye of her own ubiquitous needle, MacKinnon has even criticized the Supreme Court's landmark 1973 *Roe v. Wade* decision, which held that women have a fundamental constitutional right to choose abortion, for "facilitating women's heterosexual availability" and "freeing male aggression" by removing one of the few "legitimized reasons women had for refusing sex."[34] In fact, although MacKinnon supports a woman's right to an abortion, she says she does so for a reason that is eerily consonant with the antiabortion philosophy—namely, that women should not be forced to carry to term pregnancies that resulted from nonconsensual sex;[35] likewise, many "pro-life" activists are willing to tolerate abortion when a pregnancy results from rape. As Cardozo law professor Jeanne Schroeder has observed, summarizing MacKinnon's views:

> Women need abortion as a remedy because sexuality . . . is thrust upon them. Abortion restores choice by permitting women to reject the *consequences* of heterosexuality. . . . For MacKinnon, whether abortion would be necessary, or even ethically acceptable, in a society where sexual equality existed, cannot be known.[36]

The procensorship feminists' devalued view of women is not only that we can never freely, intelligently consent to pose for pornographic materials. In their worldview, women's bodies are merely the instruments for male sexual aggression and domination. Ironically, then, while a major rallying cry of the reproductive freedom movement has been, "A Woman's Body, A Woman's Choice," an appropriate rallying cry for the procensorship feminists would seem to be, "A Woman's Body, A Man's Choice."

CHAPTER 10

Would-Be Censors Subordinate
Valuable Works to Their Agenda

My own book, *The Feminine Mystique*, which ... helped
to start the modern women's movement, was suppressed
as pornographic in libraries in the Midwest. Why, I don't
know. Its only passion was for the personhood of women.
—BETTY FRIEDAN, founding President
National Organization for Women[1]

Given the inescapable ambiguity of the central concepts in the feminist antipornography laws—subordinating or degrading descriptions
or depictions—and the subjectivity of any interpretation of sexually
oriented expression, these laws necessarily arm individual women and
government officials with the power to impose on others their views
about what forms of sexuality are politically or morally acceptable. All
of us would be hostage to the tastes of the individual women who sued
under an antipornography law and of the judges and jurors who ruled
on their claims. To envision what this would really mean, in this chapter I address first the many types of works that could be construed, by
people with various motives, to fit the broad criteria of "subordination"
in the Dworkin-MacKinnon model law. I then consider what kinds of
works Dworkin and MacKinnon themselves find subordinating, based
on their current activism, to provide a glimpse of the law's consequences
as contemplated by its designers.

181

Who Decides for Women about Images of Women?

It is no goal of feminism to restrict individual choices or stamp out sexual imagery. . . . Women are as varied as any citizens of a democracy. . . . It is the right and responsibility of each woman to read, view or produce the sexual material she chooses without the intervention of the state "for her own good." We believe genuine feminism encourages individuals to make these choices for themselves. This is the great benefit of being feminists in a free society.

—Feminists for Free Expression, opposing the
Pornography Victims' Compensation Act[2]

As political analyst Ann Lewis has aptly observed, the key slogan of the abortion rights movement—"Who decides?"—applies equally well to the pornography controversy.[3] In this context, the fundamental questions are: Who decides which sexual expression is subordinating and which is liberating? Which contains negative imagery and which positive? Which makes the viewer feel unpleasant terror and which makes her feel pleasurable excitement? Under the procensorship feminists' model law, the government ultimately makes all of these decisions. Thus, as indicated in the last chapter, the antipornography movement's approach to sexual speech is strikingly similar to the antiabortion movement's approach to reproduction. In both cases, decisions that have an enormous impact in the quintessentially personal realm of sexuality are made not by the individual who is centrally and directly affected, but rather, by the government.

To be sure, under the civil lawsuit enforcement mechanism that procensorship feminists advocate, individual women (and men) will initiate any crackdown on particular words or images—as if it should be any consolation that the challenged materials are being outlawed in part through the efforts of a citizen vigilante rather than wholly through official government agents.

This book contains descriptions and illustrations of some of the innumerable, varied materials that would be endangered if procensorship feminists prevailed. These items not only fit within the law's sweeping definition of pornography, but many have already been attacked by procensorship feminists and others, in some cases successfully. They include examples of the following endangered species of sexual speech: celebrated paintings and sculptures by classic masters; photographs by renowned photographers; works by female, feminist artists; family photographs; erotica that is produced by women for women, including for lesbians by lesbians; nonsexual cartoons conveying witty, satirical messages about current political and social controversies; news coverage of female victims of sexual violence; materials conveying vital information about health, sexuality, contraception, and disease control; historical works about women's sexual subordination; works expressing feminist critiques of our patriarchal system and of stereotypical gender roles; and even antipornography protests by advocates of the Dworkin-MacKinnon law.

Although the Dworkin-MacKinnon model statute sets forth eight criteria for assessing whether any challenged expression depicts a woman's subordination, these criteria accentuate rather than mitigate the problems of ambiguity, subjectivity, and the resulting discretionary power handed over to those who enforce the law. These vague criteria (quoted in chapter 3) are merely open-ended invitations for value-laden interpretations. No two people could possibly agree on their precise meanings or on whether they are satisfied by any particular sexual expression.

What does it mean, for example, that "women are presented as sexual objects," a "standard" that is contained in four of the eight criteria? Or that "women are presented in postures of sexual . . . display"? Or that, through the exhibition of their "body parts—including but not limited to vaginas, breasts and buttocks," women "are reduced to those parts"? Surely these all-encompassing criteria would engulf all words or images with any sexual connotation. Indeed, since the last-mentioned criterion would also extend to women being "reduced to" *any* body parts—not just their specifically sexual parts—it would threaten any description or depiction of any portion of the female physiognomy.

Another criterion that expressly extends far beyond sexually oriented materials is the one that proscribes "women . . . shown as filthy . . . bleeding, bruised, or hurt in a context that makes these conditions sexual." This portion of the law would jeopardize news coverage

or documentaries that disclose—and hence help to galvanize constructive societal responses to—the very real suffering endured by actual
women. For example, this standard would clearly cover MacKinnon's
own graphic descriptions of the massive numbers of brutal rapes in the
Balkans.[4]

As if this indication of the law's sweeping scope is not scary enough,
recall that it is not confined to images of women. Decreeing that "[t]he
use of men [or] children in place of women . . . is pornography for purposes of this law," its proponents ensure that virtually no words or pictures would be beyond its reach. Some sense of the law's breathtaking
breadth is provided by this excerpt from the ACLU's trial court brief in
the *Hudnut* case, successfully challenging the Indianapolis antipornography ordinance:

> [T]he ordinance would deter the distribution of much unabashedly
> erotic literature of considerable literary or historic value. . . .
>
> [S]cholars could not describe, students could not study, patrons
> could not purchase, printers could not produce, institutions could not
> exhibit, and dealers could not purvey an array of visual art and sculp-
> ture comprising a principal part of our collective cultural heritage. Not
> even religious imagery—often sexually explicit—would be immune. . . .
>
> The ordinance would prohibit much clinical sexual literature. . . .
> Since the sexual subordination of women is a historical reality, the ordi-
> nance would be likely to deter much historical or anthropological work
> graphically describing such perspectives and practices. Much post-
> Freudian psychological as well as prominent philosophical literature
> involves the notion of sexual objectification. . . .
>
> The purely descriptive and academically detached nature of many . . .
> scholarly depictions would not shield them.[5]

The breadth of the Dworkin-MacKinnon model law cannot be dismissed as just the accidental product of poor draftswomanship. To
the contrary, its scope accurately reflects the procensorship feminists'
views about the scope of the underlying problem and its appropriate
solution. As they emphasize, male domination has deep and pervasive
roots in our society, so it is not surprising that our culture is permeated

by expression that reflects women's inferior status; if the answer is, as they contend, to suppress such expression, then the sweep of censorship must indeed be expansive. For this reason, the courts that struck down the Indianapolis version of the MacDworkin law concluded that it could not be salvaged through a narrowing construction. As the appellate court said, "No amount of struggle with particular words and phrases in this ordinance can leave anything in effect." This conclusion followed from the court's determination that the law's core feature—and the core conception of the procensorship analysis—is its open-ended definition of pornography, which is "defective root and branch."[6]

Frightening Feminists

A phallocentric culture is more likely to begin its censorship purges with books on pelvic self-examination for women or books containing lyrical paeans to lesbianism than with *See Him Tear and Kill Her.*

—ROBIN MORGAN, writer[7]

As Robin Morgan indicates, one of the images that would fit squarely within the MacDworkin definition of pornography is that of a woman conducting a pelvic self-examination; directly violating one of the law's criteria, the woman would be "presented being penetrated by" an "object"—namely, a speculum. No doubt this is a significant reason that Morgan, who coined the oft-quoted epigram, "Pornography is the theory and rape is the practice,"[8] has subsequently repudiated her earlier support for censoring pornography.

The classic, popular book on women's health and sexuality, *Our Bodies, Ourselves,* contains many words and images—including those of women conducting pelvic self-examinations—that would subject it to the feminist antipornography law. Not surprisingly, then, the book's publisher, the Boston Women's Health Book Collective, campaigned against the version of the MacKinnon-Dworkin law that was proposed in Cambridge, Massachusetts, in 1985. The book already had been the target of concerted censorship efforts spearheaded by fundamentalists and conservatives, who labeled it "too explicit" and "filthy." In 1977, Phyllis Schlafly's conservative Eagle Forum, apparently angered by the book's increasing availability in small-town libraries, launched a series of local campaigns to ban it, claiming that it encourages masturbation, lesbianism, premarital sex, and abortion. In Helena, Montana, the Eagle Forum succeeded in removing the book from school libraries, until the ACLU forced its reinstatement through a lawsuit. These earlier efforts to suppress *Our Bodies, Ourselves* were unsuccessful because the book clearly does not constitute proscribable obscenity. But it could well fall afoul of the broader, feminist-style antipornography laws.

Many other works that are especially important to women and feminists, which have already been subject to right-wing censorship efforts, would—ironically—also be even more endangered under a MacDworkinite measure. These include *Ms.* magazine, which has been removed from high school libraries for containing information about contraception, lesbianism, and masturbation, and Judy Blume's novels about adolescent sexuality, which are among the most widely censored books in the United States, removed from both school and public libraries all over the country. The American Civil Liberties Union's brief in the Indianapolis case made this salient point:

> Ironically, much overtly feminist scholarly material designed to address the same concerns prompting the [Dworkin-MacKinnon law] would fall within [its] sweeping definition of pornography. Prominent examples include Kate Millett's *The Basement*, a graphic chronicle of sexual torture; Dr. Paul Abramson's *Sarah: A Sexual Biography*, a detailed scholarly case study of vicious sexual abuse; sundry works on rape, wife beating and domestic violence; court testimony and photographic evidence in rape and sexual assault cases; works like [Susan] Brownmiller's *Against Our Will: Men, Women and Rape*; and psychiatric literature describing sexual pathologies and therapeutic modalities. Indeed, *Pornography: Men Possessing Women*, a work by Andrea Dworkin, one of the ordinance's original drafters, contains, by way of illustration, so many far-from-isolated passages graphically depicting the explicit sexual subordination of women that it could easily be pornographic under the ordinance.[9]

As already noted, nine years after the ACLU filed this brief, Andrea Dworkin's book *Pornography* (as well as another book she wrote) was indeed held hostage to Canada's version of the feminist antipornography law, seized by Canadian customs officials. We warned you, Andrea!

Although it is not surprising that Dworkin's antipornography manifestos contain pornographic descriptions of the works she condemns, it is noteworthy that Dworkin's fiction also contains many similar passages, some of which I quoted in chapter 7. Dworkin has acknowledged that her own work would be censored under her model law, but she apparently considers this a price worth paying for the power to censor other works that would also be viewed as pornography.[10] Even assuming that she or other procensorship feminists do take such a position, they certainly do not speak for all feminists on this point. Many may well believe that Dworkin's antipornography tracts, by depicting and deploring violence and discrimination against women, make valuable contributions to redressing those problems. And many may find her novels valuable from an artistic or political perspective. Some readers may find her novels erotically stimulating and pleasurable. The ACLU would certainly oppose any effort to suppress any of Dworkin's writings or statements.

Just as the ACLU brief accurately—alas—predicted that Dworkin's writings would be censored under her model law, the other items on the ACLU's list of endangered feminist works also cannot be dismissed as the mere fevered fears of civil libertarians. To the contrary, procensorship feminists themselves have recognized that some of these materials would be deemed punishable pornography under MacDworkinite laws; in some cases, they have even advocated that outcome.

Examples of expression that MacKinnon has deplored as pornographic, despite their clear benefits for women and feminists, include medical school textbooks[11] and the testimony of female victims of sexual assault and harassment.[12] In *Only Words,* MacKinnon writes, "When words of sexual abuse are in [women's] mouths, that is pornography. . . ."[13] University of Pennsylvania law professor C. Edwin Baker has noted that, by this logic, Anita Hill was pornographic when she repeated the words that she attributed to Clarence Thomas.[14] And writer Judith Levine reminds us, "To be safe from sexual violence, we must be able to publicly describe it in every obscene detail."[15]

Given procensorship feminists' far-reaching views of what constitutes proscribable pornography, I would feel no more comfortable giving them the power to decide what reading or viewing material will be available to me than I would feel giving that power to Phyllis Schlafly, Janet Reno, or any woman or man, whether in government or not. Both Dworkin and MacKinnon recently played key roles in situations involving the suppression of speech by feminist women, on issues of vital importance to women, including reproductive options and female sexuality. These frightening episodes confirm that Big Sister is already watching over us, and should shore up our resolve to beware of giving her even more power to do so.

Today's Procensorship Tactics, Tomorrow's Censorship Targets

Assuming for the sake of argument that the envisioned law could somehow be enforced only by Dworkin, MacKinnon, and like-minded women, it still would impose irreparable injuries upon expression by, for, and about women. This conclusion is supported by two incidents that took place in fall 1992. Whether or not these incidents involved formal censorship (as Dworkin's and MacKinnon's critics have contended but they have denied), they are nonetheless important in illuminating the formal censorship regime that the MacDworkin law would institute. The works that were targeted in these 1992 situations could all be labeled pornographic, and hence legally suppressed, under that law.

During the fall of 1992, Andrea Dworkin sought to prevent the publication, distribution, and sale of a book about women's reproductive health, written by two respected feminists, because she disagreed with one point they made in two paragraphs of the book. Moreover, although Dworkin complained to the book's (male) publisher and orchestrated a nationwide protest and boycott effort against the book, she refused to speak to the female, feminist authors of the book, or even to answer their letters.

A Woman's Book of Choices, a consumer guide to legal abortion and other means for safely ending unwanted pregnancies when legal abortions are not available, was written by Rebecca Chalker and Carol Downer, leaders of the women's health and reproductive freedom movement.[16] Chalker has long worked as an abortion counselor and writer. Downer, who was the founder and longtime director of the Federation of Feminist Women's Health Centers, has been described as a folk heroine of the women's health movement because of her 1972 trial and acquittal on charges of practicing medicine without a license; she had applied yogurt to a vaginal yeast infection.

Issued at a time when abortion rights supporters widely feared that the Supreme Court would overturn *Roe v. Wade, A Woman's Book of Choices* was warmly welcomed by leading feminists. Feminist social critic Barbara Ehrenreich, who wrote the book's foreword, called it "the most important book on reproductive rights ever written";[17] Barbara Seaman, the pioneering feminist author of *The Doctor's Case against the Pill,* lauded it as "perhaps the most important book ever written on women's rights and women's lives";[18] and the Boston Women's Health Book Collective, which publishes *Our Bodies, Ourselves,* also enthusiastically endorsed it. Andrea Dworkin, however, refused to endorse the book; worse yet, because she strenuously disagreed with one passage in it, she did everything she could to prevent it from being published and to deter anyone from buying it.

The passage at issue appears in a section of the book containing stories of women who were forced to take desperate steps to obtain abortions before *Roe v. Wade* made them legal. One of these stories, entitled "Faking Rape," recounts the experiences during the 1950s of a Miami artist named Belinda. A doctor told Belinda that she could give her an abortion if she had been raped. Belinda thereupon filed a fabricated rape complaint, thus securing a police report that served as her license to have an abortion.

After Belinda's story, the book's authors appended this comment: "Today, rape crisis and sexual abuse counseling are pretty thorough and standardized, so trying to fake such situations is not as easy as it used to be. It may require some research, preplanning and the help of sympathetic counselors."[19] The book then quotes a former rape counselor as "suggesting" that women could make false rape reports more convincing by wearing torn clothes and borrowing semen from a friend or lover to spread on their clothes or bodies.

The authors of *A Woman's Book of Choices* maintain that Belinda's story and their commentary about it simply describe a practice of women under duress, and do not suggest that either women who complain of rape, or rape counselors, are generally lying. But when the book's publisher, Dan Simon of Four Walls Eight Windows, gave Andrea Dworkin galleys of the book shortly before its scheduled publication, seeking her endorsement, Dworkin vociferously objected to this section of the book, contending that it bolstered the already widespread tendency to discount rape victims' complaints.

According to Simon, who had also published Dworkin's most recent book, *Mercy,* Dworkin threatened to (in her own words) "kill" the book if this passage were not removed.[20] Dworkin conveyed her fervent objections to various colleagues in the women's movement, who contacted the publisher to claim that this section was "dangerous" to women and to demand that it be rewritten. The publisher told Dworkin that it was too late in the publishing process to make the demanded changes, and that they would have to be deferred until the second printing.

At that point, still without having contacted the book's authors, Andrea Dworkin and her allies began a public campaign against *A Woman's Book of Choices,* faxing and calling feminists, health educators, and rape crisis counselors across the country, stating that the book encouraged the belief that women lie about being raped. In response, the publisher and authors received numerous protests, as well as threats of boycotts and lawsuits from people who, according to Chalker, had not "even seen a copy of the book, let alone read it."[21] Even worse, some bookstore owners, including owners of feminist bookstores, agreed to boycott the book.

Defending against charges that Dworkin's campaign against *A Woman's Book of Choices* was a form of censorship, Dworkin's agent, Elaine Markson, said:

> Andrea did not try to censor the authors. . . . She meant to protect the authors as well as the rape crisis centers.[22]

Just as many women do not feel "protected" by Dworkin's efforts to shield them from pornography, Rebecca Chalker and Carol Downer did not feel protected by Dworkin's efforts to shield women from their book. As Downer commented, "She's spread poison around the country. We're facing whispers and half-truths everywhere we go."[23]

Nor can Markson's rhetoric about "protection" camouflage the censorial impact of such coercive tactics as boycotts. Consider the following "reasons why feminists should think twice about boycotting books," suggested by ACLU attorney Marjorie Heins:

[T]he goal of boycotting a bookseller is to suppress, or censor, some literature, because of its offensive content. . . .

Although censorship by private individuals or groups doesn't raise the same legal questions as government censorship . . . it does raise some of the same moral and political questions. [In both cases,] censorship has the same dangerous purpose: To shrink the expressive landscape. [T]he boycotters hope, through economic coercion, to . . . impose an ideological litmus test on works that [publishers and booksellers] consider for sale or publication. . . .

Because selling books is a relatively precarious trade, publishers and booksellers are highly vulnerable to pressures from both governmental and private groups. Witness the shocking acquiescence of Waldenbooks a few years ago in removing *The Satanic Verses* from its stores after Islamic fundamentalists pronounced a death sentence on Salman Rushdie.[24]

Shortly after Simon had declared that *A Woman's Book of Choices* was too far along to be revised, he discovered that it had been printed but not bound, therefore making revision costly but possible. Accordingly, Chalker and Downer rewrote the controverted paragraph so it read:

Only in desperate situations—such as women may find themselves in in the future if states ban abortions except for certain reasons such as rape—should women even consider resorting to faking rape. Doing so has the potential to undermine the gains of the movement against violence against women which has worked to overcome the myth used by hostile prosecutors and judges that women who report rape cannot be trusted.[25]

Through her agent, Dworkin said that *A Woman's Book of Choices* was no longer "heinous" after the changes,[26] and indicated that she would cease her active campaign against the book. The authors, though, remained frustrated, because Dworkin was not as publicly forthcoming with this opinion as she had been with her previous denunciations. Consequently, they continued to face angry rape counselors and threatened boycotts. Worse yet, some major feminist bookstores that Dworkin had contacted refused to carry the book. Chalker says that Dworkin's actions hurt the book's reputation and sales, despite the change. She noted that the New York State branch of the National Organization for Women had been planning to purchase hundreds of copies of the book to distribute to chapters in small towns where it might not otherwise be sold, but "someone stopped it because of this idea it's dangerous for women."[27] As Dan Simon said in a letter to Andrea Dworkin, "[Y]ou have crossed the line from being a helpful critic to attempting to silence an important publication."[28]

Dworkin seems to blink away the historical reality that, in the pre-*Roe* days when virtually all abortions were illegal, women were driven to such desperate measures as faking rape. She also blinks away the continuing reality that, for many women, including poor women, abortion still is not a practical option in all too many instances; for them, alas, faking rape may remain the only way to terminate an unwanted pregnancy. While Congress denies Medicaid funding for virtually all abortions for poor women, for example, one of the few situations in which such funding is available is when the pregnancy is the result of rape.

But the merits of *A Woman's Book of Choices* are beside the point here. For whether or not one agrees with any or all of the book's ideas, it is indisputable, as the book's title underscores, that Chalker and Downer were trying to expand women's choices. In stark contrast, by seeking to bar women's access to the book, Dworkin was seeking to block women's choice about "choice."

Both MacKinnon and Dworkin played a role in a fall 1992 episode at the University of Michigan Law School, where MacKinnon teaches, in suppressing documentary photography and videos by seven feminist artists, five of whom are female, on the themes of sexuality and prostitution.[29] While MacKinnon has argued that the decision to censor these works was made by law students, she and Dworkin at least influenced the students' decision, as explained below. More important, MacKinnon expressly approved that decision after the fact, stating that the inclusion of pornography in an academic conference constitutes "trafficking in women" and "sets women up for harassment and rape."[30] Moreover, after MacKinnon had subsequently looked at the removed videotapes, she pronounced them to be, indeed, pornographic, and hence to have been properly removed.[31] By ratifying the students' removal of the videotapes, MacKinnon gives us a frightening indication of the works—by, about, and for feminist women—that would be subject to legal sanctions under her and Dworkin's antipornography law.

MacKinnon's and Dworkin's views on prostitution are closely related to their views on pornography. They believe that, just as women cannot voluntarily consent to pose for pornography, they cannot voluntarily consent to work in any aspect of the sex industry, including prostitution. Accordingly, just as they advocate imposing legal sanctions on pornography, they oppose lifting legal sanctions from prostitution.[32]

During the spring of 1992, the student editors of the then-new *Michigan Journal of Gender & Law,* behind which MacKinnon was a "moving force,"[33] were planning a symposium on prostitution for the fall of 1992. In conjunction with this conference, they invited artist Carol Jacobsen to curate an art exhibit on prostitution, including her own work, to present the views and experiences of prostitutes in their own voices. Although the students assured Jacobsen that the symposium would not be dominated by MacKinnon's antipornography, antilegalization-of-prostitution perspective, in fact, the symposium turned out to be exclusively for speakers with that perspective, including Dworkin and MacKinnon themselves.

Shortly before the symposium took place, student organizers admitted to Jacobsen that it had in fact become more a forum for the antipornography movement than for a discussion of prostitution. The invited antipornography, antilegalization-of-prostitution activists, following their familiar tactic, refused to appear if feminists holding different views were also invited. Although Jacobsen found these developments disturbing, they also made her feel that her exhibit would be more important than ever, since it would provide the only dissent from the MacDworkinite view at the two-day conference.

Jacobsen's exhibit included Jacobsen's own *Street Sex* (1989), candid video interviews with Detroit prostitutes who had just been released from jail; *Angelina Foxy* (1986–present), an ongoing photo-text essay by Paula Allen, documenting the life of a Jersey City prostitute; *The Salt Mines* (1990), a critically acclaimed documentary about homeless transvestite hustlers in New York City by Susanna Aikin and Carlos Aparicio; *Outlaw Poverty, Not Prostitutes* (1991), an activist video by Carol Leigh (aka "Scarlot Harlot") chronicling prostitutes' international organizing to improve their working conditions; and *Portrait of a Sexual Evolutionary* (1987) by Veronica Vera, an autobiographical account of her experiences as a former porn actress, producer of female-oriented erotic films, and prostitutes' rights activist.

The exhibit had been on display for only a few hours when a conference speaker, objecting to the sexual imagery it contained, complained to MacKinnon. MacKinnon in turn conveyed this complaint to the student organizers, who promptly removed a composite videotape containing the works of five of the exhibit's seven artists. According to Jacobsen, the student who removed the tape explained to her that she had done so under pressure from MacKinnon, who had received a complaint that the tape was pornographic.[34]

Jacobsen read a statement at the conference deploring the removal of the tape, stressing that she had selected the videos on it specifically because "they focus on prostitutes' and sex workers' own voices." She announced that she had reinstalled the tape and concluded, "If the conference organizers wish to censor or remove any part of the exhibit *again*, they must censor all of it."[35] Shortly after this statement, the student organizers met with MacKinnon, Dworkin, and two other antipornography activists who were speaking at the conference. According to press accounts, during this meeting, MacKinnon warned the students of the dangers of showing pornography, even in an academic context, and Dworkin told them that she had been harassed by men who had viewed pornography.[36] After this discussion, the students decided to tell Jacobsen that the entire exhibit would have to be removed.

As a result of this censorial action, a two-day conference purportedly on "Prostitution: From Academia to Activism," was completely stripped of any expression on behalf of the many sex industry activists who support decriminalization of prostitution. In fact, it included no voices of any current sex industry workers at all. As Veronica Vera wrote in an open letter to the University of Michigan newspaper: "If you were trying to study any other subject, you would study the experts. Carol Jacobsen offered you practical experts."[37] The voices—as well as the choices—of these women, along with the many other feminists who call for decriminalizing prostitution, were silenced by the conference organizers and speakers.

MacKinnon has sought to dissociate herself from this sorry episode by saying that she did not explicitly tell the students to remove the art exhibit. But, regardless of whether MacKinnon expressly urged them to remove the Jacobsen exhibit, a student confided to Jacobsen that she felt pressured by MacKinnon. As observed by ACLU attorney Marjorie Heins, who represented Jacobsen and the other artists in challenging this suppression of their work, "MacKinnon expressed to the students her already well-known opinions about pornography. . . . The students were practicing what the professor had frequently preached."[38]

Across the country, critics denounced this removal of feminist artworks from a law school–underwritten and—sponsored conference. In response, apologists for the episode asserted that the students were acting to protect the safety and comfort of symposium participants. As student Brian Wells said, "We really didn't think of it as a censorship issue, but as a safety issue, because two of our speakers said that based on their experience at other events, the tape would be a threat to their safety."[39]

Again, the familiar MacDworkinite tactic of eluding the appropriate—and appropriately stigmatizing—term "censorship" simply masks the real impact of the actions they initiate, influence, and endorse. In the Michigan episode, MacKinnon's and Dworkin's views at least influenced others to deprive female, feminist artists and their potential audience of an opportunity to display or view images and to express or hear views on crucially important issues concerning women's equality, women's sexuality, and women's safety. As stated by Leanne Katz, the executive director of the National Coalition Against Censorship, "The . . . suppression of an art exhibit . . . because the ideas expressed in the exhibit were 'wrong' is blatant censorship. There's no other word for it."[40]

This ugly episode demonstrates that the feminist antipornography movement will inevitably suppress not only works that are especially valuable to women and feminists because they deal with the centrally important topics of sex and gender, but also works that have broad-ranging artistic and political value. Important issues examined in the censored tapes included police abuse, prison conditions, poverty, and homelessness. It is nothing short of Orwellian that such works, in many respects as compelling artistically as they were politically, could be peremptorily confiscated as "pornography" that threatened conferees' "safety." That this action happened at a prestigious law school, and was defended by a dean who has written books about the First Amendment,[41] heightens its nightmarish quality. As Carole Vance concluded, "This case . . . shatters the illusion that restricting sexual imagery for feminist purposes is distinguishable from fundamentalist censorship—either in method or consequence."[42]

In light of the actual record of MacDworkinites' disrespect for other female, feminist voices and choices, it should be clear that the "protection" they seek to bestow would hardly be beneficial to all women. Many of us would like to be protected against such protection.

CHAPTER 11

Lessons from Enforcement

WHEN THE POWERFUL GET MORE POWER

In a male supremacist society the only obscenity law that
will not be used against women is no law at all. . . . How long
will it take oppressed groups to learn that if we give the state
enough rope, it will end up around our necks?
—ELLEN WILLIS, writer[1]

The master's tools will never dismantle the master's house.
—AUDRE LORDE, poet[2]

The last chapter showed how much we would have to fear from enforcement of their antipornography scheme by Dworkin and MacKinnon
themselves. This chapter shows how much we would have to fear from
enforcement of that scheme by any individuals or government officials.
Most ominously, the enforcement record in Canada, which in 1992
embraced the procensorship feminists' notion of pornography, has
turned anticensorship feminists' fears into realities.

The fundamental premise in the procensorship feminists'
philosophy—that our entire societal and legal system is patriarchal,
reflecting and perpetuating the subordination of women—itself conclusively refutes their conclusion that we should hand over to that
system additional power. The procensorship feminists cannot have it
both ways. If, as they contend, governmental power is inevitably used
to the particular disadvantage of relatively disempowered groups, such
as women, it follows that women's rights advocates should oppose

197

measures that augment that power, including Dworkin-MacKinnon-type laws. As columnist George Will observed: "For someone who so strenuously loathes American society, which she says is defined by pornography, MacKinnon is remarkably eager to vest in this society's representative government vast powers to regulate expression."[3]

The Conspicuous Absence
of Sexual Speech in Repressive Regimes

Under patriarchy, no woman is safe to live her life, or to love, or to mother children. Under patriarchy, every woman is a victim, past, present, and future. Under patriarchy, every woman's daughter is a victim, past, present, and future. Under patriarchy, every woman's son is her potential betrayer and also the inevitable rapist or exploiter of another woman.

—ANDREA DWORKIN[4]

[I]t is the state—not free speech—that has been the oppressor of women. It was the state, not pornography, that burned women as witches. It was 18th and 19th century law, not pornography, that defined women as chattel. . . . 20th century laws refuse to recognize rape within marriage. . . . It is the state, not pornography, that has raised barriers against women. It is censorship, not freedom, that will keep the walls intact.

—WENDY MCELROY, writer[5]

Sexual expression is an integral aspect of human freedom. Throughout history, down to the present day, the suppression of sexually explicit speech has characterized regimes that repress both free speech and human rights in general. Measures to suppress sexual expression consistently have targeted views that challenge the prevailing political, religious, cultural, or social orthodoxy.

Sexually explicit speech has been banned by the most repressive regimes, including Communism in the former Soviet Union, Eastern bloc countries, and China; apartheid in South Africa; and fascist or clerical dictatorships in Chile, Iran, and Iraq. Conversely, recent studies of Russia have correlated improvements in human rights, including women's rights, with the rise of free sexual expression. Writer Pete Hamill explains the connection:

> Recent history teaches us that most tyrannies have a puritanical nature. The sexual restrictions of Stalin's Soviet Union, Hitler's Germany and Mao's China would have gladdened the hearts of those Americans who fear sexual images and literature. Their ironfisted puritanism wasn't motivated by a need to erase inequality. They wanted to smother the personal chaos that can accompany sexual freedom and subordinate it to the granite face of the state. Every tyrant knows that if he can control human sexuality, he can control life.[6]

In places where real pornography is conspicuously absent, tellingly, works of political dissent are labeled as such. Laws banning obscene or pornographic expression have been used to suppress all kinds of expression, and the pejorative terms "obscene" and "pornographic" have been used to condemn a wide range of views, far beyond the legal or dictionary definitions of those terms, and even altogether outside the realm of sexuality. The Communist government of the former Soviet Union denounced dissenting political views as pornographic and obscene, and suppressed political dissidents under obscenity laws. In August 1987, when the Chinese Communist government dramatically increased its censorship of books and magazines with Western political and literary messages, it condemned them as "obscene," "pornographic," and "bawdy." The white supremacist South African government banned black writing as "pornographically immoral." In Nazi Germany and the former Soviet Union, Jewish writings were reviled as "pornographic," as were any works that criticized the Nazi or Communist party, respectively.[7]

Even in societies that generally respect human rights, including free speech, as we have seen, the term "pornography" tends to be used as an epithet to stigmatize expression that is politically or socially unpopular. Accordingly, the freedom to produce or consume anything called "pornography" is an essential aspect of the freedom to defy prevailing political and social mores. Pornography is not just the samizdat of individuals who are oppressed or dissident sexually, to paraphrase Stanford law professor Kathleen Sullivan; it is also the samizdat of those who are oppressed or dissident in any respect.

Legal scholar Kenneth L. Karst provides intriguing insights into the link between sexual freedom, including free sexual expression, and freedom from discrimination:

> The suppression of Unreason is rooted in the same fears that produce group subordination: men's fear of the feminine, whites' fear of blackness, heterosexuals' anxiety about sexual orientation. Historically, all these fears have been closely connected with the fear of sexuality. It is no accident that the 1960s, a period of sexual "revolution," also saw the acceleration of three movements that sought major redefinitions of America's social boundaries: the civil rights movement, the gay liberation movement, and the women's movement.[8]

Like all groups who seek equal rights and freedoms, women and feminists have an especially important stake in securing free speech. Throughout history, free speech consistently has been the greatest ally of those seeking equal rights for groups that have been subject to discrimination. Correspondingly, censorship measures have consistently been used to the particular detriment of the relatively unpopular and powerless.

Hating Speech

The pattern of disempowered groups being disproportionately targeted under censorship schemes extends even to censorship schemes that are allegedly designed for their benefit. This phenomenon is vividly illustrated by the enforcement record of laws against "hate speech"—speech that expresses racial, sexist, religious, and other forms of invidious discrimination. I addressed the First Amendment flaws of hate speech laws in chapter 3; since feminist-style antipornography laws are simply a specific kind of anti–hate speech law, it is important also to examine such laws' historical enforcement record. This record demonstrates, once again, that procensorship feminists posit a false choice between free speech and equality values. As Justice Hugo Black noted in dissenting from a 1952 Supreme Court decision upholding a hate speech law (which has been implicitly overturned by subsequent decisions),[9] "If there be minority groups who hail this holding as their victory, they might consider the possible relevancy of this ancient remark: 'Another such victory and I am undone.'"[10]

The first individuals prosecuted under the British Race Relations Act of 1965, which criminalized the incitement of racial hatred, were black power leaders. Their overtly racist messages undoubtedly expressed legitimate anger at real discrimination, yet the statute drew no such fine lines, nor could any similar law possibly do so. Rather than curbing speech offensive to minorities, this British law instead has been used regularly to curb the speech of blacks, trade unionists, and antinuclear activists. Perhaps the ultimate irony of this law, intended to restrain the National Front, a neo-Nazi group, is that it instead has barred expression by the Anti-Nazi League.

The British experience is typical. None of the anti-Semites who were responsible for arousing France against Captain Alfred Dreyfus was ever prosecuted for group libel. But Emile Zola was prosecuted for libeling the French clergy and military in his classic letter "J'Accuse," and he had to flee to England to escape punishment.

Similarly, University of Michigan Law School professor Eric Stein has documented that although the German Criminal Code of 1871 punished offenses against personal honor, "The German Supreme Court . . . consistently refused to apply this article to insults against Jews as a group—although it gave the benefit of its protection to such groups as Germans living in Prussian provinces, large landowners, all Christian clerics, German officers, and Prussian troops who fought in Belgium and Northern France."[11]

That the foregoing examples simply illustrate a long-standing global pattern was documented in a 1992 book published by Article XIX, the London-based International Centre Against Censorship (which takes its name from the free speech guarantee in the Universal Declaration of Human Rights) and the Human Rights Centre at the University of Essex in Great Britain, which draws upon contemporary analyses of the situations in fourteen different countries with various laws punishing racist and other hate speech. According to Sandra Coliver, Article XIX's legal director:

> The flagrant abuse of laws which restrict hate speech by the authorities . . . provides the most troubling indictment of such laws. Thus, the laws in Sri Lanka and South Africa have been used almost exclusively against the oppressed and politically weakest communities. . . . Selective or lax enforcement by the authorities, including in the UK, Israel and the former Soviet Union, allows governments to compromise the right of dissent and inevitably leads to disaffection and feelings of alienation among minority groups.[12]

The international pattern also holds true in specific, localized contexts—namely, on university and college campuses, where, as we have seen, antipornography feminists have made some headway. Again, the British experience is instructive. In 1974, in a move aimed at the National Front, the British National Union of Students (NUS) adopted a resolution that representatives of "openly racist and fascist organizations" were to be prevented from speaking on college campuses "by whatever means necessary (including disruption of the meeting)."[13] The rule had been designed in large part to stem an increase in campus anti-Semitism. But following the United Nations' cue, some British students deemed Zionism a form of racism beyond the bounds of permitted discussion, and in 1975 British students invoked the NUS resolution to disrupt speeches by Israelis and Zionists, including the Israeli ambassador to Great Britain. The intended target of the NUS resolution, the National Front, applauded this result. The NUS itself, in contrast, became disenchanted by this and other unintended consequences of its resolution and repealed it in 1977.

The British experience parallels what has happened in the United States, judging from the campus hate speech codes for which enforcement information is available.[14] One such code was in effect at the University of Michigan from April 1988 until October 1989. Because the American Civil Liberties Union brought a lawsuit to challenge the code (which resulted in a ruling that the code was unconstitutional),[15] the university was forced to disclose information that otherwise would have been unavailable to the public about how it had been enforced. This enforcement record, while not surprising to anyone familiar with the consistent history of censorship measures, should come as a rude awakening to any who believe that anti-hate speech laws will protect or benefit racial minorities, women, or any other group that has traditionally suffered discrimination.

During the year and a half that the University of Michigan rule was in effect, there were more than twenty cases of whites charging blacks with racist speech. More importantly, the only two instances in which the rule was invoked to sanction racist speech (as opposed to other forms of hate speech) involved the punishment of speech by or on behalf of black students. The only student who was subjected to a full-fledged disciplinary hearing under the Michigan rule was an African-American student accused of homophobic and sexist expression. In seeking clemency from the punishment that was imposed on him after this hearing, the student asserted that he had been singled out because of his race and his political views.

Others who were punished at Michigan included several Jewish students accused of engaging in anti-Semitic expression (they wrote graffiti, including a swastika, on a classroom blackboard; they said they intended it as a practical joke) and an Asian-American student accused of making an antiblack comment (his allegedly "hateful" remark was to ask why black people feel discriminated against; he said he raised this question because the black students in his dormitory tended to socialize together, making him feel isolated). Likewise, the student who in 1989 challenged the University of Connecticut's hate speech policy, under which she had been penalized for an allegedly homophobic remark, was Asian-American. She claimed that other students had engaged in similar expression, but that she had been singled out for punishment because of her ethnic background. (Representing this student, the ACLU persuaded the university to drop the challenged policy.)[16] And the first complaint filed under Trinity College's then-new policy prohibiting racial harassment, in 1989, was against an African-American speaker who had been sponsored by a black student organization, Black-Power Serves Itself.

The hate speech lesson from enforcement? Watch what you say about others, depending on not only who those others are, but also who you are. If you are a member of a group that has traditionally suffered discrimination, including women, restrictions on hate speech are especially likely to be wielded against your speech. In fact, as we now shall see, all forms of censorship have consistently been used to suppress speech of and for women.

Women in the Wake of Censorship

Censorship has been, throughout history, the single most widely used patriarchal tool for "protecting" women—from birth control, abortion, sexual satisfaction and non-heterosexual relationships. Without free speech we can have no feminist movement.
—National Organization for Women of New York State[17]

I believe that censorship only springs back against the givers of culture—against authors, artists, and feminists, against anybody who wants to change society. Should censorship be imposed . . . feminists would be the first to suffer.
—ERICA JONG, writer[18]

Although we "babes" have "come a long way," as the saying goes, could we have come further, faster without the "help" of censors? Here, the lesson from enforcement is that women should go slow on censorship, because censorship consistently has been used to slow our search for equal status.

Until recently, the "gag rule," in effect from 1988 until 1993, banned the dissemination of information about abortion at federally funded family planning clinics. (In the fall of 1994, more than three hundred Republican congressional candidates pledged to reinstate the gag rule.) As columnist Anna Quindlen observed, "What the gag rule has taught us is that reproductive freedom is not possible without free speech."[19] Indeed, that lesson should have been learned from the steady use of censorship, throughout our history, to fetter women's reproductive freedom.

Of particular note, laws permitting the suppression of sexually oriented information have often been used to suppress information that is essential not only for women's reproductive rights, but also for other aspects of the women's rights cause. Antiobscenity laws consistently have been used to suppress information about contraception. Dr. Charles Knowlton, author of the first known medical work about contraception in the United States, *Fruits of Philosophy; or, The Private Companion of Young Married People,* was prosecuted in 1839 under the Massachusetts antiobscenity law.

Likewise, the first federal antiobscenity statute, passed in 1873, criminalized the interstate mailing of both sexually oriented material and material related to contraception or abortion. This statute, which is generally known as the "Comstock" law, in honor of the leading antiobscenity crusader Anthony Comstock, who had lobbied for it, provided:

> No obscene, lewd, or lascivious book, pamphlet, picture, paper, print, or other publication of an indecent character, or any article or thing designed or intended for the prevention of conception or procuring of abortion, nor any article or thing intended or adapted for any indecent or immoral use or nature ... shall be carried in the mail.[20]

Each violation of the law could be punished with a fine of up to five thousand dollars or imprisonment at hard labor for one to ten years. Twenty-four states enacted legislation that was modeled on this federal law, prohibiting not only the intrastate transportation of obscene materials, contraceptives, and abortifacients, but also their advertisement or publications about them. Moreover, fourteen state antiobscenity statutes also enjoined speech about contraception and abortion.

Armed with this legislation, Comstock, the longtime director of the Society for the Suppression of Vice, as well as his successor, John Sumner, zealously prosecuted feminists and pioneering birth control advocates who tried to distribute information about women's sexuality and reproduction. Among those Comstock persecuted, at least fifteen women committed suicide, including Ida Craddock, who was imprisoned in 1902 for writing advice manuals on conjugal relations.

In her 1992 biography of Margaret Sanger, the leading early birth control champion, Ellen Chesler noted that the Comstock-inspired antiobscenity laws all but banned any discussion of contraception, even between doctors and patients and within the medical community.[21] Because these laws suppressed much scientific, accurate information about contraception and abortion, the only "information" readily available was in underground publications by quacks and charlatans.[22]

Sanger was persecuted under the antiobscenity laws throughout her career. Her campaign to convey accurate sexual information began in 1912 with two articles in a New York City newspaper. The first, entitled "What Every Mother Should Know," ran without incident, but the U.S. Post Office barred the second, "What Every Girl Should Know." The article contained no information on birth control, but postal officials were offended by Sanger's explanation of venereal disease and her use of words such as "gonorrhea" and "syphilis." Consequently, the newspaper's next issue contained the following announcement: "What Every Girl Should Know: 'NOTHING!' By order of the Post Office."[23]

In 1913, Anthony Comstock prosecuted Sanger for her writings on sexuality and birth control. She was criminally prosecuted again in 1917 and served thirty days in a workhouse for having operated a birth control clinic in Brooklyn. Sanger also served time in jail in Portland, Oregon, for distributing information about birth control. In 1929, she was "banned in Boston"—prohibited from speaking there.

Margaret Sanger had the dubious distinction of being one of the first victims of a new form of censorship that was applied to a then-new medium early in this century. The Supreme Court had ruled in 1915 that movies were not protected "speech" under the First Amendment,[24] and one of the first films banned under that decision was *Birth Control*, a 1917 picture produced by and featuring Margaret Sanger. The New York Court of Appeals held that this movie, a dramatization of Sanger's family planning work, could be censored "in the interest of morality, decency, and public safety and welfare."[25]

This episode underscores several significant themes explored in this book: the close connections between sex and politics, and between sexual and political repression; and the bad tendencies of the former "bad tendency" rationale for suppressing speech (that speech may be censored because it might tend to bring about some future harm), which procensorship feminists are seeking to revive. The court stressed that the film "tends to ridicule the public authorities and the provisions of . . . the Penal Law forbidding the dissemination of contraceptive knowledge," and therefore held that it could be barred, even for adult-only audiences, because it "may engender a desire to obtain" birth control information, and thus might "lead to violations of the law."

The banning of films concerning birth control and other sexual-political subjects of particular interest to women and feminists continued into the second half of this century. In support of his argument that "women who are claiming their equal citizenship should think twice about pressing the argument that pornography is not protected speech," UCLA law professor Kenneth Karst noted that, until the 1950s, New York censors routinely banned films that treated themes of particular concern to women's rights advocates: pregnancy, venereal disease, birth control, abortion, illegitimacy, prostitution, miscegenation, and divorce.[26]

From 1873, when the Comstock Act was passed, through the 1930s, other feminists and health experts who tried to present information about women's sexuality and reproductive options were also plagued by obscenity laws. Charges were brought against Emma Goldman for giving information about birth control during a lecture in New York. Mary Ware Dennett was convicted and sentenced to pay a three hundred dollar fine for her book *The Sex Side of Life: An Explanation for Young People,*[27] which she had written for the education of her adolescent sons. Marie Stopes's *Married Love,* which offered basic anatomical information and health advice to newly married couples, was prosecuted under American antiobscenity laws, even though it was an established bestseller in Europe and had already been expurgated for the American market.[28] (The ACLU represented Dennett and Stopes, and on appeal succeeded in overturning Dennett's conviction and the U.S. Customs Service's ban on both their books.)

Edward Bliss Foote, a popular health writer, was convicted in a prosecution brought by Comstock and forced to eliminate all information about contraception from his published writings. Comstock also successfully prosecuted Ezra Heywood, who had distributed a journal that advertised contraceptives. *A Marriage Manual,* by Hannah and Abraham Stone, was subjected to censorship efforts when it was first published in 1935.

The gag has been loosened or tightened at various times, but never removed. In 1990 Janet Benshoof, director of the ACLU's Reproductive Freedom Project, was charged with the misdemeanor of "soliciting abortion" under the strict antiabortion law that Guam had just passed. Her alleged crime? Benshoof said, during a speech at the Guam Press Club, that Guamanian women could still get legal, low-cost abortions in Hawaii, despite Guam's law criminalizing virtually all abortions, and she gave Guamanian women the address and phone number of Planned Parenthood in Hawaii.[29] This was eighty years after Margaret Sanger, Planned Parenthood's founding mother, was first prosecuted for providing similar information.

We women must go forward. The past is not as different from the present as the future must be. In Anna Quindlen's words:

> In the fight to keep women free it is important to remember this: freedom of speech is the bedrock of it all. Silence is what kept us in our place for too long. If we now silence others, our liberty is false. No more gag rules—that should be our goal. In clinics, in colleges, in lecture halls. Anywhere.[30]

Butler Did It: "Big Surprise" in Canada

Thanks to the Canadian Supreme Court's February 1992 decision in *Butler v. The Queen,* we have been able to observe the MacDworkinite regime in operation. As far as Canada is concerned, Erica Jong's prediction quoted earlier—that "feminists would be the first to suffer" under any newly imposed censorship—is, alas, now a description.

Andrea Dworkin has said, "The *Butler* decision is probably the best articulation of how pornography, and what kinds of pornography, hurt the civil status and civil rights of women,"[31] and Catharine MacKinnon has enthused, "[The *Butler* decision] is a stunning victory for women. This is of world historic importance. This makes Canada the first place in the world that says what is obscene is what harms women, not what offends our values."[32] Others, though they may agree about the decision's "world historic importance," offer dramatically different assessments:

> You presented a brief to the Supreme Court that has us in the shits right now. . . . [Y]ou handed them post-modern language. . . . the language that they had been looking for to come back after us, and now they are busting our bookstores.
> —ELAINE CAROL, performance artist,
> addressing feminist lawyer whose arguments
> were adopted in *Butler*, 1993[33]

> This law isn't protecting us; it's silencing us.
> —LIZ CZACH, member of feminist
> caucus of the Ontario Coalition
> Against Film and Video Censorship[34]

> Andrea Dworkin has done more damage to women's culture in her tenure as darling of the media than anyone who is a leader of the right wing. She is morally responsible for what is happening to women's literature in Canada.
> —PAT CALIFIA, feminist writer, 1993[35]

> *Butler* is just about morality. It's morality in the guise of protecting women and children. And who needs the protection of the male patriarchy anyway, of the state?
> —ELLEN FLANDERS, feminist writer[36]

The *Butler* decision has been a potent weapon to suppress free speech for all, as well as the equality rights of various disempowered groups, including the very women whose rights it was supposed to enhance. As a 1993 article in *The Nation* commented, "This epidemic of censorship shows how 'progressive' controls on expression are bound to backfire."

It concluded, "If Canada's border fiasco gives pause to MacKinnonites in other countries—the lobby for the Pornography Victims' Compensation Act in the United States, for example—maybe it will have been worth the absurdities."[37]

Because Canada's experience under *Butler* provides the only record of the actual impact of a Dworkin-MacKinnon–style law in operation, it is important to examine that record in detail. At the very least, the Canadian experience imposes a heavy burden of proof on antipornography advocates to show that the enforcement trends in Canada would not be replicated here. That burden of proof seems to be insurmountable, though, since the Canadian enforcement trends result from two factors that transcend the U.S.-Canada border: the inherently vague concept of "subordinating" or "degrading" material that is at the heart of all MacDworkinite laws; and the homophobic, antifeminist orientation that many Canadian officials share not only with their U.S. counterparts, but also with many private citizens in both countries.

Indeed, in two important respects, the Canadian version of the feminist antipornography law is less sweeping than the original Dworkin-MacKinnon model. First, notwithstanding *Butler's* incorporation of the MacDworkinite concept of pornography into the Canadian antiobscenity law, that law continues to provide that no material will be deemed obscene if it has an artistic purpose or is part of the serious treatment of a sexual theme. This is similar to the provision in the U.S. Supreme Court's definition of obscenity that excludes any material with serious literary, artistic, political, or scientific value. The Dworkin-MacKinnon model law, though, contains no comparable limitation.

Second, and relatedly, the Canadian obscenity law, again parallel to American obscenity law, applies only to works considered as a whole. Therefore, a work cannot be suppressed just because isolated passages meet the obscenity definition. Under the Dworkin-MacKinnon law, in contrast, even an isolated sexually explicit, subordinating depiction would warrant suppressing an entire work, regardless of its overall value.

The spring 1993 issue of *Feminist Bookstore News,* a Canadian publication, contained the following description of Canada's first year of experience with the antipornography definition that was supposed to be such a boon to feminists: "The *Butler* decision has been used . . . only to seize lesbian, gay and feminist material."[38] Within the first two and a half years after the *Butler* decision, well over half of all Canadian feminist bookstores had had materials confiscated or detained by customs. From Quebec to Victoria, Canadian bookstore managers had the same comment: that *Butler* increased censorship in Canada by customs, police, and lower courts, and that the predominant targets have been gay, lesbian, and women's literature.

Even those Canadian feminists who championed the *Butler* decision—working through the Women's Legal Education and Action Fund (LEAF), which MacKinnon cofounded—have been forced to acknowledge that it has become an engine for oppressing feminist, gay, and lesbian expression. Karen Busby, a lawyer who worked on the LEAF brief, made the following confession at a symposium in Toronto during the fall of 1993:

> Before the ink was dry on *Butler* . . . the Toronto police raided Glad Day Bookshop, a lesbian and gay bookstore, and confiscated *Bad Attitude,* a lesbian erotic magazine. . . . It was a shocking raid. Police ignored representations made by men of women in most cities across Canada, including . . . Toronto . . . and yet the one thing that they raid is this one magazine that sells about forty copies every two months in Canada when it comes out. It's hardly a threat to women's equality and yet that's the magazine that they chose.[39]

To add insult to injury, while Glad Day's owner and manager were arrested for selling *Bad Attitude,* a nearby mainstream bookstore that also sold it was left alone.

Bad Attitude is a magazine published by and for women—specifically, lesbian women. Its editor has explained that the magazine "is called *Bad Attitude* because that's what women who take their sexuality into their own hands (so to speak) are told they have."[40] Nonetheless, the judge who ruled in the Glad Day case found that this feminist, lesbian publication harmed women, and he therefore convicted the Glad Day principals. His ruling was based on a story (told just in words, with no photographs or illustrations) in the magazine about a sex fantasy, entitled "Wunna My Fantasies," by San Francisco writer Trish Thomas. The story is about a woman who surprises another woman in a shower, grabbing her, tying her, slapping her, and pulling her hair. While the showering woman initially resists her assailant's sexual advances, she ultimately succumbs, and they both end up enjoying their sexual encounter. Thomas has said that when she does public readings of her stories about this kind of lesbian fantasy, with some sadomasochistic elements, she is "amazed" by "not just the numbers of women that come up to me . . . to tell me that they've had these fantasies, but the diversity of women—very conservative women too."[41]

Despite the fact that women enjoy the type of fantasy described in "Wunna My Fantasies," the male judge who found it "degrading" and "demeaning," Claude Paris, explained that its fatal flaw was that it described "enjoyable sex after subordination by bondage and physical abuse at the hands of a total stranger." He dismissed the fact that the fantasy's aggressor is female as "irrelevant." Taking his cue from the Canadian Supreme Court in *Butler,* Judge Paris ruled that the ultimately consensual nature of the sex the story describes is not enough to absolve it of the criminalizing "degrading" label. He stated: "The consent . . . far from redeeming the material, makes it degrading and dehumanizing."[42]

A second lower court decision enforcing *Butler* also resulted from seizures of homosexual erotica from Glad Day Bookshop and also held homosexual expression to be "degrading." This decision, issued by Judge F. C. Hayes, held all thirteen of the confiscated gay publications to be "degrading and dehumanizing," explaining only that they showed sexual encounters "without any real, meaningful human relationship."[43] As Karen Busby of LEAF acknowledged, "Judge Hayes' decision [is] clearly homophobic. . . . He said that sex between men in and of itself was degrading and dehumanizing."[44] Chris Bearchell, a lesbian feminist journalist in Canada, commented:

> Before Hayes's ruling, some people no doubt hoped that the Butler decision might bring more enlightened obscenity rulings, because of the court's declaration that its role was to protect women and children from harm. . . . Now they are probably wondering just what pictures and descriptions of consenting men having sex with each other have to do with violence against women and children.[45]

Despite the boasting of Dworkin, MacKinnon, and (at least initially) their LEAF allies that *Butler* ushered in a brave new era of profeminist censorship, Judge Hayes's ruling makes clear instead that *Butler* simply allows censorship on traditional moralistic grounds. Indeed, precisely that interpretation of *Butler* has been made by "Project P," the antiobscenity squad of the Ontario Provincial Police. According to a spokesman, Project P interprets *Butler* to permit explicit sexual expression only if it includes romance and a story line.[46] This prompted Susan Ditta, former curator of the National Gallery of Canada and now the media arts officer at the Canada Council, to comment, "As someone who's spent a great deal of time writing about the deconstruction of narrative in contemporary video art practice, I got really worried about there having to be a story line."[47]

The fact that *Butler* merely provides a new gloss on an old notion of obscenity is underscored by its lack of any impact on the detailed regulations that Canadian Customs officials had previously followed in enforcing the obscenity law at the border. After *Butler,* government lawyers reviewed those regulations and concluded that not one word needed to be changed. As stated by Jacques Boivin, a Canadian artist, this "just goes to show that the reputedly 'feminist' definition of 'degradation' is not a departure but . . . a further reformulation of paternalistic control. Same old baloney with a recycled label."[48] Lawyer Brenda Cossman, who teaches at Canada's York University, calls the new label "sexual morality in drag."[49]

Another aspect of the Glad Day case, the singling out of publications, publishers, distributors, and stores that are relatively small and powerless, also heralded what has been a continuing enforcement pattern under *Butler.* Inland Books, a New York–based small-press book distribution company and the largest U.S. exporter of lesbian and gay literature to Canada, had 73 percent of its shipments to Canada detained during 1993. In one of the biggest book detentions in its history, Canadian Customs detained a 1993 shipment of hundreds of titles from Inland to thirty-six Canadian stores, including university bookstores, literary bookshops, and even a religious bookstore. The distributors that serve lesbian and gay bookstores often carry political publications other than those targeted specifically for the lesbian and gay audience.

214   LESSONS FROM ENFORCEMENT

Because it was part of such a shipment, a September 1993 issue of *The Nation* was detained by Canadian Customs officials.

The *Butler* decision has been used preponderantly against publications with a feminist or lesbian/gay orientation. More mainstream-oriented materials that tend to be sold in mainstream establishments have been undisturbed, benefiting from an apparent double standard in the enforcement of *Butler*. A prominent example is Madonna's *Sex*, which was published by a major commercial house and was sold in large, chain bookstores. (The book's sexually explicit contents, including scenes of rape and bestiality, were deemed sufficiently degrading by MacDworkinites that they publicly ripped it to shreds at the previously discussed 1992 feminist procensorship conference at the University of Chicago Law School.) Likewise, since *Butler*, Canadian authorities have not interfered with the importation or sale of Bret Easton Ellis's *American Psycho*, which contains extremely violent, sexually graphic accounts of the mutilation of women.

The *Toronto Star* has reported that, in many further instances, books destined for nonmainstream bookstores have been seized and banned by customs while the big chain stores are allowed to sell the very same books. Small bookstores are thus suffering substantial economic hardships. The Toronto-based *Globe and Mail* estimated that 75 percent of shipments to Glad Day and similar stores are "opened, delayed, lost, forgotten and occasionally sent back without more than a handful of Canadian citizens knowing about it."[50] According to *The Toronto Star*, "Books dealing with homosexual activities are seized regularly and often held for months, quite literally in an attempt to close down the offending stores."[51] Notes Bruce Walsh, a spokesperson for the Canadian anticensorship coalition CENSORSTOP, "[E]very gay bookseller in this country has attempted to sell their bookstores, but nobody wants to buy them."[52]

One lesbian bookstore has fought back against the Canadian government's selective suppression of lesbian sexual expression. The Little Sisters Book and Art Emporium in Vancouver brought a lawsuit claiming that it had been subjected to government harassment. After the lawsuit was instituted—and, some critics charge, specifically to blunt its allegations—Canadian officials broadened their enforcement efforts to include feminist bookstores, university bookstores, and radical bookstores.

CENSORSTOP has charged that the officials who are implementing *Butler* are "really interested in controlling radical dissent."[53] When Le Dernier Mot (LDM) bookstore published and sold transcripts of a telephone conversation that was politically embarrassing to the Canadian government, and that the government had attempted to ban from publication, customs authorities immediately began to seize books that were being shipped to LDM as allegedly violating the *Butler* obscenity standard. Prior to this incident, no LDM books had ever been seized. Likewise, just one week after Pages Bookstore in Toronto had installed a provocative anticensorship display, customs seized allegedly obscene books that were being shipped to it.

Whether or not Canadian officials have actually exercised their discretionary authority under *Butler* to target political dissent, it is indisputable that the Canadian Supreme Court's adoption of the Dworkin-MacKinnon antipornography standard has given officials a powerful weapon which they could easily aim at dissent, should they wish to do so.

Recalling that *Butler's* supposed rationale is to protect women from works that harm them, it is hard to understand how the feminist writings that have been seized under *Butler* would harm women. Indeed, some material has been suppressed under *Butler* on the ground that it is allegedly degrading and harmful not to women, but to men. For example, Canadian Customs has seized a book entitled *Weenie-Toons! Women Artists Mock Cocks* because of its alleged "degradation of the male penis."[54] Similarly, customs' banned list includes a lesbian feminist magazine entitled *Hothead Paisan,* even though it portrays no sexual activity, because it is purportedly "sexually degrading to men."[55] This comic book–style magazine depicts the adventures of a lesbian terrorist who won't take any guff from men, and who makes those who give her trouble disappear.

In one of the condemned *Hothead Paisan* strips, a white man wearing a business suit chains himself to a statue of Christopher Columbus (on which is engraved, "I found it, it's mine, kill those people") and declares, "Women will have the right to choose over my dead body!" In response, the magazine's heroine, the lesbian avenger "Hothead," springs into action. Crying "Now that's an engraved invitation!" she beats this antichoice demonstrator into the ground.[56] In addition to turning the tables on the incapacitating woman-as-victim stereotype, this strip conveys messages about other political issues, including colonialism and reproductive freedom. What a travesty that it has been suppressed in the name of feminism, under a feminist-advocated law!

And of course two books written by Andrea Dworkin herself, *Pornography: Men Possessing Women* and *Woman Hating*, were seized at the U.S.-Canada border. According to customs, they "illegally eroticized pain and bondage."[57] Dworkin's graphic, sexually explicit descriptions of men committing violent and degrading acts against women are presumably provided for purposes of persuading society to mobilize against misogynistic violence and discrimination. But neither the *Butler* decision nor any other version of the Dworkin-MacKinnon antipornography law contains any exception for subordinating sexually explicit depictions that are part of a feminist presentation. Nor could any such exception possibly be added without compounding the law's already overwhelming subjectivity. (In my view, this book—the one you are reading—is a feminist work, but would Andrea Dworkin or Catharine MacKinnon agree?)

At least one other book that described sexual violence expressly for the purpose of condemning it and aiding people to resist it was also, ironically, among the first targets of *Butler's* censorial regime. It was a novel by Robert Lally, a retired Canadian psychologist who had worked with child molesters. He wrote the book to mobilize the public to take serious action against pedophiles. Its main character, based on a composite of Lally's patients, was designed to show laypeople how pedophiles think and operate. In Lally's words, the book "was supposed to disgust people and frighten the hell out of them, so they would say, 'Let's do something about pedophiles.'" Lally sent one copy of his manuscript to a literary agent in the United States. When she returned it to him, Canadian Customs officials intercepted the manuscript pursuant to the *Butler* ruling. As Mary Williams Walsh wrote in the *Los Angeles Times:*

> Lally's project would . . . appear to be just the sort of undertaking the antipornography lobby would applaud: In his own way, he wanted to protect society from sex crimes. But the plan backfired. Under *Butler*, Lally's opus itself was found to be obscene. Three Mounties and a

Customs officer raided his house and seized his only other copy of the manuscript. Then they clapped their alleged porn kingpin into the back seat of their squad car.[58]

It is quite possible that Canadian Customs confiscated Dworkin's *Woman Hating* purely on the basis of its title. And just as Ohio law enforcement officials went after Debbie Reynolds's exercise video *Doing It Debbie's Way* because of its "provocative" title (see chapter 4), Canadian Customs recently confiscated *Hot, Hotter, Hottest,*[59] apparently for the same reason; if you look beyond the title page, you will see that this volume is a cookbook containing recipes for spicy cuisine! Laughable as these incidents may be, they illustrate the frightening force of the feminist antipornography law to suppress a limitless range of materials that are valued by diverse audiences.

Although the primary targets of Canada's *post-Butler* enforcement efforts have been feminist, lesbian, and gay materials, *Butler* also has emboldened customs officials to seize other works, including serious mainstream books. Canadian Customs seized thirty copies of Marguerite Duras's novella *The Man Sitting in the Corridor* that had been ordered by Trent University. This novella by the respected writer was detained because it includes several scenes in which a woman is beaten after passionate sex; in the last such scene, she dies. Canadian Customs also has seized books by critically acclaimed authors such as Kathy Acker, Ambrose Bierce, Langston Hughes, David Leavitt, Audre Lorde, Anne Rice, and Oscar Wilde. It has barred *Weird Smut Comics,* a publication dealing with the evils of censorship; the political journal *Lies of Our Times;* and the illustrated collection of essays published by the Feminist Anti-Censorship Taskforce, *Caught Looking.*

In 1993, customs detained a shipment of fifteen hundred copies of *Black Looks: Race and Representations,* by black feminist academic bell hooks, that were en route to several Canadian universities. Although all of the other books were seized pursuant to *Butler, Black Looks* was detained under a Canadian law prohibiting hate speech more generally, which the procensorship feminists also support.

Canadian authorities have not enforced *Butler* against the type of violent, misogynistic heterosexual materials that its advocates had hoped they would proscribe. Indeed, Catharine MacKinnon appeared to concede that enforcement of the decision had not advanced women's interests, in a telephone conversation she had with Leanne Katz, executive director of the National Coalition Against Censorship, in September 1993. MacKinnon noted that the Canadian government authorities were not going after the kind of violent, heterosexual materials that had been involved in the *Butler* case itself, to which Leanne Katz replied, "Big surprise." MacKinnon echoed, "Big surprise."[60]

And an Even Bigger Chill

As if the direct government censorship of allegedly degrading sexually oriented materials under *Butler* were not damaging enough to free speech and equality values, *Butler* has also spurred two indirect, even more expansive forms of censorship. Like all censorial schemes, it has led to self-censorship, and it also has created a "slippery slope," encouraging the adoption of additional censorship measures.

The massive self-censorship among Canadians, triggered by *Butler*, was described in a February 1994 report by the Free Expression Project of Human Rights Watch:

> The indirect effect of daily customs seizures and police raids is self-censorship by the bookstores, video stores and private citizens who for financial reasons cannot afford to mount legal challenges. Oxford University Press refused to distribute *Gay Ideas: Outing and Other Controversies,* a Beacon Press book by Canadian philosopher Richard Mohr, rather than incur the wrath of Customs. Many publishers send page proofs to the Prohibited Importations Unit in Ottawa prior to printing their Canadian editions. The Unit's staff go through the various magazines, whiting out text and replacing offending photos with black dots. Customs has even deleted safe-sex information in U.S. publications imported for Canadian gay men.[61]

The second spillover effect of *Butler* has been that Canadian government officials have been emboldened to pass other measures that suppress an even broader range of expression. As a September 1993 *Los Angeles Times* article noted, *Butler* led the Canadian House of Commons and provincial legislatures to write sweeping new laws against controversial expression, including a prohibition on serial killer trading cards and a law making it a crime to make, print, publish, import, distribute, or sell—and in some cases even possess—any depiction of a sexual act by anyone under eighteen years old, even in fiction or art,[62] and even though Canadian law recognizes that people as young as twelve may legally engage in sexual acts.[63]

The first prosecution under the draconian, *Butler*-inspired law barring sexual depictions of young people illustrates its dangerous overbreadth. Charged in the case was a twenty-six-year-old Toronto artist, Eli Langer, whose paintings and drawings were seized from the Mercer Union, one of Toronto's most respected artist-run galleries. The works portray both children and adults engaging in sexual behavior. Langer says his works were made not from models, but from his imagination. Moreover, these paintings explore the impact of child sexual abuse.

In response to pressure from the arts community, the government decided not to prosecute Langer. However, as this book went to press, prosecutors were seeking judicial permission to destroy Langer's seized paintings, and also seeking to establish a precedent for prosecuting future cases.

Although the law banning sexual depictions of young people contains an exemption for works with artistic merit (as well as educational, scientific, or medical value), it puts the burden of proof on the accused. In light of the ten-year prison sentence and fines that could be imposed following a conviction, no doubt many serious artists, scientists, and others will avoid all sexual descriptions or depictions of people under eighteen. One wonders whether Shakespeare would have written *Romeo and Juliet* or whether Nabokov would have written *Lolita* had they faced such a law. And what of Judy Blume's novels about and for adolescents? (The law contains no special provision that would exempt any of these authors—or, in the case of deceased writers, anyone who continues to circulate their works—from its general terms.)

Unavailing Apologetics

The Canadian government's use of *Butler's* feminist antipornography analysis in a discriminatory and harassing fashion has been so blatant and persistent that even LEAF (the Women's Legal Education and

Action Fund), which had worked with MacKinnon to promote that analysis, has been forced to recognize the great damage it has done. In June 1993, a group of LEAF leaders and anticensorship activists met and issued a joint news release that "unanimously condemned the use of the *Butler* decision to justify the discriminatory use of law to harass and intimidate lesbians and gays and sex trade workers." The LEAF signatories further conceded that "[s]ince . . . *Butler* . . . Canada Customs, some police forces . . . and some government funders have exploited obscenity law to harass bookstores, artists, and AIDS organizations, sex trade workers, and safe sex educators."[64]

In light of the abysmal experience with Canada's version of the feminist antipornography law, the law's feminist defenders have been unable to explain away its devastating impact on free speech and equality, on women and on lesbians and gay men. As Leanne Katz remarked, "Nearly ten percent of *Only Words* is devoted to a rhapsodic analysis of *Butler's* acceptance of her ideology. Yet MacKinnon's book says not a word about the real life consequences of her Pyrrhic victory. Only words, indeed."[65]

When (in October 1993) I debated Kathleen Mahoney, the law professor who coauthored the LEAF brief in *Butler* (in collaboration with Catharine MacKinnon) and who argued LEAF's position in the Canadian Supreme Court, she conceded that *Butler* has been used discriminatorily to harass lesbian and gay publications, but maintained that this fact was no basis for criticizing the ruling. Specifically, Mahoney argued that the *post-Butler* enforcement record simply reflected the pre-existing homophobia on the part of Canadian law enforcement authorities. She said: "We have as many homophobic police officers, I'm sure, as you do, maybe even more, as well as customs officials. . . . [P]olice activity against gays . . . has always been going on."[66]

Of course. And it always will as long as they—or their feminist allies—keep coming up with new tools to play with.

Rather than condemning the Canadian attacks on feminist and lesbian publications, Dworkin and MacKinnon apparently condone at least some of them. Referring to the conviction of Glad Day Bookshop based on the short story in *Bad Attitude,* Dworkin declared: "Lesbian porn is an expression of self-hatred. . . . When it is trafficked in the world, it becomes a social reality, and the hatred that it spreads then is not [*sic*] longer a hatred only of self, but becomes a hatred of the group."[67] Likewise, in a 1994 letter to *The New York Times,* MacKinnon wrote that "maybe the publications" that had been targeted under *Butler* "do harm on the basis of sex. . . . [T]he *Bad Attitude* publication . . . contained sex between a young girl and a nurse-caretaker."[68]

Aside from apologizing for some of the Canadian censorship under *Butler,* Dworkin and MacKinnon have made three arguments in an effort to distinguish the Canadian experience from what we could expect if their antipornography law were to be enforced in the United States. First, they sound their familiar and wrongheaded argument that the Canadian law that *Butler* interpreted is significantly different from their model law because it is criminal, rather than civil. Second, they note that some of the seizures by Canadian Customs have involved temporary detentions, rather than permanent confiscations. Third, they contend that the customs officials are following different standards from those laid down in *Butler.*[69] All three arguments are unsound. I have already discussed the "distinction without a difference" between criminal prosecutions and civil lawsuits (in chapter 3).

Dworkin and MacKinnon's observation that some customs detentions of materials have "only" been temporary shows a similar failure to come to grips with reality. For all practical purposes, just as "justice delayed is justice denied,"[70] so too, delivery delayed is delivery denied, especially when the materials in question are periodicals. The Canadian press has reported that, under *Butler,* customs officials have seized and held magazines for weeks or months, often rendering them out-of-date and unsalable. In addition, books as well as magazines that have been detained by customs may well be made unsalable because they are returned in damaged condition. According to the Canadian anticensorship organization CENSORSTOP, "Customs destructively treats materials seized, ranging from minor damages to 'accidental loss.'"[71]

Damaging as even a temporary customs detention may be, it is important to realize that many such "detentions" are in fact permanent, and thus amount to outright confiscations. Although detention decisions may be appealed, the rulings are seldom reversed unless there is a rash of adverse publicity—as there was, for example, concerning the seizures of Dworkin's books. The only alternative is court action, which is both expensive and slow. Since many booksellers cannot afford to mount such challenges, the ostensibly temporary detention, imposed by the importations bureaucracy, becomes a permanent ban.

Yet another reason why customs detentions have devastating consequences, unacknowledged by Dworkin and MacKinnon, is that these detentions have led to more self-censorship by Canadian booksellers. As reported by the Free Expression Project of Human Rights Watch:

> A bureaucratic appeals process often deters even the most committed challengers. Rather than face costly delay and interference, retailers censor their own orders of books and videos, limiting anything remotely suspect. In doing so they limit their consumers' access to alternative viewpoints. . . . Even though magazines are supposed to be reviewed on an issue-by-issue basis, [bookstores] no longer buy the magazines that have been the subject of litigation or publicity. "*Bad Attitude* and *On Our Backs* [lesbian erotic magazines] have effectively been banned in Canada," said Janine Fuller [bookbuyer for Little Sisters bookstore]. Insidiously, *Butler* has also affected the number of titles bookstores order. "Where I used to buy thirty-six copies by a famous lesbian author," said Fuller, "I now order maybe two."[72]

Dworkin and MacKinnon similarly ignore reality when they assert that the customs seizures are carried out under an independent legal authority, not the *Butler* decision. The customs legislation on obscenity incorporates Canadian Criminal Code obscenity provisions, as interpreted by the Canadian courts. As I have explained, after the *Butler* decision, Canadian government lawyers reviewed existing customs regulations to bring them into conformity with *Butler,* and found that the regulations did not need to be revised. Customs now has renewed carte blanche, not a new carte blanche.

What Have We Learned?

The enforcement record of the MacDworkinite antipornography law in Canada, and the consistent enforcement record of other censorial measures, teaches a clear lesson: *women should beware of any such measure.*

Throughout this book, we have seen that any scheme for censoring pornography would undermine women's rights and interests in many ways: it would suppress many works that are valuable to women and feminists; it would be enforced in a way that discriminates against the least popular, least powerful groups in our society, including feminists and lesbians; it would perpetuate demeaning stereotypes about women, including that sex is bad for us; it would perpetuate the disempowering notion that women are essentially victims; it would distract us from constructive approaches to countering discrimination and violence against women; it would harm women who voluntarily work in the sex industry; it would harm women's efforts to develop their own sexuality; it would reinforce the political power of factions with a patriarchal agenda; by undermining free speech, censorship would deprive feminists of a powerful tool for advancing women's equality; and since sexual freedom and freedom for sexually explicit expression are essential aspects of human freedom, censoring such expression would undermine human rights more broadly.

In contrast to these significant costs that any pornography censorship scheme would impose on feminist goals, procensorship feminists rely on only one asserted benefit of such a scheme: that it would reduce violence and discrimination against women. As we see in the next chapter, this purported benefit is at best merely speculative. Thus, from a feminist perspective, the substantial negative effects of censoring pornography are not offset by any substantial benefits.

Because reducing misogynistic discrimination and violence is so important, some feminists might be tempted to conclude that censorship would be justified by even the possibility that it might advance this goal. Such a conclusion would be unwarranted, however, because it would ignore censorship's countervailing adverse impact on the same goal.

This point is highlighted by considering some other factors, aside from pornography, that are alleged to contribute to misogynistic discrimination and violence; these include women's improving legal and economic status, women's expanding sexual options, and the associated rise of the women's movement. Susan Faludi's 1991 book, *Backlash: The Undeclared War Against American Women,* cites evidence that one of the causes of the 1980s backlash against the women's rights movement was women's increased employment outside the home, which has led to anxiety, depression, and loss of self-esteem among men.[73] Likewise, some research indicates that advances in women's rights may cause some male sexual aggression against women.[74] Furthermore, some feminist theorists and other scholars maintain that sexual assaults (as well as the consumption of pornography) have increased as a result of the women's movement and the misogynistic reactions that some men have to that movement. Andrea Dworkin herself has asserted this causal connection.[75]

Presumably, Dworkin, as well as most other feminists, would resist any effort to curb advances in women's rights, even if that effort were premised on the rationale that advances in women's rights contribute to anti-female violence. This would be a clear case of cutting off one's nose to spite one's face. As we have seen, the same is true of censoring pornography.

In an apparent nod to the dearth of evidence that pornography causes the harm she ascribes to it, Catharine MacKinnon has attempted to bolster her censorial crusade by declaring, "There is no evidence that pornography does no harm."[76] In light of the appalling Canadian experience with MacKinnon's censorship scheme, and the other enforcement lessons we have learned in this chapter, her own phrase should be recast: "There is substantial evidence that censoring pornography does substantial harm."

Why Censoring Pornography Would Not Reduce Discrimination or Violence against Women

The only thing pornography is known to cause directly is the solitary act of masturbation. As for corruption, the only immediate victim is English prose.

—GORE VIDAL, writer[1]

Most of this book has aimed to illuminate the legal flaws and misconceptions of MacKinnon-Dworkin–style antipornography laws, to show how any such law undermines rather than advances important women's rights and human rights causes, and to paint a picture of the suppressed society that this type of law would produce when put in practice. Especially given recently renewed interest in MacDworkinite laws, they—and their chilling consequences—are my immediate concern. I have accordingly exposed the overwhelming problems that are inherent in all such laws. But, for the sake of argument, let's make the purely hypothetical assumption that we could fix those problems: let's pretend we could wave a magic wand that would miraculously make the laws do what they are supposed to without trampling on rights that are vital to everyone, and without stifling speech that serves women.

Even in this "Never-Never Land," where we could neutralize its negative side effects, would censorship "cure"—or at least reduce—the discrimination and violence against women allegedly caused by pornography? That is the assumption that underlies the feminist procensorship position, fueling the argument that we should trade in our free speech rights to promote women's safety and equality rights. In fact, though, the hoped-for benefits of censorship are as hypothetical as our exercise in wishing away the evils of censorship. I will show this by examining the largely unexamined assumption that censorship would reduce sexism and violence against women. This assumption rests, in turn, on three others:

- that exposure to sexist, violent imagery leads to sexist, violent behavior;
- that the effective suppression of pornography would significantly reduce exposure to sexist, violent imagery; and
- that censorship would effectively suppress pornography.

To justify censoring pornography on the rationale that it would reduce violence or discrimination against women, one would have to provide actual support for all three of these assumptions. Each presupposes the others. Yet the only one of them that has received substantial attention is the first—that exposure to sexist, violent imagery leads to sexist, violent behavior—and, as I show later in this chapter, there is no credible evidence to bear it out. Even feminist advocates of censoring pornography have acknowledged that this asserted causal connection cannot be proven, and therefore fall back on the argument that it should be accepted "on faith." Catharine MacKinnon has well captured this fallback position through her defensive double negative with which I closed the previous chapter: "There is no evidence that pornography does no harm."

Of course, given the impossibility of proving that there is *no* evidence of *no* harm, we would have no free speech, and indeed no freedom of any kind, were such a burden of proof actually to be imposed on those seeking to enjoy their liberties. To appreciate this, just substitute for the word "pornography" in MacKinnon's pronouncement any other type of expression or any other human right. We would have to acknowledge that "there is no evidence" that television does no harm, or that editorials criticizing government officials do no harm, or that religious sermons do no harm, and so forth. There certainly is no evidence that feminist writing in general, or MacKinnon's in particular, does no harm.

In its 1992 *Butler* decision, accepting the antipornography feminist position, the Canadian Supreme Court also accepted this dangerous intuitive approach to limiting sexual expression, stating:

> It might be suggested that proof of actual harm should be required . . .
> [I]t is sufficient . . . for Parliament to have a reasonable basis for conclud-
> ing that harm will result and this requirement does not demand actual
> proof of harm.[2]

Even if we were willing to follow the Canadian Supreme Court and procensorship feminists in believing, without evidence, that exposure to sexist, violent imagery does lead to sexist, violent behavior, we still should not accept their calls for censorship. Even if we assumed that *seeing* pornography leads to committing sexist and violent actions, it still would not follow that *censoring* pornography would reduce sexism or violence, due to flaws in the remaining two assumptions: we still would have to prove that pornography has a corner on the sexism and violence market, and that pornography is in fact entirely suppressible.

Even if pornography could be completely suppressed, the sexist, violent imagery that pervades the mainstream media would remain untouched. Therefore, if exposure to such materials caused violence and sexism, these problems would still remain with us. But no censorship regime could completely suppress pornography. It would continue to exist underground. In this respect, censorship would bring us the worst of both worlds. On one hand, as we have just seen from examining the Canadian situation, suppressive laws make it difficult to obtain a wide range of sexually oriented materials, so that most people would not have access to those materials. On the other hand, though, some such materials would continue to be produced and consumed no matter what. Every governmental effort to prohibit any allegedly harmful material has always caused this kind of "double trouble." Witness the infamous "Prohibition" of alcohol earlier in this century, for example.

Let's now examine in more detail the fallacies in each of the three assumptions underlying the feminist procensorship stance. And let's start with the single assumption that has been the focus of discussion—the alleged causal relationship between exposure to sexist, violent imagery and sexist, violent behavior.

Monkey See, Monkey Do?

Aside from the mere fear that sexual expression might cause discrimination or violence against women, advocates of censorship attempt to rely on four types of evidence concerning this alleged causal link: laboratory research data concerning the attitudinal effects of showing various types of sexually explicit materials to volunteer subjects, who are usually male college students; correlational data concerning availability of sexually oriented materials and anti-female discrimination or violence; anecdotal data consisting of accounts by sex offenders and their victims concerning any role that pornography may have played in the offenses; and studies of sex offenders, assessing factors that may have led to their crimes.

As even some leading procensorship feminists have acknowledged, along with the Canadian Supreme Court in *Butler,* none of these types of "evidence" prove that pornography harms women. Rather than retracing the previous works that have reviewed this evidence and reaffirmed its failure to substantiate the alleged causal connection, I will simply summarize their conclusions.

Laboratory Experiments

The most comprehensive recent review of the social science data is contained in Marcia Pally's 1994 book *Sex and Sensibility: Reflections on Forbidden Mirrors and the Will to Censor.*[3] It exhaustively canvasses laboratory studies that have evaluated the impact of exposing experimental subjects to sexually explicit expression of many varieties, and concludes that no credible evidence substantiates a clear causal connection between any type of sexually explicit material and any sexist or violent behavior. The book also draws the same conclusion from its thorough review of field and correlational studies, as well as sociological surveys, in the U.S., Canada, Europe, and Asia.

Numerous academic and governmental surveys of the social science studies have similarly rejected the purported link between sexual expression and aggression. The National Research Council's Panel on Understanding and Preventing Violence concluded, in 1993: "Demonstrated empirical links between pornography and sex crimes in general are weak or absent."[4]

Given the overwhelming consensus that laboratory studies do not demonstrate a causal tie between exposure to sexually explicit imagery and violent behavior, the Meese Pornography Commission Report's contrary conclusion, not surprisingly, has been the subject of heated criticism, including criticism by dissenting commissioners and by the very social scientists on whose research the report purportedly relied.

The many grounds on which the Commission's report was widely repudiated include that: six of the Commission's eleven members already were committed antipornography crusaders when they were appointed to it; the Commission was poorly funded and undertook no research; its hearings were slanted toward preconceived antipornography conclusions in terms of the witnesses invited to testify and the questions they were asked; and, in assessing the alleged harmful effects of pornography, the Commission's report relied essentially upon morality, expressly noting at several points that its conclusions were based on "common sense," "personal insight," and "intuition."

Two of the Meese Commission's harshest critics were, interestingly, two female members of that very Commission, Judith Becker and Ellen Levine. Becker is a psychiatrist and psychologist whose entire extensive career has been devoted to studying sexual violence and abuse, from both research and clinical perspectives. Levine is a journalist who has focused on women's issues, and who edits a popular women's magazine. In their formal dissent from the Commission's report, they concluded:

> [T]he social science research has not been designed to evaluate the relationship between exposure to pornography and the commission of sexual crimes; therefore efforts to tease the current data into proof of a casual [sic] link between these acts simply cannot be accepted.[5]

Three of the foremost researchers concerned with the alleged causal relationship between sexually explicit materials and sexual violence, Edward Donnerstein, Daniel Linz, and Steven Penrod, also have sharply disputed the Meese Commission's findings about a purported causal relationship.[6]

Since the feminist censorship proposals aim at sexually explicit material that allegedly is "degrading" to women, it is especially noteworthy that research data show no link between exposure to "degrading" sexually explicit material and sexual aggression.

Even two research literature surveys that were conducted for the Meese Commission, one by University of Calgary professor Edna Einseidel and the other by then–Surgeon General C. Everett Koop, also failed to find any link between "degrading" pornography and sex crimes or aggression. Surgeon General Koop's survey concluded that only two reliable generalizations could be made about the impact of exposure to "degrading" sexual material on its viewers: it caused them to think that a variety of sexual practices were more common than they had previously believed, and it caused them to more accurately estimate the prevalence of varied sexual practices.[7]

Experiments also fail to establish any link between women's exposure to such materials and their development of negative self-images. Carol Krafka found that, in comparison with other women, women who were exposed to sexually "degrading" materials did not engage in more sex-role stereotyping; nor did they experience lower self-esteem, have less satisfaction with their body image, accept more anti-woman myths about rape, or show greater acceptance of violence against women.[8] Similar conclusions have been reached by Donnerstein, Linz, and Penrod.[9]

Correlational Data

Both the Meese Commission and procensorship feminists have attempted to rely on studies that allegedly show a correlation between the availability of sexually explicit materials and sexual offense rates. Of course, though, a positive correlation between two phenomena does not prove that one causes the other. Accordingly, even if the studies did consistently show a positive correlation between the prevalence of sexual materials and sexual offenses—which they do not—they still would not establish that exposure to the materials *caused* the rise in offenses. The same correlation could also reflect the opposite causal chain—if, for example, rapists relived their violent acts by purchasing sexually violent magazines or videotapes.

Any correlation between the availability of sexual materials and the rate of sex offenses could also reflect an independent factor that causes increases in both. Cynthia Gentry's correlational studies have identified just such an independent variable in geographical areas that have high rates of both the circulation of sexually explicit magazines and sexual violence: namely, a high population of men between the ages of eighteen and thirty-four.[10] Similarly, Larry Baron and Murray Straus have noted that areas where both sexual materials and sexual aggression are prevalent are characterized by a "hypermasculated or macho culture pattern," which may well be the underlying causal agent.[11] Accordingly, Joseph Scott and Loretta Schwalm found that communities with higher rape rates experienced stronger sales not only of porn magazines, but also of *all* male-oriented magazines, including *Field and Stream*.[12]

Even more damning to the attempt to rest the "porn-causes-rape-or-discrimination" theory on alleged correlations is that there simply are no consistent correlations. While the asserted correlation would not be *sufficient* to prove the claimed causal connection, it is *necessary* to prove that connection. Therefore, the existence of the alleged causal relationship is conclusively refuted by the fact that levels of violence and discrimination against women are often *inversely* related to the availability of sexually explicit materials, including violent sexually explicit materials. This inverse relationship appears in various kinds of comparisons: between different states within the United States; between different countries; and between different periods within the same country.

Within the United States, the Baron and Straus research has shown no consistent pattern between the availability of sexual materials and the number of rapes from state to state. Utah is the lowest-ranking state in the availability of sexual materials but twenty-fifth in the number of rapes, whereas New Hampshire ranks ninth highest in the availability of sexual materials but only forty-fourth in the number of rapes.

The lack of a consistent correlation between pornography consumption and violence against women is underscored by one claim of the procensorship feminists themselves: they maintain that the availability and consumption of pornography, including violent pornography, have been increasing throughout the United States. At the same time, though, the rates of sex crimes have been decreasing or remaining steady. The Bureau of Justice Statistics reports that between 1973 and 1987, the national rape rate remained steady and the attempted rape rate decreased. Since these data were gathered from household surveys rather than from police records, they are considered to be the most accurate measures of the incidence of crimes. These data also cover the period during which feminists helped to create a social, political, and legal climate that should have encouraged higher percentages of rape victims to report their assaults. Thus, the fact that rapes reported to the Bureau of Justice Statistics have not increased provokes serious questions about the procensorship feminists' theories of pornography-induced harm.[13] Similar questions are raised by data showing a decrease in wife battery between 1975 and 1985, again despite changes that should have encouraged the increased reporting of this chronically underreported crime.[14]

Noting that "[t]he mass-market pornography . . . industr[y] took off after World War II," Marcia Pally has commented:

> In the decades since the 1950s, with the marketing of sexual material . . . , the country has seen the greatest advances in sensitivity to violence against women and children. Before the . . . mass publication of sexual images, no rape or incest hot lines and battered women's shelters existed; date and marital rape were not yet phrases in the language. Should one conclude that the presence of pornography . . . has inspired public outrage at sexual crimes?[15]

Pally's rhetorical question underscores the illogicality of presuming that just because two phenomena happen to coexist, they therefore are causally linked. I have already shown that any correlation that might exist between the increased availability of pornography and *increased* misogynistic discrimination or violence could well be explained by other factors. The same is true for any correlation that might exist between the increased availability of pornography and *decreased* misogynistic discrimination or violence.

In a comparative state-by-state analysis, Larry Baron and Murray Straus have found a positive correlation between the circulation of pornographic magazines and the state's "index of gender equality," a composite of twenty-four indicators of economic, political, and legal equality.[16] As the researchers have observed, these findings may suggest that both sexually explicit material and gender equality flourish in tolerant climates with fewer restrictions on speech.

The absence of any consistent correlation between the availability of sexual materials and sexual violence is also clear in international comparisons. On the one hand, violence and discrimination against women are common in countries where sexually oriented material is almost completely unavailable, including Saudi Arabia, Iran, and China (where the sale and distribution of erotica is now a capital offense). On the other hand, violence against women is uncommon in countries where such material is readily available, including Denmark, Germany, and Japan.

Furthermore, patterns in other countries over time show no correlation between the increased availability of sexually explicit materials and increased violence against women. The 1991 analysis by University of Copenhagen professor Berl Kutchinsky revealed that, while nonsexual violent crime had increased up to 300 percent in Denmark, Sweden, and West Germany from 1964 to 1984, all three countries' rape rates either declined or remained constant during this same period, despite their lifting of restrictions on sexual materials. Kutchinsky's studies further show that sex crimes against girls dropped from 30 per 100,000 to 5 per 100,000 between 1965, when Denmark liberalized its obscenity laws, and 1982.

In the decade 1964–1974, there was a much greater increase in rape rates in Singapore, which tightly restricts sexually oriented expression, than in Sweden, which had liberalized its obscenity laws during that period. In Japan, where sexually explicit materials are easily accessible and stress themes of bondage, rape, and violence, rape rates decreased 45 percent during the same decade. Moreover, Japan reports a rape rate of 2.4 per 100,000 people, compared with 34.5 in the United States, although violent erotica is more prevalent in Japan.[17]

Anecdotes and Suspicions

As Seventh Circuit Court of Appeals Judge Richard Posner observed about MacKinnon's book *Only Words*:

MacKinnon's treatment of the central issue of pornography as she herself poses it—the harm that pornography does to women—is shockingly
casual. Much of her evidence is anecdotal, and in a nation of 260 million
people, anecdotes are a weak form of evidence.[18]

Many procensorship advocates attempt to rest their case on self-serving
"porn-made-me-do-it" claims by sexual offenders, as well as on statements by victims or police officers that sexual offenders had sexually
explicit materials in their possession at the time they committed their
crimes.

The logical fallacy of relying on anecdotes to establish a general
causal connection between exposure to sexual materials and violence
against women was aptly noted by journalist Ellen Willis: "Anti-porn
activists cite cases of sexual killers who were also users of pornography, but this is no more logical than arguing that marriage causes rape
because some rapists are married."[19]

Even assuming that sexual materials really were the triggering
factors behind some specific crimes, that could not justify restrictions
on such materials. As former Supreme Court justice William O. Douglas wrote: "The First Amendment demands more than a horrible example or two of the perpetrator of a crime of sexual violence, in whose
pocket is found a pornographic book, before it allows the Nation to be
saddled with a regime of censorship."[20] If we attempted to ban all words
or images that had ever been blamed for inspiring or instigating particular crimes by some aberrant or antisocial individual, we would end
up with little left to read or view. Throughout history and around the
world, criminals have regularly blamed their conduct on a sweeping
array of words and images in books, movies, and television.

As noted by the 1979 report of the British Committee on Obscenity
and Film Censorship, "For those who are susceptible to them, the stimuli to aggressive behavior are all around us."[21] To illustrate the innumerable crimes that have been incited by words or images, the Committee
cited a young man who attempted to kill his parents with a meat cleaver
after watching a dramatized version of Dostoyevsky's *The Brothers Kara-
mazov*, and a Jamaican man of African descent in London who raped a
white woman, saying that the televised showing of Alex Haley's *Roots*
had "inspired" him to treat her as white men had treated black women.

Additional examples cited by Ohio State University law professor Earl Finbar Murphy underscore that word blaming and image blaming extend to many religious works, too:

> Heinrich Pommerenke, who was a rapist, abuser, and mass slayer of women in Germany, was prompted to his series of ghastly deeds by Cecil B. DeMille's *The Ten Commandments*. During the scene of the Jewish women dancing about the Golden Calf, all the doubts of his life became clear: Women were the source of the world's troubles and it was his mission to both punish them for this and to execute them. Leaving the theater, he slew the first victim in a park nearby. John George Haigh, the British vampire who sucked his victims' blood through soda straws and dissolved their drained bodies in acid baths, first had his murder-inciting dreams and vampire longings from watching the "voluptuous" procedure of—an Anglican High Church Service.[22]

Were we to ban words or images on the grounds that they had incited some susceptible individuals to commit crimes, the Bible would be in great jeopardy. No other work has more often been blamed for more heinous crimes by the perpetrators of such crimes. The Bible has been named as the instigating or justifying factor for many individual and mass crimes, ranging from the religious wars, inquisitions, witch burnings, and pogroms of earlier eras to systematic child abuse and ritual murders today.

Marcia Pally's *Sex and Sensibility* contains a lengthy litany of some of the multitudinous, horrific bad acts that have been blamed on the "Good Book." She also cites some of the many passages depicting the "graphic, sexually explicit subordination of women" that would allow the entire Bible to be banned under the procensorship feminists' anti-pornography law. Pally writes:

> [T]he Bible has unbeatable worldwide sales and includes detailed justi-fication of child abuse, wife battery, rape, and the daily humiliation of women. Short stories running through the text serve as models for sex-ual assault and the mauling of children. The entire set of books is avail-able to children, who are encouraged or required to read it. It is printed and distributed by some of the world's most powerful organizations. . . .

With refreshing frankness, the Bible tells men it is their rightful place to rule women. . . . [It] specifies exactly how many shekels less than men women are worth. Genesis 19:1–8 tells one of many tales about fathers setting up their daughters to be gang raped. Even more prevalent are . . . glamorized war stories in which the fruits of victory are the local girls. . . . [P]erhaps most gruesome is the snuff story about the guy who set his maid up to be gang raped and, after her death from the assault, cut her body up into little pieces. . . . Unlike movies and television programs, these tales are generally taken to be true, not simulated, accounts.[23]

In 1992, Gene Kasmar petitioned the Brooklyn Center, Minnesota, school board to ban the Bible from school classrooms and libraries on the ground that it is lewd, indecent, obscene, offensive, violent, and dangerous to women and children. He specifically complained about biblical references to concubines, explicit sex, child abuse, incest, nakedness, and mistreatment of women—all subjects, significantly, that would trigger the feminist-style antipornography laws.

In response, the chief counsel of Pat Robertson's American Center for Law and Justice in Virginia, Jay Sekulow, flew to Minnesota and argued that the Bible "is worthy of study for its literary and historic qualities."[24] While the Brooklyn Center School Board apparently agreed with this assessment, voting unanimously to reject Kasmar's petition, it must be recalled that Sekulow's argument would be unavailing under Dworkin-MacKinnon–type antipornography laws. Under the Mac-Dworkin model law, any work could be banned on the basis of even one isolated passage that meets the definition of pornography, and the work could not be saved by any serious literary, historic, or other value it might offer. Consequently, the feminist antipornography law could be used by Kasmar and others to ban the Bible not only from public schools, but also from public libraries, bookstores, and all other venues.

The countless expressive works that have been blamed for crimes include many that convey profeminist messages. Therefore, an anecdotal, image-blaming rationale for censorship would condemn many feminist works. For example, the television movie *The Burning Bed*, which told the true story of a battered wife who set fire to her sleeping husband, was blamed for some "copycat" crimes, as well as for some acts of violence by men against women. The argument that such incidents would justify suppression would mark the end of any films or other works depicting—and deploring—the real violence that plagues the lives of too many actual women.

Under a censorship regime that permits anecdotal, book-blaming "evidence," all other feminist materials would be equally endangered, not "just" works that depict the violence that has been inflicted on women. That is because, as feminist writings themselves have observed, some sexual assaults are committed by men who feel threatened by the women's movement. Should feminist works therefore be banned on the theory that they might well motivate a man to act out his misogynistic aggression?

Studies of Sex Offenders

The scientists who have investigated the impact of exposure to sexual materials in real life have not found that either sexual materials or attitudes toward women play any significant role in prompting actual violence. In general, these studies show that sex offenders had less exposure to sexually explicit materials than most men, that they first saw such materials at a later age than nonoffenders, that they were overwhelmingly more likely to have been punished for looking at them as teenagers, and that they often find sexual images more distressing than arousing.[25]

While no evidence substantiates that viewing pornography leads to violence and discrimination against women, some evidence indicates that, if anything, there may well be an inverse causal relationship between exposure to sexually explicit materials and misogynistic violence or discrimination. One of the leading researchers in this area, Edward Donnerstein of the University of California at Santa Barbara, has written: "A good amount of research strongly supports the position that exposure to erotica can reduce aggressive responses in people who are predisposed to aggress."[26] Similarly, John Money, of Johns Hopkins Medical School, a leading expert on sexual violence, has noted that most people with criminal sexualities were raised with strict, antisexual, repressive attitudes. He predicts that the "current repressive attitudes toward sex will breed an ever-widening epidemic of aberrant sexual behavior."[27]

In one 1989 experiment, males who had been exposed to pornography were more willing to come to the aid of a female subject who appeared to be hurt than were men who had been exposed to other stimuli.[28] Laboratory studies further indicate that there may well be an inverse causal relationship between exposure to violent sexually explicit material and sexual arousal. For example, in 1991, Howard Barbaree and William Marshall, of Queen's College in Ontario, found:

> For most men, hearing a description of an encounter where the man is forcing the woman to have sex, and the woman is in distress or pain, dampens the arousal by about 50 percent compared to arousal levels using a scene of consenting lovemaking. . . . Ordinarily violence inhibits sexual arousal in men. A blood flow loss of 50 percent means a man would not be able to penetrate a woman.[29]

The foregoing research findings are certainly more consistent with what feminist scholars have been writing about rape than is the pro-censorship feminists' pornocentric analysis: namely, rape is not a crime about sex, but rather, about violence.[30]

See No Pornography, See No Sexist and Violent Imagery?

Pornography constitutes only a small subset of the sexist or violent imagery that pervades our culture and media. New York Law School professor Carlin Meyer recently conducted a comprehensive survey of the views of women's sexuality, status, and gender roles that are purveyed in nonpornographic media:

> Today, mainstream television, film, advertising, music, art, and popular (including religious) literature are the primary propagators of Western views of sexuality and sex roles. Not only do we read, see and experience their language and imagery more often and at earlier ages than we do most explicit sexual representation, but precisely because mainstream imagery is ordinary and everyday, it more powerfully convinces us that it depicts the world as it is or ought to be.[31]

Other cultural and media analysts have likewise concluded that more-damaging sexist imagery is more broadly purveyed through mainstream, nonsexual representations. Thelma McCormack, director of York University's Feminist Studies Centre, has concluded that "the enemy of women's equality is our mainstream culture with its images of women as family-centered," rather than imagery of women as sexual. According to McCormack:

> Surveys and public opinion studies confirm the connection between gender-role traditionalism and an acceptance or belief in the normality of a stratified social system. The more traditional a person's views are about women, the more likely he or she is to accept inequality as inevitable, functional, natural, desirable and immutable. In short, if any image of woman can be said to influence our thinking about gender equality, it is the domestic woman not the Dionysian one.[32]

Social science researchers have found that acceptance of the rape myth and other misogynistic attitudes concerning women and violence are just as likely to result from exposure to many types of mass media—from soap operas to popular commercial films—as from even intense exposure to violent, misogynistic sexually explicit materials.[33] Accordingly, if we really wanted to purge all sexist, violent representations from our culture, we would have to cast the net far beyond pornography, notwithstanding how comprehensive and elastic that category is. Would even procensorship feminists want to deal such a deathblow to First Amendment freedoms?

Censor Pornography, See No Pornography?

Procensorship feminists themselves have acknowledged that censorship would probably just drive pornography underground. Indeed, as recently as 1987, Catharine MacKinnon recognized that "pornography cannot be reformed or suppressed or banned."[34]

The assumption that censorship would substantially reduce the availability or impact of pornography also overlooks evidence that censorship makes some viewers more desirous of pornography and more receptive to its imagery. This "forbidden fruits" effect has been corroborated by historical experience and social science research. All recent studies of the suppression of sexual expression, including Walter Kendrick's 1987 book *The Secret Museum: Pornography in Modern Culture* and Edward de Grazia's 1992 book *Girls Lean Back Everywhere: The Law of Obscenity and the Assault on Genius,* demonstrate that any censorship effort simply increases the attention that a targeted work receives. Social scientific studies that were included in the report of the 1970 President's Commission on Obscenity and Pornography suggested that censorship of sexually explicit materials may increase their desirability and impact, and also that a viewer's awareness that sexually oriented parts of a film have been censored may lead to frustration and subsequent aggressive behavior.[35]

The foregoing data about the impact of censoring pornography are consistent with broader research findings: the evidence suggests that censorship of *any* material increases an audience's desire to obtain the material and disposes the audience to be more receptive to it.[36] Critical viewing skills, and the ability to regard media images skeptically and analytically, atrophy under a censorial regime. A public that learns to question everything it sees or hears is better equipped to reject culturally propagated values than is one that assumes the media have been purged of all "incorrect" perspectives.

Even assuming for the sake of argument that there were a causal link between pornography and anti-female discrimination and violence, the insignificant contribution that censorship might make to reducing them would not outweigh the substantial damage that censorship would do to feminist goals. From the lack of actual evidence to substantiate the alleged causal link, the conclusion follows even more inescapably: *Censoring pornography would do women more harm than good.*

CHAPTER 13

Toward Constructive Approaches to Reducing Discrimination and Violence against Women

I deplore that even a very few feminists have been diverted by the issue of pornography from the basic protection of all our rights. Now, I urge all women to have their eyes opened to the dangers to our basic rights by the pushing of antipornography legislation.

— BETTY FRIEDAN, founding President
National Organization for Women[1]

In my part of the country, the problems women suffer from images that degrade them are not real high on the list. Where I am, poverty and violence are women's most serious problems, and it always kind of amazes me to find people spending their time worrying about how women are depicted.

— MOLLY IVINS, writer[2]

Like all censorship schemes, the feminist proposal to censor sexual expression diverts attention and resources from constructive, meaningful steps to address the societal problem at which the censorship is aimed. Feminist advocates of censoring sexual materials, along with feminist opponents of such censorship, are appropriately concerned about the very real, urgent problems of discrimination and violence against women. But the MacDworkinites' pornocentrism diverts

241

attention both from the root causes of such discrimination and violence—of which violent, misogynistic sexual depictions of women are
merely one symptom—and from actual acts of discrimination and violence. In the words of Canadian feminist Varda Burstyn:

> Feminists who oppose censorship . . . do not have another slogan,
> another quick solution, another panacea to offer in its place. We do
> have a comprehensive list of tasks we must carry out to bring sexism
> and violence to an end. Working on any one of these is more helpful—
> immediately, not in the distant future—than supporting censorship of
> any kind today, for these tasks get at the structural basis of sexism and
> violence, and thus insure that we will have a future.[3]

The procensorship feminists' focus on pornography is at best myo-
pic, and at worst blinding. As law professor Carlin Meyer observes,
based on her comprehensive survey of gender stereotyping throughout
our culture:

> It seems implausible, to say the least, that pornography is more centrally
> responsible either for rendering erotic or for making possible the actu-
> alization of male violence against women than are the ideologies and
> practices of religion, law, and science. These institutions far more deeply
> and pervasively undergird male domination of women.

Furthermore, she notes, the procensorship feminists' focus on sexual
speech as a central cause of sexism and violence also underemphasizes
such institutions and practices as sports and militarism, which foster
"male bonding in physically aggressive pursuits."[4]

Focusing on the Real Causes . . . *Of Discrimination*

By asserting that pornography is a central cause—or even *the* central
cause—of sex discrimination, procensorship feminists deflect energy
and attention from the factors that feminist scholars and the U.S. Commission on Civil Rights have found to be the most significant causes
of such discrimination: sex-segregated labor markets; systematic

devaluation of work traditionally done by women; sexist concepts of marriage and family; inadequate income-maintenance programs for women unable to find wage work; lack of day care services and the premise that child care is an exclusively or largely female responsibility; barriers to reproductive freedom; and discrimination and segregation in education.[5]

Feminist sociologist Thelma McCormack has strongly denounced "the uninformed claim that pornography is in any way a factor in" causing gender inequality. She derides this view as "an insult to social scientists and the broader intellectual community for whom structural equality is the crux of social justice and [who] have laboured to develop the knowledge that would clarify and deepen our understanding of it."

McCormack urges those who want to advance women's equality to fight not the "degradation" but the *devaluation* of women that permeates our mainstream culture. She explains:

> Devaluation means that if, by some strange set of circumstances, we could eliminate all forms of pornography ... [women] would still be under-represented politically, and would still be culturally marginalized. The prohibition of obscenity ... accomplishes nothing in the struggle for equality because it confuses symbolic degradation with instrumental devaluation.[6]

The pressing work that needs to be done to eliminate women's second-class status in our society, from which the pornocentric feminists have been distracting us with their more sensational agenda, was outlined in a briefing book that the American Civil Liberties Union submitted to the Clinton Administration's transition team in 1992:

> In the late 20th century, women in the United States are still second-class citizens in virtually all aspects of economic and public life. To ... reach the ultimate goal of complete elimination of all barriers to women's full ... equality, requires our society's total commitment. ...
>
> All forms of employment discrimination against women must be eliminated, including pervasive wage discrimination, widespread occupational segregation, the "glass ceiling" on advancement, discrimination on the basis of pregnancy and childbearing capacity, rampant

sexual harassment and all other forms of discrimination against women in the workplace.

All forms of discrimination against girls and young women in education must be eradicated at all levels. Women, especially poor women, must have equal access to affordable housing, food, health care, education, job training, child care, child support enforcement and other essential services.[7]

. . . *And of Violence*

The pornocentric feminists also avoid facing the real and complex causes of and solutions for anti-female violence. Marcia Pally's comprehensive 1991 analysis of the literature on this issue, in *Sense and Censorship: The Vanity of Bonfires,* concluded:

> Leading feminists and the U.S. Commission on Civil Rights suggest that violence against women begins with educational and economic discrimination. . . . Men learn to consider women burdens, stiflers and drags on their freedom. Women, in turn, do not have the economic independence and access to day care that would enable them to leave abusive settings. Feminists also suggest that violence begins with the infantilization of women so that men hold them in contempt and see them as easily dismissed or lampooned and ready targets for anger.[8]

In arguing that exposure to pornography causes violent crimes against women, procensorship feminists dilute the accountability of men who commit these crimes by displacing some of it onto words and images, or onto those who create or distribute them. In contrast, as the ACLU has advocated, we should focus on the individual men who actually use violence or duress against women, through "[e]nforcement of criminal laws regarding assault, coerced sex, kidnapping, and trespassing; strengthening of rape laws, including elimination of the 'spousal rape' exception, under which husbands may not be prosecuted for raping their wives; [and] enforcement of . . . sex discrimination laws."[9]

The "porn-made-me-do-it" concept (anecdotes about which were discussed in the previous chapter as flawed evidence that pornography leads to violence against women) would severely set back the women's movement's efforts to ensure that our criminal justice system vigorously enforces laws criminalizing sexual assaults. The Senate Judiciary Committee members who opposed the Pornography Victims' Compensation Act (discussed in chapter 3) emphasized that suppressing pornography exonerates actual rapists and others who assault women. Their minority report explained that "the bill sends the wrong message to sex offenders. . . . Criminal defendants could use [this] to assert impaired or diminished capacity, available in many states as a defense to specific intent crimes such as rape."[10] For this reason, feminist law professor Nan Hunter observed that, to convey its actual impact, the Act should be renamed the "Rapists' Exculpation Act." Hunter further warns that to single out pornography as women's archenemy is to

repeat the mistake of some of our foremothers, the leaders of the women's temperance movement who sought to ban alcohol. Those women believed that alcohol caused much of men's violence against women, particularly domestic violence. But we have learned from the work of anti-violence groups that alcohol is not the *cause* of violence against women; it is the excuse for it. The same is true of pornography.[11]

To hold pornography, and those who produce or distribute it, responsible for crimes it allegedly prompted others to commit is fundamentally inconsistent with notions of accountability that are central to our criminal justice system. If we should accept the "logic" of this approach by holding pornographers responsible for rape, then the same "logic" would require us to hold countless other third parties responsible for rape and other crimes committed by individuals whom they allegedly influenced. Such an inverted "justice" system was effectively pilloried by Teller, of the comedy-magic duo Penn & Teller:

Of course, there are insane people who see something as innocuous as a cereal commercial and then go machine-gun shoppers at a mall. But when these nuts assert that the cereal box commanded them to kill, we lock them up. We do not accuse the corn flake maker of murder. So why blame pornographers for a rapist's actions? We do not punish his parents—though most rapists were sexually abused by their parents in childhood. We do not punish the peers who teased him at work or the

employer who fired him the afternoon before the rape. We punish the
rapist, and that is as it should be.[12]

Criminal defendants already have sought to reduce their punishments by relying on the procensorship feminist analysis of pornography. One such defendant was Thomas Schiro. He was convicted and
sentenced to death for committing a horrific, brutal rape and murder
in Indiana in 1981. Having repeatedly raped and tortured his victim,
Schiro then beat her on the head with a vodka bottle until the bottle
broke, beat her with an iron, and, when she resisted, finally strangled
her to death. Schiro followed all these atrocities with still more: he sexually assaulted and bit into his victim's corpse. (These grisly details,
set forth in the court decisions in the case, would make such decisions
sanctionable pornography under the Dworkin-MacKinnon model law).

On appeal, seeking to overturn the death penalty for what the court
called his "gruesome, sadistic acts, including necrophilia," Schiro
claimed that he had viewed violent pornography, and that this should
be deemed a "mitigating factor," reducing his culpability and hence the
harshness of his punishment. Schiro argued that his viewing of these
sexual materials should be given the same legal treatment as intoxica-
tion, or mental disease or defect, which are deemed to make defendants
unable to appreciate the criminality of their conduct and hence less
blameworthy.

In rejecting this contention, the U.S. Court of Appeals for the Seventh Circuit stressed that, if it accepted Schiro's claim, it would have to
excuse him not only from the death penalty, but also from any criminal punishment whatsoever. "Under Schiro's theory," the court said,
"pornography would constitute a legal excuse to [sic] violence against
women."[13] As it would under the procensorship feminists' scheme.

Those who agree with the Seventh Circuit's ruling should note that
Catharine MacKinnon has argued that Schiro should indeed have
been exonerated under the applicable criminal laws. Fundamental to
all our criminal laws is the concept that, to be culpable, a defendant
must have acted intentionally, and therefore must be capable of appre-
ciating the wrongfulness of his actions. In *Only Words*, MacKinnon
argued that pornography had destroyed Schiro's ability to understand

the wrongfulness of his grotesque crimes, and therefore that he should have been let off the hook.[14]

And if this conclusion isn't problematic enough, MacKinnon's proposed "remedy" for the problem, as she sees it, is at least as problematic: she wants to dispense with the intentionality requirement for criminal culpability, so that we could pin legal blame on both pornography and the rapists who are subject to its purported power to simultaneously incapacitate and incite.[15] As law professor C. Edwin Baker observes, this proposal reflects MacKinnon's "lack of concern with the moral relevance of human agency" (also reflected in her denial of agency on the part of women who choose to perform for pornography, discussed in chapter 9).[16]

Short of the revolutionary change in our criminal law that MacKinnon recommends, to dispense with the central requirement of intentional conduct, there is no way to escape the logical result of pro-censorship feminists' theories about pornography's potent effects—namely, the exoneration of all the future Thomas Schiros. Indeed, the adverse consequences could well be even more counterproductive, in terms of the critically important effort to hold rapists and murderers accountable for their crimes, as indicated by another actual case.

In an even more extreme example of the "porn-made-medo-it" defense than the one made by Thomas Schiro—and seconded by Catharine MacKinnon—Steven P. Mignogna argued that he should not be held fully responsible for raping and killing two young girls, aged twelve and thirteen, in Pennsylvania in 1988 because he had become emotionally unstable as a result of being exposed to pornography at a store he had visited two or three times. Attempting to extend the purported "porn defense" still one step further than Schiro had sought to do, Mignogna did not even show that he had bought or looked at the sexually explicit materials in question. For that reason, the court rejected Mignogna's proffered defense. Thus, the court left open the possibility that, if Mignogna *could* have demonstrated that he had seen these materials, he could have relied on them to reduce his own criminal culpability.[17]

If the procensorship feminists' theories about pornography's powerful push toward sexual violence were accepted, defenses such as Mignogna's would have to be taken seriously. In their joint book

Pornography and Civil Rights, Dworkin and MacKinnon wrote, "Pornography makes it impossible for [men] to tell when sex is forced,
that women are human, and that rape is rape."[18] MacKinnon makes
the same point more dramatically in *Only Words* by drawing an anal-
ogy between showing pornography to a man and saying "Kill!" to a
trained guard dog.[19] Surely we would not blame or punish the dog
who responded to the command by attacking; if MacKinnon's comparison is accepted, the man who responded in kind would likewise
be innocent.

Need I point out to certain women on behalf of all men that the
latter are not dogs—that men have knowledge and attitudes, which
presumably mediate their behavior? I say "presumably" because the
relationships among knowledge, attitudes, and behavior have not yet
been clearly mapped out. Until they are, we cannot know if or when
one leads to another, but we can hope that if one can be changed, so
can another.

In widely cited laboratory studies by Edward Donnerstein and other
researchers, college men appeared to be quite capable of changing their
attitudes toward women, notwithstanding massive exposure to violent,
sexually explicit, misogynistic films depicting women as welcoming
rape. These experiments thus belie procensorship feminists' belief that
seeing pornography reduces men to the mental or moral equivalent of
trained animals. The increased negative attitudes about women that
some of the men displayed after seeing the violent pornography were
more than offset by their subsequent exposure to information about
women and violence. If "porn made them think it," the facts made them
rethink it. The net impact of their exposure to the full range of materials was striking: the college men had more positive, less discriminatory, and less stereotyped attitudes toward women than they had before
the experiment. What's more, the combined exposure to misogynistic
and feminist materials reduced negative attitudes even more effectively
than exposure to the latter alone.[20]

Other studies have corroborated the finding that counter-speech can
overcome any temporary negative impact that massive exposure to violent pornography may have on viewers' attitudes toward women. As the
Surgeon General's report to the Meese Pornography Commission summarized, "Several studies have shown that presentations outlining the

ways that violent sexual material can foster or reinforce incorrect beliefs or negative attitudes have been able to prevent the expected results of exposure."[21] Capsulizing the policy implications of the social science research, Donnerstein said, "Censorship is not the solution. Education, however, is a viable alternative."[22]

More speech about sex—education, information, and the development of critical viewing skills—not less, is the answer. As the procensorship feminists themselves have demonstrated, pornography can serve as an important tool to galvanize public concern about the ongoing problems of anti-female discrimination and violence. To the extent that censorship would make such images less visible, the protest against sexism would be weakened.

Digging Out the Roots . . .

Those who are committed to assisting victims of misogynistic violence—rather than to treating their assailants as victims of pornography—and those who are committed to addressing the root causes of such violence, advocate constructive alternative measures, not the continued demonization of pornography. One prominent example is Judith Becker, a professor of psychiatry and psychology, quoted in the previous chapter, who has extensive research and clinical experience in studying sexual abuse and sexual assault. Becker has consistently opposed efforts to restrict pornography, including in her capacity as a dissenting member of the Meese Pornography Commission. Instead, she advocates government funding for services for the victims of sexual assault and abuse, as well as funding of research into the causes of, and means for preventing, sexual violence.[23]

Likewise, Shirley Feldman-Summers, a psychologist who has taught and conducted research on human sexuality, sexual victimization, and sex-role stereotypes, has suggested some of the potentially more productive strategies for reducing sexual violence, from which pornocentric feminists have diverted attention:

[C]hildren who are raised in violent homes are likely to be violence-prone. . . . How can children who are being groomed for a violent adulthood be detected at an early age, and how can intervention best be accomplished? There is also reason to believe that a significant proportion of sex offenders had a sexually repressed upbringing. . . . To what extent can sex education in our schools reduce or counteract a sexually repressive upbringing? . . . According to [social scientists], the extremely low incidence of reported rape in Japan (notwithstanding the ready availability of violent sexual materials) may be attributed to a culturally-induced sense of shame, for which one cannot make amends. In contrast, in the United States, the usual method of internal constraint is by guilt, which can be reduced by making amends. . . . Would it be effective to publicly ridicule and humiliate persons convicted of sexual assault, so as to associate shame with such acts?[24]

Another factor that contributes to male sexual violence against women is no doubt ignored by procensorship feminists not only because of their obsession with pornography, but also because of their "women-as-victims" orientation. Blinded by their victim-centric view of women, the antipornography feminists overlook the fact that most rape victims are men—and the fact that some substantial number of these male victims are likely in turn to attack women. According to conservative estimates, more than 290,000 men are sexually assaulted in jails and prisons every year, while the Bureau of Justice Statistics estimates that 135,000 women are raped annually. Even if the latter number is understated, as some critics charge, it is indisputable that there is an epidemic of male prison rape—an epidemic that preys not only on men behind bars, but also on women in the outside world. Consequently, according to Stephen Donaldson, president of Stop Prisoner Rape, "The fight against rape in our communities is doomed to failure . . . as long as it ignores the network of training grounds for rapists: our prisons, jails and reform schools." In the view of psychologists and rape counselors, he explains, the brutal, often daily, sexual assaults that many prisoners experience lead to a "pent-up rage," which

can cause victims . . . to erupt in violence once they return to their communities. Some will become rapists, seeking to "regain their manhood" through the same violent means by which they believe it was lost.[25]

Information compiled by the Bureau of Justice Statistics indicates that 23 percent of all *convicted* rapists had prior felony convictions.[26] Additionally, it seems likely that a substantial number of men who commit, but are not convicted of, rapes also served time in prison before assaulting their victims. Thus, those of us who seek to protect potential rape victims in the outside world—as well as potential rape victims in prisons—should heed Donaldson's warning.

. . . by Digging in Our Heels

The MacDworkinite idea that pornography is violence against women insults the many women who experience actual, brutal, three-dimensional violence in their real lives. Consequently, many women who are dedicating their lives to helping other women who are victims of violence have little patience for discussions of pornography as an alleged threat to women's safety.[27] I'd like you to consider the eloquent plea of one of them, whose many constructive efforts show what can and must be done to *really* help brutalized women.

Colleen Cobel, executive director of the Missouri Coalition Against Domestic Violence, was instrumental in beginning shelter service programs for battered women throughout Missouri, and for setting up the state's first toll-free hotline for victims of domestic and sexual violence. As a lobbyist, she played a key role in the passage of important legislation benefiting battered and raped women, including a domestic violence arrest statute, laws criminalizing marital rape and stalking, laws providing funding for services and shelters for battered women, and a state statute mandating the collection of law enforcement data on domestic violence crimes.

I met Colleen Cobel in 1993 when we both participated in a panel discussion about whether pornography should be censored in the name of feminism, at Washington University in St. Louis, Missouri. After listening to the other speakers, Cobel sought to shift the focus from images to human beings:

[I]f I can do honor to those women whose lives are consumed with the harsh realities of violence, it is to [address] what they experience

daily.... Women don't come into shelters saying, "This is pornography that is doing this to me." They don't call rape crisis lines saying,
"If he just wouldn't have read that magazine, I don't think I would have
been assaulted on my date." ... I put the word around the state to all of
the different shelters and sexual assault programs that I'm privileged
enough to work with. And none of the women were in a safe enough
place to distill these issues in their own personal life. To be able to name
the role that the cultural violence against women through magazines,
through film, through commercials, they couldn't name that as being a
cause.... [T]hey might have gotten raped last night because the wrong
team won in Monday night football. They might have been assaulted
because they served the wrong kind of food, because the kids were too
noisy.

When the women come into programs seeking the tools they need
to become survivors of violence, they have a long list of things that are
more paramount. It is that the judge doesn't know the law and he gave
my batterer my kids. It's that the Section 8 housing assistance list is so
long that they won't even take names for three years, and I don't have
a place to live. It's that I don't have any job skills and since I'm a rural
woman it took days to find a place to go. It's that my two-year-old thinks
that the way you get a hold of Mom's attention is you hit her in the face.

So I guess I have to expand the parameters of our discussion today in
honor of those women whose lives are being affected today by violence
and don't have the luxury of this room to sit and discuss the implications of pornography.

When the discussion later returned to antipornography proposals,
Cobel interjected along the same lines:

I want to bring us back down to the ground here. When we talk about
pornography as the injury, I don't care what causes the injury a lot of
days, all I know is that the injury is real and nobody is responding....
Our system does not work for the real life injuries and harms to women.
When today ends four women are dead and they died at the hands of
their partner, every day, every day, every day. I know our discussion
is to be in the theoretical, but it is very difficult for me to stay there
because I know that the real life devastation can come from any number

of causes. . . . And I just feel compelled to again and again say the real injury is the real injury and the real death is the real death. They come from a host of different places, different parts of society but they remain my greatest concern and my greatest focus.[28]

The pornocentric view that sexual abuse and violence stem from sexually explicit images has been disputed not only by activists who work with adult women who are actual victims of abuse, but also by activists who work with sexually abused children. Martin Morse Wooster has written that, consistent with the Meese Commission's preconceptions about the adverse impact of sexual expression, its investigators scoured Los Angeles organizations that help teenage runaways and prostitutes, in an ultimately futile quest to "see teenagers who started turning tricks after their fathers showed them *Playboy* and *Penthouse.*" As a staff member at one of these organizations noted, though, "*none* of our kids got started turning tricks because their fathers started using pornography. None. Even if you got rid of all the pornography in the world, you couldn't get rid of abusive or drunk fathers."[29]

It is important to note that the procensorship feminists' "blame-the-book" attitude closely parallels the "blame-the-victim" attitude that often characterized perceptions of female sexual assault victims, and that until recently was enshrined in American law. If a woman's skirt was "too short," or her sweater was "too tight," then it was her fault she was raped. As Marcia Pally has written, "[A]ccording to antipornography logic, it is still the woman's fault—if not the woman in the room, then the woman on the screen, calendar or wall."[30]

What "blaming the book" and "blaming the victim" have in common is the creation of a scapegoat. The many close connections between the traditional right wing and pornophobic feminists include this image-blaming approach to societal violence. In the spring of 1992, Vice President Dan Quayle criticized the title character of the television show *Murphy Brown* for choosing to become a single mother. He said the character had contributed to an erosion of "family values," which he blamed for the rioting that had occurred in Los Angeles in the wake of the acquittal of the police officers who had beaten Rodney King. Liberals promptly and savagely derided Quayle's female-image blaming. Yet as novelist Anne Rice has noted, too many liberals take a very different stance toward the same female-image-blaming strategy on the part of Dworkin and MacKinnon.

In 1992 Rice denounced the Pornography Victims' Compensation Act as "the most evil piece of legislation I have ever heard of." She astutely noted that if you give a rape victim "the right to sue and say that a magazine was the cause of the rape, there's only one step from that for the man to say, 'Yes, it was the magazine that made me do it, and it was also the way she was dressed.' Why can't he sue her?"[31]

As writer Pete Hamill has pointed out, the implications of an image- and word-blaming approach are limitless, and would surely engulf feminist writings and pictures: "Someone could claim that his family was destroyed as the result of published feminist theories attacking the family, and that feminist writers and their publishers must pay for the damage."[32]

The appeal of any censorship movement, including the one directed at pornography, is understandable insofar as it appears to offer a simple, inexpensive solution to complex, troubling societal problems. In contrast, measures that are designed to redress the root causes of these problems are less dramatic, more cumbersome, and more costly than censorship. As aptly expressed by one anticensorship feminist, Lisa Steele, "Censorship is the cheapest item on the shopping list of the women's movement."[33]

I certainly would like nothing better than to find a simple, fast route to equality and safety for women. But censoring sexual speech is really a detour or, worse, a dead end. For without free speech, where can we go but backward along our hard-forged path?

Notes

Note: The model antipornography law drafted by Andrea Dworkin and Catharine MacKinnon is quoted and referred to throughout this book. It can be found in Andrea Dworkin, "Against the Male Flood: Censorship, Pornography, and Equality," *Harvard Women's Law Journal* 8 (1985).

INTRODUCTION

1. Catharine A. MacKinnon, "Not a Moral Issue," *Yale Law & Policy Review* 2 (1984): 321–45, at 325.
2. Ad Hoc Committee of Feminists for Free Expression, letter to the members of the Senate Judiciary Committee, 14 February 1992. Reprinted in Nadine Strossen, "A Feminist Critique of 'the' Feminist Critique of Pornography," *Virginia Law Review* 79 (August 1993): 1099–1190, at 1188–90.
3. Henry Louis Gates, Jr., "To Deprave and Corrupt," review of *Girls Lean Back Everywhere: The Law of Obscenity and the Assault on Genius* by Edward de Grazia, *The Nation,* 29 June 1992, pp. 898–903, at p. 898.
4. Department of Justice, *Attorney General's Commission on Pornography, Final Report* (Washington, D.C.: Government Printing Office, 1986).
5. Alex Comfort, *The Joy of Sex* (New York: Simon & Schuster, 1972).
6. I first heard this phrase from Marcia Pally, founder of Feminists for Free Expression.
7. For this analysis by Andrea Dworkin, see: *Pornography: Men Possessing Women* (New York: E. P. Dutton, 1979); "Against the Male Flood: Censorship, Pornography, and Equality," *Harvard Women's Law Journal* 8 (1985); "Pornography's 'Exquisite Volunteers,'" *Ms.,* March 1981; "Pornography: The New Terrorism," *New York University Review of Law and Social Change* 8 (1978–79); "Pornography's Part in Sexual Violence," *Los Angeles Times,* 26 May 1981. For similar analysis by Catharine MacKinnon, see: *Only Words* (Cambridge, Mass.: Harvard University Press, 1993); "Not a Moral Issue"; "Pornography, Civil Rights, and Free Speech," *Harvard Civil Rights–Civil Liberties Law Review* 20 (Winter 1985): 1–70.
8. Cathy Crosson letter to Nadine Strossen, 6 October 1994.
9. Carole S. Vance, quoted in interviews by Sally Chew, "Pornography: Does Women's Equality Depend on What We Do about It?" *Ms.,* January/February 1994, pp. 42–45.
10. *Olmstead v. United States,* 277 U.S. 438, 479 (1928).

255

CHAPTER 1
The Sex Panic and the Feminist Split

1. Maureen Dezell, "Porn Wars," *Boston Phoenix*, 2–8 July 1993.
2. Leanne Katz, introduction to *New York Law School Law Review Symposium: The Sex Panic,* a special issue of the *Review* based on speeches at its same-titled 1992 symposium (forthcoming).
3. Marjorie Heins, "A Public University's Response to Students' Removal of an Art Exhibit" (speech given at the University of Michigan Law School, Ann Arbor, Mich., 16 October 1993).
4. *Webster's Third New International Dictionary of the English Language,* unabridged, Philip Babcock Gove, ed. (Springfield, Mass.: Merriam-Webster, 1986), p. 1767.
5. Walter Kendrick, *The Secret Museum: Pornography in Modern Culture* (New York: Viking, 1987), p. 239.
6. Andrea Dworkin, "Against the Male Flood: Censorship, Pornography, and Equality," *Harvard Women's Law Journal* 8 (1985): 1–29, at 25.
7. *Butler v. the Queen,* 1 S. C. R. 452 (1992, Canada).
8. Gayle Rubin, "Thinking Sex: Notes for a Radical Theory of the Politics of Sexuality," in *Pleasure and Danger: Exploring Female Sexuality,* ed. Carole S. Vance (Boston: Routledge & Kegan Paul, 1984), pp. 267–319, at p. 278.
9. Arts Censorship Project, *Year End Report* (New York: American Civil Liberties Union, 1992), p. 13.
10. Bernard Weinraub, "Despite Clinton, Hollywood Is Still Trading in Violence," *New York Times,* 28 December 1993.
11. Quoted in Dave Gram, "Columbus Mural Brings Charges of Harassment," Associated Press, 29 May 1992.
12. Chris Bentley, "Mall Nixes Artwork as Shocking," Springfield (Mo.) *News-Leader,* 5 March 1992.
13. Nat Hentoff, "Sexual Harassment by Francisco Goya," *Washington Post,* 27 December 1991.
14. Nancy C. Stumhofer, "Goya's 'Naked Maja' and the Classroom Climate," *Democratic Culture,* 3, no. 1 (1994): 18–22, at 19.
15. Hentoff, "Sexual Harassment by Francisco Goya."
16. Ntozake Shange, in "Where Do We Stand on Pornography?" (Round-table), *Ms.,* January/February 1994, pp. 32–41, at p. 34.
17. Joyce Price, "Breast Fetish Brouhaha Rocks Staid Vanderbilt," *Washington Times,* 6 March 1993.
18. Liza Mundy, "The New Critics," *Lingua Franca,* September/October 1993, pp. 26–33, at p. 27
19. Syracuse University, *Responding to Sexual Harassment at Syracuse University,* 8 October 1993, p. 1.
20. "75% of Female Doctors in Survey Cite Harassment by Patients," *New York Times,* 23 December 1993.
21. Ibid.
22. Joyce Price, "Art Professor Escapes Discipline: Vanderbilt Says He Must Warn Classes," *Washington Times,* 21 March 1993.
23. Ibid.

24. Malcolm Johnes, "In Defense of the Freedom to Read," *St. Petersburg Times,* 13 September 1987.
25. Price, "Breast Fetish Brouhaha."
26. Courtney Leatherman, "Dealing with Sexual Images in Iowa Classrooms," *Chronicle of Higher Education,* 8 December 1993.
27. "Free Expression Debate Had Other Flash Points," *New York Times,* 29 December 1993.
28. Dirk Johnson, "A Sexual Harassment Case to Test Academic Freedom," *New York Times,* 11 May 1994.
29. Morton M. Kondracke, "Sex, Drugs, and Pornography, Government Style," *Roll Call,* 17 January 1994.
30. Thelma McCormack, letter to the editor, *Chicago Tribune,* 28 September 1993.
31. Catharine MacKinnon, *Only Words* (Cambridge, Mass.: Harvard University Press, 1993), p. 71.
32. Indianapolis-Mercer County, Indiana, General Ordinances Nos. 24 and 25 (1984), amendments to Code of Indianapolis and Marion County, Chapter 16, "Human Relations and Equal Opportunity."
33. Brief of the American Civil Liberties Union, Indiana Civil Liberties Union, and the American Civil Liberties Union of Illinois, amici curiae, *Hudnut v. American Booksellers Association* (filed in 7th Cir. 1985), p. 28.
34. *Butler v. the Queen,* 1 S. C. R. 452 (1992, Canada).
35. Catharine MacKinnon, "Not a Moral Issue," *Yale Law and Policy Review* 2 (1984): 321–345, at 325.
36. Catharine MacKinnon, "'More Than Simply a Magazine': *Playboy's* Money," in *Feminism Unmodified* (Cambridge, Mass.: Harvard University Press, 1987), p. 145.
37. Catharine MacKinnon, quoted in Pete Hamill, "Women on the Verge of a Legal Breakdown," *Playboy,* January 1993, p. 186.
38. Andrea Dworkin, "Pornography: The New Terrorism," *New York University Review of Law and Social Change* 8 (1978–79): 218.
39. Leanne Katz, "In the Realm of the Censors," *In These Times,* 7 March 1994, pp. 24–25.
40. Quoted in Patrick Cooke, "Defending the L-Word," *Vogue,* December 1992, pp. 156–160, at p. 158.
41. Marcia Pally, letter to the editor under heading "Feminist Addenda," *Vogue,* February 1993, p. 58.
42. Kathleen Peratis, letter to Nadine Strossen, 29 November 1993.

CHAPTER 2
Sexual Speech and the Law

1. Madonna, "Rock the Vote Video," MTV Networks, 1992.
2. Susan Sontag, "The Pornographic Imagination," in *Styles of Radical Will* (New York: Anchor Books, 1969), pp. 35–73, at p. 46.
3. Garrison Keillor, statement to the Senate Subcommittee on Education, 29 March 1990. (Testimony on NEA Grant Funding and Restrictions.)
4. Sontag, "Pornographic Imagination," p. 46.
5. Catharine MacKinnon, *Only Words* (Cambridge, Mass.: Harvard University Press, 1993), pp. 45–110; Andrea Dworkin and Catharine MacKinnon, *Pornography and Civil*

Rights: A New Day for Women's Equality (Minneapolis: Organizing Against Pornography, 1988), p. 85.
6. *United States v. Schwimmer,* 279 U.S. 644, 654–55 (1929) (dissenting).
7. *Texas v. Johnson,* 491 U.S. 397, 414 (1989).
8. Ibid; *U.S. v. Eichman,* 496 U.S. 310 (1990).
9. *R.A.V. v. City of St. Paul,* 112 S. Ct. 2538 (1992). The Court recognized that this symbolic expression could be constitutionally prohibited under many laws, such as those prohibiting arson, vandalism, and trespass; it stressed, though, that this expression could not be prohibited under a law that focused on the ideas it conveyed—namely, a city ordinance that prohibited expression that "arouses anger, alarm or resentment . . . on the basis of race, color, creed, religion or gender."
10. *Schenck v. United States,* 249 U.S. 47, 52 (1919).
11. *Gitlow v. New York,* 268 U.S. 652, 673 (1925) (dissenting).
12. *American Booksellers Association v. Hudnut,* 771 F. 2d 323, 329–30 (1985).
13. *Butler v. the Queen,* 1 S.C.R. 452, 505 (1992, Canada) (stating that "[i]t might be suggested that proof of actual harm should be required. . . . [I]t is sufficient . . . for Parliament to have a reasonable basis for concluding that harm will result and this requirement does not demand actual proof of harm").
14. *Brandenburg v. Ohio,* 395 U.S. 444 (1969).
15. *National Association for the Advancement of Colored People (NAACP) v. Claiborne Hardware Co.,* 458 U.S. 886, 928 (1982).
16. *Abrams v. United States,* 250 U.S. 616, 630–31 (1919) (dissenting).
17. *Whitney v. California,* 274 U.S. 357, 375–77 (1927) (concurring).
18. Susie Bright, "I Hate to Break This to You Kitty, But . . . ," *San Diego Reader,* 18 November 1993, pp. 1–2.
19. Sontag, "Pornographic Imagination," p. 47.
20. *Webster's Third New International Dictionary of the English Language,* unabridged, Philip Babcock Gove, ed. (Springfield, Mass.: Merriam-Webster, 1986), p. 1767.
21. *Winters v. New York,* 338 U.S. 507, 510, 528 (1948).
22. President's Commission on Obscenity and Pornography, *Report* (New York: Bantam, 1970).
23. *Roe v. Wade,* 410 U.S. 179 (1973).
24. *Miller v. California,* 413 U.S. 15 (1973).
25. *Paris Adult Theatre I v. Slaton,* 413 U.S. 49 (1973).
26. *Memoirs v. Massachusetts,* 383 U.S. 413, 419–20 (1966).
27. *Miller v. California,* 24.
28. *Paris Adult Theatre I v. Slaton,* 60.
29. *Jacobellis v. Ohio,* 378 U.S. 184, 197 (1964) (concurring).
30. *Miller v. California,* 24.
31. *Brockett v. Spokane Arcades,* 472 U.S. 492, 498 (1985).
32. Quoted in Jeff Rosen, "*Miller* Time," *New Republic,* 1 October 1990, p. 17.
33. Quoted in Edward de Grazia, *Girls Lean Back Everywhere: The Law of Obscenity and the Assault on Genius* (New York: Vintage Books, 1992), p. 622.
34. *R.A.V. v. City of St. Paul* (cross); *U.S. v. Eichman* (flag); *Texas v. Johnson* (flag).
35. *Roth v. United States,* 354 U.S. 476, 487 (1957).
36. Laurence H. Tribe, *American Constitutional Law,* 2d ed. (Mineola, N.Y.: The Foundation Press, 1988), p. 905.

37. Marjorie Heins, *Sex, Sin, and Blasphemy* (New York: The New Press, 1993), p. 34.
38. *Pope v. Illinois*, 481 U.S. 497, 507 (1987) (dissenting).
39. Ibid., 504–5 (concurring).
40. *State v. Henry*, 302 Ore. 510, 732 P 2d 9 (1987); *State v. Kam*, 69 Haw. 483, 748 P 2d 372 (1988).
41. United States Department of Justice, *Attorney General's Commission on Pornography, Final Report* (Washington, D.C.: U.S. Government Printing Office, 1986), p. 251.
42. Tribe, *American Constitutional Law*, p. 919.

CHAPTER 3
The Fatally Flawed Feminist Antipornography Laws

1. Andrea Dworkin, *Letters from a War Zone* (New York: E. P Dutton, 1988), pp. 256–61; Catharine MacKinnon, *Only Words* (Cambridge, Mass.: Harvard University Press, 1993), pp. 87–89.
2. *New York v. Ferber*, 458 U.S. 747 (1982); *Osborne v. Ohio*, 495 U.S. 103 (1990).
3. Andrea Dworkin, "Against the Male Flood: Censorship, Pornography, and Equality," *Harvard Women's Law Journal* 8 (1985): 25.
4. *R.A.V. v. City of St. Paul*, 112 S. Ct. 2538, 2550 (1992).
5. *Dambrot v. Central Michigan University*, 839 F. Supp. 477 (E.D. Mich. 1993); *U.W.M. Post, Inc. v. Board of Regents of the University of Wisconsin System*, 774 F. Supp. 1163 (E.D. Wis. 1991); *Doe v. University of Michigan*, 721 F. Supp. 852 (E.D. Mich. 1989).
6. Richard Bernstein, *Dictatorship of Virtue: Multiculturalism and the Battle for America's Future* (New York: Knopf, 1994).
7. Catharine A. MacKinnon, *Toward a Feminist Theory of the State* (Cambridge, Mass.: Harvard University Press, 1989), p. 202.
8. *United States v. Levine*, 183 F. 2d 156, 157 (2d Cir. 1936). The earlier, repudiated doctrine was set forth in an 1868 British case, *Regina v. Hicklin*, L.R. 3 Q.B. 360, 368, which American courts had widely adopted. It held that the "test of obscenity" was "whether the tendency of the matter . . . is to deprave and corrupt those whose minds are open to such immoral influences. . . ."
9. *Pornography Victims' Compensation Act of 1991*, 102d Congress, 1st sess., S.R. 1521.
10. Catharine A. MacKinnon, letter to *New York Times* opinion page editor Mitchel Levitas, 1 January 1994.
11. Andrea Dworkin, in "Where Do We Stand on Pornography?" (Round-table), *Ms.*, January/February 1994, pp. 32–41, at p. 37.
12. *New York Times v. Sullivan*, 376 U.S. 254, 277 (1964).
13. *American Booksellers Association v. Hudnut*, 598 F. Supp. 1316, 1340–41 (D. Ind. 1984).
14. *New York Times Co. v. United States*, 403 U.S. 713 (1971).
15. *New York Times v. Sullivan*, 277.
16. Molly Ivins, "Havin' Fun Fightin' for Freedom," in *New York Law School Law Review Symposium: The Sex Panic* (forthcoming).
17. *New York Times v. Sullivan*, 376 U.S. 254 (1964).
18. Joyce Meskis, president of the American Booksellers Association, testifying on behalf of the association before the Senate Judiciary Committee, 23 July 1991.
19. See *Kovacs v. Cooper*, 336 U.S. 77, 87 (1949).

20. *Consolidated Edison Company v. Public Service Commission,* 447 U.S. 530, 542 (1980).
21. *Rowan v. United States Post Office Department,* 397 U.S. 728, 737 (1970).
22. *Bolger v. Youngs Drug Products,* 463 U.S. 60 (1983).
23. *American Booksellers Association v. Hudnut,* 771 F. 2d 323, 333 (7th Cir. 1985).
24. *Erznoznik v. City of Jacksonville,* 422 U.S. 205 (1975).
25. "Policy No. 3: Private Pressure Groups," *Policy Guide of the American Civil Liberties Union.* Adopted 1981.
26. Kate Ellis, Beth Jaker, Nan D. Hunter, Barbara O'Dair, and Abby Tallmer, eds., *Caught Looking: Feminism, Pornography, and Censorship* (East Haven, Conn.: Long River Books, 1986).
27. Carole Vance, in *Ideas—Feminism and Censorship,* transcript from the Canadian Broadcasting Company (Toronto: CBC Radio Works, 1993), p. 14.
28. Marcia Pally, "X-Rated Feminism: Ban Sexism, Not Pornography," *The Nation,* 29 June 1985, pp. 794–96.
29. Andrea Dworkin and Catharine MacKinnon, *Pornography and Civil Rights: A New Day for Women's Equality* (Minneapolis: Organizing Against Pornography, 1988), pp. 138–42.
30. Some versions of the MacDworkin law include a ninth criterion, that "women are presented as whores by nature." See *Caught Looking,* p. 88, quoting Minneapolis version of the Dworkin-MacKinnon model law at p. vii.
31. MacKinnon letter to Mitchel Levitas.
32. Susan J. Berkson, "Minneapolis Saw Early that Porn Causes Harm, But '84 Vetoes Stopped Ordinance from Taking Effect," *Star Tribune,* 20 February 1994.
33. Kathleen Currie and Art Levine, "Whip Me, Beat Me, and While You're at It Cancel My NOW Membership: Feminists War against Each Other over Pornography," *Washington Monthly,* June 1987, p. 17.
34. Quoted in Lisa Duggan, "Censorship in the Name of Feminism," in *Caught Looking,* p. 65. (Reprinted from *Village Voice,* 16 October 1986, pp. 11–12, 16–17, 42.)
35. Quoted in ibid., p. 65.
36. Quoted in ibid.
37. *American Booksellers Association v. Hudnut,* 598 F. Supp. 1316 (D. Ind. 1984), *aff'd.,* 771 F. 2d 323 (7th Cir. 1985), *aff'd. mem.,* 475 U.S. 1001 (1986).
38. *American Booksellers Association v. Hudnut,* 771 F. 2d 323, 325 (7th Cir. 1985).
39. *American Booksellers Association v. Hudnut,* 598 F. Supp. 1316, 1317 (D. Ind. 1984).
40. Catharine MacKinnon, "Sexual Politics of the First Amendment," in *Feminism Unmodified* (Cambridge, Mass.: Harvard University Press, 1987), p. 213.
41. *Dred Scott v. Sandford,* 60 U.S. 393 (1856).
42. *Brown v. Board of Education,* 347 U.S. 483 (1954).
43. *Village Books et al. v. City of Bellingham,* C88-1470D (W.D. Wash.). This decision is not officially reported.
44. *Dworkin v. Hustler Magazine,* 867 F. 2d 1188, 1199 (9th Cir. 1989). Interestingly, the opinion was written by a female judge, Cynthia Holcomb Hall.
45. Quoted in Karen Winkler, "Research on Pornography Gains Respectability," *Chronicle of Higher Education,* 14 June 1989.
46. *Roe v. Wade,* 410 U.S. 179 (1973).
47. For a discussion of these rulings, see Nadine Strossen, "A Feminist Critique of 'the' Feminist Critique of Pornography," *Virginia Law Review* 79 (1993): 1099–1190, at 1120–22.

48. Fred Strebeigh, "Defining Law on the Feminist Frontier," *New York Times Magazine*, 6 October 1991.

CHAPTER 4
The Growing Suppression of "Sexpression"

1. Marcia Pally, "The Soothing Appeal of Censorship," *Writer's Yearbook* (1993): 80.
2. Quoted in Digby Diehl, "Anne Rice: The *Playboy* Interview," *Playboy*, March 1993, pp. 53–64, at p. 56.
3. Isabel Wilkerson, "Foes of Pornography and Bigotry Join Forces," *New York Times*, 12 March 1993.
4. Alice Echols, "Sex and the Single-Minded," *Voice Literary Supplement*, March 1994, pp. 13, 17.
5. James R. Petersen, "Catharine MacKinnon: Again," *Playboy*, August 1992, pp. 37, 39.
6. Quoted in David Margolick, "At the Bar" (column), *New York Times*, 5 November 1993.
7. Anthony Lewis, "The First Amendment, Under Fire from the Left," *New York Times Magazine*, 13 March 1994.
8. Margolick, "At the Bar."
9. Ibid.
10. Ibid.
11. Catharine MacKinnon, "Linda's Life and Andrea's Work," in *Feminism Unmodified*, p. 133.
12. Leanne Katz, in *New York Law School Law Review Symposium: The Sex Panic* (forthcoming).
13. Wilkerson, "Foes of Pornography and Bigotry Join Forces."
14. Madonna, *Sex* (New York: Warner Books, 1992).
15. Quoted in Catherine Siemann, memo to Nadine Strossen regarding Chicago conference, 12 March 1993.
16. Maureen Dezell, "Woman's Choices," *Boston Phoenix*, 5 February 1993.
17. To correct this imbalance, the *New York Law School Law Review* is publishing a special two-issue collection of articles and essays, *The Sex Panic*, which presents feminist anti-censorship perspectives on pornography, scheduled for publication in 1994.
18. Susie Bright, "Better the Devil You Know," *San Francisco Review of Books*, May/June 1993.
19. Jean Bethke Elshtain, "The New Porn Wars," *New Republic*, 25 June 1984, p. 15.
20. "Enough Is Enough" campaign, advertising a kit for creating an antipornography billboard.
21. Carole S. Vance, in *New York Law School Law Review Symposium: The Sex Panic* (forthcoming).
22. Carole S. Vance, "Feminist Fundamentalism: Women against Images," *Art in America*, September 1993, pp. 35–39, at p. 36.
23. Judith R. Walkowitz, *Prostitution and Victorian Society: Women, Class, and the State* (New York: Cambridge University Press, 1980), p. 256.
24. ACLU Arts Censorship Project, *Above the Law: The Justice Department's War against the First Amendment* (New York: American Civil Liberties Union, 1991).
25. Deposition of Robert Marinaro in *PHE, Inc. v. U.S. Department of Justice*, 743 F. Supp. 15, 69–70 (D.D.C. 1990) 24 May 1991.

26. Chuck Philips, "A War on Many Fronts," *Los Angeles Times,* 26 December 1990.
27. *Jacobson v. United States,* 112 S. Ct. 1535 (1992).
28. Lawrence A. Stanley, "The Child Porn Myth," *Cardozo Arts & Entertainment Law Journal* 7 (1989): 295–358.
29. *United States v. Mitchell,* 915 F. 2d 521, 524 (9th Cir. 1990).
30. *Washington Revised Code,* annotated (West 1992) 9:68.050-.070, .090.
31. Susan McClary, "Getting Down Off the Beanstalk: The Presence of Woman's Voice in Janika Vandervelde's *Genesis 11,*" *Minnesota Composers' Forum Newsletter* (January 1987), cited in Christina Hoff Sommers, *Who Stole Feminism? How Women Have Betrayed Women* (New York: Simon & Schuster, 1994), p. 28. According to Sommers, "McClary also directs us to be alert to themes of male masturbation in the music of Richard Strauss and Gustav Mahler."
32. Marjorie Heins, *Sex, Sin, and Blasphemy* (New York: The New Press, 1993), pp. 61–63.
33. Ibid., p. 64.
34. Nikki Finke, "All Sides Get Worked Up over Study of Aerobics Video," *Los Angeles Times,* 12 November 1987; see also Margaret Morse, "Artemis Aging: Exercise and the Female Body on Video," *Discourse* 11 (1987–88): 20–53.
35. For example, the ACLU successfully challenged Washington's erotic-lyrics law. See *Soundgarden v. Eikenberry,* 123 Wash. 2d 750, 871 P 2d 1050 (1994).
36. 750 ILCS 5/12-18.1.
37. *An Act to Protect the Civil Rights of Women and Children,* Massachusetts 177th General Court—1992 Regular Session House Bill 5194.
38. Memorandum to Working Group, Interested Others from Leanne Katz, executive director, National Coalition Against Censorship, 11 August 1994.
39. *Finley v. National Endowment for the Arts,* 795 F. Supp. 1457 (C.D. Cal. 1992); *Bella Lewitsky Dance Foundation v. Frohnmayer,* 754 F. Supp. 774 (C.D. Cal. 1991); *New School for Social Research v. Frohnmayer,* No. 90 Civ. 3510 (LLS), Southern District of New York, February 19, 1991 (settled by stipulation).
40. Holly Hughes, quoted in interviews by Sally Chew in "Pornography: Does Women's Equality Depend on What We Do about It?" *Ms.,* January/February 1994, pp. 42–45.
41. Paul Goldberger, "Clinton Arts Dinner Whetted Appetites Still Unsatisfied," *New York Times,* 23 March 1994.
42. William Grimes, "House Votes a Cut in Arts Endowment's Budget," *New York Times,* 24 June 1994.
43. Paul Goldberger, "Clinton Arts Dinner Whetted Appetites."
44. William Grimes, "For Endowment, One Performer Means Trouble," *New York Times,* 7 July 1994; "Senate Passes 5% Arts Cut," *New York Times,* 27 July 1994.
45. Grimes, "House Votes a Cut in Arts Endowment's Budget."
46. *Finley v. National Endowment for the Arts,* 1475.
47. Barbara Isenberg and Ronald J. Ostrow, "Appeal in NEA Case Criticized," *Los Angeles Times,* 8 April 1993.
48. Quoted in Edward de Grazia, *Girls Lean Back Everywhere: The Law of Obscenity and the Assault on Genius* (New York: Vintage Books, 1992), p. 666.
49. Quoted in ibid., p. 685.
50. Judy Blume, "Is Puberty a Dirty Word?" in *New York Law School Law Review Symposium: The Sex Panic* (forthcoming).
51. Robert Brustein, "The War on the Arts," *New Republic,* 7 September 1992, p. 35.

52. Marilyn French, *The War against Women* (New York: Simon & Schuster, 1992), p. 163.
53. *Finley v. National Endowment for the Arts,* 1461.
54. Quoted in letter from Jeremiah Gutman, Jo List Levinson, and Leanne Katz to Cincinnati prosecutor Terrence Robert Cosgrove, 27 July 1994, p. 2.
55. Ibid., p. 3.
56. Andrea Dworkin, *Pornography: Men Possessing Women* (New York: E. P. Dutton, 1979), p. 23.

CHAPTER 5
Revealing Views of Women, Men, and Sex

1. Andrea Dworkin, *Woman Hating* (New York: E.P. Dutton, 1984), p. 184.
2. Lisa Duggan, Nan D. Hunter, and Carole S. Vance, "False Promises: Feminist Anti-Pornography Legislation," in *Caught Looking: Feminism, Pornography, and Censorship,* ed. Kate Ellis et al. (East Haven, Conn.: Long River Books, 1986), pp. 72–85, at p. 80.
3. Dworkin, *Woman Hating,* p. 184.
4. Quoted in Christina Hoff Sommers, "Hard-Line Feminists Guilty of Ms.-Representation," *Wall Street Journal,* 7 November 1991.
5. Carlin Meyer, "Decriminalizing Prostitution: Liberation or Dehumanization?" *Cardozo Women's Law Journal* 1 (1993): 105–20, at 117.
6. In Charles Bufe, ed., *The Heretic's Handbook of Quotations* (San Francisco: Sharp Press, 1988), p. 63.
7. Jeanne L. Schroeder, "Catharine's Wheel: MacKinnon's Pornography Analysis as a Return to Traditional Christian Sexual Theory," in *New York Law School Law Review Symposium: The Sex Panic* (forthcoming).
8. Andrea Dworkin, *Intercourse* (New York: Free Press, 1987), p. 137.
9. Ibid., pp. 42–43.
10. Andrea Dworkin, *Pornography: Men Possessing Women* (New York: E. P. Dutton, 1979), p. 23
11. Andrea Dworkin, *Letters from a War Zone* (New York: E. P. Dutton, 1988), pp. 176 and 119.
12. Andrea Dworkin, *Ice and Fire* (New York: Weidenfeld and Nicholson, 1987), p. 108.
13. Quoted in Pete Hamill, "Women on the Verge of a Legal Breakdown," *Playboy,* January 1993, p. 187.
14. Catharine MacKinnon, "Feminism, Marxism, Method, and the State: Towards Feminist Jurisprudence," *Signs: Journal of Women in Culture and Society* 8 (1983): 635–58, at 646.
15. Quoted in James R. Petersen, "Catharine MacKinnon: Again," *Playboy,* August 1992, pp. 37–39.
16. Ibid.
17. Ibid.
18. Ibid.
19. Catharine MacKinnon, "Not a Moral Issue," *Yale Law & Policy Review* 2 (1984): 334.
20. Catharine MacKinnon, "Linda's Life and Andrea's Work," in *Feminism Unmodified* (Cambridge, Mass.: Harvard University Press, 1987), pp. 127–33, at p. 130.
21. Catharine A. MacKinnon, *Toward a Feminist Theory of the State* (Cambridge, Mass.: Harvard University Press, 1989), p. 113.

22. Catharine MacKinnon, "Reflections of Sex Equality under Law," *Yale Law Journal* 100 (1991): 1281–1328, at 1302–3.
23. Catharine MacKinnon, "Francis Biddle's Sister," in *Feminism Unmodified*, pp. 163–97, at p. 171.
24. Ibid., p. 172.
25. J. Miller, "Civil Right, Not Censorship," *Village Voice*, 6 November 1994.
26. MacKinnon, "Francis Biddle's Sister," at p. 171.
27. Quoted in Tad Friend, "Yes: Feminist Women Who Like Sex," *Esquire*, February 1994, pp. 48–56, at p. 54.
28. MacKinnon, *Toward a Feminist Theory of the State*, p. 125.
29. Quoted in Petersen, "Catharine MacKinnon: Again," p. 39.
30. Quoted in Friend, "Yes: Feminist Women Who Like Sex," at p. 50.
31. Dorchen Leidholdt, "When Women Defend Pornography," in *The Sexual Liberals and the Attack on Feminism*, ed. Dorchen Leidholdt and Janice G. Raymond (New York: Pergamon Press, 1990), pp. 125–31, at p. 131.
32. Meyer, "Decriminalizing Prostitution," 117.
33. Sally Cline, *Women, Passion, and Celibacy* (New York: Carol Southern Books, 1993), p. 150, p. 1.
34. Catharine MacKinnon, *Only Words* (Cambridge, Mass.: Harvard University Press, 1993), p. 12.
35. Katie Roiphe, *The Morning After: Sex, Fear, and Feminism on Campus* (New York: Little, Brown, 1993), p. 99.
36. Dworkin, *Pornography: Men Possessing Women*, p. 55.
37. Dworkin, *Letters from a War Zone*, p. 309.
38. MacKinnon, *Toward a Feminist Theory of the State*, p. 138.
39. Brief of the American Civil Liberties Union, Indiana Civil Liberties Union, and the American Civil Liberties Union of Illinois, amici curiae, *Hudnut v. American Booksellers Association* (filed in 7th Cir. 1985), p. 28.
40. Germaine Greer, *The Female Eunuch* (New York: McGraw-Hill, 1971), p. 59.
41. Ann Snitow, "Retrenchment versus Transformation: The Politics of the Antipornography Movement," in *Women against Censorship*, ed. Varda Burstyn (Vancouver: Douglas and McIntyre, 1985), pp. 107, 120.
42. Jeanne L. Schroeder, "Feminism Historicized: Medieval Misogynist Stereotypes in Contemporary Feminist Jurisprudence," *Iowa Law Review* 75 (1980): 1135–1217, at 1136.
43. Ibid.
44. Marcia Pally, "The Soothing Appeal of Censorship," *Writer's Yearbook* (1993): 80.
45. Cathy Young, "Victimhood Is Powerful," *Reason*, October 1992, pp. 18–23, at p. 18.
46. Naomi Wolf, *Fire with Fire: The New Female Power and How It Will Change the 21st Century* (New York: Random House, 1993), p. xvii.
47. Ibid., p. 224.

CHAPTER 6
Defining Sexual Harassment: Sexuality Does Not Equal Sexism

1. Catharine A. MacKinnon, *Sexual Harassment of Working Women: A Case of Sex Discrimination* (New Haven, Conn.: Yale University Press, 1979).
2. *Meritor Savings Bank v. Vinson*, 477 U.S. 57 (1986).

3. See, for example, Catharine MacKinnon, "Not a Moral Issue," *Yale Law & Policy Review* 2 (1984): 325. ("Pornography . . . is . . . an institution of gender inequality.")
4. Katie Roiphe, *The Morning After: Sex, Fear, and Feminism on Campus* (New York: Little, Brown, 1993), p. 154.
5. Brief of Feminists for Free Expression, amicus curiae, *Johnson v. County of Los Angeles Fire Department* (filed in C.D. Cal. 1994), p. 16.
6. *Meritor Savings Bank v. Vinson,* 65.
7. Equal Employment Opportunity Commission Guidelines on Discrimination because of Sex, 29 CFR Part 1604.11(a) (1985).
8. Catharine MacKinnon, introduction to "Comment on Sexual Harassment," *Capital University Law Review,* 10 (Spring 1981): i-viii; *Only Words* (Cambridge, Mass.: Harvard University Press, 1993), pp. 56–57, 61–62; also *Sexual Harassment of Working Women.*
9. In October 1993, the EEOC issued proposed rules that define sanctionable gender-discriminatory harassment. While they cure the underinclusivity defect of the EEOC's sexual harassment guidelines noted in the text, they raise significant problems of their own, purporting to proscribe a broad range of "verbal conduct" on the basis of its content or viewpoint. These proposed new guidelines do not alter the EEOC's previous guidelines concerning sexual harassment. Federal Register Vol. 58, No. 189, October 1, 1993, p. 51266, Proposed Rules; 29 CFR Part 1609, Guidelines on Harassment Based on Race, Color, Religion, Gender, National Origin, Age, or Disability.
10. *Harris v. Forklift Systems,* Inc., 114 S. Ct. 367 (1993).
11. Ibid.
12. *Robinson v. Jacksonville Shipyards, Inc.,* 760 F. Supp. 1486 (M.D. Fl. 1991).
13. Ibid., 1542.
14. David Moshman, "Banned at UN-L," *Academic Freedom Coalition of Nebraska Newsletter* 4 (2): 2.
15. Nat Hentoff, "Sexual Harassment by Francisco Goya," *Washington Post,* 27 December 1993.
16. Nancy C. Stumhofer, "Goya's 'Naked Maja' and the Classroom Climate," *Democratic Culture,* 3, no. 1 (1994): 18–22.
17. Liza Mundy, "The New Critics," *Lingua Franca,* September/October 1993, pp. 26–33, at p. 27.
18. Ibid., pp. 29–30.
19. Brief of Feminists for Free Expression, amicus curiae, *Johnson v. County of Los Angeles Fire Department,* p. 5.
20. *Stanley v. Georgia,* 394 U.S. 557 (1969).
21. *Johnson v. County of Los Angeles Fire Department,* U.S. District Court for the Central District of California, CV 93-7589 SVW (JGX), Findings of Fact, Conclusions of Law and Judgment, entered 10 June 1994 (holding that the policy was unconstitutional as applied to the quiet reading and possession of sexually oriented materials during a firefighter's personal time).
22. Brief of Feminists for Free Expression, amicus curiae, *Johnson v. County of Los Angeles Fire Department,* pp. 24–26.
23. Roiphe, *The Morning After,* pp. 100–101.
24. Sexual Harassment and Academic Freedom, Statement 3, National Association of Scholars, 1993.

25. Naomi Wolf, *Fire with Fire: The New Female Power and How It Will Change the 21st Century* (New York: Random House, 1993), p. 195.

26. Rudy Platiel, "Adult Magazine Complaint Enters New Phase," *Toronto Globe and Mail,* 4 January 1994; Reva Landau, "Bread, Milk, and Pornography," *Toronto Star,* 22 February 1993.

27. Tom Puleo, "Market Mores: Who Should Censor?" *Hartford Journal,* 13 January 1992.

28. Thomas McGevran, "Bookstore Charged with Harassment: Complaint Says Pornography Magazines Violate Sexual Harassment Policy," *Carleton College Carletonian,* 29 May 1992; Chris Youngquist, "VP Decides R.A.P. Case: Disputed Magazines Will Remain in Bookstore," *Carletonian,* 9 October 1992.

29. Laurence H. Tribe, *American Constitutional Law,* 2d. ed. (Mineola, N.Y.: The Foundation Press, 1988), pp. 920–28.

30. James R. Petersen, "The *Playboy* Read-in," *Playboy,* February 1992, pp. 37–39.

31. *Civil Rights Act of 1964* at 201, Pub. L. No. 88-352, 78 Stat. 243 (codified at 42 U.S.C. at 2000a [1982]) prohibiting discrimination and segregation in places of public accommodation.

32. Brief of Feminists for Free Expression, amicus curiae, *Johnson v. County of Los Angeles Fire Department,* pp. 6–7.

33. Mark Schapiro, "The Fine Art of Sexual Harassment: Aphrodite Gets Her Day in Court," *Harper's,* July 1994, pp. 62–63.

34. Editorial, "Hillary the Stupendous," *Washington Times,* 10 April 1993.

35. Quoted in Schapiro, "The Fine Art of Sexual Harassment," p. 63.

36. Cynthia Grant Bowman, "Street Harassment and the Informal Ghettoization of Women," *Harvard Law Review* 106 (1993): 517. The following three quotes appear on pages 575, 562, and 523, respectively.

37. Quoted in "A Move to Protect Women from 'Street Harassment,'" *New York Times,* 2 July 1993.

38. Marcia Pally, *Sex and Sensibility: Reflections on Forbidden Mirrors and the Will to Censor* (Hopewell, N.J.: Ecco Press, 1994), pp. 73, 75.

39. *In the Interest of Joseph T., a minor,* 430 S.E. 2d 523, 524 (1993).

40. Susan Fall telephone conversation with Thomas Hilbink, 25 July 1994.

41. *Bradwell v. Illinois,* 83 U.S. (16 Wall.) 130, 140 (1873) (concurring).

42. *Bailey v. State,* 219 S.W. 2d 424, 428 (Ark. 1949).

43. Kingsley R. Browne, "Title VII as Censorship: Hostile-Environment Harassment and the First Amendment," *Ohio State Law Journal* 52 (Spring 1991): 488.

44. *Muller v. Oregon,* 208 U.S. 412 (1908).

45. *Frontiero v. Richardson,* 411 U.S. 677, 684 (1973).

46. Sarah J. McCarthy, "Cultural Fascism," *Forbes,* 9 December 1991, p. 116.

CHAPTER 7
"Different Strokes for Different Folks": The Panoply of Pornographic Imagination

1. Richard A. Posner, "Obsession," review of *Only Words* by Catharine A. MacKinnon, *New Republic,* 18 October 1993, pp. 31–36, p. 36.

2. Brief of the American Civil Liberties Union and the Indiana Civil Liberties Union, amici curiae, *American Booksellers Association v. Hudnut* (Filed in D. Ind. 1984), p. 1.

3. Carlin Meyer, "Sex, Censorship, and Women's Liberation" (unpublished), pp. 42–43. [A revised version of this manuscript was published in *Texas Law Review* 72 (1994): 1097–1201.]

4. Sallie Tisdale, "Talk Dirty to Me: A Woman's Taste for Pornography," *Harper's*, February 1992, pp. 37–46, p. 45.

5. Marjorie Heins, *Sex, Sin, and Blasphemy* (New York: The New Press, 1993), p. 142.

6. Tad Friend, "Yes: Feminist Women Who Like Sex," *Esquire*, February 1994, pp. 48–56.

7. Heins, *Sex, Sin, and Blasphemy*, p. 35; John R. Wilke, "Porn Broker: A Publicly Held Firm Turns X-Rated Videos into a Hot Business," *Wall Street Journal*, 11 July 1994.

8. Carin Rubinstein and Carol Tavris, "Survey Results," *Redbook*, September 1987, pp. 147–49, 214–25, at p. 214.

9. Marc Speigler, "Lust Be a Lady," *New City*, 12–18 May 1994, pp. 8–9.

10. Susan Sontag, "The Pornographic Imagination," in *Styles of Radical Will* (New York: Anchor Books, 1969), p. 36.

11. Tisdale, "Talk Dirty to Me," p. 45

12. Thelma McCormack, "If Pornography Is the Theory, Is Inequality the Practice?" (presented at public forum, *Refusing Censorship: Feminists and Activists Fight Back*, York, Canada, 12 November 1992), p. 32.

13. Pete Hamill, "Women on the Verge of a Legal Breakdown," *Playboy*, January 1993, p. 189.

14. McCormack, "If Pornography Is the Theory," p. 22.

15. Lisa Duggan, Nan D. Hunter, and Carole S. Vance, "False Promises: Feminist Anti-Pornography Legislation," in *Women against Censorship*, ed. Varda Burstyn (Vancouver: Douglas and McIntyre, 1985), pp. 130–151, at p. 140.

16. Carole S. Vance, epilogue to *Pleasure and Danger: Exploring Female Sexuality* (Boston: Routledge & Kegan Paul, 1984), p. 433.

17. Evelyn C. White, "Alice Walker Says Award Is No Treasure: State Presents Her with 'Decapitated' Art," *San Francisco Chronicle*, 16 April 1994.

18. Peter Hecht, "Hearings Set on Writings' Removal from Test," *San Diego Union-Tribune*, 8 March 1994; Carl Ingram, "Stories Deleted from Tests Reinstated," *Los Angeles Times*, 12 March 1994.

19. David Link, "In the Eye—or the Mind—of the Beholder; Art: Alice Walker's Criticism of the Robert Graham Art Echoes the Small-Mindedness of Her Own Critics," *Los Angeles Times*, 21 April 1994.

20. Caitlin Sullivan, "Bookstores Vandalized over 'Lesbian Porn' Issue," *Seattle Gay News*, 18 June 1993.

21. Ibid.

22. Christine Wenz, "In Our Heads," *Stranger*, 5–11 July 1993.

23. Ibid.

24. Heather Findlay, "Dyke Porn 101: How to Enjoy (and Defend) Your Porn," *On Our Backs*, November/December 1993, pp. 14–15, 42–43, at p. 14.

25. Wenz, "In Our Heads."

26. Suzanne "Zan" Scommodau and Tanya Turkovich, letter to the editor, *Seattle Gay News*, 25 June 1993.

27. Quoted in Jack Kammer, "Men and Women: Who's Got the Power?," *The Sun* (Baltimore), 21 December 1993.

28. Quoted ibid.

29. Veronica Vera, "Censored Artist, Activist Speaks Out," *Michigan Daily,* 30 November 1992.

30. Kammer, "Men and Women: Who's Got the Power?"

31. Quoted in Susan Brownmiller, *Against Our Will: Men, Women and Rape* (New York: Bantam, 1976), p. 363.

32. Sara Diamond, "Pornography: Image and Reality," in *Women against Censorship,* pp. 40–57, at p. 51.

33. Wendy McElroy, "Talking Sex, Not Gender," *Liberty* (in press).

34. Ibid.

35. Gary Day and Clive Bloom, eds., *Perspectives on Pornography: Sexuality in Film and Literature* (New York: St. Martin's Press, 1988), pp. 1–8, at p. 5.

36. Posner, "Obsession," p. 36.

37. Katie Roiphe, *The Morning After* (New York: Little, Brown, 1993), p. 151.

38. Hammill, "Women on the Verge," p. 188.

39. Heins, *Sex, Sin, and Blasphemy,* p. 145.

40. Shortly after this ad aired, President George Bush fired then-NEA chair John Frohn-mayer. Heins, *Sex, Sin, and Blasphemy,* pp. 135, 167.

41. Edward de Grazia, *Girls Lean Back Everywhere: The Law of Obscenity and the Assault on Genius* (New York: Vintage Books, 1992), p. 589

42. Ibid., p. 588.

43. Susie Bright, telephone conversation with Thomas Hilbink, 21 July 1994.

44. Walter Kendrick, *The Secret Museum: Pornography in Modern Culture* (New York: Viking, 1987), p. 234.

45. Carole S. Vance, "More Danger, More Pleasure: A Decade after the Barnard Sex-uality Conference," in *New York Law School Review Symposium: The Sex Panic* (forthcoming).

46. Catharine MacKinnon, *Only Words* (Cambridge, Mass.: Harvard University Press, 1993), p. 3.

47. Walter Berns, "Dirty Words," *Public Interest,* Winter 1994, pp. 119–125, at p. 121.

48. James Lindgren, "Defining Pornography," *University of Pennsylvania Law Review* 141 (April 1993): 1153–1275, at 1200.

49. Andrea Dworkin, *Ice and Fire* (New York: Weidenfeld and Nicholson, 1987), at, respec-tively, pp. 54, 64, 84–85, 101–102.

50. The two books by Dworkin that were seized were *Pornography: Men Possessing Women* and *Woman Hating.* Albert Nerenberg, "Fear Not, Brave Canadian: Customs Stands on Guard for Thee," *Montreal Gazette,* 22 January 1993.

51. *Ulrich's International Periodicals,* 32d ed. (New Providence, N.J.: R. R. Bowker, 1993).

52. John R. Wilke, "Porn Broker: A Publicly Held Firm Turns X-Rated Videos into a Hot Business," *Wall Street Journal,* 11 July 1994.

53. David Landis, "Regulating Porn: Does It Compute?" *USA Today,* 9 August 1994.

54. John Tierney, "Porn: The Low-Slung Engine of Progress," *New York Times,* 9 January 1994.

55. Catharine MacKinnon, "On Collaboration," in *Feminism Unmodified* (Cambridge, Mass.: Harvard University Press, 1987), pp. 198–205, at p. 199.

56. U.S. Department of Justice, *Beyond the Pornography Commission: The Federal Response* 6 (1988) (estimating the amount spent on sexually oriented magazines, films, telephone services, cable television, and videos).

57. Sontag, "Pornographic Imagination," p. 72.
58. *Cohen v. California*, 403 U.S. 15, 25 (1971).

CHAPTER 8
Positive Aspects of Pornographic Imagery

1. Quoted in Wendy Kaminer, "Exposing the New Authoritarians," *San Francisco Examiner*, 29 November 1992.
2. Sallie Tisdale, "Talk Dirty to Me: A Woman's Taste for Pornography," *Harper's*, February 1992, pp. 37–46, at p. 45.
3. Quoted in Kathleen Sullivan, book review of *Girls Lean Back Everywhere* by Edward de Grazia, *New Republic*, 28 September 1992, pp. 35–40, at p. 39.
4. Quoted in Edward de Grazia, *Girls Lean Back Everywhere: The Law of Obscenity and the Assault on Genius* (New York: Vintage Books, 1992), p. 613.
5. Tisdale, "Talk Dirty to Me," p. 45.
6. Quoted in Kathleen Currie and Art Levine, "Whip Me, Beat Me and While You're at It Cancel My NOW Membership: Feminists War against Each Other over Pornography," *Washington Monthly*, June 1987, p. 17.
7. Jack Kammer, "Men and Women: Who's Got the Power?" *The Sun* (Baltimore), 21 December 1993.
8. United States Department of Justice, *Attorney General's Commission on Pornography, Final Report*, (Washington, D.C.: U.S. Government Printing Office, 1986), p. 1028.
9. Patti Britton, letter to the Honorable Patrick A. Leahy, 10 February 1992.
10. Quoted in Hugh Hefner, "The Place of Pornography: A Symposium in *Harper's* on Pornography and the Media," *Playboy*, March 1985, p. 24.
11. Barbara Faye Waxman, quoted in interviews by Sally Chew, "Pornography: Does Women's Equality Depend on What We Do about It?" *Ms.*, January/February 1994, p. 45.
12. Paula Webster, "Pornography and Pleasure," in *Caught Looking: Feminism, Pornography, and Censorship*, ed. Kate Ellis et al. (East Haven, Conn.: Long River Books, 1986), pp. 30–35, at p. 35.
13. Judith Kegan Gardiner, "What I Didn't Get to Say about Pornography, Masculinity, and Repression," in *New York Law School Law Review Symposium: The Sex Panic* (forthcoming).
14. Quoted in John Strausbaugh, "Making Book," *New York Press*, 30 March-5 April 1994, pp. 12–13.
15. Lisa Palac, "How Dirty Pictures Changed My Life," *Playboy*, May 1994, pp. 80, 88.
16. Quoted in *On Our Backs*, November/December 1993.
17. Heather Findlay, "Dyke Porn 101: How to Enjoy (and Defend) Your Porn," *On Our Backs*, November/December 1993, p. 15.
18. Susie Bright, "Politics of Porn," *San Francisco Review of Books*, June/July 1994, pp. 12, 13.
19. Kathleen Sullivan, book review of *Girls Lean Back Everywhere* by Edward de Grazia, *New Republic*, 28 September 1992, pp. 35–40, p. 39.
20. Chris Bearchell, "Gay Porn Is Getting Skinned Alive," *Toronto Star*, 15 January 1993.
21. Pat Califia, "Among Us, Against Us," in *Caught Looking*, pp. 20–25, at p. 23.
22. Findlay, "Dyke Porn 101."

23. John Preston, "Whose Free Speech?" *Boston Phoenix,* 8 October 1993.
24. Quoted in Tim Kingston, "Canada's New Porn Wars: 'Little Sister' Gay/Lesbian Bookstore Battles Canadian Customs," *San Francisco Bay Times,* 4 November 1993.
25. Norma Ramos, in "Where do We Stand on Pornography?" (Roundtable), *Ms.,* January/February 1994, pp. 32–41.
26. Caitlin Sullivan, "Bookstores Vandalized over 'Lesbian Porn' Issue," *Seattle Gay News,* 9 July 1993.
27. Susan Estrich, *Real Rape* (Boston: Harvard University Press, 1987).
28. Catharine MacKinnon, *Only Words* (Cambridge, Mass.: Harvard University Press, 1993), p. 26.
29. Ibid., p. 58.
30. Kaminer, "Exposing the New Authoritarians."
31. Statute of Treasons, 25 Edward 3 St. 5, Chap. 2, (1350), in effect until 1694.
32. Quoted in Barry Brown, "Canada's New Pornography Laws Drawing Charges of Censorship," *Buffalo News,* 10 January 1994.
33. Catharine MacKinnon, "Turning Rape into Pornography: Postmodern Genocide," *Ms.,* July/August 1993, pp. 24–30.
34. MacKinnon, *Only Words,* p. 15.
35. Carlin Romano, "Between the Motion and the Act," *The Nation,* 15 November 1993, pp. 563–70.
36. Quoted in David Streitfeld, "Rape by the Written Word?" *Washington Post,* 4 January 1994.
37. Lindsay Waters, Harvard University Press (with cosigners Claire Silvers, Maria Eugenia Quintana, Paul Adams, Christopher Palma, Stephanie Gouse, Aida Donald), letter to the editor, *The Nation,* 27 December 1993, p. 786.
38. Jare Hester, "Critic Blasted for Rape Fantasy," *New York Daily News,* 22 November 1993.
39. Ibid.
40. Richard Lacayo, "Assault by Paragraph," *Time,* 17 January 1994, p. 62; Jeffrey Moussaieff Masson, letter to Carlin Romano, 28 November 1993.
41. Streitfeld, "Rape by the Written Word?"
42. Nancy Friday, *Women on Top* (New York: Simon & Schuster, 1991), pp. 4–5.
43. Jean MacKellar, in collaboration with Menacham Amir, *Rape: The Bait and the Trap: A Balanced, Humane, Up to Date Analysis of Its Causes and Control* (New York: Crown, 1975), p. 260.
44. Quoted in Digby Diehl, "Anne Rice: The *Playboy* Interview," *Playboy,* March 1993, pp. 53–64.
45. Ellen Willis, "Feminism, Moralism, and Pornography," in *Caught Looking,* pp. 54–59, p. 56.
46. Kathleen Sullivan, book review of *Girls Lean Back Everywhere,* p. 35.
47. Ann Snitow, Christine Stansell, and Sharon Thompson, eds., *Powers of Desire: The Politics of Sexuality* (New York: Monthly Review Press, 1983); Varda Burstyn, ed., *Women against Censorship* (Vancouver: Douglas and McIntyre, 1985); Carole S. Vance, ed., *Pleasure and Danger: Exploring Female Sexuality* (Boston: Routledge & Kegan Paul, 1984); Kate Ellis, Beth Jaker, Nan D. Hunter, Barbara O'Dair, and Abby Tallmer, eds., *Caught Looking: Feminism, Pornography, and Censorship* (East Haven, Conn.: Long River Books, 1986).
48. Ann Snitow, "Retrenchment versus Transformation: The Politics of the Antipornography Movement," in *Women against Censorship,* p. 107, pp. 115–16.

49. Myrna Kostash, "Second Thoughts," in *Women against Censorship*, pp. 32–38, p. 37.
50. Nan D. Hunter and Sylvia Law, Brief Amici Curiae of Feminist Anti-Censorship Task-force, *University of Michigan Journal of Law Reform* 21 (1987–88): pp. 69–136, at p. 121.
51. Lisa Duggan, Nan D. Hunter, and Carole S. Vance, "False Promises: Feminist Anti-Pornography Legislation," in *Caught Looking*, pp. 72–85, at p. 82.
52. Sara Diamond, "Pornography: Image and Reality," in *Women Against Censorship*, pp. 40–57, at p. 57.
53. Ann Snitow, "Retrenchment vs. Transformation: The Politics of the Anti-Pornography Movement," in *Caught Looking*, pp. 10–17, at pp. 14–15.
54. Lynn Hunt, ed. *The Invention of Pornography: Obscenity and the Origins of Pornography, 1500–1800* (New York: Zone Books, 1993).
55. Walter Kendrick, *The Secret Museum: Pornography in Modern Culture* (New York: Viking, 1987), pp. 144–45.
56. Ibid., p. 219.
57. Ibid.

CHAPTER 9
Posing for Pornography: Coercion or Consent?

1. Karen, letter to *Ms.*, May/June 1994, p. 4.
2. See Nadine Strossen, "The Convergence of Feminist and Civil Liberties Principles in the Pornography Debate," review of *Women against Censorship*, ed. Varda Burstyn, *New York University Law Review* 62 (1987): 201–35, at 210 n. 42, citing legal authorities regarding these potential remedies.
3. Quoted in Pete Hamill, "Women on the Verge of a Legal Breakdown," *Playboy*, January 1993, p. 186.
4. Wendy McElroy, "The Unholy Alliance," *Liberty*, February 1993, p. 56.
5. Leora Tanenbaum, "The Politics of Porn: Forced Arguments," *In These Times*, 7 March 1994, pp. 17–20.
6. Andrea Dworkin quoted in "Where Do We Stand on Pornography?" (Roundtable), *Ms.*, January/February 1994, pp. 32–41, 37–38; Catharine MacKinnon quoted in Fred Strebeigh, "Defining Law on the Feminist Frontier," *New York Times Magazine*, 6 October 1991.
7. Quoted in Tanenbaum, "Politics of Porn," p. 19.
8. Quoted in Dan Greenberg and Thomas H. Tobiason, "The New Legal Puritanism of Catharine MacKinnon," *Ohio State Law Journal* 54 (Fall 1993): 1375–1424, at 1402–3
9. Ibid.
10. Tanenbaum, "Politics of Porn," p. 18.
11. Quoted ibid., p. 20.
12. Veronica Vera, testimony before the Senate Judiciary Committee, 30 October 1984.
13. Quoted in "The War against Pornography," *Newsweek*, 18 March 1985, pp. 58, 66.
14. Veronica Vera, testimony before the Senate Judiciary Committee, 30 October 1984.
15. Quoted in Tanenbaum, "Politics of Porn," p. 18.
16. Edward de Grazia, *Girls Lean Back Everywhere: The Law of Obscenity and the Assault on Genius* (New York: Vintage Books, 1992), p. 586.
17. Quoted in ibid., p. 593.
18. Quoted in ibid., pp. 594–95.

19. Karen De Crow, "Women Are Victims Again," *USA Today*, 5 October 1993.

20. Andrea Dworkin, *Intercourse* (New York: Free Press, 1987), p. 133.

21. *Butler v. the Queen*, 1 S. C. R. 452, 479 (1992, Canada).

22. Karen DeCrow, "Burger King and America's Real Family Values," *Penthouse*, May 1991, pp. 84–85.

23. Tanenbaum, "Politics of Porn," p. 19.

24. Quoted in ibid., pp. 19–20.

25. Susie Bright, "I Hate to Break This to You, Kitty, But . . . ," *San Diego Reader*, 18 November 1993, p. 36.

26. Richard Lacayo, "Accidents: A Death on the Shop Floor," *Time*, 16 September 1991, p. 28.

27. "About a Sixth of U.S. Crime Is at Job Sites," *New York Times*, 25 July 1994.

28. Richard A. Posner, "Obsession," review of *Only Words* by Catharine A. MacKinnon, *New Republic*, 18 October 1993, pp. 31–36, at p. 34.

29. Leonore Tiefer, "On Censorship and Women," *American Theatre*, January 1991, pp. 50–51.

30. Karen, letter to Nadine Strossen, 20 January 1993.

31. Cathy Young, untitled, in *New York Law School Law Review Symposium: The Sex Panic* (forthcoming).

32. Ibid.

33. Dworkin, *Intercourse*, pp. 222–23.

34. Catharine A. MacKinnon, "Privacy v. Equality: Beyond Roe v. Wade," in *Feminism Unmodified* (Cambridge, Mass.: Harvard University Press, 1987), p. 99.

35. Catharine A. MacKinnon, "Reflections on Sex Equality under Law," *Yale Law Journal* 100 (1991): 1281–1328, at 1300; *Toward a Feminist Theory of the State* (Cambridge, Mass.: Harvard University Press, 1989), p. 112, pp. 185–86; "Privacy v. Equality: Beyond Roe v. Wade," *Feminism Unmodified*, pp. 93–102, at pp. 94–96.

36. Jeanne Schroeder, untitled, in *New York Law School Law Review Symposium: The Sex Panic* (forthcoming).

CHAPTER 10
Would-Be Censors Subordinate Valuable Works to Their Agenda

1. Betty Friedan, "Feminism," in *The Meese Commission Exposed: Proceedings of a National Coalition Against Censorship Public Information Briefing on the Attorney General's Commission on Pornography* (New York: National Coalition Against Censorship, 1987), pp. 24–25.

2. Ad Hoc Committee of Feminists for Free Expression, letter to the members of the Senate Judiciary Committee, 14 February 1992. Reprinted in Strossen, "A Feminist Critique of 'the' Feminist Critique of Pornography," *Virginia Law Review* 79 (August 1993): 1099–1190, at 1188–90.

3. Ann Lewis, "Speaking for Ourselves," in *New York Law School Law Review Symposium: The Sex Panic* (forthcoming).

4. Catharine MacKinnon, "Turning Rape into Pornography: Postmodern Genocide," *Ms.*, July/August 1993, pp. 24–30.

5. Brief of the American Civil Liberties Union and the Indiana Civil Liberties Union, amici curiae, *American Booksellers Association v. Hudnut* (filed in D. Ind. 1984), pp. 1a–7a.

6. *American Booksellers Association v. Hudnut,* 771 F. 2d 323, 332, 334 (7th Cir. 1986).

7. Robin Morgan, "Theory and Practice: Pornography and Rape," in *Take Back the Night,* ed. Laura Lederer (New York: William Morrow, 1980), pp. 134–47, at p. 137.

8. Robin Morgan, *Going Too Far: The Personal Chronicle of a Feminist* (New York: Random House, 1977), p. 169.

9. Brief of the American Civil Liberties Union and the Indiana Civil Liberties Union, amici curiae, *American Booksellers Association v. Hudnut* (filed in D. Ind. 1984), p. 8a.

10. Samuel Walker, *In Defense of American Liberties: A History of the ACLU* (New York: Oxford University Press, 1990), p. 351.

11. *American Booksellers Association v. Hudnut,* 771 F. 2d 323, 325–26 (7th Cir. 1985) (noting MacKinnon's statement that medical school textbooks meet her definition of pornography); Catharine MacKinnon, "The Palm Beach Hanging," *New York Times,* 15 December 1991 (referring to the rape prosecution against William Kennedy Smith, then a medical student, MacKinnon observed that "pornography [is] used in some medical schools to desensitize students").

12. James R. Petersen, "Catharine MacKinnon: Again," *Playboy,* August 1992, pp. 37–39. (Quotes MacKinnon as saying, "Women's sexual histories would be made into live oral pornography in court.")

13. Catharine MacKinnon, *Only Words* (Cambridge, Mass.: Harvard University Press, 1993), p. 66.

14. C. Edwin Baker, "Of Course, More Than Words," book review of *Only Words* by Catharine MacKinnon, *University of Chicago Law Review* 61 (1994): 1181–1182 n. 3 (quoting *Only Words* at pp. 65–66).

15. *NCAC Censorship News,* vol. 2, no. 53, 1994, p. 2.

16. Rebecca Chalker and Carol Downer, *A Woman's Book of Choices: Abortion, Menstrual Extraction, and R.U. 486* (New York: Four Walls Eight Windows, 1993).

17. Barbara Ehrenreich, foreword to *A Woman's Book of Choices* by Chalker and Downer, p. vii.

18. Barbara Seaman on *A Woman's Book of Choices,* back cover.

19. Chalker and Downer, *A Woman's Book of Choices,* p. 34.

20. Daniel Simon (co-publisher, Four Walls Eight Windows Press), letter to Andrea Dworkin, 18 September 1992.

21. Rebecca Chalker, letter to Erica Jong, president of The Authors Guild, 4 November 1992.

22. Clare McHugh, "In Feminist Abortion Book Squall, Bigfoot Dworkin Stops the Presses," *New York Observer,* 26 October 1992.

23. Ibid.

24. Marjorie Heins, "Why Boycotting Booksellers Is a Bad Idea," *On the Issues,* Fall 1991, pp. 22–23.

25. Chalker and Downer, *A Woman's Book of Choices,* p. 40.

26. Maureen Dezell, "Porn Wars: NOW's ongoing struggle with Censorship," *Boston Phoenix,* 2–8 July 1993.

27. Ibid.; Rebecca Chalker, telephone conversation with Thomas Hilbink, 7 July 1994. Chalker stated, "It wasn't just someone, it was a pro-Andrea faction within the New York State chapter."

28. Dan Simon letter to Andrea Dworkin, 18 September 1992.

29. ACLU Arts Censorship Project, 'Anti-Censorship Feminists Condemn Suppression of Art Exhibit," news release, 16 November 1992; Marjorie Heins, "A Public University's

Response to Students' Removal of an Art Exhibit," in *New York Law School Law Review Symposium: The Sex Panic* (forthcoming); Carol Jacobsen, "First Amendment Rights Need to Be Upheld," *Michigan Daily*, 6 November 1992; Reed Johnson, "Sex, Laws, and Videotape," *Detroit News*, 7 December 1992.

30. Tamar Lewin, "Furor on Exhibit at Law School Splits Feminists," *New York Times*, 13 November 1992.

31. Catharine MacKinnon letter to Ira Glasser, 12 August 1993.

32. Andrea Dworkin, "Pornography and Male Supremacy" and Catharine A. MacKinnon, "Pornography and Civil Rights," *Michigan Journal of Gender & Law* 1 (1993).

33. Lewin, "Furor on Exhibit."

34. Carol Jacobsen, "Anti-Porn Feminism vs. Feminist Art: Notes on the Censorship of 'Porn'im'age'ry: Picturing Prostitutes,'" in *New York Law School Law Review Symposium: The Sex Panic* (forthcoming).

35. Carol Jacobsen, 'Anti-Porn Feminism"; Heins, "A Public University's Response"; Tamar Lewin, "Furor on Exhibit at Law School Splits Feminists," *New York Times*, 13 November 1992.

36. Liza Mundy, "The New Critics," *Lingua Franca*, September/October 1993, pp. 26–33, at p. 29; Laura Fraser, "Hear No Evil," *San Francisco Weekly*, 11 November 1992.

37. Veronica Vera, "Censored Artist, Activist Speaks Out," *Michigan Daily*, 30 November 1992.

38. Heins, in *New York Law School Law Review Symposium: The Sex Panic* (forthcoming).

39. Lewin, "Furor on Exhibit."

40. National Coalition Against Censorship, "NCAC Decries University of Michigan Censorship," press release, 16 November 1992.

41. See Lee Bollinger, "The Return of Porn'im'age'ry," *Law Quadrangle Notes*, Spring 1994, pp. 2–7.

42. Carole Vance, "Feminist Fundamentalism: Women against Images," *Art in America*, September 1993, pp. 35–39.

CHAPTER 11
Lessons from Enforcement: When the Powerful Get More Power

1. Ellen Willis, "An Unholy Alliance," *New York Newsday*, 25 February 1992.

2. Audre Lorde, "The Master's Tools Will Never Dismantle the Master's House," in *Sister Outsider Essays and Speeches* (San Francisco: Crossing Press, 1984), pp. 110–113.

3. George F. Will, "Pornography Scare," *Washington Post*, 28 October 1993.

4. Andrea Dworkin, *Our Blood: Prophecies and Discourses on Sexual Politics* (New York: Harper & Row, 1976), p. 20.

5. Wendy McElroy, "The Unholy Alliance," *Liberty*, February 1993, p. 53.

6. Pete Hamill, "Women on the Verge of a Legal Breakdown," *Playboy*, January 1993, p. 189.

7. Alan Dershowitz, "What Is Porn?" *ABA Journal*, 1 November 1986, p. 36.

8. Kenneth L. Karst, "Boundaries and Reasons: Freedom of Expression and the Subordination of Groups," *University of Illinois Law Review* 1990 (1990): 95–149, at 103–4.

9. See Laurence H. Tribe, *American Constitutional Law*, 2d ed. (Mineola, N.Y.: The Foundation Press), pp. 926–27.

10. *Beauharnais v. Illinois*, 343 U.S. 250, 275 (1952) (dissenting).

11. Eric Stein, "History against Free Speech: The New German Law against the 'Auschwitz'—and Other—'Lies,'" *Michigan Law Review* 85 (November 1986): 277–324, at 286.
12. Sandra Coliver, "Hate Speech Laws: Do They Work?" in *Striking a Balance: Hate Speech, Free Speech, and Non-Discrimination*, ed. Sandra Coliver. (Essex: Article 19, 1992), pp. 363–74, at pp. 373–74.
13. Aryeh Neier, *Defending My Enemy* (New York: E. P Dutton, 1979), pp. 155–57.
14. Nadine Strossen, "Regulating Racist Speech: A Modest Proposal?" *Duke Law Journal* 1990 (1990): 484–583, at 554–55.
15. *Doe v. University of Michigan*, 721 F. Supp. 852 (E.D. Mich. 1989). The ACLU also successfully challenged a hate speech code at the University of Wisconsin. *UWM Post, Inc. v. Board of Regents of University of Wisconsin System*, 774 F. Supp. 1163 (E.D. Wis. 1991).
16. *Wu v. University of Conn.* (No. Civ. H89-649 PCD) (D. Conn. 1989).
17. NOW-New York State, "Canada Sounds Death-Knell for Free Speech," press release, 28 February 1992.
18. Quoted in Mary Kay Blakely, "Is One Woman's Sexuality Another Woman's Pornography?" *Ms.*, April 1985, pp. 37–38.
19. Anna Quindlen, "The Gag Rules," *New York Times*, 7 October 1992.
20. Quoted in Margaret A. Blanchard, "The American Urge to Censor: Freedom of Expression versus the Desire to Sanitize Society—From Anthony Comstock to 2 Live Crew," *William and Mary Law Review* 33 (1992): 741–851, at 766.
21. Ellen Chesler, *Woman of Valor: Margaret Sanger and the Birth Control Movement in America* (New York: Simon & Schuster, 1992), p. 70.
22. Ibid.
23. Cited in Blanchard, "The American Urge to Censor," 766.
24. *Mutual Film Corp. v. Industrial Commission*, 236 U.S. 230 (1915). This decision was reversed by *Winters v. New York*, 333 U.S. 507 (1948) and *Joseph Burstyn, Inc. v. Wilson*, 343 U.S. 495 (1952).
25. *Message Photo-Play Co. v. Bell*, 166 N.Y.S. 338 (1917).
26. Karst, "Boundaries and Reasons," 114, n. 79.
27. Mary Ware Dennett, *The Sex Side of Life: An Explanation for Young People* (New York: Published by Author, 1928).
28. *U.S. v. One Obscene Book Entitled "Married Love,"* 48 F. 2d 821 (S.D.N.Y. 1931); *U.S. v. One Book Entitled "Contraception,"* 51 F. 2d 525 (S.D.N.Y. 1931).
29. Tamar Lewin, "Guam's Abortion Law Tested by A.C.L.U. Lawyer's Speech," *New York Times*, 21 March 1990.
30. Quindlen, "The Gag Rules."
31. Quoted in Tim Kingston, "Canada's New Porn Wars: 'Little Sister' Gay/Lesbian Bookstore Battles Canadian Customs," *San Francisco Bay Times*, 4 November 1993.
32. Quoted in Tamar Lewin, "Canada Court Says Porn Harms Women," *New York Times*, 28 February 1992.
33. Elaine Carol, in *Ideas—Feminism and Censorship*, transcript from the Canadian Broadcasting Company (Toronto: CBC Radio Works, 1993), p. 16.
34. Quoted in Rashida Dhooma, "Gay Demo Rakes Pornography Charges," *Toronto Sun*, n.d.
35. Quoted in Kingston, "Canada's New Porn Wars."
36. Ellen Flanders, in *Ideas—Feminism and Censorship*, p. 9.

37. Carl Wilson, "Northern Closure: Anti-Pornography Campaign in Canada," *The Nation*, 27 December 1993, p. 788.
38. "Canada Customs Hits Feminist Stores and Others," *Feminist Bookstore News*, March/April 1993, p. 21.
39. Karen Busby, "LEAF and Pornography: Litigating on Equality and Sexual Representations" (unpublished), p. 17.
40. Quoted in Camilla Gibb, "Project P Targets Lesbian Porn," *Quota*, May 1992, pp. 4–5, at p. 5.
41. Trish Thomas, in *Ideas—Feminism and Censorship*, p. 9.
42. *Her Majesty The Queen against John Bruce Scythes, Thomas Frank Ivison, and Ontario Corporation #620704 Operating as Glad Day Bookshop, Inc.*, Ontario Court of Justice (Provincial Division), 16 February 1993, C.H. Paris, j.
43. *Glad Day Bookshop v. Deputy Minister of National Revenue for Customs and Excise (DMVR)*, Ontario Court of Justice (General Division), 14 July 1992.
44. Busby, "LEAF and Pornography," p. 17.
45. Chris Bearchell, "Gay Porn Is Getting Skinned Alive," *Toronto Star*, 15 January 1993.
46. Susan Ditta, in *Ideas—Feminism and Censorship*, p. 15.
47. Ibid.
48. Jacques Boivin, letter to Leanne Katz, 17 November 1993.
49. Brenda Cossman, *Ideas—Feminism and Censorship*, p. 16.
50. Editorial, "Reading between the Borderlines," *Toronto Globe and Mail*, 30 June 1992.
51. Pierre Berton, "How Otto Jelinek Guards Our Morals," *Toronto Star*, 29 May 1993.
52. Quoted in Bill Redden, "O for Christ's Sake Canada," *PDXS* (Portland), 30 August–12 September 1993.
53. Berton, "How Otto Jelinek Guards Our Morals."
54. "Canada Customs Hits Feminist Stores," *Feminist Bookstore News*.
55. Redden, "O for Christ's Sake Canada."
56. Diane DiMassa, *Hothead Paisan: Homicidal Lesbian Terrorist* (San Francisco: Cleis Press, 1993), pp. 120–21.
57. Sarah Scott, "Porn Police: Who Decides What to Ban at the Border," *Montreal Gazette*, 14 April 1993.
58. Mary Williams Walsh, "Chill Hits Canada's Pornography Law," *Los Angeles Times*, 6 September 1993.
59. Kingston, "Canada's New Porn Wars."
60. Leanne Katz, memo to Roz Udow, 23 September 1993. See also letter from Catharine A. MacKinnon to Leanne Katz, 11 November 1993 (expressing MacKinnon's disagreement with some aspects of Katz's description of the telephone call, but not the aspect described in the text).
61. Human Rights Watch Free Expression Project, *A Ruling Inspired by U.S. Anti-Pornography Activists Is Used to Restrict Lesbian and Gay Publications in Canada*, February 1994, pp. 8–9.
62. NCAC Working Group on Women, Censorship, and "Pornography," "MacKinnon/Dworkin 'Theories' Flunk Reality Test," press advisory, 10 November 1993; Mary Williams Walsh, "Chill Hits Canada's Porn Law," *Los Angeles Times*, 6 September 1993.
63. Act of June 30, 1987, ch. 24, 1987 Statute of Canada 633 (Can.) sec. 139.(2) Sexual Offenses: exception. 1994 Tremear's Criminal Code Section 163.1.

64. LEAF News Release, "Historic Gathering Condemns Targeting of Lesbian and Gay Materials and Sex Trade Workers," Toronto, 21 June 1993.

65. NCAC Working Group, "MacKinnon/Dworkin 'Theories' Flunk Reality Test."

66. Kathleen Mahoney, panel and group discussion at the 19th Annual Olin Conference, Washington University, St. Louis, Missouri, 20 October 1993.

67. Quoted in Kingston, "Canada's New Porn Wars."

68. Catharine MacKinnon, letter to *New York Times* opinion page editor Mitchel Levitas, 1 January 1994.

69. The three arguments were presented in the following: MacKinnon letter to Mitchel Levitas; MacKinnon answers to questions at National Press Club, 22 November 1993; Dworkin-MacKinnon press release, 26 August 1994; MacKinnon letter to Leanne Katz.

70. Attributed to William Ewart Gladstone, 1809–1898 in John Bartlett and Justin Kaplan, eds., *Bartlett's Familiar Quotations*, 16th ed. (Boston: Little, Brown, 1992), p. 446.

71. CENSORSTOP, "Canada Customs Evades Little Sister's Trial Action . . . Again," press release, 29 September 1993.

72. Human Rights Watch, *A Ruling Inspired by U.S. Anti-Pornography Activists*, p. 9.

73. Susan Faludi, *Backlash: The Undeclared War Against American Women* (New York: Crown, 1991), pp. 40–41.

74. Larry Baron and Murray A. Straus, "Sexual Stratification, Pornography, and Rape in the United States," in *Pornography and Sexual Aggression*, ed. Neil M. Malamuth and Edward Donnerstein (Orlando, Fla.: Academic Press, 1984), pp. 185, 205–6

75. Faludi, *Backlash*, p. xxi; Jeffrey Weeks, *Sexuality and Its Discontents* (New York: Routledge, Chapman and Hall, 1986) p. 233; Alan Soble, *Pornography: Marxism, Feminism, and the Future of Sexuality* (New Haven: Yale University Press, 1986), pp. 82, 84; Naomi Wolf, *The Beauty Myth: How the Images of Beauty Are Used against Women* (New York: William Morrow, 1991); Andrea Dworkin, "Why So-Called Radical Men Love and Need Pornography," in *Take Back the Night*, ed. Laura Lederer (New York: William Morrow, 1980), pp. 148, 153.

76. Catharine MacKinnon, *Only Words* (Cambridge, Mass.: Harvard University Press, 1993), p. 37.

CHAPTER 12
Why Censoring Pornography Would Not Reduce Discrimination or Violence against Women

1. Quoted in David Futrelle, "The Politics of Porn, Shameful Pleasures," *In These Times*, 7 March 1994, pp. 14–17.

2. *Butler v. the Queen* 1 SCR 452 (199), p. 505.

3. Marcia Pally, *Sex and Sensibility: Reflections on Forbidden Mirrors and the Will to Censor* (Hopewell, N.J.: Ecco Press, 1994).

4. Albert J. Reiss, Jr. and Jeffrey A. Roth, eds., *Understanding and Preventing Violence* (Washington, D.C.: National Academy Press, 1993), p. 111. (A project for the National Research Council.)

5. Judith Becker and Ellen Levine, paper presented to a meeting of the National Coalition Against Censorship, New York, N.Y., 17 June 1986.

6. Daniel Linz, Steven D. Penrod, and Edward Donnerstein, "The Attorney General's Commission on Pornography: The Gaps between 'Findings' and Facts," *American Bar Foundation Research Journal* 4 (Fall 1987): 713–36, at 723.

7. Edward Mulvey and Jeffrey Haugaard, *Surgeon General's Workshop on Pornography and Public Health* (Arlington, Virginia: U.S. Department of Health and Human Services, 1986).

8. Carol Krafka, "Sexually Explicit, Sexually Violent, and Violent Media: Effects of Multiple Naturalistic Exposures and Debriefing on Female Viewers" (Ph.D. dissertation, University of Wisconsin, 1985), p. 29.

9. Daniel Linz, Edward Donnerstein, and Steven Penrod, "The Effects of Long-Term Exposure to Violent and Sexually Degrading Depictions of Women," *Journal of Personality and Social Psychology* 55 (1988): 758–68.

10. Cynthia Gentry, "Pornography and Rape: An Empirical Analysis," *Deviant Behavior: An Interdisciplinary Journal* 12 (1991): 277–88, at 284.

11. Larry Baron and Murray Straus, "Four Theories of Rape: A Macro-sociological Analysis," *Social Problems* 34, no. 5 (1987): 467–89.

12. Joseph Scott and Loretta Schwalm, "Pornography and Rape: An Examination of Adult Theater Rates and Rape Rates by State," in J. E. Scott and T. Hirchi (eds.), *Controversial Issues in Crime and Justice* (Beverly Hills: Sage, 1988).

13. Bureau of Justice Statistics, *Criminal Victimization in the United States* (Washington, D.C.: Government Printing Office, 1990); Pally, *Sex and Sensibility*, p. 22.

14. Richard J. Gelles and Murray Straus, *Intimate Violence: The Causes and Consequences of Abuse in the American Family* (New York: Touchstone, 1989), p. 112.

15. Pally, *Sex and Sensibility*, pp. 21, 23.

16. Baron and Straus, "Four Theories of Rape."

17. Pally, *Sex and Sensibility*, pp. 57–61.

18. Richard Posner, "Obsession," review of *Only Words* by Catharine MacKinnon, *New Republic*, 18 October 1993, pp. 31–36, at p. 34.

19. Ellen Willis, "An Unholy Alliance," *New York Newsday*, 25 February 1992, p. 78.

20. *Memoirs v. Massachusetts*, 383 U.S. 413, 432 (1966) (concurring).

21. Williams Committee, *The British Inquiry into Obscenity and Film Censorship* (London, England: Home Office Research and Planning Unit, 1979).

22. Earl Finbar Murphy, "The Value of Pornography," *Wayne Law Review* 10 (1964): 655–80, at 668.

23. Pally, *Sex and Sensibility*, pp. 99–100.

24. Associated Press, "Atheist Loses Fight to Ban Bible at School," *Chicago Tribune*, 11 November 1992.

25. Pally, *Sex and Sensibility*, pp. 25–61.

26. Edward Donnerstein, "Erotica and Human Aggression," in *Aggression: Theoretical and Empirical Reviews*, ed. Richard Green and Edward Donnerstein (New York: Academic Press, 1983), pp. 127–28.

27. Quoted in Jane Brody, "Scientists Trace Aberrant Sexuality," *New York Times*, 23 January 1990.

28. Pally, *Sex and Sensibility*, p. 50.

29. Howard Barbaree and William Marshall, "The Role of Male Sexual Arousal in Rape: Six Models," *Journal of Consulting and Clinical Psychology* 59, no. 5 (1991): 621–30; Pally, *Sex and Sensibility*, pp. 44–45.

30. Susan Brownmiller, *Against Our Will: Men, Women, and Rape* (New York: Simon & Schuster, 1975); Susan Estrich, *Real Rape* (Boston: Harvard University Press, 1987).
31. Carlin Meyer, "Sex, Censorship, and Women's Liberation" (unpublished), pp. 42–43. [A revised version of this manuscript was published in *Texas Law Review* 72 (1994): 1097–1201.]
32. Thelma McCormack, "If Pornography Is the Theory, Is Inequality the Practice?" (presented at public forum, *Refusing Censorship: Feminists and Activists Fight Back,* York, Canada, 12 November 1992), p. 12.
33. Edward Donnerstein, Daniel Linz, and Steven Penrod, *The Question of Pornography: Research Findings and Policy Implications* (New York: Free Press, 1987), p. 107.
34. Catharine MacKinnon, "Not a Moral Issue," *Yale Law & Policy Review* 2 (1984): 321–45, at 325.
35. Percy H. Tannenbaum, "Emotional Arousal as a Mediator of Communication Effects," *Technical Report of the U.S. Commission on Obscenity and Pornography* 8 (1971), p. 353.
36. Timothy C. Brock, "Erotic Materials: A Commodity Theory Analysis of Availability and Desirability," *Technical Report of the U.S. Commission on Obscenity and Pornography* 6 (1971), pp. 131–37.

CHAPTER 13
Toward Constructive Approaches to Reducing Discrimination
and Violence against Women

1. Betty Friedan, "Feminism," in *The Meese Commission Exposed: Proceedings of a National Coalition Against Censorship Public Information Briefing on the Attorney General's Commission on Pornography* (New York: National Coalition Against Censorship, 1987), pp. 24–25.
2. Molly Ivins, "Havin' Fun Fightin' for Freedom," in *New York Law School Law Review Symposium: The Sex Panic* (forthcoming).
3. Varda Burstyn, "Beyond Despair: Positive Strategies," in *Women against Censorship,* ed. Varda Burstyn (Vancouver: Douglas and McIntyre, 1985), pp. 152, 179.
4. Carlin Meyer, "Sex, Censorship, and Women's Liberation" (unpublished), p. 32. [A revised version of this manuscript was published in *Texas Law Review* 72 (1994): 1097–1201.]
5. Nan D. Hunter and Sylvia Law, Brief of Amici Curiae of Feminist Anti-Censorship Taskforce, *University of Michigan Journal of Law Reform* 21 (1987–88): pp. 69–136, at pp. 134–35.
6. Thelma McCormack, "If Pornography Is the Theory, Is Inequality the Practice?" (presented at public forum, *Refusing Censorship: Feminists and Activists Fight Back,* York, Canada, 7–8 November 1992), p. 26.
7. American Civil Liberties Union, *Restoring Civil Liberties: A Blueprint for Action for the Clinton Administration* (1992), p. 66.
8. Marcia Pally, *Sense and Censorship: The Vanity of the Bonfires* (New York: Americans for Constitutional Freedom and the Freedom to Read Foundation, 1991), p. 14.
9. "Policy No. 4: Censorship of Obscenity, Pornography and Indecency," *Policy Guide of the American Civil Liberties Union.* Adopted 1985.
10. S. Rep. No. 372, 102nd Congress, 2d sess. 34 (1992).
11. Nan D. Hunter, "S. 1521: A Rapist's Exculpation Act?" (unpublished), pp. 10–11.

12. Teller, "Movies Don't Cause Crime," *New York Times*, 17 January 1992.
13. *Schiro v. Clark*, 963 F. 2d 962, 972 (7th Cir., 1992).
14. Catharine MacKinnon, *Only Words* (Cambridge, Mass.: Harvard University Press, 1993), pp. 95–97.
15. Ibid., p. 96.
16. C. Edwin Baker, "Of Course, More Than Words," review of *Only Words* by Catharine MacKinnon, *University of Chicago Law Review* 61 (1994): 1181, 1207–8.
17. *Commonwealth v. Mignogna*, 585A.2d 1, 10 (Pennsylvania Superior Court, 1990).
18. Quoted in Tad Friend, "Yes: Feminist Women Who Like Sex," *Esquire*, February 1994, pp. 48–56, p. 54.
19. MacKinnon, *Only Words*, p. 12.
20. Neil Malamuth and Edward I. Donnerstein, "The Effects of Aggressive Pornographic Mass Media Stimuli," *Advances in Experimental Psychology* 15 (1982): 103, 129, 150–85.
21. Pally, *Sense and Censorship*, p. 34 (citing the report of the Surgeon General's Workshop on Pornography and Public Health, p. 50).
22. Edward I. Donnerstein and Daniel G. Linz, "Debate on Pornography," *Film Comment*, December 1984, pp. 34–35, at p. 35.
23. Dr. Judith Becker, professor of psychiatry and psychology, letter to Senator Hank Brown, 3 April 1992.
24. Shirley Feldman-Summers, "A Comment on the Meese Commission Report and the Dangers of Censorship," *Sexual Coercion and Assault* 1, no.6 (n.d.):179, 182.
25. Stephen Donaldson, "The Rape Crisis Behind Bars," *New York Times*, 29 December 1993.
26. Kathleen Maguire, Ann L. Pastore, Timothy J. Flanagan, eds. *Bureau of Justice Statistics Sourcebook of Criminal Justice Statistics—1992*. (Washington, D.C.: U.S. Department of Justice, 1993), p. 532, table 5.59.
27. Wendy Kaminer, "Feminists Against the First Amendment," *Atlantic Monthly*, November 1992, pp. 111–117, at p. 115.
28. Colleen Cobel, panel and group discussion at the 19th Annual Olin Conference, Washington University, St. Louis, Mo., 20 October 1993.
29. Edward de Grazia, *Girls Lean Back Everywhere: The Law of Obscenity and the Assault on Genius* (New York: Vintage Books, 1992), p. 586, citing Martin Morse Wooster, "Reagan's War on Porn," *Reason*, April 1986, pp. 29–33.
30. Pally, *Sense and Censorship*, p. 31.
31. Quoted in Digby Diehl, "Anne Rice: The *Playboy* Interview," *Playboy*, March 1993, pp. 53–64, at p. 56.
32. Pete Hamill, "Women on the Verge of a Legal Breakdown," *Playboy*, January 1993, pp. 138–40 and 184–90, at p. 188.
33. Lisa Steele, "A Capital Idea: Gendering in the Mass Media," in *Women against Censorship*, ed. Varda Burstyn, pp. 58–78, at p. 61.

Index

Photo insert images between pages 144–145 are indicated by *p1*, *p2*, *p3*, etc.

abortion, 42, 46, 60, 69, 116, 177–78, 179–80, 182; censorship of information on, xv, xxi, 204, 205, 208; free speech about, xxiii; mifepristone used for early stage, xiv–xv; National Right to Life Committee on, xxvin20; *A Woman's Book of Choices* and, 189–93
Above the Law (ACLU), 80
Abrams, Floyd, 73
Abramson, Paul, 186
Abrams v. United States, 37–38
The Accused (film), 156–57
Acker, Kathy, 217
ACLU. *See* American Civil Liberties Union
aerobics videos, 84, 217
AFA. *See* American Family Association
Agatha (saint), *p6*
AIDS, 46, 88, 102, 148; safer sex and, 14, 218
Aikin, Susanna, 194
Alexander, Jane, 88
Allen, Paula, 194
American Association of University Professors, 110–11
American Booksellers Association v. Hudnut, 67–69, 70, 184
American Civil Liberties Union (ACLU), 14, 26, 60, 76, 80, 84, 88, 91, 111, 112–13, 115–16, 123, 125, 132, 202–3, 207, 243–44; antipornography laws opposed by, 24, 68–69, 99, 184, 186–87; CDA challenge under, xiii
American College Health Association, 116
American Family Association (AFA), 87, 139
American Psycho (Ellis), 214
anticensorship feminists, 7–9, 261n17; debates, xi–xii; educational settings

focus for, xxv; feminists attack of, xi; Gates support of, xii; procensorship feminists' condemnation of, 25–26; "prosex" stance ascribed to, 93, 97; vigilance and victories for, xxiv–xxv
anticommunism, 38–39
antiobscenity laws, 24, 29–30, 35, 61, 132, 164–65; antipornography laws compared with, 49–50, 52–53, 210; contraception information suppressed under, 204–8; enforcement of, 44–45, 46–48, 79–83, 91; opposed by procensorship feminists, 49–50; respected artists prosecuted under, 80–81
antipornography laws, 40, 48, 49–70; antiobscenity laws compared with, 49–50, 52–53, 210; in Canada, 13, 24–25, 35, 51–52, 53–54, 65, 67, 70, 92, 99, 142, 153, 187, 197, 208–22, 227; civil censorship and, 53–58; "coercion" provision of, 63, 64; constitutional flaws of, 33–34, 50–61, 67–69, 70; equality undermined by, 27, 68; feminist works vulnerable under, 99, 102–3, 182–83, 185–87, 208–11, 214, 215–16, 223–24; First Amendment and, xix; "forbidden fruits" effect and, 240; "forced" exposure provision of, 58–61, 63, 64; government enforcement of, 197–98, 208–22; history of MacKinnon-Dworkin model for, 63–69; indicia of subordination in, 64, 65, 92, 96, 183–84, 210; injurious to sex industry workers, 168–69, 174–77; judicial defeats for, 67–69, 70, 184; LGBTQ+ works vulnerable under, 92, 151–53, 211–17, 220–21, 222, 223; locales

antipornography (*cont.*)
considering introduction of, 65, 85; overall value of work not considered in, 52–53; pornography pushed underground by, 227; private persuasion and counterspeech as alternatives to, 55–56; reduction of violence and discrimination against women as goals of, 223, 225–28, 240; self-censorship triggered by, 218, 222; trafficking provision of, 63, 64–65; types of works subordinated to, 181–87, 236
antipornography movement, ix, xii; gender equality impacted by, 99; religious conservatism relation to, xiii
anti-Semitism, 199, 201, 202, 203
Aparicio, Carlos, 194
Aphrodite (Bettiol), *p2–p3*
Arkansas laws, xvi, xxiv–xxv, 123
art: governmental funding policies and, 86–91, 139; hindered by climate of fear, 89–90; sexual harassment notions and, 113–14, 120. *See also* nudity or sexual themes
Article XIX (anti-censorship group), 201–2
Athey, Ron, 88
Atkinson, Ti Grace, 101
Augustine, Saint, 101

Backlash (Faludi), 223–24
Bad Attitude (magazine), 128, 211–12, 220–21, 222
Baker, C. Edwin, 187, 247
Barbaree, Howard, 238
Barker, Sara Evans, 68
Baron, Larry, 231, 232
Barrie, Dennis, 44–45
Bearchell, Chris, 151, 212
Beck, Marianna, *p1*, 128
Becker, Judith, 229, 249
Beethoven, Ludwig van, 83
Benshoof, Janet, 208
Berger, John, 114
Berns, Walter, 140
Bette's Oceanview Diner (Berkeley, Calif), 118
Bettiol, Zoravia, *p2–p3*, 120

Beyond the Pornography Commission, 268n56
the Bible, 235–36
Bierce, Ambrose, 217
birth control, 21–22, 42, 46, 116; censorship of information on, 24, 204–8; Comstock Act cited in banning, xiv–xv. *See also* abortion
Black, Hugo, 201
Black Looks, 217
Blake, Toni, 21–22
Blakeslee, Laurie, 17
Blume, Judy, 27, 90, 186, 219
Boivin, Jacques, 213
Bondanella, Peter, 91
books, banning, xvi–xvii, xxv
Boston Women's Health Book Collective, 100, 185–86, 189
Bowman, Cynthia Grant, 120–21
boycotts, 188, 190–92
Bradley, Joseph, 122–23
Brandeis, Louis, 8, 33, 35, 37, 38–39, 55
Brandenburg v. Ohio, 35–36, 50
Brase, Robert, 82
Brennan, William, 47
Bright, Susie, 40, 78, 128, 139, 150–51, 173
British Committee on Obscenity and Film Censorship, 234
British Race Relations Act (1965), 201
Britton, Patti, 147
Brockway, Laurie Sue, 150
Browne, Kingsley, 123
Brownmiller, Susan, 186
Brown v. Board of Education, 68
Brustein, Robert, 90
Buchanan, Pat, 139
Bureau of Justice Statistics, 232, 250
The Burning Bed, 236–37
Burstyn, Varda, 242
Busby, Karen, 212
Bush, George, 79, 89
Butler v. The Queen, 13, 227, 228; enforcement of, 208–18, 222; indirect forms of censorship spurred by, 218–22

Califia, Pat, 151, 209
California, 120

campuses. *See* educational settings; schools; *specific universities*

Canada: antipornography law in, 13, 24–25, 35, 51–52, 53–54, 65, 67, 70, 92, 99, 142, 153, 187, 197, 208–22, 227; enforcement record in, 197, 208–22; expanded definition of sexual harassment in, 117

Canadian Customs, 213–14, 215, 217, 218, 220, 221–22

Canadian Supreme Court, 13, 35, 54, 65, 67, 70, 171–72, 208, 212, 215, 220, 227, 228

Carleton College, 118

Carol, Elaine, 209

Cassell, Carol, 134

Caught Looking, 217

CDA. *See* Communications Decency Act

celibacy, 98

censorship, 33; allure of, 71–72; boycotts and, 188, 190–92; civil, 53–58; disempowered groups targeted in, 52, 200–204; double standard for "protectors" and "protected" in, 138–39, 142; internet, xii–xiii, xxv; one-sided legal forums on, 76–77; as outcome of procensorship feminists' tactics, 189–96; women's rights and interests curbed by, 23–25, 27, 204–8. *See also* anticensorship feminists; antiobscenity laws; antipornography laws; procensorship feminists

CENSORSTOP, 214, 215, 221

Center for Constitutional Rights, 88

cesarean sections, 179

Chalker, Rebecca, 189–93

Chaucer, Geoffrey, 19–20

Chesler, Ellen, 206

Chicago Theological Seminary, 21

child pornography, 49, 81, 82, 165–66; Supreme Court on, x

children, accessing sexual expression online, ix, xvii, xxv

China, 199, 233

Christian Coalition, 87, 139

Cincinnati, 91

Cincinnati Contemporary Art Center, 44–45

Citizens for Community Values, 84

civil lawsuits: censorial impact of, 53–58; governmental role in, 55, 56; procedural safeguards lacking in, 57–58

Civil Rights Act (1964), 108, 118, 119

Civil Rights Commission, U.S., 242–43, 244

civil rights movement, 36, 51, 200

Cline, Sally, 98

Clinton, Bill, 89

Clinton administration, 243–44

clothing: as protection from male gaze, 18; "provocative," 16

Cobel, Colleen, 251–52

Cohen, Roberta, *p6–p7*

Coliver, Sandra, 202

come shots, 136–37

Communications Decency Act (CDA), xiii–xiv; Comstock Act links to, xiv; LGBTQ+ rights and, xiv

Comstock, Anthony, xiv, 160, 205–6, 207–8

Comstock Act (1873), xiv

Concerned Women for America, 78

Confronting Your Fears (Cohen), *p6–p7*

Congress, U.S., 29–30, 70, 85, 148, 192; NEA and, 88, 89, 91

contraceptives. *See* birth control

Cossman, Brenda, 213

Coughenour, Beulah, 66

counterspeech, 33, 39, 55–56, 60, 248

Court of Appeals, U.S.: for Ninth Circuit, 69, 82; for Seventh Circuit, 67–68, 246–47

COYOTE (Call Off Your Old Tired Ethics), 101

Crosson, Cathy, 7, 116, 119

cultural feminism, 62–63

Customs, U.S., 82, 207

Czach, Liz, 209

DAP. *See* Dykes Against Porn

Day, Gary, 137

Decriminalize Sex Work (advocacy group), vii–viii

DeCrow, Karen, 27, 171, 173

Deep Throat (film), 166–68

de Grazia, Edward, 139, 169–70

democracy, 159
Deneuve, Catherine, xviii
Denmark, 233
Dennett, Mary Ware, 23–24, 207
Dezell, Maureen, 11, 76
Diamond, Sara, 135, 159
disability rights, 148
discrimination: in enforcement of
    censorship, 44–45, 51–52, 200–204;
    sexual harassment relation to, xvii–xviii,
    xxi
discrimination, gender-based, 27, 30, 46,
    223–24, 265n9; all sexual expression
    equated with, 18, 105, 106–8, 118;
    anti-male rhetoric and, 98–99;
    antipornography laws as supposed
    cure for, 223, 225–26, 240; constructive
    approaches to reduction of, 241–42;
    pornography allegedly as, 7, 63, 64–65,
    106–7; pornography as supposed cause
    of, 7, 23, 31, 35, 36–37, 62–65, 85, 225,
    227–38, 242–44; sexual harassment
    as form of, 106, 108–9; women's
    reproductive role as purported basis for,
    123–24
Ditta, Susan, 213
Dixon, Greg, 65–66
Dobbs decision (2022), xiv–xv
Dodson, Betty, 101, 150
Doing It Debbie's Way, 84, 217
domestic violence, 173
Donaldson, Stephen, 250
Donnerstein, Edward, 229–30, 237, 248–49
Dornan, Robert K., 88
Douglas, William O., 234
Downer, Carol, 189–93
drag performances, xvii, xxiv–xxv
Dreyfus, Alfred, 201
Duggan, Lisa, 93–94, 131, 158–59
Duras, Marguerite, 217
Dworkin, Andrea, *p1, p4,* 6–7, 8n, 13, 16,
    30, 31, 59–60, 72, 73, 78, 124, 130, 145,
    181, 198, 209, 224, 246, 247–48; anti-
    male rhetoric of, 99; antiobscenity laws
    opposed by, 49–50; "antisex" stance
    ascribed to, 92, 94, 95–97; Canadian
    experience and, 187, 208, 216, 217,
    221–22; civil censorship and, 53–55;

criticism of LGBTQ+ sexual expression
    by, 92, 93, 152–53, 220–21; divisive rhe-
    toric of, 25; involvement in suppression
    of feminist artists' works, 192–95;
    model antipornography law drafted
    by, 24–25, 49, 53–55, 63–71, 92, 96–97;
    pornography examined closely by,
    138, 139; "rape" imagery and, 178–79;
    sex industry workers as viewed by,
    164–65, 166, 167; on sexual expression
    suppression, viii–ix, xi, xix; on sexual
    intercourse, 92, 94, 95, 171; sexually
    explicit descriptions in writings of, 140,
    141–42, 187, 216; *A Woman's Book of
    Choices* and, 189–93
Dykes Against Porn (DAP), *p8,* 133–34,
    153

Eagle Forum, 78, 186
Easterbrook, Frank, 34, 58–59, 67–68
Echols, Alice, 72
educational settings: anticensorship efforts
    in, xxv; censorship impacting free
    speech in, xx, xxv; First Amendment
    protection in, 110–11; free speech about
    abortion in, xxiii; gender expression
    in, xix, xxiii, xxiv; hate speech codes
    in, 202–3; LGBTQ+ expression in, xix;
    "radical" feminists targeting, xxii–
    xxiii; sex education in, 46; sex panic in,
    17–18, 19–22; sexual expression bans
    in, 115–17; sexual harassment and, xxi,
    xxii–xiii; sexual harassment rules in,
    115–17, 119, 120; stifling of sex-related
    speech in, 105, 106, 116–17, 120; trans
    women facilities in, xxiii–xxiv. *See also*
    law schools; schools; *specific universities*
EEOC. *See* Equal Employment
    Opportunity Commission
Ehrenreich, Barbara, 27, 189
Einsiedel, Edna, 230
Ellis, Bret Easton, 214
Elshtain, Jean Bethke, 77–78
Equal Employment Opportunity
    Commission (EEOC), 108–9, 265n9
equality, 99, 102, 106, 107; availability of
    sexual materials related to, 233; free
    speech related to, 23–25; protectibility

of expression about, 51; sexual
egalitarianism and, 145–47; suppression
of sexual expression impact on, 122;
undermined by antipornography laws,
27, 68; women's sexuality related to,
17–18, 22
Equal Rights Amendment (ERA), 51,
62, 66
ERA. *See* Equal Rights Amendment
Esquire, p4, 127
Estrich, Susan, 153
Evans, Don, 19–20
Ezra, Alan, ix, xvii

FACT. *See* Feminist Anti-Censorship
Taskforce
Fall, Susan, 122
Faludi, Susan, 223–24
Feldman-Summers, Shirley, 249
The Female Eunuch (Greer), 100
The Feminine Mystique (Friedan), 181
feminism and feminists, 62–63; anticensorship feminists attacked by, xi; on
free speech, xii; NEA (non)funding of,
87, 90–91; pornography debate among,
25–27, 72–75; "radical," ix, xiii, xix, xxii–
xxiii; suppression of artworks about
and of, 190–94; works endangered by
antipornography laws, 99, 102–3, 182–
87, 208–11, 214, 215–16, 223–24. *See also*
anticensorship feminists; procensorship
feminists
Feminist Anti-Censorship Taskforce
(FACT), 25, 27, 62, 68, 69, 158, 217
Feminist Bookstore News, 210–11
Feminists Fighting Pornography (FFP),
60–61
Feminists for Free Expression, 5, 27, 69,
107–8, 116, 119, 182
FFP. *See* Feminists Fighting Pornography
Fight Online Sex Trafficking Act (FOSTA),
vii–viii
Findlay, Heather, 133–34, 150, 152
Finley, Karen, 5, 89, 90, 120
First Amendment, 8, 14, 24, 29–30, 30n,
31; anticensorship feminists' vigilance
around, xxiv–xxv; antipornography laws
and, xix; Bettiol's *Aphrodite* and, *p2–p3;*

private actors not subject to, 110–11,
113, 119; view pointneutrality and, xi.
See also free speech
Flanders, Ellen, 209
Fonda, Jane, 84
Foote, Edward Bliss, 207
FOSTA. *See* Fight Online Sex Trafficking
Act
Fraser, Arvonne, 65
Fraser, Donald, 65
Free Expression Project, 218, 222
free speech, 29–48, 209; on abortion,
xxiii; on abortion, bans, xv; adversely
affected by attacks on sexual expression,
85; anticensorship feminists' vigilance
around, xxiv–xxv; bad tendency
argument and, 33–34, 35, 37, 206–7;
civil censorship and, 53–58; "clear
and present danger" requirement and,
33–34, 35–36, 39; content or viewpoint
neutrality and, 33, 45, 50, 67–68, 86, 88;
counterspeech and, 33, 39, 55–56, 60,
248; and distinction between protected
advocacy and unprotected incitement,
36–37; educational settings censorship
impacting, xx, xxv; equality related
to, 23–25; forced public exposure and,
58–61; gender equality relationship
with, xii; governmental funding of
artwork and, 86–87, 88–89, 90–91; hate
speech laws and, 50–51, 75, 76, 200–204,
217; hypocrisy around, xxv; "least
restrictive alternative" concept and,
39–40; LGBTQ+ individuals impacted
by suppression of, xv; NOW on, xii; and
political dimension of sexual expression,
30, 46–48, 50; political dimension of
sexual expression and, 159–61; sexual
expression as special case for, ix, 30, 35,
40–44, 46, 47–48, 58; sexual harassment
and, xxii, 110–11, 113, 115–16, 119;
suppressed in repressive regimes, 198–
200; Supreme Court's jurisprudence on,
30, 31, 32–48, 53, 54–59, 61, 67–68, 70,
86, 110n, 115, 143, 201, 206, 210; violence and, ix. *See also* censorship; First
Amendment
French, Marilyn, 90

Friday, Nancy, 27, 134, 156
Friedan, Betty, 27, 181, 241
Frighten the Horses (magazine), 103
fundamentalists, 87, 102, 185–86;
    antipornography movement relation to,
    ix, xiii; procensorship feminists' alliance
    with, 6–7, 70, 77–78

Gans, Olivia, 178–79
Gardiner, Judith Kegan, 149
Gates, Henry Louis, Jr., xii, 5–6
Gay Ideas (Mohr), 218
gay men. *See* LGBTQ+ individuals
gender equality: antipornography
    movement impact on, 99; free speech
    relationship with, xii; workplace, xviii
gender expression: in educational settings,
    xix, xxiii, xxiv; legislation banning,
    xvii; schools censoring, xix. *See also*
    LGBTQ+ individuals
gender stereotyping, 78, 107, 122–23; by
    procensorship feminists, 98–100, 105
Gentry, Cynthia, 231
Germany, 199, 201, 233
Gersen, Jeannie Suk, xx–xxi
Ginsburg, Ruth Bader, xviii, 109, 123
Girls Lean Back Everywhere (de Grazia),
    169–70, 240
Glad Day Bookstore (Toronto), 211–12,
    213, 214, 220–21
Goldman, Emma, 94, 207
Goya, Francisco de, *p2*, 15–16, 113–14
Graham, Robert, 132
de Grazia, Edward, 240
Great Britain, 201–2
Greenberg, Dan, 167
Greer, Germaine, 100
Guam, 208
Guerreri, Dexter, 155

Hafferkamp, Jack, *p1*
Haigh, John George, 235
Hamill, Pete, 130, 138, 199, 254
Hand, Learned, 53
Harlan, John Marshall, 143
Harris v. Forklift Systems, Inc., 109, 111
Hartley, Nina, 168, 169
Harvard Law Review, 120–21

hate speech laws, 50–51, 75, 76, 200–204,
    217; debates, xi–xii
Hawaii Supreme Court, 47
Hayden, Tom, 121
Hayes, F. C., 212–13
Heins, Marjorie, 12, 46, 114, 139, 191, 195
Helms, Jesse, 45, 77, 87
Hentoff, Nat, 16, 113–14
Heywood, Ezra, 207–8
Hill, Anita, 106, 187
Hite, Shere, 101
Holmes, Oliver Wendell, 31, 33–34, 35, 37,
    38, 55
"hostile environment" harassment, 108–9,
    111
Hot, Hotter, Hottest, 217
Hothead Paisan, 215–16
Hudnut, William, 66, 67
Hudnut case. *See American Booksellers
    Association v. Hudnut*
Hughes, Holly, 5, 87, 120
human rights, 198–200, 223
Human Rights Watch, 218, 222
Hunt, Lynn, 159
Hunter, Nan, 93–94, 131, 146, 158–59, 245
Hustler, 69, 142

Ice and Fire (Dworkin), 95–96, 141–42
Illinois, 85
Indianapolis, antipornography law in, 24,
    34, 54, 65–69, 99, 184, 186
Inland Books, 213
Intercourse (Dworkin), 95
International Centre Against Censorship,
    201–2
internet: age restrictions for viewing
    sexual expression on, ix, xvii, xxv;
    CDA on sexual expression on, xiii–xiv;
    censorship, xii–xiii, xxv; FOSTA and,
    vii–viii
The Invention of Pornography (Hunt, ed.),
    159
Iowa Board of Regents, 20
Ivins, Molly, 27, 56, 241

Jacob, Margaret, 159–60
Jacobsen, Carol, 193–95
Jacobson, Keith, 82

Japan, 233, 250
Jefferson, Thomas, xxiv
Jennings, Peter, 73
Johnson, Lyndon B., 41–42
Johnson, Steven W, 115
Jong, Erica, 27, 204, 208
The Joy of Sex, 6, 96–97, 147
Justice Department, U.S., *p4*, 89, 142, 174;
    National Obscenity Enforcement Unit
    of, 79–82

Kaminer, Wendy, vii, viii, xii, xv, 154
Kammer, Jack, 134, 146
Karst, Kenneth L., 200, 207
Kasmar, Gene, 236
Katz, Leanne, 11, 25–26, 76, 195, 218, 220
Keillor, Garrison, 29
Kelly, Howard, 150
Kendrick, Walter, 12, 139–40, 160–61,
    240
Kennedy, Sheila Suess, 66
Kensington Ladies Erotic Society, 128
Kernberg, Otto, 147–48
Kerson, Sam, 15
Kipnis, Laura, xxii
Knowlton, Charles, 205
Koop, C. Everett, 230, 248–49
Kostash, Myrna, 158
Kovic, Kris, 150
Krafka, Carol, 230
Ku Klux Klan, 35, 50
Kutchinsky, Berl, 233

LaHaye, Beverly, 78
Lally, Robert, 216–17
La Mama Experimental Theatre (New York
    City), 89
Lambda Legal Defense & Education Fund,
    Inc., 91
Langer, Eli, 219
Law, Sylvia, 69
law journals, 77, 120–21
Lawrence, Charles, 76
law schools: forums on censorship at,
    76–77; sexual misconduct education
    censorship in, xx–xxi; University of
    Michigan, 77, 192–94
LDM. *See* Le Dernier Mot

LEAF. *See* Women's Legal Education and
    Action Fund
Leavitt, David, 217
Leavy, Deborah, 74
Le Dernier Mot (LDM), 215
Leidholdt, Dorchen, 97
Leigh, Carol, 194
lesbianism. *See* LGBTQ+ individuals
Letters from a War Zone (Dworkin), 95, 99
Levine, Ellen, 229
Levine, Judith, 187
Le Viol (the rape) (Magritte), *p5*
Lewis, Ann, 182
LGBTQ+ individuals, vii, 45, 46, 51, 52,
    60, 66, 102, 200; Arkansas banning
    books about, xvi; CDA and rights of,
    xiv; facilities for, xxiii–xxiv; FOSTA
    and, viii; free speech restrictions impact
    for, xv; NEA funding and, 88, 90–91,
    139; pornography and, 132–34, 151–53,
    211–12, 220–21, 222; schools censoring
    sexual expression and, xix; Texas law on
    expression of, xvii; works endangered
    by antipornography laws, 92, 151–53,
    211–17, 221, 222, 223, 224
Libido (journal), *p1*, 128
library materials, Arkansas laws on, xvi,
    xxv
Library of Congress, 148
Lies of Our Times, 217
Linda Lovelace. *See* Marchiano, Linda
Lindgren, James, 141
Link, David, 132
Linz, Daniel, 229–30
Little Sisters Book and Art Emporium
    (Vancouver), 214, 222
Lorde, Audre, 197, 217
Los Angeles County Fire Department,
    115–16, 119, 265n21
Los Angeles Times, 81, 217, 218–19

MacArthur Foundation, 76
MacKellar, Jean, 156
MacKinnon, Catharine, *p4*, 5, 6–7, 8n, 12,
    13, 17, 23, 30, 31, 37, 70, 82–83, 124, 127,
    128, 130, 131, 134, 145, 146–47, 177, 181,
    183–84, 187, 188, 198, 211, 239; abortion
    rights and, 179–80;

MacKinnon, Catharine (*cont.*)
anti-male rhetoric of, 99; antiobscenity laws opposed by, 49–50; "antisex" stance ascribed to, 94, 95, 96–97, 101–2; Canadian experience and, 208, 217–18, 221–22; civil censorship and, 53–55; debates with anticensorship feminists refused by, 73–75; divisive rhetoric of, 25; on harm allegedly done by pornography, 224, 225–26, 234; involvement in suppression of feminist artists' works, 192–95; media coverage of, 72–74; model antipornography law drafted by, 24–25, 49, 53–55, 63–71, 92, 96–97; pornography examined closely by, 138; radical premises of, absorbed into culture, 107; rapists' culpability as viewed by, 246–47; real and fictionalized rape distinction blurred by, 154–56; sex industry workers as viewed by, 164–65, 166, 167, 169, 172; on sexual expression suppression, viii–ix, xi, xix; sexual harassment as viewed by, 106, 108–9; on sexual intercourse, 94, 96, 97; sexually explicit descriptions in writings of, 140, 142; women infantilized by, 165–66
Madonna, 29, 76, 214
Magritte, René, *p5*
Mahoney, Kathleen, 220
Mailer, Norman, 146
mailings, erotic, 58
male gaze, 18, 114
The Man Sitting in the Corridor (Duras), 217
Mapplethorpe, Robert, 19, 29, 45, 87
Marchiano, Linda ("Linda Lovelace"), 166–68, 169, 170, 173
Margolick, David, 74
Marinaro, Robert, 80
Markson, Elaine, 190–91
marriage, prostitution equated with, 95–96
Marshall, Thurgood, 47, 115
Marshall, William, 238
The Martyrdom of St. Agatha (del Piombo), *p6*
Massachusetts, 85
Masson, Jeffrey, 155

masturbation, 150, 225
Maus (Spiegelman), xvi–xvii
McCarthy, Sarah J., 124
McClary, Susan, 83
McClure, William, 120
McCormack, Thelma, 23, 130, 154, 239, 243
McElroy, Wendy, 137, 198
media: mainstream, sexist imagery in, 126, 238–39; procensorship feminists as covered by, 71, 72–74; sexist imagery in mainstream, 227
Medical Gynecology, 150–51
Meese, Ed, *p4*, xiii, 77, 82–83
Meese Pornography Commission, *p4*, 6, 12–13, 47, 66–67, 69–70, 72–73, 77, 79, 147, 229, 230, 248–49, 253; bipartisan support of, xiii; sex industry workers and, 169–71; sexually explicit report of, 139–40, 142
men: innate violence ascribed to, 99–100; #MeToo movement and, xvii, xviii; as rape victims, 250
Menlo Park, California, 120
Mercy (Dworkin), 141, 190
Mereu, Mike, 131–32
Meskis, Joyce, 57, 259n18
#MeToo movement, xvii, xviii
Meyer, Carlin, 94, 97, 126, 238, 242
Meyer, Dottie, 170, 171
Michigan Journal of Gender & Law, 193
mifepristone, xiv–xv
Mignogna, Steven P, 247
military schools, xvii
Miller v. California, 42, 43–44, 47
Millett, Kate, 27, 186
Minneapolis, 63–65, 165–66
Minnesota, 117
Mohr, Richard, 218
Money, John, 237
Moral Majority, 65–66
Morgan, Robin, 185
Morse, Margaret, 84
Ms. Magazine, *p1*, 16, 54, 101, 153, 154, 166, 167, 186
Mundy, Liza, 17
Murphy, Earl Finbar, 235
Murphy, Marilyn, 16–17

Murphy Brown, 253
music, erotic or sexual, 83

NAACP. *See* National Association for the Advancement of Colored People
NAS. *See* National Association of Scholars
The Nation, 62–63, 154–55, 209–10, 214
National Association for the Advancement of Colored People (NAACP), 36
National Association of Scholars (NAS), 117
National Association of Women Judges (NAWJ), 74–75
National Campaign for Freedom of Expression, 88
National Coalition Against Censorship, 25, 27, 69, 75–76, 91
National Coalition Against Pornography, 78
National Endowment for the Arts (NEA), 14, 29, 45, 46, 86–91, 139; LGBTQ+ and funding from, 90–91
National Front, 201, 202
National Organization for Women (NOW), xii, 66, 117, 175, 192, 204
National Research Council, 229
National Right to Life Committee, xxviin20
National Union of Students (NUS), 202
Navy, U.S., 168
NAWJ. *See* National Association of Women Judges
NEA. *See* National Endowment for the Arts
New England Journal of Medicine, 18
Newsweek, 139
New York Civil Liberties Union (NYCLU), 61
New York Law School Law Review, 261n17
New York Times, 65, 72, 74, 76, 142, 221
New York Times Magazine, 70, 72, 73, 166
New York Times v. Sullivan, 56–57
Nin, Anaïs, 135
Ninth Circuit Court of Appeals, 69, 82
Nixon, Richard M., 41–42, 160–61
Northwestern University, xxii
NOW. *See* National Organization for Women
nude dancing, 163, 176–77
The Nude Maja (Goya), p2, 15–16, 113–14
nudity or sexual themes, 46–47, 183, 184, 192–94; as allegedly inherently harassing,

114–15, 120; in art, 15–17, 19–20, 87–88, 113–14, 120, 131–32; art with, 44–45; censoring art with, xvi–xvii, 15–17
NUS. *See* National Union of Students
NYCLU. *See* New York Civil Liberties Union

objectification of women, 121, 129, 149
obscenity, 12, 13, 30–31, 35; legal definition of, 42–44, 47, 52, 210. *See also* antiobscenity laws
O'Connor, Sandra Day, xviii, 109
Only Words (MacKinnon), 12, 23, 72, 98, 140, 153–55, 187, 220, 233–34, 248
On Our Backs (magazine), p8, 128, 132–34, 153, 222
Ontario Human Rights Commission, 118
Ontario Provincial Police, 213
Ordeal (Marchiano), 166–68
Oregon, 47, 85
orgasms, 98; come shots and, 136–37
Our Bodies, Ourselves (Boston Women's Health Book Collective), 5, 100, 185–86, 189
Out of Bondage (Marchiano), 167

Pages Bookstore (Toronto), 215
Palac, Lisa, 127, 150
Pally, Marcia, 26, 62–63, 71, 102, 121, 228, 235–36, 244, 253; on defining pornography, 13, 255n6. *See also* Feminists for Free Expression
paraphilias, 147
Paris, Claude, 212
Paris Adult Theatre I v. Slaton, 42
Pasolini, Pier Paolo, 91
patriarchy, 197, 198
PEN America, vii
Pennsylvania State University, p2, 15–16, 113–14
Penrod, Steven, 229–30
Pentagon Papers, 54
Penthouse, 117, 142, 151–52, 170, 171
Peratis, Kathleen, 26
Perspectives on Pornography (Day), 137
Philadelphia Inquirer, 155–56
Pierce, Charles P., xvii
Pink Pyramid (Cincinnati), 91

Piombo, Sebastiano del, *p4*
Playboy, 6, 117, 118, 142, 148, 151–52
Playgirl, 117
Poets & Writers, p1, 16
Pommerenke, Heinrich, 235
"Porn, the Low-Slung Engine of Progress" (Tierney), 142
"The Pornographic Imagination" (Sontag), 128, 142–43
pornography: anthologies of feminist writings on, 158–61; child, 49, 81, 82; "coercion into," 63, 64; come shots in, 136–37; discrimination and violence against women as supposed outcomes of, 7, 23, 31, 35, 36–37, 62–65, 85, 225–26, 228–38, 242–46, 251–54; "forced" public exposure to, 58–61, 63, 64; individualized interaction of viewers and, 126, 128–29; legal definitions and protections, x–xi; LGBTQ+, 132–34, 151–53, 211–12, 220–21, 222; literary value of, 128; negative connotations of, x; one-sided legal forums on, 76–77; opponents of, fascinated with subject, 138–40; political implications of, 30, 159–61; posing for, 163–80; positive aspects of, 145–61; poststructuralist approach to, 129–34; in procensorship feminists' writings, 140–41; profeminist aspects of, 158–59; public opinion on, 142; public perception of feminist stance toward, 72–77; public sympathetic to suppression of, 73; purported aim or effect of, 40; as purported form of gender-based discrimination, 7, 63, 64–65, 106–7; rape scenes in, 127, 129, 134–36, 154–57; sex lives improved by, 147–49; sexual egalitarianism and, 145–47; "snuff" films and, 173; as source of sexual information or pleasure, 148–49; speaking, writing, and demonstrating against, 55–56; Supreme Court defining, x–xi; in treatment of sexual dysfunctions, 147; use of word, 11–13, 23, 25, 27, 49, 50, 63, 78, 92, 182–83, 199–200; women as audience for, 126–28; women as producers of, 128, 150, 177; women's self-images and, 230.

See also antipornography laws; sexual expression
Pornography and Civil Rights (Dworkin and MacKinnon), 247–48
Pornography (Dworkin), 95, 99, 179, 186, 216
Pornography Victims' Compensation Act, 53, 57, 65, 69, 85, 147, 210, 245, 254
Portrait of a Sexual Evolutionary (video), *p4*
Posner, Richard, 125, 138, 174–75, 233–34
Post Office, U.S., 82, 206
Powers of Desire (Snitow, ed.), 158
President's Commission on Obscenity and Pornography, 41–42, 160, 240
Preston, John, 152
Princeton University, 116
privacy rights, 58–59, 115–16
procensorship feminists, 11–26, 46; anticensorship feminists condemned by, 25–26; anti-male rhetoric of, 98–100, 101–2; "antisex" stance ascribed to, 13–22, 92, 94–98, 100–103; awareness of misogyny heightened by, 125; categorical approach of, 126, 128–29; debates with anticensorship feminists refused by, 73–75; free speech in educational settings impacted, xx; fundamentalist alliance with, 6–7, 70, 77–78; legal forums dominated by, 76–77; media coverage of, 71, 73–75; mistakenly assumed to speak for all feminists, 7–8, 73–78; NEA funding and, 87; "pornography" term as used by, 11–13, 23, 25, 49, 50, 63–64, 78, 92; public support for, 72–73; on rape, expression about, xx–xxi; Reagan and Bush administrations and, 79; real and fictionalized rape distinction blurred by, 154–57; sex industry as viewed by, 163–72; sexism in mainstream media overlooked by, 126, 227, 239–40; sexual harassment as viewed by, 105–6; sexual subjugation of women assumed by, 134; statutes promulgated by (*See* antipornography laws); woman-as-male-pawn worldview of, 177–80

prostitution, 101, 175; marriage equated with, 95–96; suppression of videotapes on, 192–95
purdah, 18
puritanism, 199

Quayle, Dan, 253
"quid pro quo" harassment, 108, 121–22
Quindlen, Anna, 204–5, 208

racism, 31, 35–36, 50–51, 60
"radical" feminism and feminists, ix, xiii, xix, xxii–xxiii
Ramos, Norma, 26, 153
rape, 99, 102, 174, 189–92, 193; availability of sexual materials and rates of, 231, 235–36; fictionalized distinction from actual, 154–57; intercourse equated with, 94, 95, 96, 178–79; male victims of, 250; #MeToo movement and, xviii; in pornography, 127, 129, 134–36, 154–57; procensorship feminists on expression about, xx–xxi; romance equated with, 95–96; women's fantasies about, 156–57
Rape (MacKellar), 156
rape myth, 129, 135–36, 239
R.A.V. v. City of St. Paul, 258n9
Reagan, Ronald, 6, 62, 79
Religious Right. *See* fundamentalists
reproductive freedom: Comstock Act and, xiv–xv. *See also* abortion; birth control
Reynolds, Debbie, 84, 217
Rice, Anne, 27, 72, 157, 217, 253–54
Robertson, Pat, 87
Robinson, Lois, 112
Robinson v. Jacksonville Shipyards, Inc., 112–13
Roe v. Wade, 42, 69, 178, 179–80, 189, 192
Roiphe, Katie, 98, 102, 107, 116, 138
Romano, Carlin, 154–55
Roth v. United States, 46
Royalle, Candida, 128, 168, 173
Rubin, Gayle, 13

safer sex, 14, 21–22, 218
Salò, 120 Days of Sodom (film), 91

San Francisco Chronicle, 131–32
Sanger, Margaret, xiv, 5, 23–24, 206
Sarris, Kathy, 66
Scalia, Antonin, 47, 50–51, 110
Schapiro, Mark, 119
Schiro, Thomas, 246–47
Schlafly, Phyllis, 66, 77, 78, 186
schools: gender expression censorship in, xix; military, xvii. *See also* educational settings; law schools; *specific universities*
Schroeder, Jeanne, 95, 101, 180
Schwalm, Loretta, 231
Scott, Joseph, 231
Seaman, Barbara, 189
Seattle Gay News, 134
The Secret Museum (Kendrick), 160, 240
Sekulow, Jay, 236
self-censorship, 218, 222
Senate, U.S., 85; Judiciary Committee, 53, 65, 147, 169, 245
Sense and Censorship (Pally), 244
Seventh Circuit Court of Appeals, 67–68, 246–47
sex, societal wariness toward, 14–16, 42
Sex and Sensibility (Pally), 228, 235–36
sex education, 42, 46, 98
sex industry workers, 220, 223; antipornography laws opposed by, 168–69, 175–77; censorship injurious to, 168–69, 174–77; consent of, ignored by procensorship feminists, 172; criminal and civil remedies available to, 163, 164, 175; economic factors and, 172–73; empowerment of, 169, 177; Meese Commission and, 169–71; relative safety of, 174; supposed coercion of, 163–73, 176, 244; suppression of videotapes about, 192–95; woman-as-male-pawn worldview and, 177–80
sexism, 62, 97; antipornography laws and alleged reduction of, 226, 227–28, 240; in mainstream media, 126, 227, 239–40; pornocentric vision and, 125–26; sexual expression equated with, xvii–xviii, xxi–xxiv; sexuality equated with, 105, 108–9
Sex (Madonna), 214

sex offenders, 228; availablity of sexual materials and, 231; studies on, 237–38; words and images blamed by, 234, 244–46, 254

The Sex Panic, 261n17

sexual activity: egalitarianism in, 145–47; outlawing of, 29, 42; pornography as aid in, 147–49; viewed as inherently degrading to women, 92, 94–98, 100–103, 105, 122; women's power and, 134, 146

sexual assault: teaching about, xx–xxi. *See also* rape; violence against women

sexual dysfunctions, 147

sexual expression, 125–43; as allegedly inherently discriminatory, 18, 105, 106–8, 118; as allegedly inherently harassing, 14–16, 17–18, 19–22, 70, 105, 106, 107–8, 112–17, 122; American legal system and, 29–48; anticensorship feminists' vigilance around, xxiv–xxv; awareness of sexist content in, 125; bipartisan support of suppressing, xiii, xvi; 1992 campaign against, 78; censorship support in 2022 and 2023, xvi–xvii; constitutional protections of, x; government assaults on, 79–92; human rights correlated with, 198–200, 223; obscenity definition and, 42–44, 47, 52; political dimension of, 30, 46–48, 50, 159–61; "protecting" women from, 122–23; "prurient interest" and "patently offensive" criteria for, 43–44; schools censoring, xix; as serious literary, artistic, political, or scientific value, 42, 43–44, 52–53; sexist conduct equated with, xvii–xviii, xxi–xxiv; sexual harassment viewed as all, xvii–xviii; as special case for free speech, 30, 35, 40–44, 46, 47–48, 58; subjective views of, xi; suppressed in repressive regimes, 198–200; Texas law on age restrictions for viewing online, ix, xvii, xxv; varied nature of responses to, 126, 129–34; war on, 13–22 (*See also* antiobscenity laws; antipornography laws); women as audience for, 126–28, 131, 132–34; workplace and educational settting

bans on, 115–17. *See also* LGBTQ+ individuals

sexual harassment, 102; all sexual expression viewed as, xvii–xviii, xxii, 14–16, 18, 19–22, 70, 105, 106, 107, 108, 112–17, 122, 258n9; discrimination and, xvii–xviii, xxi; educational settings and, xxi, xxii–xiii; expanded definition of, 117–21; First Amendment protection and, 110–11, 114, 115–16, 119; free speech and, xxii; and incentive to err on side of strong antiharassment policies, 113; legal definition of, 108–11; legitimate instances of, 19, 108–10, 111–12, 116, 122; looks and gestures as, 17, 19, 116, 120; MacKinnon on discrimination and, xxi; nineteenth-century views and, 122; practical definition of, 111–17; rape contrasted with, xviii; sale of sexually oriented magazines allegedly as, 117–18; Supreme Court on educational settings, xxii; Supreme Court on workplace, xvii–xviii, xxii; women's job opportunities and, 123–24; workplace and educational settings rules on, 115–17, 119, 120

Sexual Harassment of Working Women (MacKinnon), 106

sexual liberation, 42, 101, 200

sexually transmitted diseases, 20, 46, 88, 102, 148; safer sex and, 14, 21–22, 218

"sexual revolution," 41–42, 200

Shafer, Martin, 14–15

Shange, Ntozake, *pl,* 16

Silva, J. Donald, 20–21

Simon, Dan, 190, 191, 192

Singapore, 233

"SLAPS" test, 42, 43, 52–53

Snitow, Ann, 101, 158, 159

"snuff" films, 173

Snyder, Graydon, 21

Sontag, Susan, 29, 30, 40, 128, 142–43

South Africa, 199, 202

South Carolina Supreme Court, 122

Soviet Union, 199, 202

speech, freedom of. *See* free speech

Spiegelman, Art, xvi–xvii

Stanley, Dolores, 118

state and local governments: antiobscenity laws and, 79, 82–83; antipornography laws enacted by, 85. *See also specific states and localities*
Steele, Lisa, 254
Stein, Eric, 201
Stevens, John Paul, 47
Stewart, Ellen, 89
Stewart, Potter, xi, 43, 84
sting operations, 82
Stone, Hannah and Abraham, 208
Stopes, Marie, 207
Straus, Murray, 231, 232
Stumhofer, Nancy, *p2*, 16, 113–14
Sturges, Jock, 80–81
Sullivan, Kathleen, 44, 151, 157, 200
Sumner, John, 205
Sunstein, Cass, 76
Supreme Court, U.S., 12, 118, 123; abortion rights and, 178, 179–80, 189; *American Booksellers Association v. Hudnut*, 67–69, 70, 184; CDA censorship ruling by, xiii; on child pornography, x; civil censorship and, 54–55, 57–58; Comstock Act and, xiv–xv; *Dobbs* decision in 2022, xiv–xv; extremist prosecutorial efforts and, 80–81; free speech jurisprudence of, 30, 31, 32–48, 53, 54–59, 61, 68–69, 70, 86, 110n, 115, 143, 201, 206, 210; governmental funding policies and, 86, 87; Indianapolis antipornography law and, 68–69; pornography defined by, x–xi; privacy rights and, 58–59; sexual harassment cases and, xvii–xviii, xxii, 106–13
Sweden, 233
Swept Away (Cassell), 134
Swept Away (film), 135–36
Syracuse University, 17, 19

Tailhook scandal, 106, 168
Talmud, 21
Tanenbaum, Leora, 167–68, 173
Tashima, A. Wallace, 88–89, 90–91
teachers, censorship of, xx–xxi
Teller (comedian-magician), 245–46
"test of obscenity," 259n8
Texas, age verification law, ix, xvii, xxv

Thelma and Louise (film), 156–57
Thomas, Clarence, 72, 106, 187
Thomas, Trish, 211–12
Tiefer, Leonore, 175–76
Tierney, John, 142
Tisdale, Sallie, 126–27, 129, 145, 146
Tobiason, Thomas H., 167
Today (show), 73–74
Tongues Untied (film), 139
Toronto *Globe and Mail*, 214
Toronto Star, 214
Transgender Law Center, viii
trans women, facilities for, xxiii–xxiv
Traynor, Chuck, 166
Tribe, Laurence, 47–48
Trinity College, 203
2023 Banned Books Update (PEN America), vii
2 Live Crew (band), 44–45

universities. *See* educational settings; *specific universities*
University of Arizona, 17
University of Central Florida, xxiii
University of Chicago Law School, 76–77
University of Connecticut, 203
University of Michigan, 202–3; Law School, *p4*, 77, 192–94
University of Minnesota, 117
University of Nebraska at Lincoln, 21–22, 113
University of New Hampshire, 20–21

Vance, Carole, 7, 62, 78, 93–94, 114, 131, 140, 158–59, 196
Vanderbilt University, 16–17, 19–20
Ventura County Fire Department, 115, 119
Venus de Milo (statue), 15
Vera, Veronica, *p4*, 134, 168–69, 170, 194, 195
victimhood, 39, 102, 223, 250
Vidal, Gore, 225
videotapes: aerobics, 84, 217; pornographic, 142, 147, 148–49; purportedly obscene, 84, 91; X-rated, "sin tax" on, 85

violence: as allegedly inherent male trait, 98–99; free speech and, ix; societal tolerance of, 14–15; in workplaces, 174
violence against women, 27, 223–24; antipornography laws as supposed cure for, 223, 225–26, 240; compensation for victims of, 53, 57, 65, 69, 85, 147, 210, 245, 254; constructive approaches to reduction of, 241–42, 244–46, 248–54; in pornography, 127, 129, 134–36, 154–57, 233; pornography as supposed cause of, 7, 23, 31, 35, 36–37, 62–65, 85, 225, 227–38, 244–49, 251–54. *See also* rape
Violence Against Women Act, 85
Vogue, 26
Voice Literary Supplement, 72

Walker, Alice, 131–32
Walkowitz, Judith, 78–79
Walsh, Bruce, 214
Walsh, Mary Williams, 217
Wan, Dawn, *p8,* 133–34, 153
WAP. *See* Women Against Pornography
The War Against Women (French), 90
WAS. *See* Women Against Sex
Washington (state), 83
Washington Times, 120
Waxman, Barbara Faye, 148
Ways of Seeing (Berger), 114
Webster, Paula, 149
Weenie-Toons! Women Artists Mock Cocks, 215
Weinstein, Harvey, xviii
Weird Smut Comics, 217
Wellesley College's Center for Research on Women, 117
Wells, Brian, 195
Wenz, Christine, 134
Wertmuller, Lina, 135–36
Whicher, Jane, 76
Whitney v. California, 38–39
Wilde, Oscar, 217
Wildmon, Donald, 77, 87, 139
Wilkerson, Isabel, 76

Wilkes, John, 46
Will, George, 198
Williams, Patricia, 12
Willis, Ellen, 157, 197, 234
Wolf, Naomi, 102
Woman Hating (Dworkin), 216, 217
A Woman's Book of Choices (Chalker and Downer), 189–93
women: as alleged male pawns, 177–80; as audience for sexual expression, 126–28, 131, 132–34; books on health and sexuality of, 185–86, 189–93, 207–8; censorship in suppression of, 23–25, 27, 204–8; infantilization of, 105, 164–66, 178; "objectification" of, 121, 129, 149; "protected" from sexual expression, 122–23; self-images of, 230; sexuality of, 17–18, 22, 100–101; stereotypes about, 78, 105, 107, 122–23; victim-centric view of, 39, 102, 223, 250. *See also* equality; rape; violence against women
women, discrimination against. *See* discrimination, gender-based
Women, Passion, and Celibacy (Cline), 98
Women Against Pornography (WAP), 61–62, 63
Women Against Sex (WAS), 98
Women Against Violence Against Women, 63
Women Against Violence and Pornography in the Media, 63
Women on Top (Friday), 156
Women's Legal Education and Action Fund (LEAF), 211, 212–13, 219–20
"women's liberation movement," 42, 200, 223–24; sexual liberation and, 101
Wooster, Martin Morse, 253
World War I, 35
"Wunna My Fantasies" (Thomas), 211–12

Young, Cathy, 102, 177

Zionism, 202
Zola, Émile, 201